Microsoft 365 and SharePoint Online Cookbook

Over 100 actionable recipes to help you perform
everyday tasks effectively in Microsoft 365

Gaurav Mahajan
Sudeep Ghatak

BIRMINGHAM - MUMBAI

Microsoft 365 and SharePoint Online Cookbook

Commissioning Editor: Pavan Ramchandani
Acquisition Editor: Sandeep Mishra
Content Development Editor: Akhil Nair
Senior Editor: Hayden Edwards
Technical Editor: Deepesh Patel
Copy Editor: Safis Editing
Project Coordinator: Kinjal Bari
Proofreader: Safis Editing
Indexer: Tejal Daruwale Soni
Production Designer: Aparna Bhagat

First published: June 2020

Production reference: 1260620

Published by Packt Publishing Ltd.
Livery Place
35 Livery Street
Birmingham
B3 2PB, UK.

ISBN 978-1-83864-667-7

www.packt.com

I would like to dedicate this book to my parents for showing me the true meaning of hard work and for all their sacrifices; my wife for taking care of everything else while I was busy writing, and for letting me do the talking in the book; the little munchkins in our lives - my niece, nephew, and daughter for keeping us inspired with their infectious laughter and energy.

- Gaurav

I would like to dedicate this book to my parents for helping me along the path of knowledge and for making constant sacrifices so that I could have a good future, my wife for taking care of me and the family, my brother for his continued encouragement, and my lovely daughter for her unending love.

- Sudeep

Packt>

Packt.com

Subscribe to our online digital library for full access to over 7,000 books and videos, as well as industry leading tools to help you plan your personal development and advance your career. For more information, please visit our website.

Why subscribe?

- Spend less time learning and more time coding with practical eBooks and Videos from over 4,000 industry professionals

- Improve your learning with Skill Plans built especially for you

- Get a free eBook or video every month

- Fully searchable for easy access to vital information

- Copy and paste, print, and bookmark content

Did you know that Packt offers eBook versions of every book published, with PDF and ePub files available? You can upgrade to the eBook version at www.packt.com and as a print book customer, you are entitled to a discount on the eBook copy. Get in touch with us at customercare@packtpub.com for more details.

At www.packt.com, you can also read a collection of free technical articles, sign up for a range of free newsletters, and receive exclusive discounts and offers on Packt books and eBooks.

Foreword by Sandy Ussia

Microsoft 365 is a huge and fairly complex collection of interrelated cloud applications, many of which could be the subject of an entire book. Gaurav and Sudeep have taken this enormous, ever-changing body of content, and have broken it down into a cookbook-style collection of practical "recipes" which you can use as needed and can come back to time and time again.

This book is aimed at beginner to intermediate "chefs" who want to know how to perform a specific task in one of the Microsoft 365 applications, and who is also interested in learning how and why things work in the background, to come to a deeper understanding of the platform. Each recipe follows a pattern similar to a cooking recipe, with sections on **Getting ready** (kitchen/utensil prep), **How to do it** (ingredients and the method), **How it works** (cooking theory), and in many cases, **There's more** (a deep dive into related topics).

My favorite cookbooks contain not only lists of ingredients and what to do with them, but also notes about cooking basics and practical ideas that allow me to extend my skills beyond the written recipe. Although the specifics may change – ingredients may be unavailable, for instance – a good cookbook gives me the foundational knowledge of what's important to the recipe, so I can cook well no matter what I have on hand. Similarly, the *Microsoft 365 and SharePoint Online Cookbook* will give you a strong understanding of key concepts that you can continue to use, even as applications and features change.

I suggest using this book as you would any cookbook: study the fundamentals of each broad topic, then delve into individual recipes as per your requirements. Bookmark your favorite recipes, and combine and use what you learn to create your own digital transformation menus!

Sandy Ussia (@SandyU)

Microsoft Business Applications MVP

Technical Evangelist, Lightning Tools

Partner, NLightning

June 2020

Foreword by Nate Chamberlain

Office 365 apps and services vary widely in their usage and abilities. Becoming familiar with them all can be a challenge when sifting through the extensive amount of (outdated and current) information available on the internet. Without a clear, easily digestible resource it can be difficult at times to know where to start and how deep to get into any one topic.

What's wonderful about the Cookbook you're about to dive into is that it's divided into 100+ recipes across thoughtfully presented topic areas. Each recipe will guide you, step-by-step, through some of the most essential and important functions across the entire Office 365 suite. While each recipe includes the how, you'll also get to know the when and why of the recipes.

The authors of this book are long-time community champions, whose own career journeys helped me kickstart my career in Office 365 in 2015. Their expertise on the subject has helped countless organizations and individuals learn what they need to properly utilize, govern, and drive the adoption of Office 365 apps and services.

Having had the privilege of benefiting from the work of these authors before, I am confident that you'll find value within these pages, which will propel your professional growth and stimulates your creativity. By choosing to become more familiar with SharePoint and Office 365, you're expanding your abilities and potential to create the most innovative and productive digital workplace possible.

Nate Chamberlain

Creator, NateChamberlain.com

Microsoft MVP

M365 Certified Enterprise Administrator Expert

Contributors

About the authors

Gaurav Mahajan is a technology evangelist with a focus on Microsoft 365, SharePoint, and AI. He has over 19 years of technical consulting experience and is passionate about helping organizations envision, build, and deploy solutions focused on solving practical problems. Gaurav has a Bachelor in Engineering, is Stanford certified in machine learning, and holds a PG Diploma in management from the Indian Institute of Management. He is also a Microsoft Technology Solutions Professional (P-TSP) and holds various other Microsoft certifications. He occasionally blogs, and speaks at and organizes technical events, code camps, and conferences. He is a co-chair of the M365 & SharePoint Saturday, Pittsburgh (US) annual conference. In his free time, he likes to travel and spend time with his family.

I would like to thank my amazing colleagues at CEI for their cooperation, without which this book would not have been possible. My special thanks to Mike Snell and Brian Massey for their never-ending support and encouragement; and to Brandon Hammond and Zac Sloane for their valuable reviews.

Sudeep Ghatak has over 17 years of experience working with Microsoft technologies. He started as a .NET programmer, later moving to SharePoint back in 2007. Sudeep currently works as a senior solution architect in NZ and designs solutions based on Office 365 and the Azure platform. He is a certified Solutions Developer (MCSD) and holds a postgraduate degree in instrumentation engineering. He is an active member of the Microsoft community in New Zealand and runs an Azure meetup group. He is also an active speaker and advocate of Office 365 and Azure. He is often seen speaking at user groups and conferences in and around Christchurch, New Zealand. Outside of work, Sudeep loves to spend time with his family and has a strong interest in music and astrophysics. He loves playing guitar and is currently taking violin lessons with his 7-year-old daughter.

I would like to thank Dr. Krishna Badami, Hikmat Noorebad, JP Van Heerden, and Joseph Mckenna for their valuable input.

And from the both of us:

Our special thanks to Sandy Usia and Nate Chamberlain for taking the time to provide their valuable input for the book and for their all-round encouragement. Our thanks also to Monica Grover for her valuable input.

We thank everyone in the Packt team who helped us along the way, especially Akhil, Deepesh, Divij, Hayden, and Sandeep for their efforts, guidance, and contributions from the start till the end.

We would like to acknowledge with gratitude the love and support of our friends and family whose encouragement kept us going.

This acknowledgement would be incomplete without conveying our special thanks to Megan Bowen, who let us use her account to help write this book (you will get to know her once you read the book).

About the reviewer

Vignesh Ganesan works as a technical specialist for Modern Workplace at Microsoft. He has close to 9 years of experience in various technologies, such as SharePoint, Windows Server, Office 365, Azure, and GSuite. In his current role at Microsoft, he helps customers in their digital transformation journey so that they can get the best out of their SharePoint and Office 365 implementation. He spends his free time writing technical blogs and delivering webinars and you can find all his work on his blogsite and his YouTube channel. Besides actively writing articles and delivering webinars, he organizes most of the technical events in India, such as SharePoint Saturday events, Microsoft 365 developer bootcamps, Global Power Platform bootcamps, and so on.

Packt is searching for authors like you

If you're interested in becoming an author for Packt, please visit authors.packtpub.com and apply today. We have worked with thousands of developers and tech professionals, just like you, to help them share their insight with the global tech community. You can make a general application, apply for a specific hot topic that we are recruiting an author for, or submit your own idea.

Table of Contents

Preface

We have been working on SharePoint and related technologies since 2007, when Microsoft 365 wasn't around, and we have seen it go through several transformations since then. One of the questions we have often been asked as consultants is "What is SharePoint?". We have, at times, struggled to answer that question because, unlike some other Microsoft products that focus on solving one problem, SharePoint is a platform that can be leveraged to help implement a multitude of business solutions.

The question is even harder to respond to when someone asks "What is Microsoft 365?" because it is even bigger than SharePoint. With this book, our goal is to answer those questions by providing practical guidance on and insights into how to carry out various tasks in all the different areas of Microsoft 365. While we have provided the necessary background and best practices where possible, we have deliberately stayed away from getting too technical to keep the recipes simple for those who are new to Microsoft 365.

Microsoft 365 is an ever-changing platform with frequent updates being made to it. As you can imagine, it is often hard to write a book on such a rapidly changing platform. We have tried to keep the book as close to the latest updates and as we can. However, you should expect to see some variations in the steps and images provided in this book. Having said that, the underlying concepts that guide these steps should remain the same.

This book covers all the major applications in the Microsoft 365 suite, with the aim to provide the reader with a head start. To attain expert status, however, you will require additional study and lots and lots of hands-on practice.

Who this book is for

While writing this book, we had the following people in mind:

- End users who would like to get familiar with various Microsoft 365 services in order to use them.
- Business stakeholders who would like to consider Microsoft 365 tools to solve business problems.
- IT administrators who want to put governance around the use of various Microsoft 365 tools.

- Developers who would like to get familiar with the potential customizations.
- Architects who want to gain insights into best practice recommendations.

What this book covers

Chapter 1, *Overview of Microsoft 365*, provides an overview of Microsoft 365.

Chapter 2, *Introduction to SharePoint Online*, provides an introduction to various aspects of working with SharePoint Online in general.

Chapter 3, *Working with Modern Sites in SharePoint Online*, explores sites in SharePoint in greater detail.

Chapter 4, *Working with Lists and Libraries in SharePoint Online*, dives deep into content management in SharePoint.

Chapter 5, *Document Management in SharePoint Online*, explains how to manage documents and files in SharePoint.

Chapter 6, *Term Store and Content Types in SharePoint Online*, discusses the workings of taxonomy in SharePoint.

Chapter 7, *OneDrive for Business*, covers various aspects of OneDrive and its sync client.

Chapter 8, *Search in Microsoft 365*, shows you how to search for content across Microsoft 365 in the optimal way.

Chapter 9, *Office Delve*, shows how to discover and view content focused on you, your work, and the people you work with.

Chapter 10, *Microsoft 365 Groups*, describes how to work with Microsoft 365 groups.

Chapter 11, *Microsoft Teams*, explains how to make calls, set up meetings, and collaborate using Teams.

Chapter 12, *Yammer – The Enterprise Social Network*, explains how to communicate within interest groups.

Chapter 13, *Power Automate (Microsoft Flow)*, demonstrates how to automate business processes.

Chapter 14, *Power Apps*, provides steps to build online forms by connecting to various data sources.

Chapter 15, *Power BI*, demonstrates ways to visualize and analyze information.

Chapter 16, *Power Virtual Agents*, describes how you can build powerful chatbots.

Chapter 17, *Planner*, shows how to build and manage a task board.

Chapter 18, *Custom Development – SharePoint Framework*, provides an overview of custom development in SharePoint and Teams.

Chapter 19, *Microsoft 365 on Mobile*, covers the mobile apps available for Microsoft 365 applications.

Appendix, discusses additional topics that are not covered in the rest of the book.

To get the most out of this book

All you need is access to and licenses for the various apps and workloads in Microsoft 365. If you already have access to your organization's Microsoft 365 subscription but are still unable to work your way through a recipe, you may need to reach out to your IT department to grant you the appropriate licenses and/or access required to complete the steps in that recipe.

Alternatively, you can also sign up for a Microsoft 365 trial account here: https://www.microsoft.com/en-us/microsoft-365/try. This will give you one month's free access to a newly created Microsoft 365 environment. This option is recommended for organizations or users that want to try the service first. You will need to enter your billing information first, but you can cancel the subscription at any time.

Another option is to sign up for the developer program by visiting https://developer.microsoft.com/en-us/microsoft-365/dev-program. This will provide you access to a Microsoft 365 environment containing all the workloads and apps, with fictitious user accounts, along with a lot of dummy test content. This environment has a 90-day validity, after which it is deleted unless it is renewed. The developer program provides a great opportunity to learn about Microsoft 365 and its entire suite of apps.

Download the example code files

You can download the example code files for this book from your account at
`www.packt.com`. If you purchased this book elsewhere, you can visit
`www.packtpub.com/support` and register to have the files emailed directly to you.

You can download the code files by following these steps:

1. Log in or register at `www.packt.com`.
2. Select the **Support** tab.
3. Click on **Code Downloads**.
4. Enter the name of the book in the **Search** box and follow the onscreen instructions.

Once the file is downloaded, please make sure that you unzip or extract the folder using the latest version of:

- WinRAR/7-Zip for Windows
- Zipeg/iZip/UnRarX for Mac
- 7-Zip/PeaZip for Linux

The code bundle for the book is also hosted on GitHub
at `https://github.com/PacktPublishing/Microsoft-365-and-SharePoint-Online-Cookbook`. In case there's an update to the code, it will be updated on the existing GitHub repository.

We also have other code bundles from our rich catalog of books and videos available at `https://github.com/PacktPublishing/`. Check them out!

Conventions used

There are a number of text conventions used throughout this book.

`CodeInText`: Indicates code words in text, database table names, folder names, filenames, file extensions, pathnames, dummy URLs, user input, and Twitter handles. Here is an example: "Scaffold a web part template by typing `yo @microsoft/sharepoint` and respond to the questions that are asked."

A block of code is set as follows:

```
Syntax:
Set(variable_name,value)
```

Any command-line input or output is written as follows:

```
npm install -g @microsoft/generator-sharepoint
```

Bold: Indicates a new term, an important word, or words that you see onscreen. For example, words in menus or dialog boxes appear in the text like this. Here is an example: "Click the **Sync** option in the header menu."

 Warnings or important notes appear like this.

 Tips and tricks appear like this.

Sections

In this book, you will find several headings that appear frequently (*Getting ready, How to do it..., How it works..., There's more...,* and *See also*).

To give clear instructions on how to complete a recipe, use these sections as follows:

Getting ready

This section tells you what to expect in the recipe and describes how to set up any software or any preliminary settings required for the recipe.

How to do it...

This section contains the steps required to follow the recipe.

How it works...

This section usually consists of a detailed explanation of what happened in the previous section.

There's more...

This section consists of additional information about the recipe in order to make you more knowledgeable about the recipe.

See also

This section provides helpful links to other useful information for the recipe.

Get in touch

Feedback from our readers is always welcome.

General feedback: If you have questions about any aspect of this book, mention the book title in the subject of your message and email us at customercare@packtpub.com.

Errata: Although we have taken every care to ensure the accuracy of our content, mistakes do happen. If you have found a mistake in this book, we would be grateful if you would report this to us. Please visit www.packtpub.com/support/errata, selecting your book, clicking on the Errata Submission Form link, and entering the details.

Piracy: If you come across any illegal copies of our works in any form on the Internet, we would be grateful if you would provide us with the location address or website name. Please contact us at copyright@packt.com with a link to the material.

If you are interested in becoming an author: If there is a topic that you have expertise in and you are interested in either writing or contributing to a book, please visit authors.packtpub.com.

Reviews

Please leave a review. Once you have read and used this book, why not leave a review on the site that you purchased it from? Potential readers can then see and use your unbiased opinion to make purchase decisions, we at Packt can understand what you think about our products, and our authors can see your feedback on their book. Thank you!

For more information about Packt, please visit packt.com.

Overview of Microsoft 365

1

Microsoft is the reigning leader in business collaboration and productivity. Over 400,000 companies worldwide use Microsoft products and services. Over 100 million monthly active users use SharePoint. A recent Gartner Report (`https://m365book.page.link/gartner`) places Microsoft as the leader in the provision of content services platforms that focuses on the following key areas:

- **Content management**: A content management solution (also sometimes known as Enterprise Content Management or ECM) lets you store, manage, and optionally share an organization's content, which includes documents and/or web pages. Microsoft's first true CMS came with WSS 3.0, a product that later came to be known as **SharePoint**, which soon became a widely popular document- and content-management platform. While SharePoint serves as the document management solution for a team, **OneDrive for Business** is meant to host and manage employees' personal files.

- **Collaboration**: Collaboration is the exchange of information and ideas between *collaborators* within or even outside an organization. More recent advancements in technology allow for those collaborating to be located across different geographical locations and still be able to effectively work together as if they were collocated. **SharePoint** and **Teams**, coupled with your ever-favorite Office apps, such as **Word, Excel, PowerPoint, OneNote**, and so on, are a few of the Microsoft solutions around to help boost business collaboration.

- **Communication**: Communication is vital to every business. It reflects the culture of an organization and helps align the goals of individuals within an organization toward a common objective. To effectively communicate with employees, organizations should offer multiple channels for both formal and informal communication. Besides communicating the organization's vision and goals, these channels can be used to update their employees on news, events, and policies to prepare them for a crucial situation, ensure safety, or effectively listen to the opinions and ideas of other employees. Microsoft has several apps that offer communication channels for different engagement levels, such as the following:
  - **Outlook**: For formal communication
  - **Teams**: For instant communication
  - **Yammer**: For communication between interest groups
  - **Kaizala**: For first-line workers

- **Process automation**: Business-process automation is the use of technology to execute repeatable tasks or processes. It helps accelerate and standardize business processes, thereby improving the quality of the outcome while reducing costs at the same time. You can streamline both simple and complex processes, such as employee onboarding, accounts payable, contract management, time management, and more. Microsoft provides the following selection of apps, grouped under the **Power Platform** umbrella, to help you build business process automation apps. Power Platform lets the experts in the subject build no-code business solutions using the following:
  - **Power Apps**: To build online forms
  - **Power Automate**: To automate repetitive processes
  - **Power BI**: To analyze and visualize data
  - **Power Virtual Agents**: To build chatbots

- **Productivity**: Besides the applications mentioned previously, there are several other applications that target specific use cases, which can be broadly divided into the following categories:
  - **Office Online**: Outlook, Word, Excel, and PowerPoint to author and share content
  - **Project and task management**: Using **To do** to manage personal tasks, **Planner** to manage simple project tasks, and **Project Online** for more complex scenarios

- **Digital forms**: Using **Power Apps** to build online forms and **Forms** to build surveys
- **Video streaming**: Using **Stream** to upload and manage videos

All these products and services are now integrated and offered as a unified service called **Microsoft 365** (earlier known as **Office 365**). With Microsoft 365, Microsoft has allowed organizations to provide these services to their employees through a subscription model. It comes with different plans tailored equally well for large, medium, and small companies. We will see the different plans and licensing models later in this chapter.

The infrastructure business is changing!

Gone are the days when companies had dedicated data centers or server rooms with racks and racks of servers. Outsourcing the maintenance of infrastructure to a cloud provider has proved beneficial in several ways. Let's see how!

Traditionally, companies built data centers to store sensitive, competitive, and critical information. The facility had to be well protected with both physical and virtual security and access measures. Other running costs included server licenses, hardware costs, higher than normal power consumption, and facility maintenance costs. Usually, such companies also needed to invest in building a *disaster recovery* center, which served as a secondary backup—a precautionary measure, should the primary data center go down.

Although it seems that having a private data center makes sense for a company, given that it has full control over it, in reality, it is both risky and challenging to safeguard your applications from cyber attacks and other potential hackers. Even financially, it doesn't make sense to keep servers running around the clock when the usage of the applications is low, such as during a local holiday season. On top of that, you would need dedicated staff that is responsible for applying patches, installing updates, and ensuring that all applications are running smoothly.

This is where cloud computing and hosting comes to the rescue!

The term **cloud** refers to the infrastructure and/or services that are hosted and maintained by a provider and that can be accessed over the internet. Microsoft, Google, and Amazon are some of the well-known cloud providers, but there are certainly many more that provide various cloud services. There are primarily three service models that the cloud providers offer:

- **Infrastructure-as-a-service** (**IaaS**): In this model, instead of purchasing and maintaining their own computing hardware, organizations *borrow* the necessary infrastructure from one or more service providers by paying a fee. They then install and maintain the required software on this infrastructure.
- **Platform-as-a-service** (**PaaS**): In this model, in addition to the infrastructure, the service provider also provides the operating system and development tools required to build applications.
- **Software-as-a-service** (**SaaS**): In this model, the applications are provided by the service provider. These applications can be accessed over the internet. The responsibility of upgrading the software and fixing the bugs lies with the service provider.

The evolution of Microsoft 365

The journey of Microsoft's productivity suite started in the '80s when it was first introduced by Bill Gates as **Microsoft Office**, with three applications: Word, Excel, and PowerPoint. Since then, Office applications have captured the corporate world and home users alike. Anyone who has ever used a PC has had some experience with Microsoft Office at some point. It is hard to imagine a world without Word, Excel, and PowerPoint. These applications have transformed the world since the day they were launched.

While one team in Microsoft was busy improving the already popular office suite of applications, another team was busy shaping an enterprise-scale collaboration and content-management platform called SharePoint. This platform offered online document storage and enabled collaboration between teams. In addition, and since its days of inception, SharePoint was built to be a highly extensible and customizable platform that allows developers and non-developers alike to extend its capabilities by building business solutions on top of it. SharePoint was initially released as a standalone application for installation on a server (there are several companies that still use it on-premises) before becoming available on the cloud as SharePoint Online and as a member of the Microsoft 365 family.

Advancements in SharePoint have given birth to other technologies and tools that have now evolved into fully-featured products in themselves. The following are just some of those products:

- **OneDrive for Business**: Older versions of SharePoint included a service called My Sites. My Sites were personal sites for every SharePoint user, a place where they could store their personal files. My Sites have now been replaced by OneDrive for Business.
- **Microsoft Teams:** Teams has been through several pit stops before becoming Microsoft 365's default communication tool. In 2011, Microsoft acquired **Skype**, a free piece of software that enables you to make VOIP calls and host video conferencing. After the acquisition of Skype, Microsoft replaced the business communication tool named **Lync** with a corporate version of Skype, called **Skype for Business**. Skype for Business has now been deprecated and replaced by Microsoft Teams.
- **Power Automate**: SharePoint as a platform had a workflow solution referred to as **SharePoint workflows**. The workflows were designed using a free tool called **SharePoint Designer**. Although SharePoint workflows were powerful, managing them was hard because of the lack of a visual tool. SharePoint workflows got deprecated with the advent of Power Automate, which had a nice web-based visual designer that was so easy to use that even non-developers could build workflow solutions themselves.
- **Power Apps**: **Microsoft Infopath** was a popular tool for designing, editing, and distributing electronic forms. Infopath forms could be connected to a variety of data sources and often used along with SharePoint to extend the capabilities of SharePoint list forms. Infopath has been deprecated and replaced with a web-based forms designer known as Power Apps. Again, with this move, Microsoft has tried to make designing forms easier for non-developers.
- **Power BI**: In 2006, Microsoft acquired ProClarity and launched Performance Point as a BI solution. It was discontinued in 2009 and paved the way for Power BI.

Over the years, Microsoft has made other strategic acquisitions, such as Yammer and Mover, to consolidate its Microsoft 365 offering. They were soon joined by other online services, such as Stream, Planner, Sway, To do, and so on.

Hopefully, that provides you with some context on how **Microsoft 365** evolved. The next section explains why Microsoft 365 is right for any organization.

What is Microsoft 365?

Microsoft 365 is a SaaS and PaaS offering by Microsoft. It is a collection of several products, services, and platforms, each tailored for a specific use case. Microsoft 365 applications can be accessed online at `www.office.com`. In addition to online applications, it also lets you download the license-based client version of certain applications, such as Microsoft Office (Word, Excel, and PowerPoint), OneDrive, Teams, and so on.

Moving to Microsoft 365 provides you with the following benefits:

- **One subscription service for everything**: Microsoft 365 provides you with an ecosystem of applications. Every application is designed to cater for a specific use case. You get applications that let you build electronic forms and business process automation, create insights into your business data, and so on. This saves you buying multiple point solutions for every use case.

- **No installation required**: All Microsoft 365 apps are accessible through a web browser, including the ones that have a web and client version. Client versions are available for some applications, such as Word, Excel, PowerPoint, Outlook, Teams, Power BI, and so on. Although the web versions provide limited features compared to the desktop version, the web versions are catching up with their client counterparts pretty rapidly.

- **Choose your own device**: Microsoft 365 runs on PC, Mac, and Linux machines. It is compatible with all major browsers, such as Microsoft Edge, Internet Explorer 11, Mozilla Firefox, Google Chrome, and Safari 10+. More information on the operating system and browser compatibility can be found at `https://m365book.page.link/browser-compatibility`.

- **Mobile friendly**: All Microsoft 365 services are *responsive* (meaning that they adjust to the viewing area of the device) when viewed on mobile browsers. Most of these services also have a mobile app that lets you leverage the native mobile features (such as camera and GPS). To read about the mobile compatibility of the various Microsoft 365 apps, visit `https://m365book.page.link/mobile-compatibility`.

- **Always get the latest**: Microsoft 365 is continuously being updated with new features and capabilities. Users do not have to worry about upgrades; they can experience improvements as soon as Microsoft updates are released to their organization's tenant. Your organization can try new features before they are released to the general public by opting in for **Targeted release**. Your IT administrator can designate a set of users to try out these new features before these get rolled out to the rest of the company. You can read more about **Standard** and **Targeted** release here: `https://m365book.page.link/first-release`.

- **High availability**: Microsoft 365 offers 99.9% uptime. The information at `https://m365book.page.link/office-continuity` shows uptime data across the world over the last three years. Microsoft notifies you at least five days before any scheduled maintenance job. You also receive notifications in case of unplanned outages. Administrators can check the status of the Microsoft 365 services from the administration Service Health portal during partial outages.

- **State of the art security**: One of the main reasons why companies are reluctant to move to the cloud is that they are not sure how secure their data is. Some of these security concerns are as follows:

    - **Who can access my data**: Your data belongs to you. There are well-laid policies and checks to ensure that no one can access your data without permission. There could be exceptional scenarios where the government or law enforcement agencies can request your data. To read more about this, refer to `https://m365book.page.link/data-access`.

    - **Protect data from hackers**: All Microsoft 365 data is stored in highly secured environments. However, to further secure your Microsoft 365 environment, Microsoft has laid out certain security guidelines (`https://m365book.page.link/security`) that should be followed. These guidelines reduce the risks of hacking, if not eliminating them completely.

    - **Data ownership:** Even though your data is saved on Microsoft infrastructure, they do not own your data. If you cancel your Microsoft 365 subscription, your data gets deleted from their servers after 90 days. During this time, you can renew your subscription or back up the data from Microsoft 365. You can read more about data ownership at `https://m365book.page.link/ownership`.

- **Compliance and information security**: Microsoft 365 also provides features such as data loss prevention and device management that let you store your company's data and information without the risk of information leakage. It offers additional capabilities surrounding data compliance and information security. Since these are very highly specialized areas, focused on the administrative side of Microsoft 365, we have not covered the topics in this book. If you are an administrator and implementing Microsoft 365 for your organization, we recommend that you should familiarize yourself with these areas. You can read more about Microsoft 365 compliance features here: `https://m365book.page.link/M365-Compliance`. You can read here more about the Microsoft 365 security features here: `https://m365book.page.link/M365-Security`

Licensing

Microsoft 365 has several subscription plans for the following entities:

- **Small and medium businesses**: In this category, there are **Basic**, **Standard**, and **Premium plans**. The Basic plan offers Office apps (Outlook, Word, Excel, PowerPoint, and OneNote) for online, mobile-only use, and grants 1 TB storage per user. The Standard and Premium tiers include the corresponding desktop Office apps along with additional services.
- **Schools**: Microsoft offers plans to schools under the "Education" banner. The plans are **A1**, **A2**, and **A3**. A1 offers Office apps (Outlook, Word, Excel, PowerPoint, and OneNote) for online and mobile-only use. The A2 plan additionally provides access to the corresponding desktop apps. Power BI is only available with the A3 plan.
- **Nonprofit organizations**: This category includes a basic and a standard plan. The primary difference between the two plans being that the standard plan lets you download Office Apps for desktop whereas the basic plan lets you access office applications only on the web.
- **Home users**: For home users, Microsoft offers a **one-time** purchase or two subscription-based plans (**family** and **individual**) to choose from. The one-time purchase plan lets you use only three apps (Word, Excel, and PowerPoint) on a single device. Family and individual plans offer additional apps.

- **Enterprises**: Enterprises can choose between the **E3** and **E5** plans. The E5 plan is the premium version that includes all Microsoft 365 apps and services.
- **First-line workers**: The first-line workers are the first ones to represent your organization. Microsoft 365 offers the **F3** plan to help such workers stay productive. The F3 plan offers Office web and mobile apps, OneDrive for Business, and a few other Microsoft 365 services.
- **Standalone plans**: Besides the plans mentioned above, some services are also available with Standalone plans. These can even be included in plans that do not offer these services by default. The standalone plans are listed here: `https://m365book.page.link/standalone-plans`

You get access to a set of applications in Microsoft 365 based on the subscription plan assigned to you by your organization. To get access to other applications, you can either request your administrator to upgrade you to a higher plan or assign you a license for that specific application. We have mentioned the license requirements in the *Getting started* section of each recipe.

The Microsoft 365 plans get updated from time to time. You can check the plans by browsing to `https://www.office.com/` and looking under **Products** menu in the top navigation or referring to this page `https://m365book.page.link/m365-plans`

Microsoft 365 Apps

Microsoft 365 comprises the following key applications and services (in alphabetical order):

- **Calendar**: This app lets you view your daily, weekly, or monthly schedule, book meetings, share meetings, and event times. It also lets you view your organization's shared calendars and the calendars of your colleagues.
- **Delve**: This app uses machine learning and artificial intelligence to display information relevant to you based on what you work on and who you work with. The information is pulled from different applications within Microsoft 365, such as SharePoint, OneDrive, and Teams. Delve is covered in `Chapter 9`, *Office Delve*.
- **Dynamics 365**: Microsoft Dynamics 365 offers customer-relationship management and enterprise resource-management services. It lets you build business applications for your organization. It comes with purpose-built data models that can then be customized as per your needs.

- **Excel**: Excel is one of the most popular programs that are used for organizing and manipulating data. It lets you connect to various databases and also visualize data using pivot charts and tables. With Microsoft 365, you can access your Excel spreadsheets in a web browser.

- **Forms**: Microsoft Forms lets you create surveys, team quizzes, and opinion polls by designing simple electronic forms using several input options. The responses received can then be analyzed individually or collectively within Forms or by exporting the responses in Excel. To learn more about Forms, check out Chapter 20, *Appendix*.

- **Kaizala**: Kaizala is a chat-based secured phone app that lets you have secure conversations with internal staff, as well as people external to your organization.

- **MyAnalytics**: This app provides insights into your work habits by looking into your interactions with people. It also lets you mute notifications that might distract you and book time to focus on your daily calendar.

- **OneDrive**: OneDrive lets you save and share your files in one place. You can share these files securely with your colleagues, vendors, or partners. Your OneDrive files can be downloaded on any device and synchronized with the cloud to ensure that your work is never lost. You can find more details on OneDrive in Chapter 7, *OneDrive for Business*.

- **OneNote**: OneNote is a note-taking app that can capture and organize your notes into notebooks, sections, or pages. It lets you take handwritten as well as audio notes. To learn more about OneNote, check out Chapter 20, *Appendix*.

- **Outlook**: Outlook lets you stay on top of your emails. It has features such as spam detection and auto filter. It also has features such as attachment reminders, attendee tracking, and the ability to attach a document as a link (as opposed to a duplicate copy).

- **People**: People lets you maintain a list of your contacts. This includes internal staff, as well as all your friends, family, and acquaintances.

- **Planner**: Planner lets you manage your tasks by organizing them into plans, assigning them to individuals, and notifying people. You and your team can track tasks on a planner board and track them to completion. The planner is covered in Chapter 17, *Planner*.

- **Power Automate**: Formerly known as **Flow**, this app lets you automate business processes by using conditional logic and connecting a host of data sources. Power Automate is covered in Chapter 13, *Power Automate (Microsoft Flow)*.

- **Power BI**: This app lets you visualize data using built-in and custom visuals, lets you build dashboards and share these with others. Power BI is covered in Chapter 15, *Power BI*.
- **Power Virtual Agents**: This service lets you design chatbots for your organization that can integrate with other Microsoft 365 services. PVAs are covered in Chapter 16, *Power Virtual Agents*.
- **Power Apps**: This app lets you develop electronic forms that let you interact with your organization's data. They can be built for both web and mobile. Power Apps have been discussed in Chapter 12, *Power Apps*.
- **PowerPoint**: Using PowerPoint lets you build presentations using visual effects and animations and share them with your colleagues. PowerPoint has both a client and a web version and supports coauthoring.
- **SharePoint**: SharePoint is a platform for your organization to boost team collaboration, document, and content management. It lets you securely share content and information with your colleagues and partners. Chapter 2, Chapter 3,
  Chapter 4, Chapter 5, and Chapter 6 discuss SharePoint in detail.

- **Stream**: Stream is your company's own video portal, where your staff can upload and share videos of classes, meetings, presentations, and training sessions. It also lets you categorize videos under channels. To know more about Stream, check out *Appendix*.
- **Sway**: Microsoft Sway is a professional digital storytelling app for your organization that helps produce rich marketing material and presentations to be cataloged and shared. See *Appendix* for more information.
- **Tasks**: The Tasks app lets you manage tasks in Outlook. It lets you assign due dates to tasks and marks them as complete.
- **Teams**: Teams is your collaboration hub with a chat-based team workspace that lets you work collaboratively with your colleagues. It allows you to have group chats, online meetings, calling, and web conferencing. Chapter 11, *Microsoft Teams* covers Teams in details.
- **To Do**: This app lets you manage, prioritize, and complete the most important things you need to achieve every day. See *Appendix* for more information.
- **Whiteboard**: Whiteboard is an app that lets you use your device as a whiteboard to ideate and exchange ideas. It supports text, shapes, and free-form drawing.

- **Word**: This app lets you create professional documents and share them with your colleagues. The app has a client and a web version and supports the co-authoring of documents.
- **Yammer**: Yammer is your organization's social network that drives employee engagement in your organization. Yammer has been covered in Chapter 12, *Yammer - The Enterprise Social Network*.

Signing in to Microsoft 365

Microsoft 365 uses a single sign-in for all its apps and services. The initial sign-in page for Microsoft 365 can vary slightly depending on the device that you are signing in from, and the app which you are signing in to. However, you will see a consistent Sign in option on all such apps and devices. For example, the initial sign-in page when you use a browser to sign-in to Microsoft 365 through its landing page at www.office.com looks like this:

This Microsoft support article walks you through the login experience when signing in from apps on various devices: https://m365book.page.link/M365-SignIn

The login experience becomes consistent after you click the **Sign in** button. Clicking this button will first prompt you for an email id. For your work or school subscription, this will be your corresponding work or school email id. If you have a personal Microsoft account, then this will be your personal email id.

For work or school accounts, entering the email id and clicking **Next** will take you to your organization's sign-in page, where you will need to enter your usual password for your organization. Then click **Sign in** again. Note that you may be asked for more information here depending on whether your organization has configured additional security.

If you are navigating to one of the Microsoft 365 services from the browser, you will also be asked if you would like to **Stay signed in?**. Confirming **Yes** to this prompt will mean that you will not need to sign in again every time you access an app or service using the same browser. You can also select **Don't show this again** to reduce the number of times you are prompted to sign-in. Please be sure to do this only on a device that belongs to you and is not shared with others.

That's it! You are now ready to benefit from all the Microsoft 365 apps and services using this one sign-in. Next, we will explore the various components of the Microsoft 365 user interface in a bit more detail.

Microsoft 365 user interface

Microsoft 365 comes with a very simple and intuitive user interface. You are presented with a landing page that looks like this when you first log in to the Microsoft 365 home page at www.office.com:

Let's look at the various sections of this page in a bit more detail.

Page header - the suite bar

The suite bar appears on top of all Microsoft 365 apps. This one component consistently spans across all the Microsoft 365 applications. The suite bar has the following links:

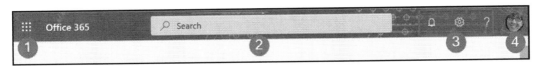

1. The set of squares on the extreme left is known as the Microsoft 365 **App launcher** (also called the **waffle**). It is the Start menu equivalent to Windows 10. The waffle displays the frequently used Microsoft 365 apps. In addition to the Microsoft 365 apps, your organization can add their own apps in this section. You can then navigate to your apps from here. In addition, you will also see your recent documents if you scroll all the way to the bottom of the App launcher. You can also click **All apps** towards the bottom of the app launcher panel to be taken to a page that shows you a listing of all the apps that you have access to:

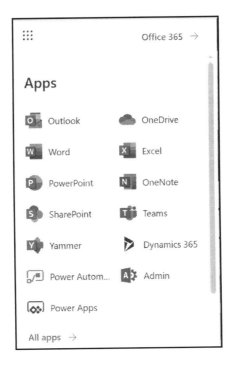

2. The Microsoft 365 **Search** box in the middle lets you search across your organization's entire Microsoft 365 tenant. **Search** allows you to find relevant content from across all SharePoint sites and OneDrive for Business. We will cover **Search** in much more detail in subsequent chapters, but it is worth mentioning here that **Search** will always only show you content that you have access to.

3. Next to the **Search** box are three Microsoft 365 icons:

   1. **Notification icon**: Notifies you when you receive an email.
   2. **Settings icon**: This is explained in the following section.
   3. **Help icon**: To get help on Microsoft 365. The help icon is the context-aware, in clicking this icon will show you help relevant to the area or page that you were browsing when you clicked it.

4. Towards the extreme right is the profile picture (or your initials, if the picture is unavailable). You can update your contact details by clicking on the profile picture and then selecting **My Office Profile**. You can also view your subscriptions and license information and update your account details (privacy settings, password, and so on) from here.

Settings icon

The **Settings** menu is represented by the *gear* icon. The settings icon lets you change your personal preferences, including your notification settings and your password for Microsoft 365, as shown in the following screenshot:

You can update the following from here:

- Your personal Microsoft 365 look and feel (if your organization allows this)
- Certain Microsoft 365 notifications preferences
- Your organization account password
- Additional security and privacy settings

Further, the settings panel is context-aware, meaning that the settings that you see in this panel will depend on the Microsoft 365 workload or app within which you are working. For example, when you are viewing the settings panel from within a page in SharePoint, you will see settings that are relevant to that specific page or area in SharePoint. We will cover the settings for individual apps separately in the chapters for these apps.

Page content

While the header consistently appears across all the Office 365 workloads, the content for the individual apps varies depending on the type of app. The Microsoft 365 home page contains the following sections (from top to bottom).

Apps section

This section displays all the apps that you have access to based on your assigned licenses:

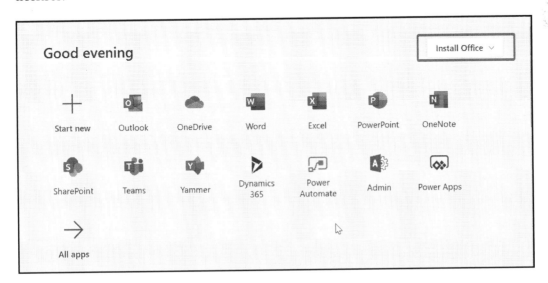

The **Install Office** option in the top right-hand corner lets you install Office applications (such as Word, Excel, and PowerPoint) on your machine. This link is visible only if your subscription plan lets you install Office applications.

Recommended

The next section displays all the documents that might be relevant to you. Microsoft 365 uses machine learning and artificial intelligence to create a personalized list for each user based on the projects that you are working on and the people you are working with:

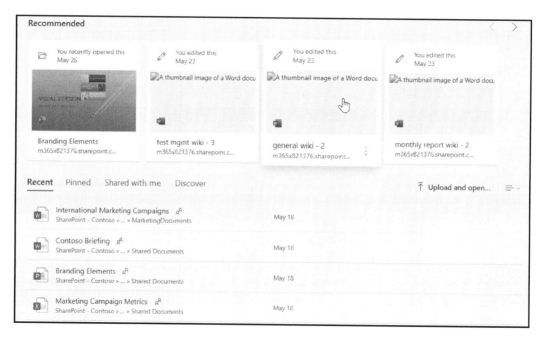

The section below the **Recommended** section displays the documents you have been working on or those that have been shared with you. Microsoft 365 lets you pin a document from the **Recent** tab and it will stay here forever until it's deleted.

OneDrive and SharePoint locations

Towards the bottom of your Microsoft 365 homepage are your recently accessed OneDrive locations and frequently accessed SharePoint sites or sites that you follow. You can see more listings by visiting the individual applications by either clicking **Go to OneDrive** or **Go to SharePoint**:

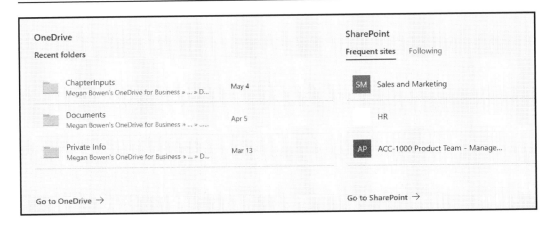

Microsoft 365 admin interface

Microsoft 365 is a very powerful platform, but with power comes responsibility. The Microsoft 365 Admin Center lets you manage various aspects of the platform. Only designated administrators in your organization can access the Admin Center. They can access it through the Admin app after they log into www.office.com.

The following screenshot shows the landing screen of the Microsoft 365 Admin Center:

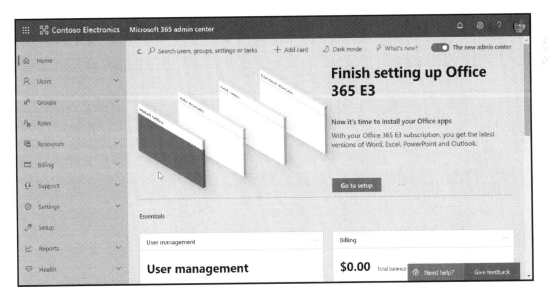

You can perform the following actions from the Microsoft 365 Admin Center:

- Add or remove users in your organization's Microsoft 365 environment.
- Manage app licenses for these users.
- Manage organization-wide admin role assignments.
- Create and manage Azure Active Directory groups and mailboxes.
- Manage app licenses and billing information.
- Log a support ticket with Microsoft Support.
- Register your company domain with Microsoft 365.
- View usage and compliance reports and perform audits.
- Monitor Microsoft 365 health and performance.
- Administer and govern individual Microsoft 365 apps using the corresponding admin center.

Since this book is focused more on using the different workloads of Microsoft 365, discussing the admin capabilities is beyond the scope of this book.

Microsoft 365 admin roles

Microsoft 365 has various administrator roles, each specific to the nature of the work that the admin is involved in. These roles can be divided into three broad categories:

Global roles: Users with these roles can access all Microsoft 365 admin features. The two global roles are as follows:

- **Global admin**: This is the highest privilege you can get in the Microsoft 365 Admin Center. Global admins can perform all tasks within the Microsoft 365 Admin Center. They can also add other individuals as global admins. This role should be granted with caution.

 The person who signed up for Microsoft Online Services automatically becomes a global admin.

- **Global reader**: Individuals with this role can view admin features but cannot change them.

Administrator roles: These roles are assigned to individuals responsible for maintaining the different administrative aspects of your Microsoft 365 services, such as licensing, billing, users, helpdesk requests, and so on. Some key roles under this category are as follows:

- **Helpdesk admin**: To reset passwords and manage service requests
- **User admin**: To create users and groups
- **Compliance admin**: To maintain data governance
- **Guest invited**: To allow external users to the organization's Active Directory
- **License admin**: To assign licenses to users

Admins for a specific app or workload: It is a best practice to assign individuals admin access only to the services that they are responsible for. Some noteworthy admin roles for specific services are as follows:

- **Exchange admin**: To manage Exchange Online
- **Groups admin**: To manage Microsoft 365 groups
- **SharePoint admin**: To manage SharePoint and OneDrive for Business
- **Teams service admin**: To administer the Teams application
- **Power platform admin**: To manage Power Apps and Power Automate
- **Power BI admin**: To administer Power BI admin tasks

There are other admin roles in addition to the ones mentioned here. A full list of admin roles and their descriptions is available at `https://m365book.page.link/ admin-roles`.

Let's get started!

Our goal is to empower you to make the most of your Microsoft 365 subscription. Since knowing the Microsoft 365 ecosystem in entirety seems like a daunting task, this book focuses on explaining what each Microsoft 365 application does, how you can use it, and when should you use one over another.

Microsoft 365 runs on a multitude of devices but experience on all devices is similar. However, the recipes in this book have been only been tested on Windows 10 devices and using the Chrome browser. So, you may see some minor variations if you are using a different OS or browser.

While this book covers all the major applications in Microsoft 365 stack, the technology itself is evolving with each passing day. Some services are being deprecated while other services are being added. With this book, we have tried to stay as close to the current offering as possible. We hope that this book will help you in your Microsoft 365 endeavors. As a reminder, we encourage you to reach out to us via customercare@packtpub.com and mention the book title in the subject for any feedback or concerns that you may have. We always welcome your inputs in helping make this book better.

Best of luck. Let's get started!

Introduction to SharePoint Online

2

SharePoint Online is part of the Microsoft 365 ecosystem that lets you create and share content, knowledge and applications thus empowering collaboration and productivity in organizations. At its core, it is a content management system that gives its users *areas* (**sites**, **lists**, and **libraries**) where they can organize and collaborate on **documents**, **data**, and **news**. It also lets users **securely share** the content, not just with their peers, but also with collaborators outside the organization. Users are also able to find this content through powerful enterprise **search** capabilities. Additionally, SharePoint enables an organization to effectively communicate through rich **pages** and engaging tools and **web parts**.

SharePoint integrates well with a lot of other tools within and outside of the Microsoft 365 family, such as Microsoft Teams, Groups, One Drive, and Microsoft Office Suite, to name a few. SharePoint can be accessed through a variety of browsers, such as Edge, Chrome, Firefox, and Safari, as well as on various desktop and mobile platforms.

We briefly discussed in `Chapter 1`, *Overview of Microsoft 365*, that SharePoint is available both as a standalone installation (on-premises) and as a cloud offering (through Microsoft 365). However, our book is focused on SharePoint Online. The recipes and related details in the next 4 chapters are focused on SharePoint Online but the key concepts apply to both the versions of SharePoint. All references of SharePoint in these chapters and in general throughout the book refer to SharePoint Online unless mentioned otherwise.

In this introductory chapter, we will look at the following recipes, which will show you how to carry out some of the more common tasks in SharePoint Online:

- Getting to the SharePoint start page
- Creating a modern site
- Viewing site contents
- Creating a list
- Adding an item to a list
- Creating a document library
- Uploading documents to a library
- Sharing a document
- Searching content

While this chapter covers the more commonly used scenarios, dedicated chapters later in this book will dive into many of the different areas of SharePoint in more detail. You will find references to these chapters in the *See also* sections of each recipe in this chapter.

Getting to the SharePoint start page

The SharePoint start page is the central location that shows you relevant content from all the SharePoint sites that you have access to in your organization. From here, you can easily get to the sites that you are following, frequently visit, or have recently visited. This page also lets you search for content across all the SharePoint sites that you may have access to.

This recipe shows you how to log in to Microsoft 365 and then browse to the SharePoint Online home page from there.

Getting ready

To be able to browse to the SharePoint start page, your organization should have purchased one of the Microsoft 365 products that contain SharePoint. In addition, they should have assigned you a license to use SharePoint Online.

How to do it...

To access the SharePoint Online home page, follow these steps:

1. Browse to `www.office.com` and click the **Sign in** button, as shown in the following screenshot:

2. Log in using the email ID and password provided, as described in the *Signing in to Microsoft 365* topic in `Chapter 1`, *Overview of Microsoft 365*.

3. As shown in the following screenshot, you will be directed to the Microsoft 365 home page upon a successful sign-in:

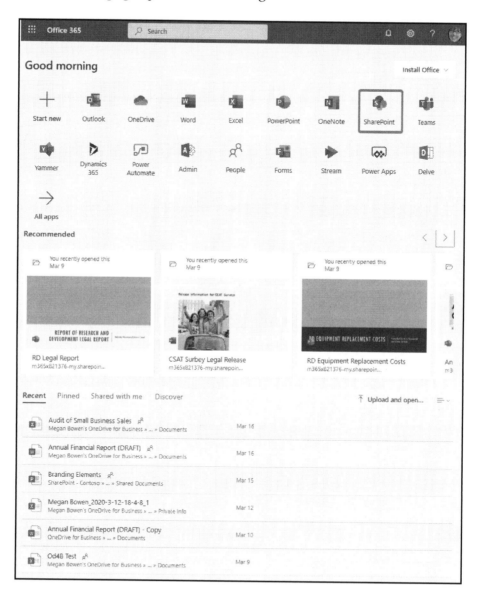

4. Click the **SharePoint** icon highlighted in the preceding screenshot.
5. Doing so will take you to the SharePoint start page, which should look similar to the following:

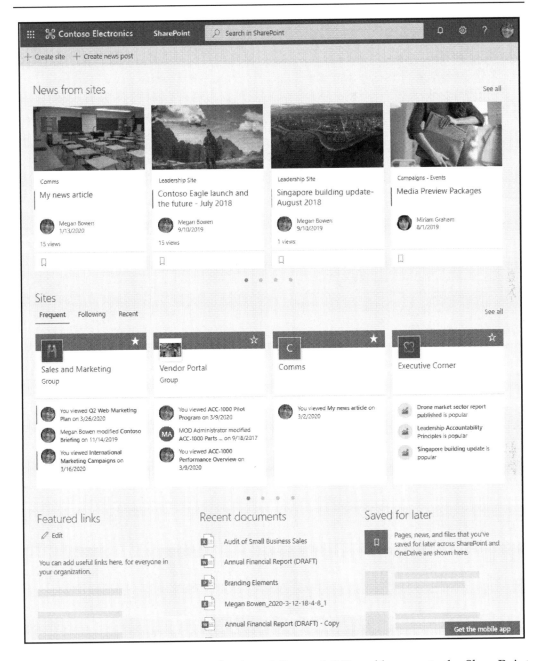

That's it! You just learned how to log in to Microsoft 365 and browse to the SharePoint start page of your organization. The content that you will see on this page is personalized to you and can be customized by your organization.

How it works...

The SharePoint start page shows your interactions across all SharePoint sites that you may have access to. In short, this page lets you get to what's most relevant to you, even without you having to search for the content. The following is a brief description of the functionality and different sections on this page, starting from the top left and going toward the bottom right:

- **Microsoft 365 Suite Bar**: The blue bar at the top is called the **Suite Bar** in Microsoft 365. We discussed the suite bar as part of `Chapter 1`, *Overview of Microsoft 365*.

- **Create site** and **Create news post**: Clicking **Create Site** walks you through the steps of creating a new site in your SharePoint environment. We'll discuss this in more detail as part of the *Creating a modern site* recipe later in this chapter. Clicking **Create news post** helps you publish a new news post from within a site of your choice. Please note that these options are only available to you through the SharePoint start page if they are enabled by your organization. We'll discuss this in more detail as part of the *Adding a page* recipe in `Chapter 3`, *Working with Modern Sites in SharePoint Online*.

- **News from sites**: As the title suggests, this section shows you the news from your sites in one single place. You can also bookmark (that is, **Save for later**) a news item so that it shows up in your list of **Saved** items on this page.

- **Sites - Frequent** tab: As the title suggests, this section shows you *tiles* containing information about your most visited sites. In addition to the name of the site and a link to it, each tile shows statistics about when you last visited the site, when and who last modified anything on the site, and, optionally, what's popular in the site.

- **Sites - Following** tab: This section shows you a list of the sites that you are following. The information shown for each site is similar to that shown on the **Frequent** tab. When you create a site, SharePoint automatically adds it to the list of sites that you are following. To follow an existing site, you can click the **Not following** text toward the top right of any page on that site, as shown in the following screenshot:

- **Sites - Recent** tab: This section shows a list of sites that you recently visited. The information shown for each site is similar to that shown on the **Frequent** tab.
- **Featured links**: This section lets you manage links that you may want to bookmark for the entire organization to view. Any changes that you make to this section by adding, editing, or removing links will show up for the entire organization. Only users that have the requisite admin access can maintain the **Featured links** in this section.
- **Saved for later**: This section shows content, such as news items, that you may have saved for later.
- **Recent documents**: This section shows you a list of your recent documents across all of SharePoint and OneDrive for Business.
- **Get the mobile app**: SharePoint has a very robust mobile app that lets you access your SharePoint Online content on the go. Clicking the **Get the mobile app** button takes you to a page that helps you download the mobile app. You will need to enter a mobile number or email ID on this page. Microsoft 365 will then send a link to this mobile number or email ID. You can then use this link to download the SharePoint app and log in to it to view your content on the go.

See also

- Chapter 1, *Overview of Microsoft 365*
- The *Creating a modern site* recipe in this chapter
- The *Adding a page* recipe in Chapter 3, *Working with Modern Sites in SharePoint Online*

Creating a modern site

SharePoint provides various templates or site types so that you can create sites. These templates use similar building blocks but target different scenarios. They differ from each other in various ways, such as how they store information, how they present it, and even the nature of the functionality that they have to offer.

This recipe shows you how to create a site using the **Team site** template, which is the most commonly used site template for team collaboration.

Getting ready

Your organization should do the following before you can create sites from the SharePoint start page:

- Grant you access to SharePoint as part of the Microsoft 365 suite
- Enable the creation of sites from the SharePoint start page
- Enable the creation of modern sites in your Microsoft 365 environment

How to do it...

To create a new site from the SharePoint start page, follow these steps:

1. Browse to the SharePoint start page, as described in the previous recipe.
2. Click on the **Create site** option and then **Team site**, as shown in the following screenshot:

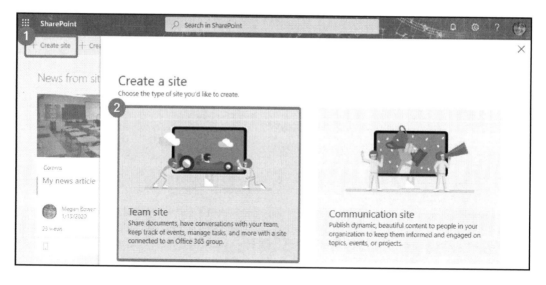

What we're creating through this page is something called a **Site collection**. Please refer to the *There's more...* section, later in this recipe, to find out the difference between a site and a site collection. If you can't see the **Create site** option, your organization has likely disabled the creation of site collections for you. Please refer to Chapter 3, *Working with Modern Sites in SharePoint Online*, for steps on creating a (sub) site if that's the case.

3. Enter a title and description for your site, and confirm or change the pre-selected **Group email address**, **Privacy settings**, and language (more about these settings later in this recipe). Then, click the **Next** button, as shown in the following screenshot:

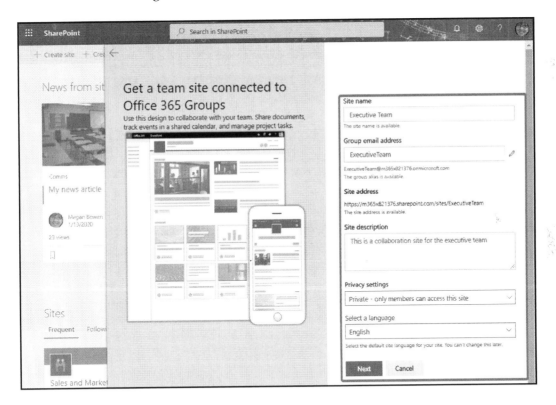

The group email address that you can see in the previous screenshot is used for the corresponding Microsoft 365 group that gets created along with the **Team site**. You can read more about groups in `Chapter 10`, *Microsoft 365 Groups*.

Furthermore, you should carefully choose **Privacy settings** on this screen. Choosing **Private** for this setting means only selected members that you have allowed on the next screen will have access to view and modify content within the site. Selecting **Public** for this setting would mean that **everyone** in your organization, by default, will be able to view and modify content within this site. You can always change the site's permissions after it has been created.

4. At this point, SharePoint will start creating the site in the background.
5. Even as it does that, SharePoint will prompt you to optionally invite other users to your site. These users are typically people from your organization who you'd like to grant owner or member access to this site. This can be seen in the following screenshot:

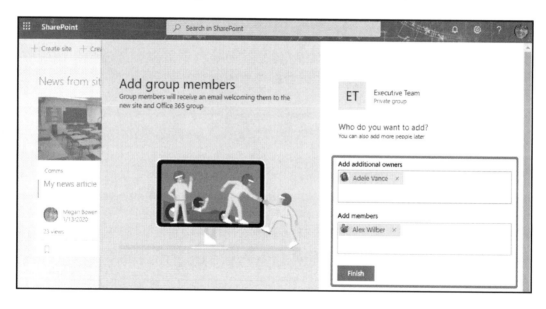

Owners and members who are added through this screen are granted two different levels of permissions in SharePoint. Users who are granted **owner access** to the site will be able to alter site permissions, add and customize pages, and change other key elements of the site. This access should only be granted to a select few users from your team.

People with **member access** are granted the ability to contribute to the content on your site. They can carry out tasks such as adding, editing, and deleting documents and/or list items. They can also view all the content within your site.

There is a third permission setting that isn't shown here, and that is visitor access. Visitors to your site can view the content within your site. This content can be presented through informational lists, documents, or pages within your site.

Who you grant member and visitor permissions to should be carefully considered, but know that these permissions can be changed after the site has been created.

6. Clicking **Finish** will then redirect you to the home page of this newly created site.

Congratulations! You just created a new site in SharePoint Online.

How it works...

At its core, a SharePoint Site is a website that lets us store information and then present it in different ways. Information can be stored as data in lists and in the form of documents and/or files in libraries within the site. SharePoint uses pages and, optionally, web parts in these pages to show this information in a variety of formats. When you create a new site in SharePoint, it automatically creates one or more of these artifacts for you within that site. Finally, every site that gets created comes with search capabilities built into it. Search in SharePoint is a quick way to find information relevant to you, not only from within your site but also other sites and workloads that your organization may have enabled in Microsoft 365. We will learn more about Search as part of the *Searching content* recipe in this chapter and then go through it in more detail as part of `Chapter 8`, *Search in Microsoft 365*.

Types of modern site collections

At the time of writing this book, Microsoft has made a variety of templates available for modern site collections. Let's go over them now.

Team site

This type of site collection is primarily used for collaboration within a team or a department actively working on shared content. As mentioned earlier, this is by far the most common type of site template used for creating SharePoint Sites. SharePoint Team Sites are also connected to Microsoft 365 groups, which, in turn, are connected to other components such as Planner and Outlook. Examples of team sites include sites created for individual project teams to collaborate on, extranet sites created to work with external partners or vendors, and sites created for internal departments (such as the Human Resource department or Finance department) for their team collaboration. This means your organization would typically have a lot of team sites.

 While this recipe described creating a group-associated **Team Site**, you can also have your designated SharePoint admin(s) create modern Team Sites for you without an underlying group. They can create such Team Sites through the SharePoint admin center.

Communication site

This type of site collection is used to broadcast a message or simply tell a story to your organization. Communication sites can be used to share news, reports, strategies, and other information in a visually compelling way. The content in a typical communications site will be shared with a large audience (potentially the entire organization). Examples of communication sites include your intranet landing site, a training site, a site where members in your organization would view key business metrics, and a site that's created to gather information for an organizational merger. This means your organization would typically have very few communication sites.

Hub site

SharePoint hub sites are a way to bring together (roll up) information such as news and activity from a family of related site collections. As the owner (administrator) of your site collection, you can either register your site as a hub site or associate it with an existing hub site collection. If you choose to associate your site with an existing hub, your site will inherit the look and feel (theme) of the hub site.

Your site will also inherit other properties of the hub site, such as the navigation bar, additional navigation links, applications, or custom lists with specific columns.

Additionally, the users who have been granted access to the hub site will start seeing content, news, and activity being rolled up from your site, along with any other sites that are associated with that hub site. This makes it easier for users to discover related content from across all these sites. An example of a hub site could be an enterprise Sales portal providing shared resources for the organization-wide sales teams and connecting multiple regional sales team sites and communication sites.

Hub sites need special permissions to be created and cannot be created by end users through the SharePoint start page. They can only be created by special users designated as SharePoint admins by your organization. You can read more about the SharePoint admin role here: `https://m365book.page.link/SP-Admin`

Home site

A home site is your organization's designated intranet landing site. Behind the scenes, the home site is just another communication site, but with the following differences:

- It aggregates content from your entire organization through news, events, videos, conversations, and other resources.
- The search experience in the home site defaults to the entire organization. This means that if you perform a search from the home site, it will bring back results from the entire organization.
- You can only designate one site from your entire organization as the organization's home site.

It is highly recommended that you create a home site as a place to aggregate content that is of utmost importance to your organization.

You can read more about the home site and the best practices surrounding its setup here: `https://m365book.page.link/Home-Site`

There's more...

In this section, we will briefly review the concept of site collections. We will then look at the difference between the deprecated classic user interface versus the more modern experience.

Site versus site collection

As noted earlier, what we created through this recipe was a **site collection**. Simply put, and as the name suggests, a site collection is a *collection* of one or more sites that are grouped under the same URL. More often than not, all sites within a site collection will share identical navigation, branding, audience type, and sometimes even similar security.

When you first create a site collection, SharePoint will create a top-level site, or what is known as the **root site**, for you. You can then create as many **subsites** as you'd like to create under this root site. You could also create as many subsites as you wish under these sites. All these sites and subsites may or may not be based on the same template as the root site.

Modern versus classic experience

SharePoint supports two different **user interface (UI)** experiences:

- The more modern, fluid, and mobile-friendly experience
- The classic experience, which is now being deprecated

The modern experience makes it easy for you to create dynamic sites and pages that automatically adjust to the resolution of the device that they are being viewed on and are, hence, mobile-friendly. The modern site experience also includes a newer, modern way of working with lists and libraries. Since the classic experience is being deprecated and no longer recommended for creating new content, we will only be discussing the modern experience in this book. For those of you with the inquisitive mind, here is a great article on the SharePoint community blog explaining the modern experience and why you should use it for creating new content: `https://m365book.page.link/Why-Modern`

See also

- `Chapter 3`, *Working with Modern Sites in SharePoint Online*

Viewing site contents

The **Site Contents** page in SharePoint provides a one-stop view of all the lists, libraries, and other apps on their site. Any subsites within that site will also appear here. Provided you have appropriate access, you can also add new lists, libraries, pages, apps, and subsites to the site from this page.

Getting ready

You should have at least **Read** or **View** access to a site in order to be able to view the contents within that site.

How to do it...

To view the contents of your site, follow these steps:

1. Browse to your site in SharePoint.
2. Click on the settings icon in the top-right corner of any page on the site and then click on the **Site contents** menu option, as shown in the following screenshot:

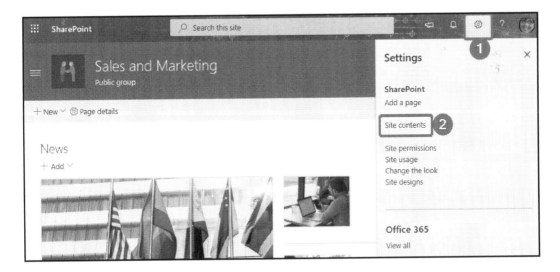

3. You will be directed to the **Site contents** page, as shown in the following screenshot:

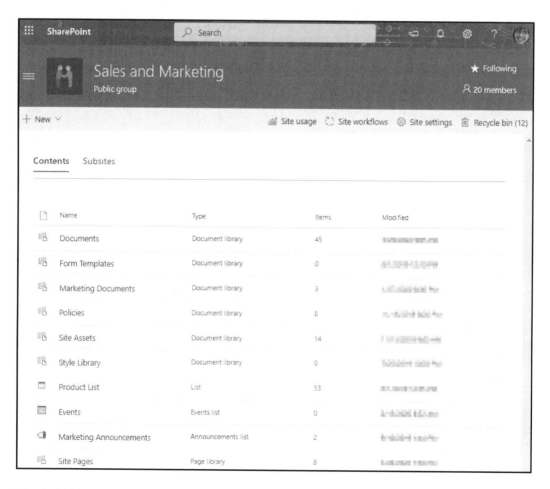

That's it! You can now view the various assets of your site from here.

How it works...

The **Site Contents** page lets you view a list of all the lists and libraries within your site. The view shows various information for each list and/or library, including its name, type, number of items in that list or library, and when anything was last modified in it.

If the site has subsites, you can also view a list of such sites through this page. The view shows various information for each subsite, including its name, description, number of user views, when the site was created, and when anything was last modified in it.

In addition to this, you can also perform various actions from this page, as shown in the following screenshot:

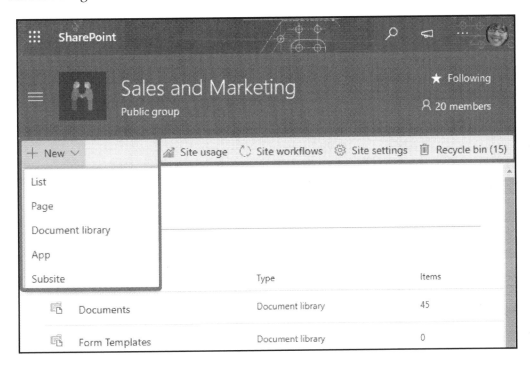

Let's go over these actions here:

- Use the **New** menu to create various artifacts in the site: We discussed the different types of items that you can create in a SharePoint site using this menu through various recipes in this chapter and will continue to do so in Chapter 3, *Working with Modern Sites in SharePoint Online*.
- View the **Site usage** reports: You can view these reports to understand how users interact with your site and what content is popular among the users of your site. Assuming you have the required access, this is also where you can generate and view reports about the content permissions within your site. You can read more about site usage reports here: https://m365book.page.link/Usage-Data

- View the **Site workflows**: SharePoint workflows are now deprecated and we discussed them as part of the *SharePoint Workflows* topic in the *Appendix*. However, if you are still using SharePoint workflows and have appropriate access in SharePoint, you can click this link to view the Site workflows.

 The modern way to implement process automation and workflows is to use **Power Automate** in Microsoft 365. We will discuss Power Automate in great detail in Chapter 13, *Power Automate (Microsoft Flow)*.

- View and manage **Site settings**: We'll discuss site settings in the *Viewing and changing site settings* recipe in Chapter 3, *Working with Modern Sites in SharePoint Online*. However, given that you have appropriate access, you can get to the site settings page by clicking this link.
- View the site's **Recycle bin**: The SharePoint recycle bin is just like the recycle bin on your computer, and it lets you view the items that have been deleted from your site. The following section provides more details about the site's Recycle bin.

Recycle bin

Just like the recycle bin on your computer, you can either restore deleted items or permanently delete them from here. However, a number of key differences between the recycle bin on your computer and the site recycle bin are as follows:

- The site recycle bin not only contains deleted files and folders but also deleted items of other types, such as list items, calendar items, contacts from the contact lists, entire lists or libraries, and even subsites. In that sense, it is a catch-all for anything that gets deleted from your site.
- You can only view content that you have access to based on your permissions within a site. So, unless you had permissions to that content before it was deleted from the site in the first place, you will not see it in the site recycle bin. An exception to this rule is for the site admins – since site admins have access to all content on the site, they also can view and restore any and all content that was deleted from the site.

- Two recycle bins: Deleted something from your site and deleted it again from the recycle bin? Don't worry! SharePoint's got your back. In addition to the primary recycle bin that you can see within a site, site admins also have access to a second- stage recycle bin (or the site collection recycle bin). This is where items go once they've been deleted from your recycle bin. Just as in the primary recycle bin, admins can restore or permanently delete items from the second-stage recycle bin.
- 93-day retention: The total retention period for items in the recycle bin is 93 days. You can restore content or have your site admins restore content within the site for 93 days. After that, the content is permanently deleted.

> Deleted subsites are stored in the second-stage recycle bin and can only be restored from there by your site admin.
>
> We also read about site collections as part of the *Creating a modern site* recipe earlier in this chapter. Deleted site collections will need to be restored by a designated SharePoint admin from your organization.

You can read more about the SharePoint Online site recycle bin here: `https://m365book.page.link/recycle-bin`
You can read more about the second-stage recycle bin here: `https://m365book.page.link/recycle-bin-2`

See also

- `Chapter 3`, *Working with Modern Sites in SharePoint Online*
- The *Viewing and changing site settings* recipe in `Chapter 3`, *Working with Modern Sites in SharePoint Online*
- *SharePoint Workflows* in the *Appendix*

Creating a list

SharePoint uses lists as the primary way to store information that end users such as you or I create. Almost all of the information in SharePoint is stored in some type of list.

This recipe shows how to create a new list from scratch. For illustrative purposes, we will use this list to store details of the products from our company's product line. This list will contain the following columns to store the product information:

- Title
- Code Name
- Product Line
- Date Released
- Notes

Getting ready

You will need either an **Edit**, **Design**, or **Full Control** permission on the site where you'd like to create the list.

How to do it...

To create a new SharePoint list, follow these steps:

1. Browse to the **Site contents** page for the site where you'd like to create the list.
2. Click the **New** menu and then click **List**.
3. Provide a descriptive name for the list so that others can identify the nature of the information that it stores. We are going to use `Products List` as the name for our list:

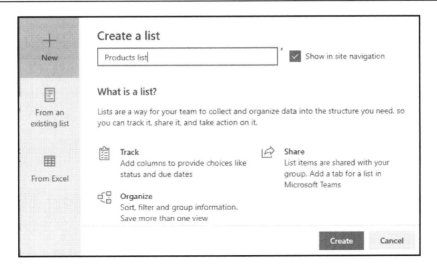

Instead of creating a new list from scratch, you can also choose to start **From an existing list**. Doing so will show you a list of existing sites that you have access to. Selecting the site will then show you all the lists from that site. You can then click on an existing list and click **Create**. Doing so will create a new list with the same columns, views, and formatting as the list that you had selected.

You can additionally create a list **From Excel**. You can select an excel file from one of the libraries in the site or upload a new file to create a list using the columns and data from the files. You can read more about this capability in the following support article: `https://m365book.page.link/CreateList-FromExcel`

4. We will leave the **Show in site navigation** box checked. This will result in the list to be shown on the left-hand side navigation menu for the site.

5. We will then click the **Create** button, toward the bottom of the screen, to create the list.

6. This will create the new list and show us the newly created list in the browser.

7. You will notice that the list already has a **Title** column created for us. We can now add the remaining columns to our list.

8. To add the `Code Name` column, click on the **Add column** option and select **Single line of text**. Then, enter `Code Name` as the column name, optionally provide an appropriate description for the column, and click the **Save** button.

9. To add the `Product Line` column, click on the **Add column** option and select **Choice** as the column type. Then, enter `Product Line` as the column name. Enter `Computers & Tablets`, `Gaming`, and `Home Theater` in three separate lines in the **Choices** field. Then, click the **Save** button, as shown in the following screenshot:

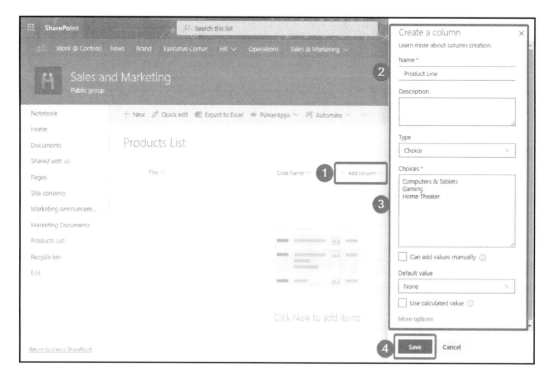

10. To add the `Date Released` column, click on the **Add column** option and select **Date** as the column type. Then, enter `Date Released` as the column name and click the **Save** button.

11. To add the `Notes` column, click on the **Add column** option and select **Multiple lines of text** as the column type. Then, enter `Notes` as the column name, optionally enter a description, and click the **Save** button.

12. When a new list is created in SharePoint, it creates a few additional columns that are not shown to the users by default. The **Modified** and **Modified By** columns are two such columns that get created with the list. We are going to add them back to the view of the list so that we can track who added the items to the list and when.

13. Click the **Add column** option and then **Show/hide columns**. Then, select the **Modified** and **Modified By** columns, as shown in the following screenshot:

14. This is what your list will look like in the end if you followed the preceding steps:

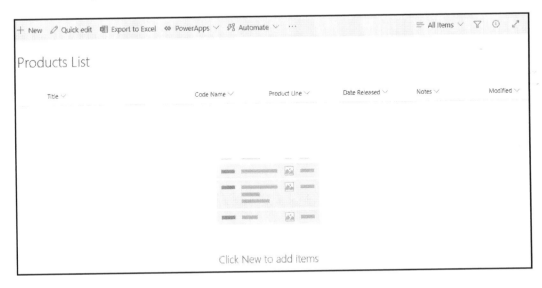

Congratulations! You just learned how to create a custom list and added new columns to it.

How it works...

In its simplest form, a list in SharePoint is a table-like container for information, similar to an Excel spreadsheet or a database table. It lets you store a collection of data in a way that enables you and your co-workers to organize and share information flexibly. Just like a spreadsheet or a database table, it lets you add and manage columns so that you can store and display different types of data such as text, number, date, and currency. You can also specify various column properties, such as setting a default or calculated value for your column, and making it required. The properties you can specify for a column also vary, depending on the type of column. The *Adding a column* recipe in Chapter 4, *Working with Lists and Libraries in SharePoint Online*, discusses list columns in greater detail.

In addition to the ability to define columns, a SharePoint list also lets you create **views** for it. List views enable you to filter, sort, group, and format the data in a list so you can easily highlight the information that's the most important to your audience.

Content in lists exists in the form of list items. Items in a list can include file attachments, people, and links. Furthermore, SharePoint provides pre-created forms that you can use to add or update the information in lists. You can also create your own customized forms to add or edit information in lists. You can use tools such as Microsoft Power Apps to create mobile-friendly forms and apps around this data. Additionally, you can configure email alerts for when list items are added, updated, or deleted. We will look at **alerts** as part of the *Adding alerts* recipe in Chapter 4, *Working with Lists and Libraries in SharePoint Online*.

Finally, SharePoint lets you create a blank list from scratch and also provides a set of pre-built list types. Examples of such lists include Tasks, Announcements, Contacts, Links, and Issue Tracking. We will discuss these pre-built lists and other advanced list capabilities in more detail in Chapter 4, *Working with Lists and Libraries in SharePoint Online*.

Deleting a list

You can delete a list by browsing to the **List settings** page. Please refer to the *How it works...* section of the *Viewing and changing list settings* recipe in Chapter 4, *Working with Lists and Libraries in SharePoint Online*, for more information about browsing to the **List settings** page and deleting a list.

See also

- Chapter 4, *Working with Lists and Libraries in SharePoint Online*

Adding an item to a list

You can add items to a list in various ways. These methods will be covered in greater detail in Chapter 4, *Working with Lists and Libraries in SharePoint Online*. This recipe will show the most commonly used method to add items to the representative list we created as part of the previous recipe. Even though this recipe uses the Product List as an example, the steps here are true for other scenarios where there's a need to store data in SharePoint.

Getting ready

You will need **Contribute** permissions or higher for the list you would like to add the new item to.

How to do it...

To add a new item to a list, follow these steps:

1. Browse to the list where you'd like to add the new item.
2. Click the **New** button above the section that shows the title of the list.

Selecting an item from a list replaces the top menu bar with the **item-actions** menu. So, if you have the required permissions for the list and are still not seeing the **New** menu, make sure you have not accidentally selected an item from the list of items below it.

3. Enter information for the required fields (highlighted by a red *) and, optionally, the non-required fields, as shown in the following screenshot:

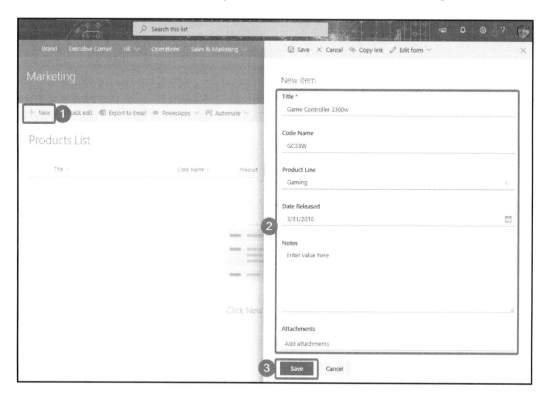

4. You can also optionally add file attachments for this item by clicking the **Add attachments** hyperlink toward the bottom of the form. File attachments include a variety of file types – images and documents, to name a few.
5. Click the **Save** button to add the item to the list.
6. Congratulations! You just added a new item to a SharePoint list.

How it works...

Information in lists is stored one item at a time (although there are ways to work with multiple items at a time). You can imagine a list item as a single row in an Excel spreadsheet, except that this row can hold a variety of rich information. Each list comes with a set of forms to add, edit, and view these items. Each list item can optionally also contain one or more attachments. Furthermore, the add, edit, and view forms can be customized to meet specific user needs. Every time an item is added or edited in a list, SharePoint also stores additional information (or metadata) against that item. This metadata includes information such as who created and/or edited the item and when. SharePoint also lets you create follow-up actions when items are added or updated in a list. You can do this using Power Automate, which we will discuss in depth in Chapter 13, *Power Automate (Microsoft Flow)*.

There's more...

Provided you have appropriate access, you can also delete one or more list items from a list and documents from a library. Let's learn how to do that here.

Deleting an item

To delete a list item, simply browse to your list, select the file you would like to delete, and then click the **Delete** option from the list's menu bar, as shown in the following screenshot:

Alternatively, you can also right-click the list item or click the three dots to the right of the title field to open the context menu and then click **Delete** to delete the item. This is shown in the following screenshot:

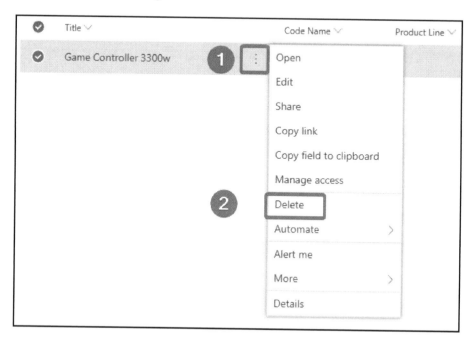

Deleting an item from a list or library sends it to the recycle bin, where it stays there for a couple of days until it gets moved to the second stage recycle bin or until it gets permanently deleted. You can restore deleted items as long as they are still in the recycle bin and have not been permanently deleted. Please refer to the *Viewing site contents* recipe, earlier in this chapter, to read more about the site recycle bin.

Additionally, if you look closely at the preceding screenshot, you will notice that the various list item-related actions in the menu bar of the list are also available through the context menu. The context menu also shows quite a few other actions that you can perform on the selected list item. This is also true for the context menu that appears against the files or documents in SharePoint libraries. Please note that the steps provided here for deleting list items are also true for deleting files from SharePoint libraries.

See also

- The *Viewing site contents* recipe in `Chapter 2`, *Introduction to SharePoint Online*
- `Chapter 4`, *Working with Lists and Libraries in SharePoint Online*
- The *Adding alerts* recipe in `Chapter 4`, *Working with Lists and Libraries in SharePoint Online*

Creating a document library

A library is a secure place in SharePoint where you can upload, create, and manage files for online sharing and collaboration with your team. Just like lists, each library comes with key built-in columns that store information about each file, such as who created the file and when, and who last modified it and when. You can always add to the columns in a library, just as you would do for a list. Almost all site types ship with a default library so that you can store the documents within that site. Libraries can be of different types. A **Document library** is the most commonly used library and, as the name suggests, it is used to store, manage, and share documents.

For this recipe, we will create a document library from scratch. We will use this library to store marketing documents. This library will enable you to classify each document using the **Document Type** and **Document Classification** columns.

Getting ready

You will need either an **Edit**, **Design,** or **Full Control** permission on the site where you'd like to create the library.

How to do it...

To create a new document library in your site, follow these steps:

1. Browse to the **Site contents** page.
2. Click the **New** menu and then the **Document library** option under that menu.
3. Provide a name and description for the library so that others can identify the nature of the information that it stores. We are going to use `Marketing Collateral` as the library name and `This library contains collateral for use of the Marketing team` as its **Description**.
4. We will leave the **Show in site navigation** box checked. This will result in the library being shown on the left-hand side navigation menu for the site.
5. We will then click the **Create** button to create the new document library.
6. This will create the new library and redirect us to it in the browser.
7. You will notice that the library already has the following columns created for us: **Name**, **Modified**, and **Modified By**. We can now add the remaining columns to our library.
8. To add the **Document Type** column, click on the **Add column** option and select **Choice** as the column type. Then, enter `Document Type` as the column name. Enter `Campaign`, `Case Study`, `Product Overview`, and `Product Pitch` in four separate lines in the **Choices** field. Then, set **Require that this column contains information** to **Yes** and click the **Save** button, as shown in the following screenshot:

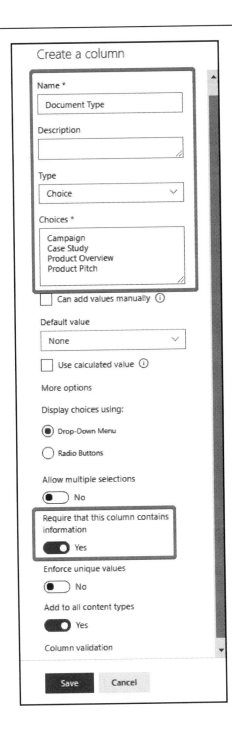

9. To add the **Document Classification** column, click the **Add column** option and select **Choice** as the column type. Then, enter `Document Classification` as the column name. Enter `Confidential`, `Restricted`, `Internal use`, and `Public` in four separate lines in the **Choices** field. Then, slide **Require that this column contains information** to **Yes** and click the **Save** button.

10. We will also change the position of the two newly created columns so that they show up next to the **Name** column (before the **Modified** and **Modified By** columns). To do so, simply click on the **Document Type** column name and drag it left, before the **Modified** column. Do the same for the **Document Classification** column, as shown in the following screenshot:

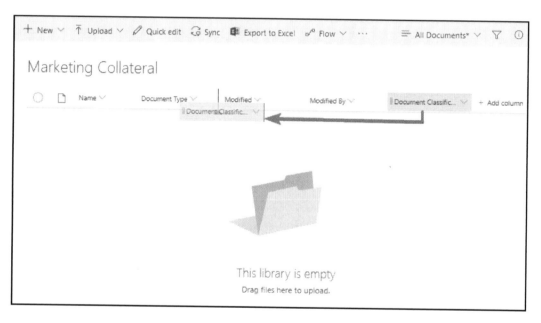

That's it – congratulations! You just created and configured your first SharePoint document library.

How it works...

A document library is a type of list that is centered around documents. Just like a list, it lets you add, edit, view, and delete documents and metadata related to those documents. One of the most popular capabilities that a document library enables is the ability for multiple users to concurrently work on the same document. Users can not only concurrently edit documents but can also view each other's edits in real-time. SharePoint also lets you create complex approval workflows on these documents. Similar to regular lists, you can set email alerts for when documents in a library are added, updated, or deleted.

Just like lists, SharePoint provides a set of pre-built libraries. Some notable examples of such libraries include the **Picture Library**, **Form Library**, and **Site Pages Library**.

See also

- Chapter 4, *Working with Lists and Libraries in SharePoint Online*
- Chapter 5, *Document Management in SharePoint Online*

Uploading documents to a library

SharePoint lets you create new documents directly within the library through the **New** menu. It also lets you upload documents that have been authored offline.

In this recipe, we are going to learn how to upload an existing document to a document library and then *tag* it with the appropriate metadata. Even though this recipe uses the **Marketing Collateral** library as an example, the steps here are true for libraries of all types.

Getting ready

You will need **Contribute** permissions or higher for the library where you would like to upload the document.

How to do it...

To upload a document to your document library, follow these steps:

1. Browse to the library where you'd like to upload the document.
2. Click **Upload** and then choose the **Files** option to open the file selection dialog, as shown in the following screenshot:

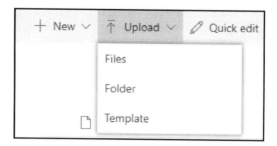

3. Browse to the file that you'd like to upload and click the **Open** button.

   You can upload multiple files or entire folders to a library using this method if you so desire.

 SharePoint also supports drag and drop capabilities, which work with a wide variety of browsers. Simply drag and drop the files or folders anywhere in the browser window when viewing the library. This will result in SharePoint uploading the files or entire folders and any subfolders with the contents of these folders to the library, resulting in the same outcome as that of *steps 2* and *3* here.

4. This will initiate the file upload process. SharePoint will show the newly uploaded file in the library, as shown in the following screenshot:

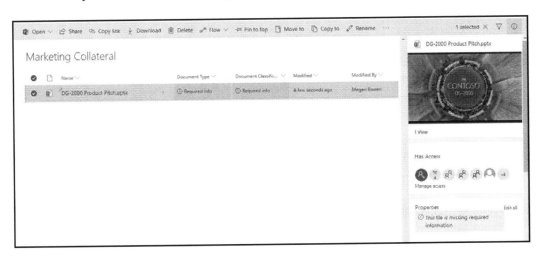

5. You will notice that SharePoint shows information about the file as well as a preview.

Clicking on the preview in the right-hand side pane activates the file and lets you preview the entire contents of the file right from within that pane.

6. Before the document becomes visible to everyone, you will need to enter information in the required fields for this document. You will also want to give your file a friendly title at this point. Click on the **Edit all** link in the **Properties** pane for this document. Make sure the document is selected if you can't see the properties pane.

7. Enter or select the required information for the document and click the **Save** button, as shown in the following screenshot:

After you've uploaded a document to a library, SharePoint will maintain a history of all edits that have been made for that document. You can view the previous versions of the document, when and who modified it, and even revert the document to one of these previous versions. This is particularly useful when a document is going through multiple cycles of updates by multiple users and you need to "undo" the last set of changes because they were inaccurate or incorrect, for example.

That's it! You have now uploaded your first document to a SharePoint document library. We will learn how to view and modify these documents in the *Viewing and editing documents in the browser* recipe in `Chapter 5`, *Document Management in SharePoint Online*.

How it works...

Documents are stored in libraries one document at a time. SharePoint also lets you upload or delete multiple documents at a time. If your documents have associated metadata, SharePoint lets you edit the metadata of multiple documents at once. The metadata that you add against the documents will also show up in the information panel in regular **Office** desktop apps or programs such as Microsoft Word, Excel, or PowerPoint. This can be seen in the following screenshot:

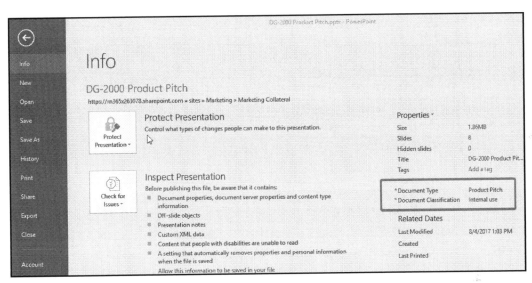

In addition to custom metadata, SharePoint will also store and show you additional information about who created or last modified the document and when. SharePoint also lets you create follow-up actions when documents are added, modified, or deleted. You can do this by using workflows in SharePoint or by using *Microsoft Power Automate*, which was added recently. For example, if a user uploads an expense report, you can send it through an automated approval process in your organization. Please refer to `Chapter 13`, *Power Automate (Microsoft Flow)*, for more details.

Finally, SharePoint enforces some restrictions on file sizes and paths. You can view those restrictions here: `https://m365book.page.link/File-Size-Path-Restrictions`

Uploading a folder

You can upload an entire folder and any subfolders along with their entire contents to a SharePoint document library. To do so, simply browse to your library, click **Upload**, and choose the **Folder** option. You will then be prompted to select a folder from your computer. Selecting a folder will create a copy of that folder in the document library and copy all the contents of that local folder to the newly created folder in SharePoint online. Note that, as we mentioned earlier in this recipe, you can also simply drag and drop multiple folders into your document library view. Doing so will recreate the folders and their contents within the document library.

See also

- Chapter 5, *Document Management in SharePoint Online*
- The *Adding alerts* recipe in Chapter 4, *Working with Lists and Libraries in SharePoint Online*

Sharing a document

Once you've uploaded a document to SharePoint Online, you can use the **Share** or **Copy Link** features in SharePoint to easily share a link to it with your colleagues. This recipe shows you how to share a link to a document using the **Share** feature.

Getting ready

You should have at least **Read** access to the document you'd like to share.

How to do it...

To share a document with a member of your team, follow these steps:

1. Browse to the document you'd like to share.
2. Click on the **Share** icon next to the document. Alternatively, select the document and then click the **Share** option on the top menu bar, as shown in the following screenshot:

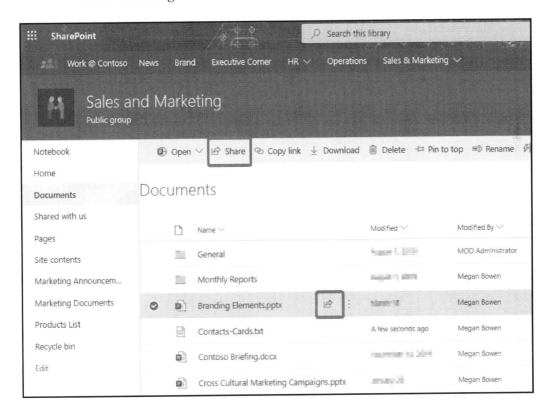

3. On the pop-up box that appears, click on the **People you specify can view** option (note that the exact verbiage may differ, based on your organization's settings) and choose whether the people or groups you are sharing this document with should be able to edit it:

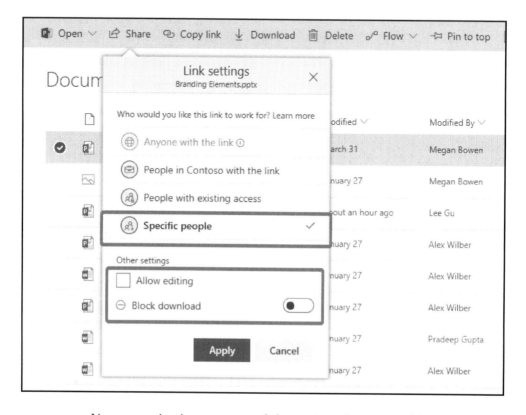

Your organization can control the options that are enabled and selected by default in the **Link settings** box, as shown in the preceding screenshot. Most organizations have the **Allow editing** option not selected by default. This means that the people who you are sharing the document with will be able to view it but will not be able to edit it unless you select the **Allow editing** option. You can additionally select the **Block download** option to prevent users from being able to download the documents. When this option is selected, they can only view the documents in the browser. This is useful when you do not want the users to maintain a local copy of the document. Note that the **Block download** option is only available when you are sharing the document with a view-only link.

4. Click the **Apply** button and then enter the name(s) of the people you would like to share the document with.

5. Enter a message to be sent with the sharing invitation email and click the **Send** button, as shown in the following screenshot:

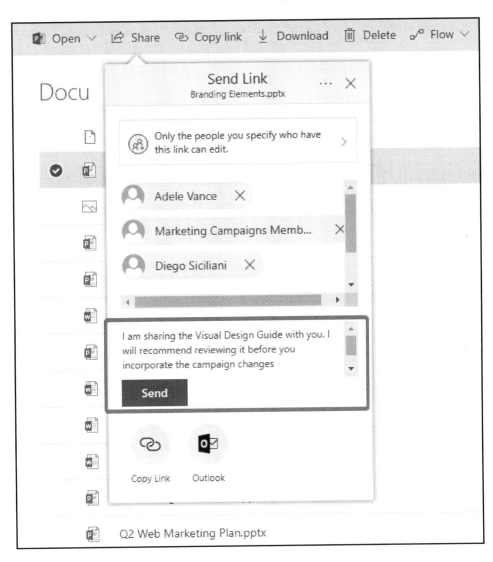

As shown in the preceding screenshot, and depending on how your organization has been set up, you may be able to directly share documents with entire groups, in addition to sharing them with individuals. Just start typing the name of your group or team and, depending on your organization settings, you might be able to select it as a recipient of the message.

6. SharePoint then sends the recipients an email with your message and a link to the document, as shown in the following screenshot:

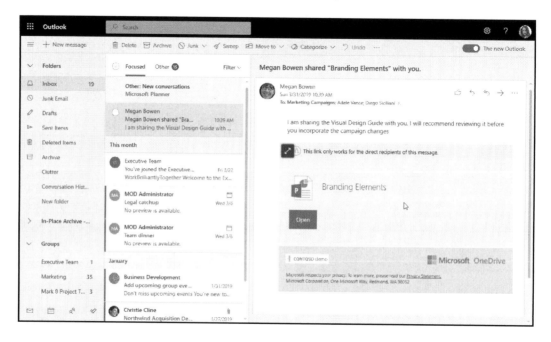

Congratulations! You just learned how to share a document with other members within your organization. The recipients of your sharing invitation can now view or edit this document, depending on the permission that was granted to them.

How it works...

There are a couple of things that happen when a document is shared:

- SharePoint checks to see if the person that the document is being shared with already has the required permissions. If not, SharePoint alters the permissions for the document so that the appropriate rights (Read or Contribute) are granted to the person that the document is being shared with. You can read more about managing document permissions in the *Viewing and changing document permissions* recipe in `Chapter 5`, *Document Management in SharePoint Online*.

 SharePoint also checks your permissions during the sharing process. If you do not have the permission to edit the document and try to share it with the **Allow editing** box checked, SharePoint will send an email requesting access to members of the site that have the authority to approve such requests. An email with a link to the document will be sent to the requested users after the sharing request gets approved. Additionally, note that the request approver can also control the level of access that will be granted to the requested user(s). They can restrict permissions and inversely grant greater access than what you had originally requested.

- It generates a link specific to the people that the document is being shared.
- It sends an email with the generated link, along with a message, if you specified one.

This recipe showed you how to share a document with specific people. Three other sharing options that you will see in the **Link settings** dialog are as follows:

- **Anyone with the link**: Use this option to share the document with anonymous users that are outside your organization. People with this link can view or edit the document without having to sign in to Microsoft 365. Since this option enables you to share your organization's content with **anonymous** external users, there's a good chance that it may have been disabled by your SharePoint site or organization administrators. When sharing a link through this option, it is recommended to set an expiration date, along with a password, for added security:

If you do decide to password-protect your file, you will need to share it with the users of the link. They will then be required to enter the password every time they use the link, as shown in the following screenshot:

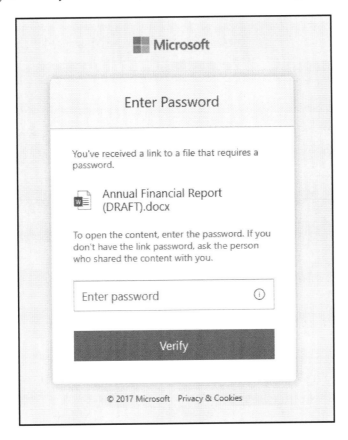

- **People in <your organization name> with a link**: This option generates a link that anyone in your organization can use to view or edit the document. Note that unlike the previous option, users of the link will be required to sign in to the site.
- **People with existing access**: This option enables you to simply get a link to the document without changing its permissions. Just like with the other options, if needed, you can directly send a message containing a link to the document right from within this dialog.

There's more...

As we just saw, the **Share** option sends an email message with a link to the intended recipients. You may, however, need to just copy the link so that you can then share it through different means (such as a Teams channel or even an existing email chain). The **Copy link** menu option, which is right next to the **Share** option, enables you to do just that.

Copy link

You can access the **Copy link** option from either the top navigation bar or the context menu for a list or library item:

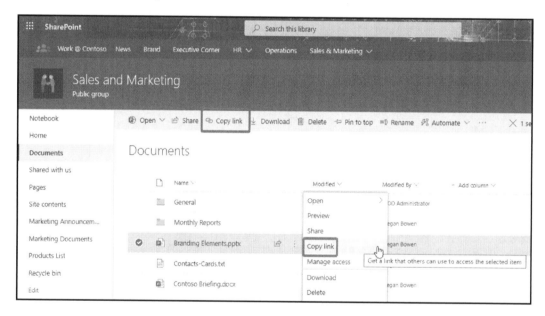

See also

- The *Creating a new document* recipe in Chapter 5, *Document Management in SharePoint Online*
- The *Determining and revoking permissions in a site* recipe in Chapter 3, *Working with Modern Sites in SharePoint Online*
- The *Sharing a file* recipe in Chapter 7, *OneDrive for Business*

Searching content

Search is a core part of the SharePoint user experience. It enables users to find relevant business information and documents more quickly and easily than ever before.

For this recipe, as a marketing manager in my organization, I am going to search for the visual design guide called "Branding Elements" that my team just helped put together.

Getting ready

All you need is **Read** access to the site where you will be performing your search. The results that SharePoint returns are "security trimmed," which means you will only see content that you have access to through permissions.

How to do it...

To perform a search within a site, follow these steps:

1. Browse to any page on the site where you'd like to perform the search.

2. Start typing your search keywords to see the relevant results. In this case, we will start typing `Branding Elements`. We'll notice that we immediately start seeing the results after entering the first two letters, as shown in the following screenshot:

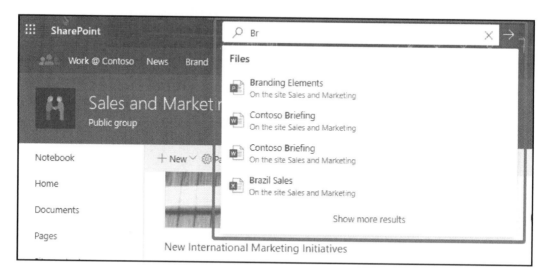

3. At this point, we can click the appropriate result if we've found what we're looking for.
4. Otherwise, we can finish entering the search keyword(s) and then click the **See more results** link, toward the bottom, to be taken to the search results page to see the matching results from the current site. Note that these results are sorted in order of their predicted relevance to you.

5. We can then expand individual results to see the matching text in context, as well as an inline preview of the matching document. You can also filter the results by the type of result and apply additional filters by clicking the **Filters** link, as shown in the following screenshot:

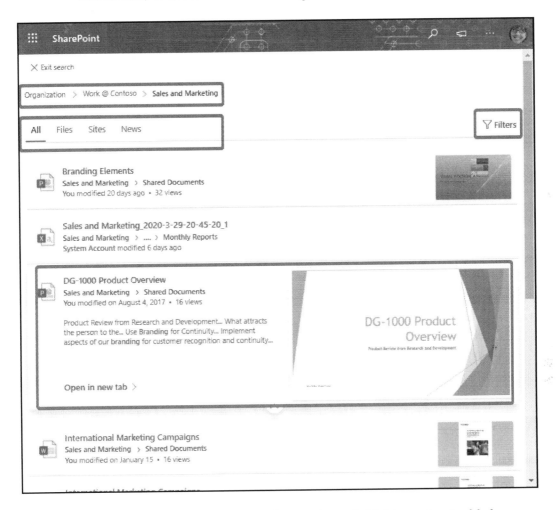

 The whole SharePoint search experience is highly customizable by your organization. For example, your organization can define additional filters that you can utilize. Another search customization that's widely used is to define "Best Bets," which are results that would show up at the top, depending on your search keywords.

6. Finally, the results you will initially see are those from within the site where you performed the original search. Clicking the **Work @ Contoso** link on the top, however, brings back results from the hub that this site is part of. Furthermore, clicking the **Organization** link on the top will expand the scope of the search results to the entire organization. Bear in mind that the results you see are always security trimmed, which means that you will only see documents and content that you have access to in the first place.

How it works...

Microsoft Search is a component of Microsoft 365 that helps you find information that you already have access to but do not know where to look for it. This information could be a document that you had previously created or it could be information that was shared by your colleagues. In its simplest form, SharePoint Search **crawls** and **indexes** information in lists and libraries. For libraries, the content that gets indexed includes the metadata associated with the respective documents. In addition to lists and libraries, SharePoint Search also indexes content in pages and the profiles of the employees in your organization. It then lets you **search** this indexed content using advanced filter criteria. Finally, it lets you **view the results** through a user-friendly presentation experience.

Some of the salient features of the search results page shown in the preceding screenshot are as follows:

- **Search scope**: Earlier, we discussed the ability to expand the scope of the search results from the current site to the current hub, and then to the entire organization. When you expand the search scope, you will still see what's most relevant to you first. So, if you have been working on a document in the recent past and that closely matches the search term, it will always be shown to you at the top, irrespective of whether you are searching within the current site, the hub that it belongs to, or the entire organization. Searching from within the Microsoft 365 home page or the SharePoint start page automatically defaults the search scope to the organization level. Similarly, performing a search from the hub site defaults the scope to the entire hub, meaning that it will show you results from all the sites within that hub.

- **Search result verticals**: The various tabs shown in the preceding screenshot are also commonly known as search verticals. Verticals are a way to group content of different types. The preceding screenshot shows verticals for **Files** (which only shows file and folder results), **Sites** (which only shows matching sites), and **News** (which only shows matching news posts). It also provides an **All** vertical that shows combined results from all the verticals. In addition to these, you may also be able to see a **People** vertical, which, as the name suggests, will show you matching people results. The People vertical is only shown when you expand your search scope to the organization level. We'll discuss People search in more detail in the *Finding experts and people* recipe in `Chapter 8`, *Search in Microsoft 365*.

- **Result previews**: Clicking anywhere in the blank area against the search result opens up the search preview. Here, you can see a preview of the text where the search result occurred within the document. As shown in the following screenshot, you will also see a small preview of the document within this section. You can scroll through the document using this preview capability. This is particularly helpful since it enables you to review the result inline to validate its usefulness, even before you click on it:

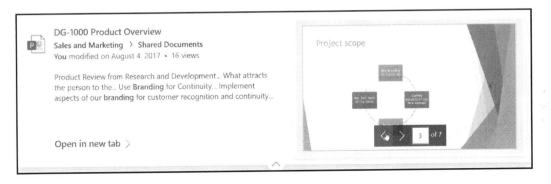

- **Filters**: Clicking this option currently lets you further filter the results by the last modified time. You should expect more capabilities to be available in this area in the future. However, the idea behind all the improvements being made to Microsoft Search is that the relevant content should automatically come to you, instead of you having to perform a search, apply filters, and so on.

Microsoft has been investing heavily in Search, resulting in numerous improvements being made to it. These improvements include things such as showing results based on their relevance to you. This relevance score could be based on the things you work on the most, the people you interact with the most, and the freshness of the content, to name a few. Recent enhancements to the platform have resulted in users being able to get the results back instantly, even as you click in the search box and start typing your keywords, and even before you click the search button to perform an actual search.

At the time of writing this book, Microsoft is rolling out a unified search experience through all of its Microsoft 365 workloads. This means that the search experience is going to be identical, regardless of whether you perform the search from SharePoint, Outlook, Teams, or other workloads in Microsoft 365.

See also

- Chapter 8, *Search in Microsoft 365*
- Chapter 9, *Office Delve*

Working with Modern Sites in SharePoint Online

3

In the previous chapter, we looked at some basic recipes explaining how you interact with a site in SharePoint. This chapter dives deeper into the workings of sites in SharePoint. We will look at various aspects of site customization, such as changing the site theme, modifying the navigational elements, working with pages in a site, and the web parts on those pages. We will also look at some additional scenarios, such as modifying site permissions and creating a subsite.

When your site's users first browse to a SharePoint site, they are presented with the **home page** of that site. If you are the owner of a site, you should carefully plan the information and layout of your site's home page. The information that is presented on the home page can vary significantly, depending on the purpose and type of your site. For a department site, for example, the home page could show key news about the department, important documents or forms, department events, key contacts, KPIs, and/or links to key information and areas within the site.

Besides the page content itself, every page in a SharePoint site consists of the following sections, which are also shown in the following screenshot:

- **The Office Suite Bar (1)**: The Office Suite Bar gives you a consistent navigation experience across all the workloads of Microsoft 365. It also gives you access to context-aware settings and your profile details, among other things. The Office Suite Bar was discussed in greater detail in Chapter 1, *Overview of Microsoft 365*.

- **Hub navigation (2)**: This area is visible only on sites that are part of a hub. It is used for cross-site navigation between various sites that are part of the hub. We discussed hub sites as part of the *Creating a modern site* recipe in Chapter 2, *Introduction to SharePoint Online*.

- **Site header and top navigation (3)**: The site header section appears on every page on the site. It contains the site logo and the site title. Clicking the site title from any page within that site will take you to the home page for that site. For certain types of sites, it also contains top navigation for that site. We will discuss the top navigation as part of the *Modifying the top navigation* recipe, later in this chapter. This section also contains links so that you can do the following:

  - **Follow or unfollow a site**: We saw this as part of the *Getting to the SharePoint home page* recipe in Chapter 2, *Introduction to SharePoint Online*.

  - **Share the site with others in the organization**: We will learn how to modify permissions on a site as part of the *Determining and revoking permissions in a site* recipe, later in this chapter.

  - **Create Site**: This option is only available on hub sites. Clicking this link creates a new site collection and associates it with the selected hub.

  - **Group membership count**: For group-connected Team sites, this section also shows the members in that group. You will learn more about this in Chapter 10, *Microsoft 365 Groups*.

- **New menu and page editing toolbar (4)**: This section contains the following options:
    - **New menu**: Clicking this menu lets you add new lists, libraries, pages, posts, and other types of apps and artifacts to your site.
    - **Page details**: Clicking this link lets you view and edit various properties of the page.
    - **Published date**: This shows you the last date when the page was first published or when updates to it were published again.
    - **Edit**: Clicking this option lets you make changes to the page and republish it. We will learn how to add and edit pages as part of the *Adding a page* recipe, later in this chapter.
- **Left navigation menu (5)**: This section lets you define the navigation menu in order to help users easily navigate between the various lists, libraries, pages, and other areas in your site. The left navigation menu is only available for certain types of sites. We will discuss the left navigation menu as part of the *Modifying the left navigation* recipe, later in this chapter.
- **Page content (6)**: This section contains the actual page content and will vary for every page within the site. You can modify content in modern pages by using **web parts** in sections of the page. We will discuss web parts as part of the *Adding a web part* recipe, later in this chapter.

- **Page footer (7)**: The footer appears at the bottom of all the pages within your site. You can enable or disable the footer for your site via the **Site settings** menu. We will mention the footer as part of the *Changing the look* recipe, later in this chapter:

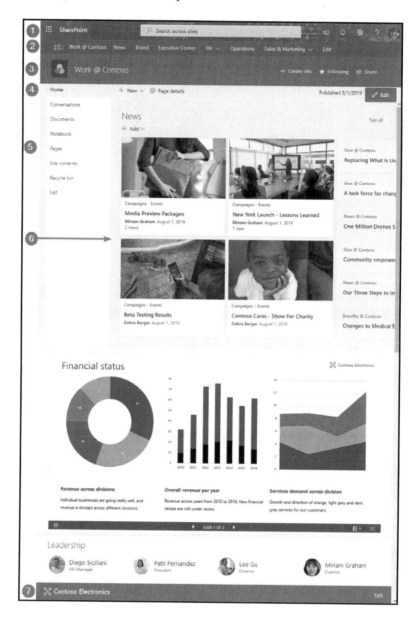

Please note that the options mentioned here and the actions that you can perform through these options are highly dependent on the type of the site and your level of access to that site.

In this chapter, we will cover the following topics:

- Changing the look
- Adding a page
- Adding a web part
- Adding an app
- Modifying the top navigation
- Modifying the left navigation
- Viewing and changing site settings
- Determining and revoking permissions in a site
- Creating a subsite

Let's get started!

Changing the look

SharePoint lets you apply custom styles and colors to your site so that it closely aligns with the branding guidelines defined by your organization.

In this recipe, we will look at how to change the look and feel of a SharePoint site, primarily by changing its theme.

Getting ready

You will need **Design** or **Full Control** permissions in your site to be able to apply a custom theme.

How to do it...

To change the theme of your site, browse to the site and follow these steps:

1. Click on the **Settings** gear icon in the top-right corner.
2. Click **Change the look**, as shown in the following screenshot:

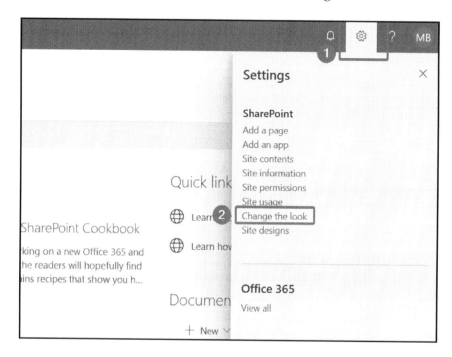

3. Click **Theme** and select the theme you would like to apply.

 The options you can see here can be controlled by your organization. A lot of organizations have a set of pre-created company themes available for their users to select from. Some organizations also lock down the themes entirely so that users cannot change them.

4. Click **Customize** (**1** in the following screenshot) if you'd like to change the theme colors; otherwise, click **Save** (**2** in the following screenshot):

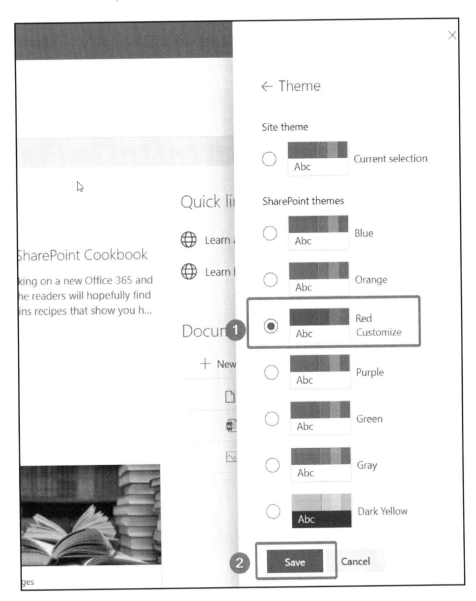

Congratulations! You just changed the theme for your site.

How it works...

There are multiple ways in which you can "brand" a SharePoint site so that it matches other sites and areas in your organization's Microsoft 365 tenant. The following is a list of some of the customizations you can make to your SharePoint site:

- Changing the logo for your site
- Changing the header area at the top
- Changing the top navigation (only for **Communication Sites**)
- Applying a footer (only for **Communication Sites**)
- Defining and applying a custom color scheme or theme
- Creating custom page templates
- Advanced branding using custom code and third-party tools

The options that are available to you depend on your role in the organization and the permissions that have been granted to you. If you have been granted access to brand your site, you will likely want to make sure that it adheres to your organization's branding and theming guidelines. That way, it will align better with other organization's content or websites and thus give your site's users a more consistent and familiar experience. Here's a great infographic from the Microsoft support team on how to customize your site: https://m365book.page.link/Customize-Site-Infographic.

An important caveat to note is that Microsoft pushes updates to Microsoft 365 and SharePoint online from time to time. Therefore, you will want to make sure that any changes you make using custom code or third-party tools adhere to Microsoft's guidance regarding branding customizations so that they are compatible with such updates.

Finally, if you are working with the classic experience, this support article will show you how to change the look for such a site: https://m365book.page.link/Classic-Design.

We discussed the modern versus classic experience as part of the *Modern versus classic experience* topic of the *Creating a modern site* recipe in Chapter 2, *Introduction to SharePoint Online*.

See also

- *Modifying the top navigation* recipe in this chapter

Adding a page

Pages in SharePoint are a means to display information and content to the users of your site. A SharePoint page is just like a page on any other website, except that you, as a contributor to or owner of the site, have access to modify it through easy-to-use page editing tools built into the platform. You can use these tools to format and style the pages, as well as maintaining a variety of content on them.

In this recipe, you will learn how to add a new page to your site.

Getting ready

You will need one or more of the following permission levels in your site to be able to add pages to it: **Contribute**, **Edit**, **Design**, or **Full Control**.

How to do it...

To add a new page to your site, browse to the site's home page and follow these steps:

1. Click on **New** and then **Page** from the navigation bar, as shown in the following screenshot:

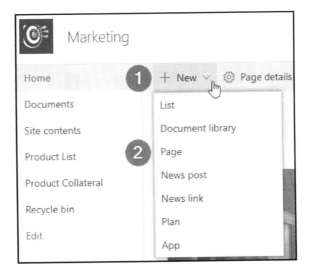

2. Then, select a template from the list of available page templates. For our example, we will select the **Blank** page template.

A page template is a pre-created design layout for your page. Instead of having to design a page from scratch, selecting a page template lets you start with a design that closely matches the anticipated layout and design needs for your page. In addition to the templates available through SharePoint, your site owner might have pre-created templates, which may mimic the design needs for the site more closely.

3. Click **Create page** to create the new page.
4. SharePoint will then take you to the newly created page. Here, you can give it a title and, optionally, start adding content to this page.
5. You can then click the **Save as draft** button to save the page as a draft, as shown in the following screenshot:

6. At this point, SharePoint will generate a URL for the page.

Draft pages are not visible to the **visitors** of your site and help you save your progress while you are working on them. It is recommended that you keep saving the draft page as frequently as possible. This will ensure that you don't lose your work if you lose your internet connection or due to other unforeseen issues. Please note that anyone with **Contribute** access or higher to the **Site Pages** library (more on this shortly) will be able to view such drafts.

7. If you'd like to, you can also click the **Publish** button toward the top right of the page to make your page visible to others.

Congratulations! You just published your first page.

How it works...

Pages in SharePoint are similar to documents that live in a document library. The main differences between documents and pages are as follows:

- Pages are typically stored in special libraries, called **Site Pages**.
- The permissions needed to edit pages are different from the permissions required to edit documents in a library.
- You can edit the content of a page using tools built right into SharePoint.

Once you've created your page, you can enter or modify some basic information.

Entering basic page information

For your new page, you can do the following:

- Give it a **Title**
- Change the name of the contact person for the page (or completely remove it from the page)
- Change the layout for the title area
- Show or hide the date that the page was published
- Enable or disable page comments

At this point, you can also start adding content to your page, but we'll cover that in more detail in the next recipe. Once you have added content to the page, you will need to publish it so that it is visible to other users.

Publishing a page

A page can go through various stages in the publishing process before it is visible to others in your organization.

When you create a **New** page, the page gets saved as a **Draft**. At this point, the page is only visible to you and to others who have contributor access or higher to the **Site Pages** library. The site visitors will not see any draft pages or versions.

While you will likely have several members who have Contribute access to the site, you may not necessarily want them to be editing pages on your site. It may be a good idea to set *custom permissions* on this library by *stopping permissions inheritance*. We will learn more about permissions inheritance as part of the *Determining and revoking permissions in a site* recipe, later in this chapter, and as part of the *Viewing and changing list permissions* recipe in `Chapter 4`, *Working with Lists and Libraries in SharePoint Online*.

You can then continue to edit the page and save it as a draft until you are satisfied with the changes. You can **Publish** the page once you have finalized its content. This changes the status of your page to **Published**. The page and its content now become visible to others that have access to your site. Your page will now also start showing up in the relevant searches. Additionally, you may want to add a link to your page from one of the navigation menus or from another page so that users can easily locate it. We'll discuss the SharePoint navigation menus in more detail as part of the *Modifying the top navigation* and *Modifying the left navigation* recipes, later in this chapter.

Once the page has been published, you can come back to it any time and **Edit** it to make changes to it. To do so, simply browse to your page and click the **Edit** button in the top-right corner of the screen, as shown in the following screenshot:

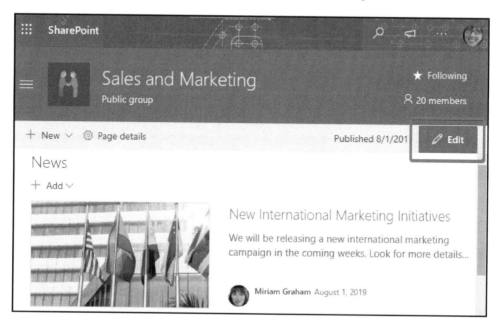

From that point on, you will go through the same editing and publishing process that you followed while creating a new page. Similar to before, you can continue to save your changes as drafts (which means they will only be visible to you and other contributors of the site). You can also **Republish** the page to make your changes visible to others:

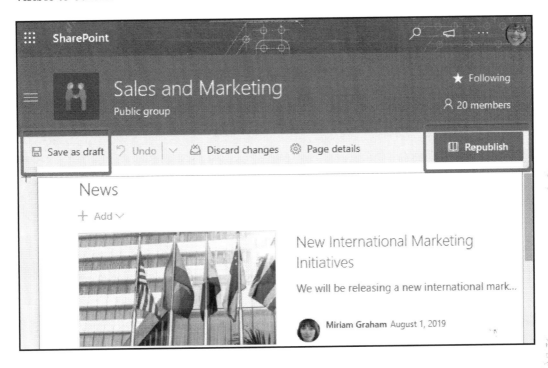

You can also configure the publishing process via the **Site Pages** library so that all the pages on your site go through a formal approval workflow before they become visible to others.

The Site Pages library

All pages get stored in a special library called **Site Pages**. This library is just like any other document library, except that it has certain capabilities tailored toward creating and managing pages. To browse to the **Site Pages** library, simply browse to the **Site contents** page, as described in the *Viewing Site contents* recipe in Chapter 2, *Introduction to SharePoint Online*. Then, click **Site Pages**.

The first thing that you will notice in this library is that the pages are grouped by the page author. You can change this view by selecting the various view options toward the top-right corner of the library, as shown in the following screenshot:

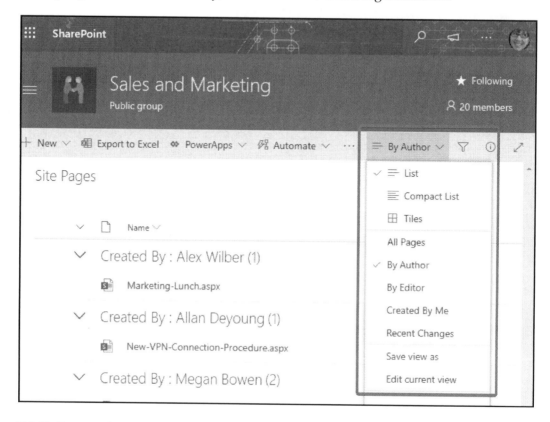

We'll discuss **views** in more detail in the *Creating a custom list view* recipe in `Chapter 4`, *Working with Lists and Libraries in SharePoint Online*.

The next thing you will notice if you are in a **Team site** is that the list of pages in the **New** menu shows **Wiki Page** and **Web Part Page** options, in addition to the usual option to create a **Site Page**. Please note that these page types are now deprecated and should not be used to render the modern site experience.

Thirdly, if you click **Automate** and then **Power Automate** from the library menu, you will notice an option to **Configure page approval flow**:

There's more...

In this section, we will understand a little bit about the page approval workflow. We will then review a special type of modern SharePoint page called the **News post**. Finally, we will look at how to delete a page from a site.

Content approval

A lot of large organizations require that page additions and modifications go through an approval process before new pages or changes to existing pages become visible to others. The *Configure page approval flow* option enables you to do just that. We will learn more about automating such approval tasks in Chapter 13, *Power Automate (Microsoft Flow)*. Please read this Microsoft Docs article if you want to learn more about the page approval flow: https://m365book.page.link/Page-Approvals.

You will start seeing the **Submit for approval** button instead of the **Publish** and **Republish** buttons once you turn on approvals for your library:

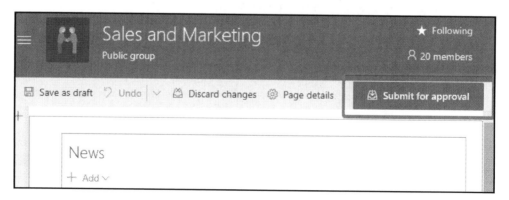

Clicking **Submit for approval** will result in the approval flow starting, which lets you add a message and submit the page for approval:

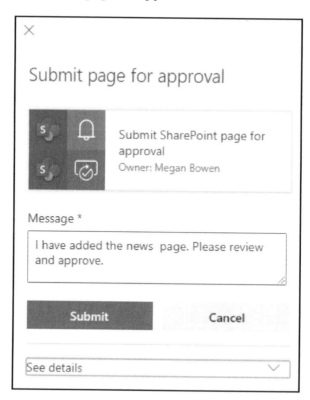

The respective approvers will then receive an email, notifying them of the approval request. They can then click the **Approve** link from that email to view the approval request and approve the page through Power Automate:

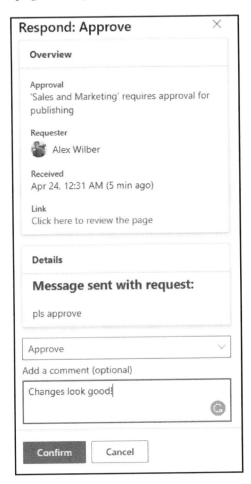

Once approved, the changes you made to the page will become visible to the site's visitors.

To turn off page approvals again, simply turn off the **Content Approval** setting from the **Versioning settings** page for the library. Please refer to the *Versioning settings, content approval, and document checkout* recipe in `Chapter 5`, *Document Management in SharePoint Online*, to learn more about how to do that.

News post and news link

A **news post** is a type of page that enables you to publish news, announcements, and updates, and create engaging stories about your department or organization. This content can then be automatically surfaced in different places through the various web parts and channels within and outside of SharePoint. The two ways that a news post differs from a regular site page in SharePoint are as follows:

- News posts surface through various pre-built web parts and channels.
- You cannot create news posts directly using the **New** menu from the **Site Pages** library. However, you can create them from the **Create news post** option from the top of the SharePoint home/start page. Please refer to the *Getting to the SharePoint home page* recipe in `Chapter 2`, *Introduction to SharePoint Online*, for details on how to browse to the SharePoint home page. You can also create news posts by clicking the **New** menu option and then **News post** from the top of any page in your modern Team or Communications site.

One of the other options that you will notice when you click the **New** menu mentioned in this recipe is a **news link**. While a news post lets you create and publish new content as a news post, a news link lets you create a link to existing content and surface it as a news post. In addition to promoting content from within your SharePoint sites, you can also promote external content such as the news from your external site.

Creating, maintaining, and having news posts or news links surface in various places is a relatively large topic and beyond the scope of this book. You can, however, refer to the following Microsoft support articles for more details on how to do that:

- **Create and share news on your SharePoint sites**: `https://m365book.page.link/Create-News`
- **Use the News web part on the SharePoint page**: `https://m365book.page.link/News-WebPart`
- **Create an organization news site**: `https://m365book.page.link/News-Site`

Finally, this resource lists some compelling use cases for creating SharePoint news pages: `https://m365book.page.link/SP-News`

Deleting a page

The only way to delete a page is from the **Site Pages** library. To delete a page, simply browse to the **Site Pages** library within the site, select the page you would like to delete, and then click the **Delete** option from the library menu, as shown in the following screenshot:

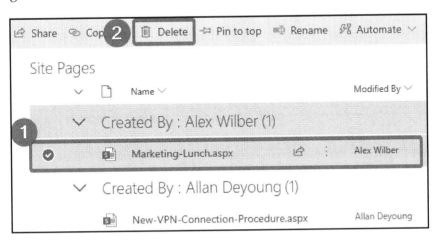

In general, this is also how you can delete documents from within any document library, or items from with any list in SharePoint. Please refer to the *Deleting an item* section of the *Adding an item to a list* recipe in Chapter 2, *Introduction to SharePoint Online*, for more details about deleting items and documents from SharePoint lists and libraries. Additionally, the *Viewing Site contents* recipe in Chapter 2, *Introduction to SharePoint Online*, discusses the site recycle bin. The site recycle bin is where deleted pages are stored until they are permanently deleted.

See also

- The *Viewing Site contents* recipe in Chapter 2, *Introduction to SharePoint Online*
- The *Audience targeting* topic of the *Adding a web part* recipe, later in this chapter
- The *Creating a custom list view* recipe in Chapter 4, *Working with Lists and Libraries in SharePoint Online*

- The *Versioning settings, content approval, and document checkout* recipe in Chapter 5, *Document Management in SharePoint Online*
- Chapter 13, *Power Automate (Microsoft Flow)*

Adding a web part

Web parts are the smallest building blocks of a page. Each web part is a self-contained widget that lets you add text, images, files, videos, and other dynamically generated content to your page. This content can exist within your Microsoft 365 environment or can even exist externally.

In this example, we will add a **news** web part to our recently created page. This news web part will show a summary of all the news items within the current SharePoint site or from other SharePoint sites within your tenant.

Getting ready

You will need to have one or more of the following permission levels in your site to edit pages and add web parts to them: **Contribute**, **Edit**, **Design**, or Full Control.

How to do it...

To add a web part to a page, browse to the page you wish to add a web part to and follow these steps:

1. Click the **Edit** link from the page editing bar in the top-right corner of the page that you'd like to edit.
2. Click the + symbol at the bottom of the title area to reveal a list of web parts that you can add to your page.

3. Select a web part you would like to add. In this case, we will add the **News** web part, which aggregates news from your site, as shown in the following screenshot:

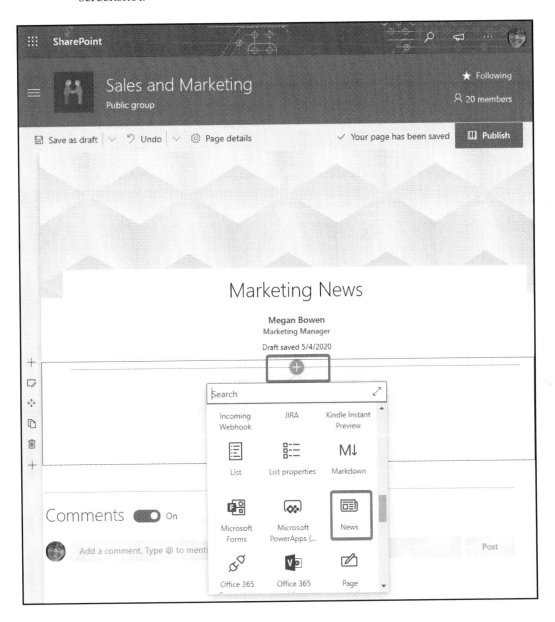

4. Click **Edit web part** (the pencil icon) to the left of the web part to optionally edit properties for the web part:

The properties you see will vary, depending on the type of web part that you are editing. For the **News** web part, you can select the source of news, its layout within the section, any filters you'd like to apply to the news, and how you'd like to organize the news.

5. You can then either save your changes as a draft or **Republish** the modified version of your page so that your changes are visible to other users.

That's it! You just learned how to add a web part to a page in SharePoint.

How it works...

When you edit a page, its status changes to **Draft** as an indicator. Other users will continue to see the previously published version of the page, and the changes that you make to the page aren't visible to others unless you publish it again. It's only when you **Republish** the page that users will see the changes that you made to it.

A page in SharePoint can have multiple horizontal **sections**. Each section, in turn, can be subdivided into one or more vertical subsections or *columns*. You can then add web parts to the appropriate columns in these sections. You can add a section by clicking the **+** sign toward the left of your page:

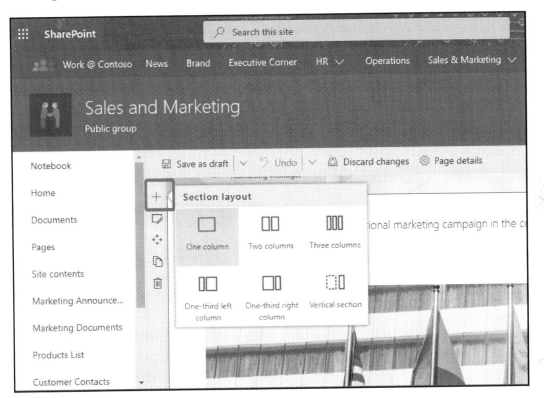

SharePoint offers a variety of web parts that you can add to your page:

- You can add web parts that let you enter text or wiki-like markdown on your page.
- There's also a web part that, given an address, shows you the current weather information on your page.
- There are also web parts for embedding images, documents, or content from secure (HTTPS only) third-party websites (such as YouTube) on your page.
- You can show commonly used links on your page using the **Quick links** web part.

- You can also show content from existing lists or libraries on your site using the corresponding list or document library web parts.
- Your organization can develop custom web parts using one of the modern SharePoint development frameworks, such as the SharePoint Framework, which will be discussed in greater detail in `Chapter 18`, *Custom Development - SharePoint Framework*.
- You also download a variety of third-party apps and web parts from the SharePoint store. We will discuss this in more detail in the *Adding an app* recipe, later in this chapter.

This is just a limited subset from the list of all the web parts that SharePoint has to offer. There are a ton of other web parts that enable interesting capabilities, which we encourage you to explore. You can view the complete list of web parts and an overview via this Microsoft support article: `https://m365book.page.link/WebParts-List`.

Remember that each web part comes with a set of properties that you can use to somewhat customize yours and your customers' experience.

There's more...

In this section, we will look at the concept of audience targeting, which lets you provide relevant content to users based on their profile attributes, such as their department or role, to name a couple.

Audience targeting

Audience targeting in SharePoint enables you to serve up relevant content to your users. It does this by allowing you to selectively restrict access to the following content to a *targeted* set of users:

- **Navigation links**: This enables you to show certain links to particular groups. For example, you could potentially set a target audience on the HR menu link, from the top navigation menu, so that it only shows up for members of the HR department.
- **Pages and news**: This enables you to target certain pages and news posts at certain groups. For example, you could set a target audience for a marketing news page so that it only shows for the members of the Marketing department.

- **Various web parts**: Turning this *filter* on for the News and Highlighted content web parts enables these web parts to respect the target audience values that have been defined for the published news posts or various SharePoint list or library items.

Please note that audience targeting, in a sense, employees *security by obscurity* to only show relevant content (or rather hide irrelevant content) to the targeted users. This means that it does not change the underlying permissions of the underlying content but merely *hides* it from being shown up in the UI for users who are not part of the groups that the content is targeted at. For example, even if you set the audience for the HR site navigation link so that the link is only visible to HR department users, users that are not part of the HR department can still directly browse to the HR department site if they know the URL.

Using audience targeting is a great way to create a personalized experience for the users of your site. For example, you could have the same set of web parts on your site's home page and yet show different content to various users, depending on the departments or teams that they belong to.

The following Microsoft support articles provide a deep dive into the various concepts and how-tos of audience targeting:

- **Overview of audience targeting in modern SharePoint sites**: `https://m365book.page.link/Audience-Targeting-Overview`
- **Target navigation, news, and files to specific audiences**: `https://m365book.page.link/Audience-Targeting-Uses`

Adding an app

You can extend the functionality of your SharePoint site by adding apps to it. Just like the apps on a mobile device, SharePoint apps are ready-to-use standalone widgets or applications that help address specific business needs.

In this recipe, we will learn how to add an app from the SharePoint Store.

Getting ready

You need to have **Full Control** access to the site you would like to add the app to.

How to do it...

To add an app from the SharePoint Store, follow these steps:

1. Browse to the home page of your site.
2. Click **New** from the page editing menu and then click **App**, as shown in the following screenshot:

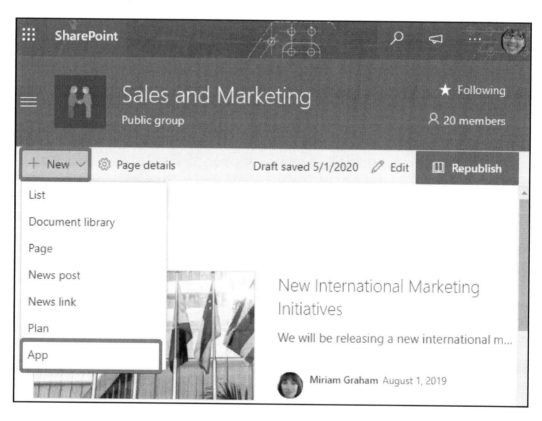

3. Doing so will take you to the **Apps You Can Add** screen of the **Your Apps** section. Here, you can view a list of the intrinsic SharePoint Apps (usually various kinds of lists and libraries) that you can add to your site. You will also see any apps that your organization has created or previously purchased but that haven't been added to your site yet. You can add an app from this screen by simply clicking on the app. The **Facebook Integration** app shown in the following screenshot is an example of one such app that my organization had purchased previously:

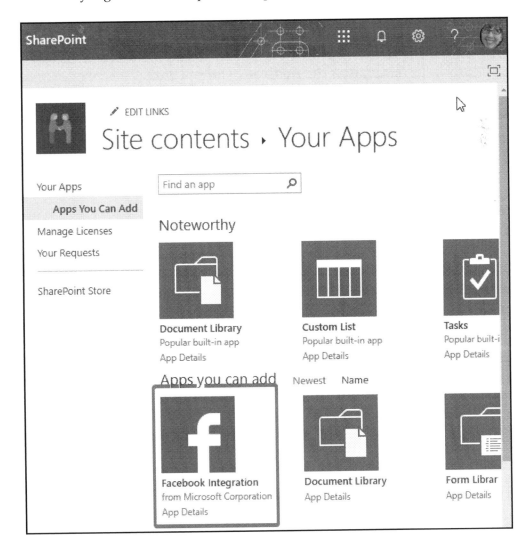

4. Next, click the **SharePoint Store** link from the left navigation menu to be taken to the **SharePoint Store**. As shown in the following screenshot, you can perform various actions on this screen (clockwise from the top right):

- Change the purchase currency or select a different language to view the apps.
- Search for apps by typing the full or partial name in the search box.
- Filter apps by category.
- Choose between paid or free apps.
- Sort the results by various criteria.
- Finally, as shown in the following screenshot, you can hover over any app to read a brief description of that app:

5. Search for your app by using one of the search and filter criteria. We will search using the text `Microsoft Dynamics` for our example.

6. Click the desired app once you are satisfied with your search results. You will then be taken to the app details screen. Make sure you click the **Permissions** link on this screen, as highlighted in the following screenshot, to view the permissions that the app will acquire once deployed to your site:

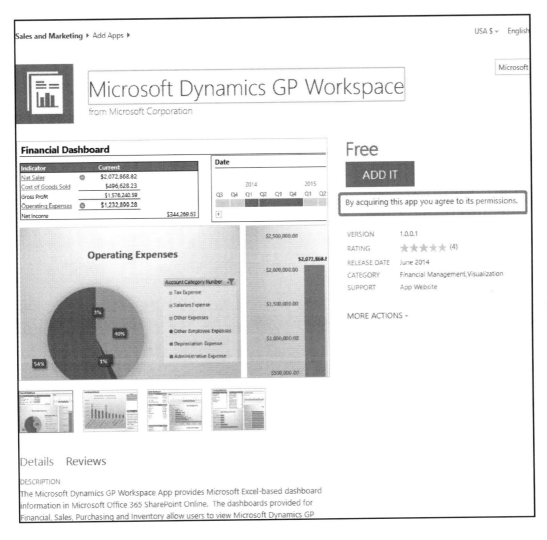

7. Click **ADD IT** to purchase the app for your organization.

8. Click **Continue** on the confirmation screen. You will then be taken to a screen that does the following:

   - Informs you that the app was added to your organization's *App catalog*. From this point on, owners of all sites will start seeing the app on the **Apps you can add** screen, as we saw earlier. They will be able to simply click on the app to add it to their site.

   - It allows you to continue adding the app to your site. Deselecting **Allow adding this app to <site name>** will still add the app to your organization's app catalog but will not add it to your site. You can add the app later to your site through the **Apps you can add** screen, even if you deselect this option for now:

9. Click **Return to site** to be taken back to your site. If you did leave the **Allow adding this app to <site name>** option selected, you will see the following message, informing you of the permissions that the app will acquire and the actions that it can perform once it has been added to your site:

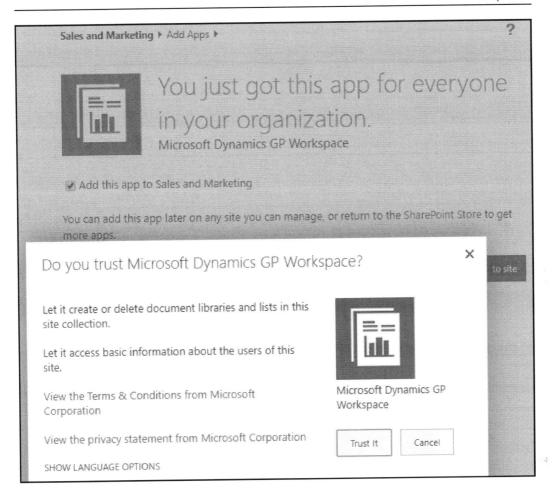

10. Click **Trust it** to confirm that you are fine with the access that the app has to your site and its users. Doing so will add the app to your site and will also redirect you to the **Site contents** page, where you can view the app and any other apps on your site.

Just like various other app stores, the apps on the SharePoint Store are thoroughly vetted before they are allowed to be hosted there. It is, however, always a good idea to make sure you review the actions that the app can perform on your site before you enable it.

Congratulations! You just learned how to purchase an app from the SharePoint Store and add it to your site. From this point on, depending on the type of app, you can either add it as an app part to a page on your site or click the app to explore its functionality. Some of the more complex apps may require your company administrators to download additional apps and components from the respective app vendor's website before the app you purchased can work. Besides this, someone in your organization may need to work on procuring the appropriate licenses from the app vendor. Almost all apps that you will find on the SharePoint Store will indicate they are free to add to your tenant. Some of them, however, will actually require you to purchase licenses directly from the vendor. For both scenarios mentioned here, you will receive appropriate messages while adding the app from the SharePoint Store.

How it works...

In addition to adding apps using the **New** menu from a page on your site, you can add SharePoint apps from the following places:

- By clicking on the gear icon in the top-right corner of your site and then clicking **Add an app**, as shown in the following screenshot:

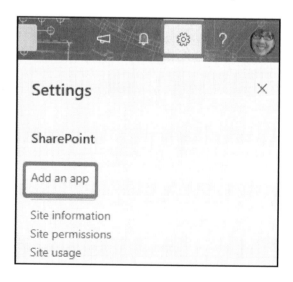

- By using the **New** menu option of the **Site contents** page. Please refer to the *Viewing Site contents* recipe in `Chapter 2`, *Introduction to SharePoint Online*, for more details of the **Site contents** page.

Types of add-ins

SharePoint custom apps are also commonly known as **add-ins**. From a functional perspective, SharePoint add-ins can provide three types of functionality:

- **App parts**: These are usually simple apps that can be added as app parts or web parts on existing **Site Pages**. We looked at web parts as part of the previous recipe in this chapter. An example of this could be an app that gathers information from your organization's Facebook page and shows it on the home page of your SharePoint site.
- **Full page apps**: These are usually more complex apps that provide a single-page or multipage experience for implementing a larger business functionality. These apps are usually meant to automate more complex business processes.
- **SharePoint extensions**: These apps can be used to extend SharePoint's features, such as adding to the existing ribbons, menus, or buttons.

From a technical perspective, SharePoint add-ins come in two flavors:

- **SharePoint hosted add-ins**: These add-ins are completely hosted within your organization's SharePoint tenant. All the components for this add-in exist within the SharePoint site where the add-in is hosted.
- **Provider hosted add-ins**: These add-ins usually have one or more business components hosted in a remote *provider (vendor)-hosted* location. These remote components could include the following:
  - Business logic
  - Data hosted as databases, blobs, caches, and so on
  - Any other type of components that may or may not be built and/or hosted using the Microsoft technology stack

There's more...

Your organization can decide to create their own add-ins. Please refer to Chapter 18, *Custom Development - SharePoint Framework,* to learn more about how to create your own add-ins, along with other aspects of SharePoint development. Your organization can publish these add-ins either to the SharePoint Store or to an internal app catalog.

App catalog

An app catalog is a site collection that is created within the organization's tenant. The purpose of this site collection is to host any add-ins that have been created by your organization. It can also be used to host third-party add-ins. At its core, the app catalog contains a document library where authorized users can upload the application's *packages*. These packages can then optionally go through an approval process before they are enabled in their sites by the respective site owners:

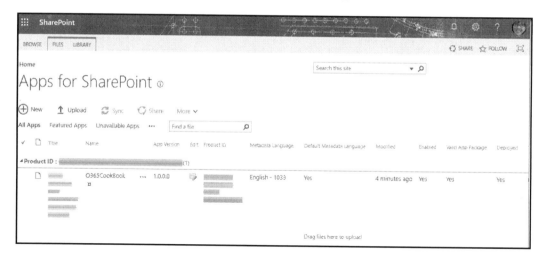

Once approved and deployed, these apps become available for the site owners to deploy through the **Apps you can add** screen, which we discussed previously in this recipe. Please refer to the *Deploying your SPFx web part to a Microsoft 365 tenant* recipe in Chapter 18, *Custom Development - SharePoint Framework,* for more details on the app catalog.

Removing an app from your site

Site owners can remove add-ins that were previously deployed to their site by browsing to the **Site contents** page, clicking the three dots next to the app, and then clicking **Remove** from the context menu, as shown in the following screenshot:

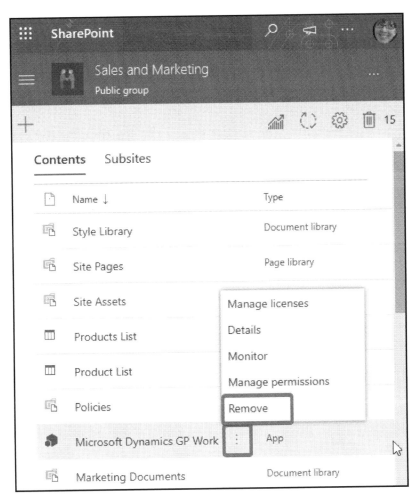

Please note that at the time of writing, you will receive the following message when you try to remove the app from the **Site contents** page:

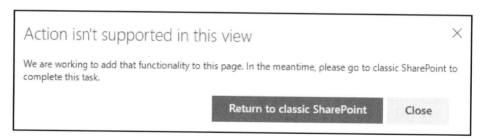

While this is expected to change in the future, for now, you will need to click the **Return to classic SharePoint** button to be taken to the **Site contents** page in *classic* SharePoint. You will then need to follow similar steps to delete the app from the classic **Site contents** page, as shown by steps **(1)**, **(2)**, and **(3)** in the following screenshot:

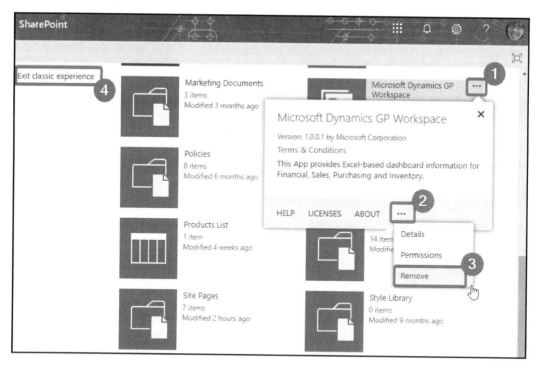

You will then need to click **Exit classic experience**, as shown by step **(4)** in the preceding screenshot, to return back to the modern SharePoint experience.

While removing the app completely removes any files that it uses internally, the app may have created artifacts in your site that may still be in use and will likely not be deleted by this operation. An example is as follows: if your app created custom pages or provisioned custom lists or libraries in your site, there's a good chance that you will need to manually delete those pages and/or lists from your site.

Please note that even though the remove operation removes the app from your site, the app will still be available for other site owners to use in their sites. This is because when the app was first installed, it was *licensed* to be used by the entire organization.

Removing the app license

Once you are sure no one else in your organization is using the app and provided you have the necessary permissions, you can remove the app's license by browsing to the **Your Apps** page, which was mentioned earlier in this recipe.

Since this operation affects multiple sites that you may not be the owner of, it is highly recommended that this step be carried out in consultation with, or by, someone designated as a global SharePoint admin by your organization.

You will then need to click the **Manage Licenses** link in the left navigation, click your app, click **ACTIONS**, and then click **Remove this license**, as shown in the following screenshot:

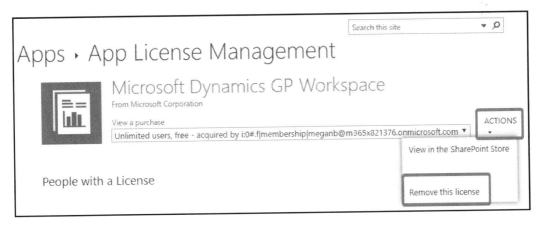

Doing so will completely remove the app and its license from your organization's tenant.

See also

- The *Viewing Site contents* recipe in Chapter 2, *Introduction to SharePoint Online*
- Chapter 18, *Custom Development - SharePoint Framework*

Modifying the top navigation

When you create a new **Communication site** or register a site as a **hub**, SharePoint also creates a navigation menu toward the top of the site. You can use the Global Navigation menu to help your site's users quickly browse to different areas in your site.

In this recipe, we will learn how to modify the Global Navigation in a site in order to add a new header and sublink menu items.

Getting ready

You will need either the **Edit**, **Design**, or **Full Control** permission level in your site to be able to modify the Global Navigation. The site you will be modifying should either be a **Communication site** or designated **hub** site.

How to do it...

To change the Global Navigation in your site, follow these steps:

1. Browse to any page within the site.
2. Click the **Edit** link toward the end of the top navigation bar, as shown in the following screenshot:

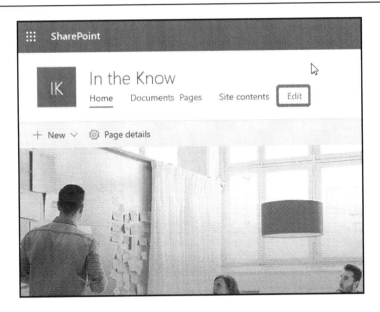

3. This results in the Global Navigation opening up in **Edit** mode. Position the mouse cursor below an existing item where you would like to add the new menu item.

4. Click the **+** sign and then select the **Header** option from the **Choose an option** drop down, as shown in the following screenshot:

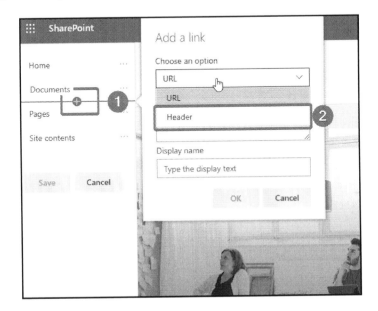

5. Give your menu a **Display name** and then click the **OK** button. This will result in a new **Header** being created.

6. To add a link underneath the newly created **Header** item, position the mouse cursor directly below it.

7. Click the **+** sign and then select **URL** from the **Choose an option** drop down.

8. Enter values for the **Address** and **Display name** text boxes, as shown in the following screenshot:

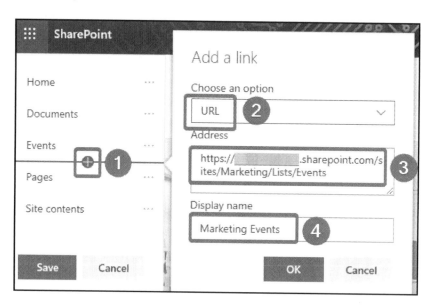

9. Click the **OK** button to save your URL.

10. Click the three dots next to your newly added link menu.

11. Click the **Make sub link** menu option, as shown in the following screenshot:

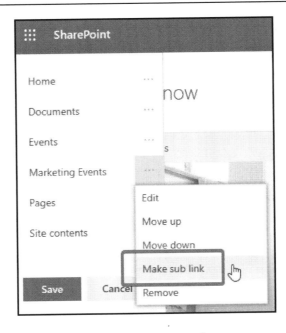

12. Then, click the **Save** button to save your changes.

Congratulations! You just added new navigation items to your Global Navigation.

How it works...

Communication and **hub** sites are typically used in communication or intranet type scenarios, where users are likely to be presented with content from across multiple pages and/or sites. Such sites are typically designed so that users can easily get to the content they are looking for. This is typically done through an enriched search experience. Even then, users typically start looking for content using the top navigation. Creating a robust cross-site Global Navigation in such scenarios aides the user experience by helping users quickly browse to the information they are specifically looking for.

There's more...

SharePoint lets you create the Global Navigation menu using two different widely accepted styles. We will discuss these here.

Cascading menu and Megamenu

SharePoint lets Global Navigation to be styled as either **Cascading menus** or **Mega menus**. A cascading menu uses the classic multi-level navigation to help you display your navigation hierarchy using multiple sub-level menus, as shown in the following screenshot:

On the other hand, the **Mega menu** option, which was recently introduced in SharePoint, lets you display multiple levels of navigation without you having to go through the various flyouts shown in the following screenshot:

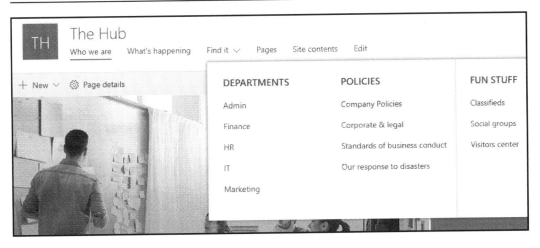

You can switch between either of these menu styling options through the **Change the look** setting, which was described earlier as part of the *Changing the look* recipe.

See also...

- The *Audience targeting* topic of the *Adding a web part* recipe, earlier in this chapter

Modifying the left navigation

When you create a new **Team site**, SharePoint also creates a navigation menu toward the left of the page. This menu is called the **Quick Launch** menu. The purpose of the **Quick Launch** menu is to help the users of your **Team site** quickly get to the different areas within your site.

In this recipe, we will learn how to modify the **Quick Launch** menu in your site and how to add a link to an existing list within the site.

Getting ready

You will need to have the **Edit**, **Design**, or **Full Control** permission levels in your site to be able to modify the **Quick Launch** menu. The site you are modifying should be a **Team site** or a **Team site** registered as a **hub**.

How to do it...

To modify the **Quick Launch** menu of your site, follow these steps:

1. Browse to any page on your **Team site**:

2. Click the **Edit** link below the **Quick Launch** on the left-hand side.
3. Click the + sign and then select **URL** from the **Choose an option** drop down.
4. Enter the link address and a display name for the link. Then, click the **OK** button.

5. Click the **Save** button to save your changes, as shown in the following screenshot:

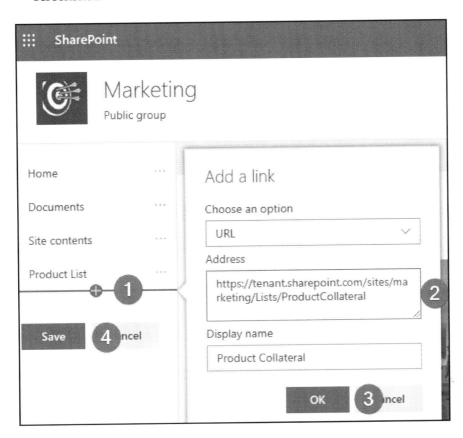

That's it! You just learned how to modify the **Quick Launch** menu for your site.

How it works...

The purpose of a **Team site** is to facilitate collaboration within a team. From that perspective, the users of your site are expected to navigate more within the different areas within the site than across other sites. The **Quick Launch** navigation menu helps to facilitate the process of browsing to relevant content within the site for such team members. Just like the top navigation menu, the **Quick Launch** menu also allows multiple levels of submenus to help you better organize the navigation within your site.

Note that in addition to defining your custom link, you can also use some pre-defined links, such as the ones shown in the following screenshot:

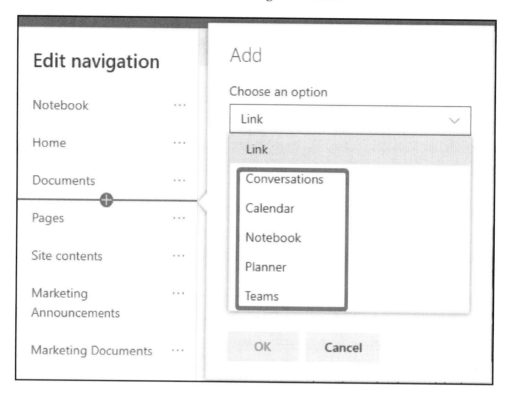

Clicking on **Notebook** in the preceding screenshot, for example, will create a link to the OneNote notebook for the site.

Finally, if you need to, you can completely disable the left navigation menu by browsing to the **Navigation Elements** setting under **Site Settings** and deselecting the **Enable Quick Launch** option, as shown in the following screenshot:

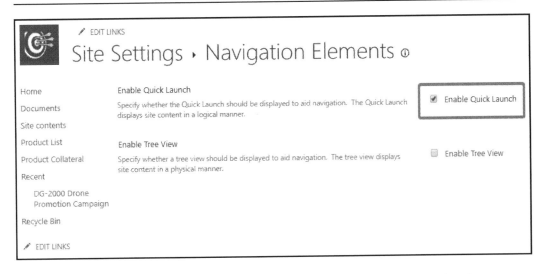

Note that the **Enable Tree View** option shown in the preceding screenshot is deprecated in the modern experience and is therefore not discussed here. A few classic pages, such as the **Site settings** page, which we will learn about in the *Viewing and changing site settings* recipe, later in this chapter, will still show the tree view if this option is checked. However, modern pages will not show the tree view, even if it is selected here.

See also...

- The *Viewing and changing site settings*, later in this chapter
- The *Audience targeting* topic of the *Adding a web part* recipe, earlier in this chapter

Viewing and changing site settings

SharePoint lets you view and modify various aspects of your site any time after it's been created.

In this recipe, we will learn how to view and change the basic information for a site, such as its title, description, or logo. We will also learn how to change advanced settings for a site, such as disabling the left navigation for a **Team site**.

Getting ready

Which settings you are allowed to change depends on your permissions within the site. The **Edit** and **Design** permission levels allow you to change certain features, such as the ability to edit site navigation and the site theme. The **Full Control** permission level gives you the greatest control over various site settings.

This recipe assumes you have **Full Control** access to the site.

How to do it...

To disable the **Quick Launch** for your site, follow these steps:

1. Browse to the site that you would like to change the settings of.
2. Click on the **Settings** gear icon in the top-right corner.
3. Click **Site information**, as shown in the following screenshot:

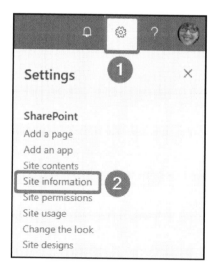

4. This takes you to the edit **Site Information** page. You can carry out the following actions on this page:
   - Change the site logo, name, and description
   - Change the privacy settings of the site
   - Change the hub association for the site (refer to the *Creating a modern site* recipe in `Chapter 2`, *Introduction to SharePoint Online*, to learn what a hub site is)

- View or change advanced site information
- Delete the site (you can use this link to delete a site if you have **Full Control** access to it)

5. Click **View all site settings**, as shown in the following screenshot:

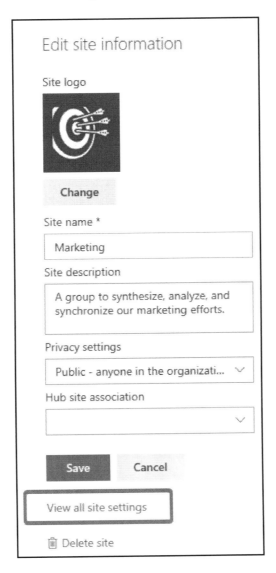

View all site settings

6. Click **Navigation Elements** under the **Look and Feel** heading.
7. Uncheck the **Enable Quick Launch** checkbox and click the **OK** button.
8. Browse to the home page of your site.
9. You will notice that the **Quick Launch** menu no longer shows up for your **Team site**.

That's it! You just learned how to browse to the **Site settings** page and modify the settings for your site.

How it works...

You can change the various properties and settings of your site after it has been created. The type of settings that you can change not only depend on your permissions within the site but also on the type of site you have. For example, a **Communication Site** will not contain the **Navigation Elements** option we discussed in this recipe since communication sites do not contain the **Quick Launch** navigation menu to begin with.

The following screenshot shows a few other settings you can change within a **Team site** if you have **Full Control** access to it:

Site Settings

Look and Feel	Web Designer Galleries
Quick launch	Site columns
Navigation Elements	Site content types
Change the look	
	Site Administration
Site Actions	Regional settings
Manage site features	Language settings
Enable search configuration export	Export Translations
Reset to site definition	Import Translations
	Site libraries and lists
	User alerts
Search	RSS
Result Sources	Sites and workspaces
Result Types	Workflow settings
Query Rules	Term store management
Schema	
Search Settings	
Search and offline availability	
Configuration Import	
Configuration Export	

Most of the settings on this page are advanced admin settings and are beyond the scope of this book or have now been deprecated in the modern experience. Others, such as **Site columns**, **Site content types**, and **User alerts**, are covered throughout the various chapters and recipes in this book.

Determining and revoking permissions in a site

SharePoint lets you view who has access to your site and what level of access they have.

This recipe will show you how to determine the level of access that a user may have to your site. We will also learn how to use SharePoint permissions management to revoke permissions for an existing user of the site.

Getting ready

You will need at least **Read** access to the site where you'd like to check user permissions. You will need **Full Control** access to be able to view advanced permissions or to revoke user permissions on your site.

For this recipe, we will assume that you have **Full Control** access to the site where you'd like to check permissions.

How to do it...

To view and update user permissions on a site, browse to your site and follow these steps:

1. Click on the **Settings** gear icon in the top-right corner.

2. Click **Site permissions**, as shown in the following screenshot:

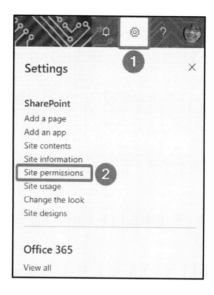

3. Here, you can view the members that are part of the different site permission groups in SharePoint.
4. Click the **Advanced permissions settings** link toward the bottom of the screen, as shown in the following screenshot:

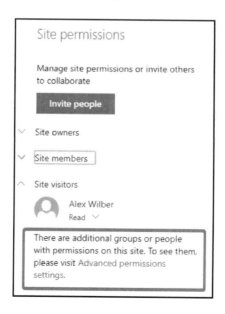

The link to where you can view advanced permissions will only be visible to you if you have been granted the **Full Control** permission level in the site.

5. Click on **Check Permissions** from the menu at the top.
6. Enter the name of the user or group that you would like to check the permissions of and click **Check Now**.
7. You can now view the permissions that have been granted to this user:

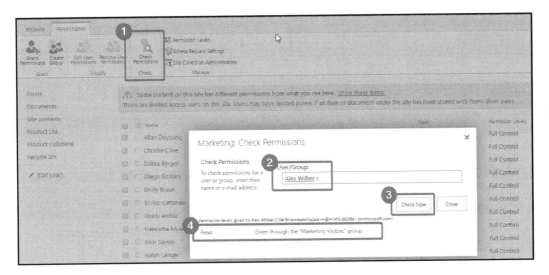

8. Note the names of any such groups that the user is part of. In this case, the user, **Alex Wilber**, has been granted **Read** access through the **Marketing Visitors** group.
9. Close this dialog box and click on the **Marketing Visitors** group from the **Permissions** screen.
10. Select the checkbox against the user's name from the list of users that shows in the **Marketing Visitors** group.

11. Click the **Actions** menu and then **Remove Users from Group**, as shown in the following screenshot:

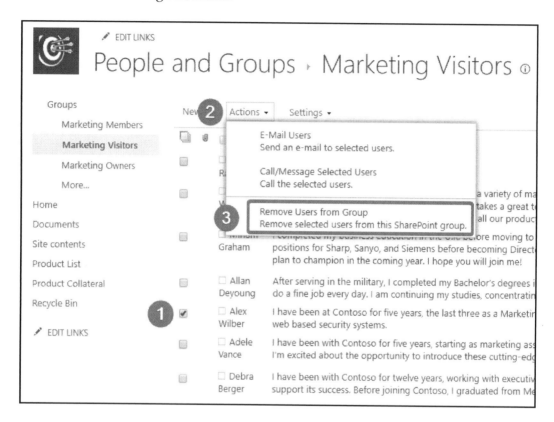

12. Click **OK** on the confirmation message that appears.

Congratulations! You've learned how to determine and update user permissions to your sites.

How it works...

SharePoint offers very granular permission and access control not only to your site but all the way down to lists, document libraries, and further down to list items, documents, lists, and files in it. We will review the various permission-related settings here.

Site permissions

Permissions in SharePoint start at the site level. There are typically three permission groups that get created along with the site:

- **Site Owners:** Members of this group have **Full Control** access to the site and all content in it.
- **Site Members:** Members of this group have **Edit** access to the site.
- **Site Visitors:** Members of this group have **Read** access to the site.

In addition to these groups, which are created by default, you can grant or revoke site permissions for individual users or groups through the **Site permissions** page.

We will review various aspects of permissions in SharePoint later in this topic.

Permission levels

Full Control, **Edit**, and **Read** are called **Permission Levels**. These can be accessed through the **Site permissions** page. SharePoint comes with five pre-defined permission levels, with each permission level shown in the following screenshot:

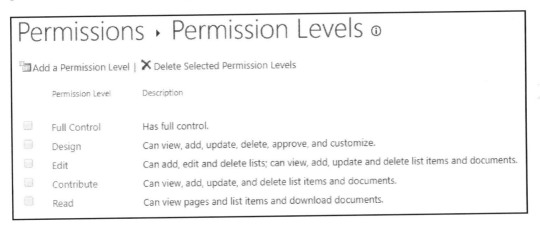

Each permission level includes or excludes several individual permissions. Permissions on the add/edit **Permission Levels** page are categorized under the following headings:

- **List Permissions**: This subsection contains all permissions related to lists and list items, such as whether this permission level allows users to add/edit or delete items. The following screenshot shows various permissions that can be controlled within this category and the permissions that are selected by default for the **Edit** permission level:

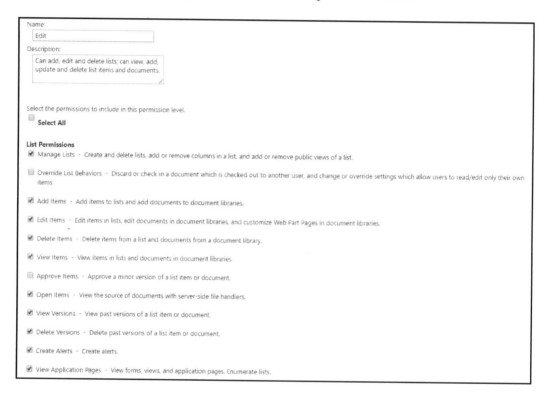

- **Site Permissions**: This subsection lists all permissions that can be controlled for a site. The following screenshot shows various permissions that fall under this category and the permissions that are selected by default for the **Edit** permission level:

Site Permissions

☐ Manage Permissions - Create and change permission levels on the Web site and assign permissions to users and groups.

☐ View Web Analytics Data - View reports on Web site usage.

☐ Create Subsites - Create subsites such as team sites, Meeting Workspace sites, and Document Workspace sites.

☐ Manage Web Site - Grants the ability to perform all administration tasks for the Web site as well as manage content.

☐ Add and Customize Pages - Add, change, or delete HTML pages or Web Part Pages, and edit the Web site using a Microsoft SharePoint Foundation-compatible editor.

☐ Apply Themes and Borders - Apply a theme or borders to the entire Web site.

☐ Apply Style Sheets - Apply a style sheet (.CSS file) to the Web site.

☐ Create Groups - Create a group of users that can be used anywhere within the site collection.

☑ Browse Directories - Enumerate files and folders in a Web site using SharePoint Designer and Web DAV interfaces.

☑ Use Self-Service Site Creation - Create a Web site using Self-Service Site Creation.

☑ View Pages - View pages in a Web site.

☐ Enumerate Permissions - Enumerate permissions on the Web site, list, folder, document, or list item.

☑ Browse User Information - View information about users of the Web site.

☐ Manage Alerts - Manage alerts for all users of the Web site.

☑ Use Remote Interfaces - Use SOAP, Web DAV, the Client Object Model or SharePoint Designer interfaces to access the Web site.

☑ Use Client Integration Features - Use features which launch client applications. Without this permission, users will have to work on documents locally and upload their changes.

☑ Open - Allows users to open a Web site, list, or folder in order to access items inside that container.

☑ Edit Personal User Information - Allows a user to change his or her own user information, such as adding a picture.

- **Personal Permissions**: The actions in this section pertain to changes that users can make to their personal views. These actions do not alter the content that other users see within the site. Through the permissions in this section, you can control the actions that the users can perform on their personal views. The following screenshot shows various permissions that fall under this category and the permissions that are selected by default for the **Edit** permission level:

Personal Permissions

☑ Manage Personal Views - Create, change, and delete personal views of lists.

☑ Add/Remove Personal Web Parts - Add or remove personal Web Parts on a Web Part Page.

☑ Update Personal Web Parts - Update Web Parts to display personalized information.

You cannot edit the permissions in the SharePoint default permission levels, but you can create your own permission levels by selecting the permissions you'd like to include in those permission level. This means you can be very specific about what kind of access you would like to have for each permission level in SharePoint. For example, one of the frequently requested features is the ability for users to be able to edit or contribute content but not to be able to delete it. This can simply be achieved by creating a permission level by copying the **Edit** permission level (shown in the preceding screenshot) and then deselecting the **Delete Items** permission under the **List Permissions** category.

Here's a recommended Microsoft article if you would like to understand SharePoint permission levels in greater detail: `https://m365book.page.link/Permission-Levels`.

Permission inheritance

When you create a new subsite, list, or library within a SharePoint site, it *inherits* the permissions from the parent site. This means the object uses the same permissions as the site that it was created within. These permissions further trickle down to the item level in a list or to the individual document level in a document library. This means that items in lists or documents in document libraries automatically inherit permissions from the parent list or library. SharePoint, on the other hand, allows you to **Stop Inheriting Permissions** and assign unique permissions to individual lists/libraries or items/documents within them. This enables you to set different permissions for individual lists or libraries within your site. The *Viewing and changing list permissions* recipe in `Chapter 4`, *Working with Lists and Libraries in SharePoint Online*, discusses this in more detail.

 It is not recommended to *break* permission inheritance too frequently since it tends to confuse users. It can also quickly become a maintenance nightmare when you are trying to figure out permissions for different objects within a site.

Permission groups in SharePoint

Permission groups in SharePoint are a way to manage a set of users that are expected to have the same permissions in SharePoint. You will have one or more users in a SharePoint group that you can then assign permissions to. Just like the Site owners, members, and visitors groups we mentioned earlier, you can create additional groups of your own in SharePoint and assign them custom permissions.

In addition to assigning permissions to users through SharePoint groups, you can also assign permissions to users that are part of **Active Directory Domain** groups in your organization. This way, you can utilize the user's categorization through those AD groups, provided that your organization is actively maintaining them.

Site collection administrator

When a site is created, there is one permission *role* that gets created in addition to the three groups mentioned earlier. This role is the **site collection administrator**. Site collection administrators not only have full access to all content within all sites and any subsites in that site collection but they also have access to additional settings and admin functionality in the site. This list of site collection administrators can be managed through the **Site settings** page. Only existing site collection administrators or the global **SharePoint Admins** that have been designated by your organization can manage the site collection administrators list.

See also...

- The *Sharing a document* recipe in Chapter 2, *Introduction to SharePoint Online*
- The *Viewing and changing list permissions* recipe in Chapter 4, *Working with Lists and Libraries in SharePoint Online*

Creating a subsite

SharePoint lets you create subsites under existing sites. Subsites are useful when you want to organize content through a subset of lists, libraries, or pages but the audience that will have access to this content is the same or a subset of the users of the parent site. For example, a large organization might have a site for the HR department, and they are likely to have a payroll subsite within it for a small set of members that help manage the organization's payroll.

This recipe shows you how to create a subsite using the modern **Team site** template.

Getting ready

You need **Full Control** access to the site that you would like to create the new subsite for.

How to do it...

To create a subsite, follow these steps:

1. Browse to the site that you would like to create the subsite for.
2. Click on the **Settings** gear icon in the top-right corner and then **Site contents**.
3. Click **New** and then **Subsite**.
4. On the **New SharePoint Site** page, enter or select the following:
   - A title, description, URL name, language, and template for your site.
   - Whether or not the site will use the same permissions as the parent site. Clicking **Use unique permissions** will let you specify permissions that are different from that of the parent site.
   - Whether or not the site will show up on the **Quick Launch** of the parent site (typically set to **No**).
   - Whether or not the site will show up on the Global Navigation of the parent site (typically set to **Yes**).

- Whether or not the site will use the same Global Navigation as the parent site (typically set to **Yes**):

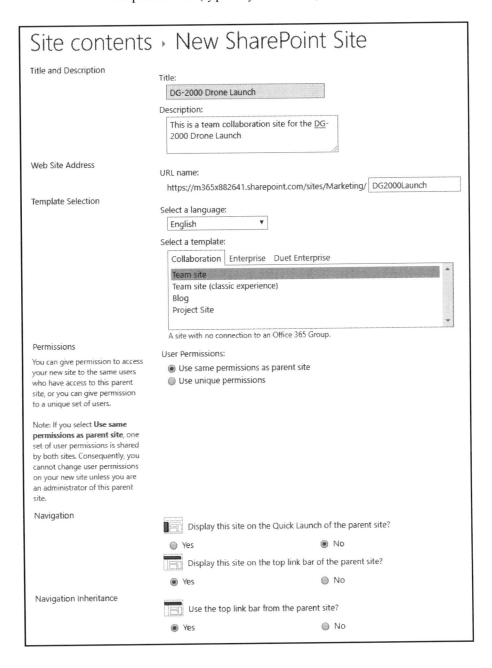

5. Click the **Create** button once you have finished setting this up or confirmed the information you provided here.

Congratulations! You just created your new subsite.

How it works...

For reasons beyond the scope of this book, the general guidance from Microsoft at the time of writing is to not create subsites. Microsoft recommends creating sites (that is, site collections) instead to accomplish your goals and using a **hub** to connect related sites. Having said that, subsites may still make sense in some scenarios. One such scenario was described at the onset of this recipe with the HR site and the payroll subsite. Another example could be a temporary collaboration area within a "Research" **Team site**, for a smaller team to collaborate on a new idea or upcoming product. Here is some good independent guidance on the pros and cons of each: https://m365book. page.link/Why-Subsites and https://m365book.page.link/Why-Sites At the time of writing, the maximum number of subsites that you can have within a SharePoint site collection is 2,000. On the other hand, the maximum number of site collections per organization tenant is 2 million.

There's more

In the topics in this section, we will look at how to use custom site provisioning to create SharePoint sites that contain extended or custom capabilities right off the bat, as soon as they are created. We will then look at the concept of using templates to replicate the structure, design, and features of your favorite SharePoint sites.

Custom provisioning using Site Designs and Site Scripts

SharePoint lets you create sites that use a customized provisioning experience tailored by you for your users. You can accomplish this using **site designs** and **site scripts**. A site-design is a collection of site scripts that let you provision your designs and customizations as part of the site creation experience. These designs and customizations can include reusable lists, themes, layouts, pages, or custom actions so that your users can quickly build new SharePoint sites with the features they need. Site designs are useful in helping drive consistency across your sites. You can apply site designs while creating a site, as shown in the following screenshot:

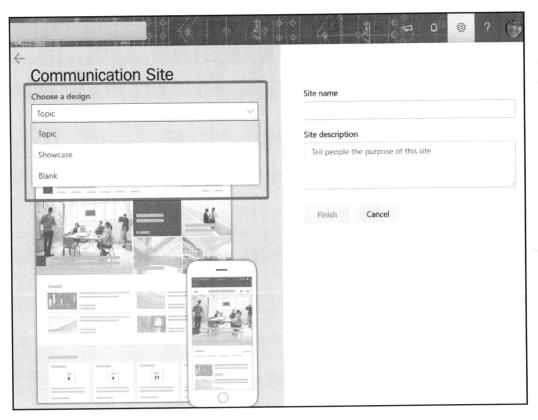

For existing sites, you can apply site designs by clicking on the gear icon and then clicking **Site designs**, as shown in the following screenshot:

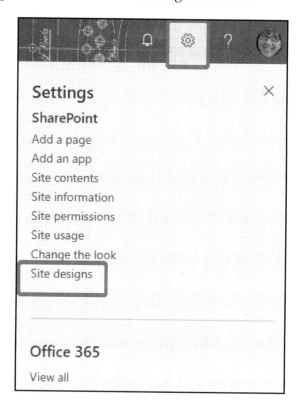

Creating site scripts and site designs is an advanced capability and will require administrative and development expertise to accomplish it. The following Microsoft Docs article and sub-articles provide a detailed walk-through of implementing and using site scripts and site designs in your organization: `https://m365book.page.link/Site-Designs`.

Reusing a site as a template

You may, however, need to recreate the functionality, designs, structure, and/or some or all of the content of an existing site. The way you would go about doing so in the classic SharePoint experience was by saving the site as a *template* and then creating new sites using that template. This capability, however, is now deprecated in the modern SharePoint experience.

There are two ways to export existing sites as templates in the more modern experience, and we will look at both here.

Exporting a site using a site script

Site designs and site scripts allow you to create sites using a complex and customizable provisioning experience. They are a great way to create standardized sites from scratch. You can also use site scripts to export your existing site and its settings so you can use the generated script to create a new site.

Please refer to the `Get-SPOSiteScriptFromWeb` command here to export your site as a script: `https://m365book.page.link/Get-SPOSiteScriptFromWeb`.

 The `Get-SPOSiteScriptFromWeb` command is part of the SharePoint Online PowerShell module. You can read more about SharePoint Online PowerShell in the *Powershell* section of the *Appendix*

Once the site is exported as a script, you can use it in a site design for users to create a new site based on that template. We also discussed site designs and site scripts in the previous topic on *Custom provisioning using Site Designs and Site Scripts*.

In addition to using PowerShell for site designs and site scripts, you can also use the Microsoft 365 Rest API to carry out the same tasks, as described here: `https://m365book.page.link/SiteDesign-RestAPI`.

Exporting a site using PnP provisioning

The PnP engine has made developer and admin commands available that can be used to save a site of your choice as a template. You can then optionally make changes to the features of the saved site template and then use similar PnP commands again to provision one or more sites using the saved template.

 PnP (short for **Patterns and Practices**). You can read more about it in the *SharePoint PnP* topic of the *Office Development Frameworks* section in the *Appendix*.

You can use the `Get-PnPProvisioningTemplate` command to export the site as a template, as described here: `https://m365book.page.link/Get-PnPProvisioningTemplate`.

You would then use the `Apply-PnPProvisioningTemplate` command to use this template to create a new site: `https://m365book.page.link/Apply-PnPProvisioningTemplate`.

You can read more about the PnP provisioning engine and its templating capabilities here: `https://m365book.page.link/PnP-Provisioning-Engine`.

See also...

- The *Creating a modern site* recipe in `Chapter 2`, *Introduction to SharePoint Online*
- The *SharePoint PnP* topic in the *Office Development Frameworks* section of the *Appendix*

4

Working with Lists and Libraries in SharePoint Online

Lists in SharePoint are containers that let you view and maintain information, just as with an Excel spreadsheet or a database table. Just like spreadsheets or database tables, lists have columns and rows. Each column identifies the type of information that gets stored in the list. Each row, also called a list item, stores said information. SharePoint comes with a set of ready-to-use *templates* that can be used to create lists with built-in functionality. Examples of such lists are **Announcements**, **Contacts**, and **Tasks** lists. All lists come with some standard and useful features, such as the following:

- The ability to add or remove various types of columns as needed
- The ability to specify validations for the columns (such as maximum field lengths, whether a field is required or not, and so on)
- The ability to customize the organization of information presented through views
- Native forms to view and edit the information
- The ability to embed information from these lists in other pages in Microsoft 365
- Allowing permissions to be specified for the entire list or individual items within the list
- The ability to search through the list information, depending on your permissions for the list or individual items
- Item-level versioning and history
- The ability to subscribe to alerts for changes in the list

Lists further extend out as libraries, in that libraries are lists that are centered around documents. We will learn more about libraries in Chapter 5, *Document Management in SharePoint Online*. However, for this chapter, it is sufficient to note that almost all concepts that apply to lists also apply to libraries. The recipes surrounding the lists that we will review in this chapter will therefore also apply to libraries.

The following recipes in this chapter will show us how to work with lists in SharePoint:

- Creating a list using a built-in template
- Adding a column
- Creating a custom list view
- Using **Quick Edit** to bulk-edit list items
- Viewing and changing list settings
- Viewing and changing list permissions
- Adding alerts

Creating a list using a built-in list template

In Chapter 2, *Introduction to SharePoint Online*, we saw how to create a custom list from scratch. In this chapter, we'll see how to create lists using predefined list templates. For our recipe, we will use the **Announcements** list template. You can use the Announcements list to easily share news, updates, and announcements about your department or organization. You can use the inbuilt rich text editor to add images, links, and rich formatting to these announcements. You can then add this list as a web part on the home page of your site so that the announcements are prominently visible to your site visitors. You can additionally set an expiration date for each announcement so that it *drops off* the list after that date.

We will now see how to use this list template to create a Marketing Announcements list on our site.

Getting ready

You will need **Edit**, **Design**, or **Full Control** permissions in your site to be able to create lists.

How to do it...

To create a new list based on the Announcements template, follow these steps:

1. Browse to the site in which you would like to create the list.
2. Click the settings gear icon in the top-right corner.
3. Click **Add an app**, as shown in the following screenshot:

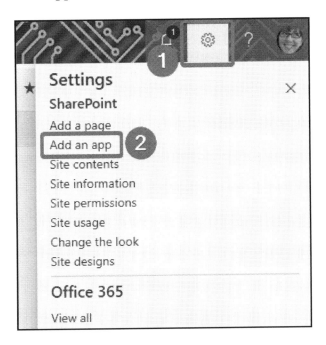

4. Search for the term Announcement in the **Find an app** search box.

Note that sites based on certain templates, such as the modern communications site, need an extra step for the additional list templates, such as the **Announcements** template, to show up. You will need to enable the **Team Collaboration Lists** feature in the site for such templates to show up. Features in SharePoint are modules of functionality that can be enabled or *activated* as needed. To enable this feature, browse to the **Site Features** page, as described in this support article: https://m365book.page.link/Activate-Features. Then, search for the text **Team Collaboration Lists** and click the **Activate** button next to it. You will now start seeing the additional list and library templates on the **Add an app** page.

5. Click the **Announcements** search result.

6. Enter `Marketing Announcements` for the list name and click the **Create** button.

The name you enter while creating a list or a library is also used as the **Uniform Resource Locator** (**URL**) to your list. For example, the list we just created would have the following URL:
`https://tenant-`
`name.sharepoint.com/sites/Marketing/Marketing%20Annou`
`ncements/`.

For that reason, you should avoid entering spaces or other special characters when creating lists or libraries in SharePoint. Doing so will ensure that the URL for your list is clean and does not contain any special characters. In the preceding example, you would want to enter `Marketing Announcements` as the list name. This would create a list with the following URL:
`https://tenant-name.sharepoint.com/sites/Marketing/Ma`
`rketingAnnouncements` (without the `%20` in the URL).

Once the list is created, you can go back and rename it to add the spaces and special characters to it as desired (`Marketing Announcements` in our example, with a space in between). Renaming the list after it's created does not change the URL of the list, and your users would still see the same clean URL that got generated while creating the list, at the same time benefiting from a more user-friendly title.

Congratulations! You just created a list using the **Announcements** list template in SharePoint.

How it works...

In addition to the ability to create lists from scratch, SharePoint also provides *templates* that you can use to create lists and libraries in your site. When you create a list or library using one of the existing templates, SharePoint will automatically create and configure predefined columns, views, and settings based on that template. As is, such lists and libraries are generally geared toward addressing very focused needs so that you can start using them right away. If required, however, you can also customize them to meet any specific needs that you may have.

As an example, the `Marketing Announcements` list that we just created comes with fields that let you create an announcement, giving it a title, body, expiration date, and—optionally—add file attachments to it. The next few recipes will show you how to further customize the `Marketing Announcements` list by adding new columns and creating custom views for it.

Finally, in addition to creating a list this way, you can also create a list based on the following:

- Click on the **New** menu from the home page (or any other modern page) on your site and then click **App**, as shown in the following screenshot:

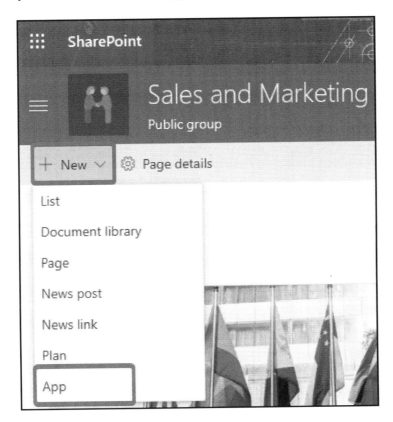

- Similarly, you can click the **New** menu and then **App** from the **Site contents** page to be taken to the **Apps you can add** page. If you are not familiar with the **Site contents** page, you can view the *Viewing site contents* recipe in `Chapter 2`, *Introduction to SharePoint Online*, to see how to browse to it from your site.

There's more...

Just like the Announcements list template, SharePoint comes with multiple other inbuilt list and library templates. You can also create lists based on existing lists that you may have created within your site.

In this section, we will first see a brief list of the other such native list and library templates that SharePoint offers. We will then discuss a few advanced ways to export the list so that it can be recreated within your site, other sites in your organization, or even across organizations.

Inbuilt list and library templates

SharePoint comes with multiple inbuilt templates that you can use to quickly create lists and libraries with predefined capabilities. The following is a list of all such templates in SharePoint:

Template Name	Type	Description
Announcements	List	A list of news items, statuses, and other short bits of information.
Calendar	List	A calendar of upcoming meetings, deadlines, or other events. Calendar information can be synchronized with Microsoft Outlook or other compatible programs.
Contacts	List	A list of people that your team works with, such as customers or partners. Contacts lists can synchronize with Microsoft Outlook or other compatible programs.
Custom List	List	Create your own list from scratch.
Custom List in Datasheet View	List	A custom list that is displayed as a spreadsheet to allow easy data entry. You can add your own columns and additional views, just like in a regular list.
Discussion Board	List	A place to have newsgroup-style discussions. Discussion boards make it easy to manage discussion threads and can be configured to require approval for all posts.
Document Library	Library	Use a document library to store, organize, sync, and share documents with people.
Issue Tracking	List	A list of issues or problems associated with a project or item. You can assign, prioritize, and track issue status.
Links	List	A list of web pages or other resources.
Picture Library	Library	A place to upload and share pictures.
Promoted Links	List	Use this list to display a set of link actions in a tile-based visual layout.

Survey	List	A list of questions that you would like to have people answer. Surveys let you quickly create questions and view graphical summaries of the responses.
Site Assets	Library	This library is used to store files and other assets required for the functioning of the site. Examples of files stored in this library are page images and videos, OneNote notebook, site logo, and so on.
Site Pages	Library	This library contains the pages used within the site.
Style Library	Library	The purpose of this library is to store style elements for your site.
Tasks	List	A place for team or personal tasks.

 Please note that some lists and libraries may or may not be available depending on the configuration or type of your site. The type or configuration of your site also dictates the lists and libraries that automatically get created when you create your site.

For more information regarding the list templates listed previously, please view the *Types of lists* section at: `https://m365book.page.link/List-Types`. For more information regarding the library templates, please view the *Types of libraries* section at: `https://m365book.page.link/library-types`.

Saving a list as a template

In addition to using the inbuilt templates to create lists, you can also create lists based on existing lists that you may have already created within your site.

We saw how to create a new list that is based on an existing list as part of the *How to do it...* section in the *Creating a list* recipe in `Chapter 2`, *Introduction to SharePoint Online*. For the most part, you should be able to use it to recreate an existing list with its columns, views, and formatting. There are, however, a few limitations in that approach:

- When selecting the source list, you will only see sites and lists that you have access to, via permissions. Consequently, you will not be able to see or create lists based on other lists that you do not have access to.
- You will not be able to copy over data using this approach.
- You will be unable to copy over any list settings that you may have changed from the defaults.
- You cannot use this approach if you would like to automate the creation of certain predefined lists when provisioning new sites.

This is where some of the additional methods discussed in this recipe come in handy. Using these methods, your SharePoint admins, or others who have access to the existing list, can export it as a template and share it with you so that you can recreate a new list in your site based on that template. The one drawback of these methods is that you will require administrator or developer help to be able to use them to export and import your lists.

We will briefly discuss these additional methods to save existing lists as templates and then reuse them to create new lists. Note that you can reuse the exported list templates to not only recreate lists within the same site or other sites in your organization but even across organizations/tenants if you need to do so.

Exporting a list using site scripts

We discussed site designs and site scripts as part of the *Custom provisioning using site designs and site scripts* topic of the *Creating a subsite* recipe in Chapter 3, *Working with Modern Sites in SharePoint Online*.

We can use the Get-SPOSiteScriptFromList command to export the list as a script. For more details, go to the following link: https://m365book.page.link/Get-SPOSiteScriptFromList.

 The Get-SPOSiteScriptFromList command is part of the SharePoint Online PowerShell module. You can read more about SharePoint Online PowerShell in the *Powershell* section of the *Appendix*

Once the list is exported, you can import it to an existing site or make it part of a site's design, to be provisioned to a new site.

Remember that in addition to using PowerShell for site designs and site scripts, you can also use the Microsoft 365 **representational state transfer (REST) application programming interface (API)** to carry out the same tasks, as described here: https://m365book.page.link/SiteDesign-RestAPI.

Exporting a list using PnP

The **PnP** (short for **Patterns and Practices**) provisioning engine also gives us commands for exporting your lists as reusable templates.

 You can read more about PnP in the *SharePoint PnP* topic of the *Office development frameworks* section of the *Appendix*.

You can use the `Export-PnPListToProvisioningTemplate` command to export the list, as described here: `https://m365book.page.link/Export-PnPListToProvisioningTemplate`.

You would then use the `Apply-PnPProvisioningTemplate` command to recreate the list in a new or existing site, as described here: `https://m365book.page.link/Apply-PnPProvisioningTemplate`.

You can read more about the PnP provisioning engine and the templating capabilities here: `https://m365book.page.link/PnP-Provisioning-Engine`.

Exporting a list using list settings

Finally, you can also use the **Save list as template** list setting to save a list as a template. To do so, browse to the **List settings** page, as described in the *Viewing and changing list settings* recipe later in this chapter. Then, click the **Save list as template** heading under the **Permissions and Management** heading.

 If you are not seeing this option under list settings, your site administrator might need to allow **Custom Script**. Please refer to this article from Microsoft to enable **Custom Script** on your site: `https://m365book.page.link/Custom-Script`.

You can then enter the values on this screen, as shown in the following screenshot, and then click the **OK** button to save the list as a template:

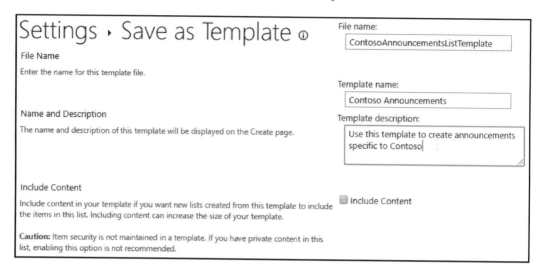

You will now start seeing this list in the **Add an app** screen, as shown in the following screenshot:

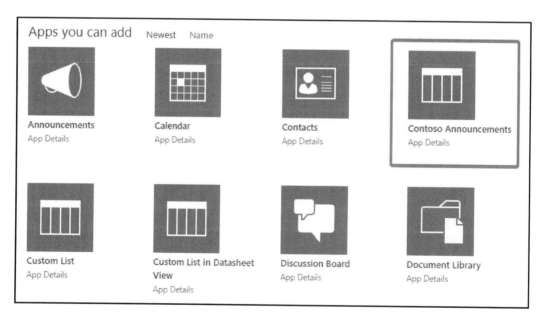

You can also download the list template file and use it to create lists on other sites. You can also read more about saving and using list templates here: `https://m365book.page.link/Manage-list-templates`.

See also

- The *Creating a list* recipe in `Chapter 2`, *Introduction to SharePoint Online*
- The *There's more...* section of the *Creating a subsite* recipe in `Chapter 3`, *Working with Modern Sites in SharePoint Online*
- The *SharePoint PnP* topic in the *Office development frameworks* section of the *Appendix*

Adding a column

Columns in lists define the nature and type of information that is stored in those lists. We briefly saw how to create new columns on a custom list as part of the *Creating a list* recipe in `Chapter 2`, *Introduction to SharePoint Online*.

In this recipe, we'll see how to add a new column to the `Marketing Announcements` list that we just created. We will add a new `Announcement Start Date` column to the list. We will then discuss some more advanced concepts around column creation in the sections to follow.

Getting ready

You will need **Edit**, **Design**, or **Full Control** permissions in your site to be able to add columns to your list.

How to do it...

To add a new column to your list:

1. Browse to the list for which you would like to add the new column.
2. Click **Add column** to see a list of the types of columns that you can add to the list.
3. Click **Date** to create a column that lets you store dates or date-time values.

4. In the **Create a column** window, enter or select values for various column properties, as shown in the following screenshot:

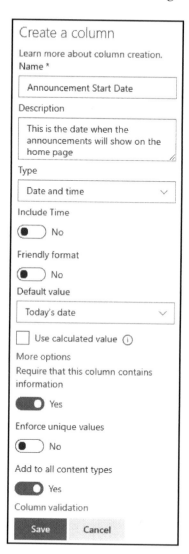

5. Click the **Save** button to save the properties and create your new column.

That's it! You just learned how to create a new column to your list.

How it works...

Columns allow for information to be associated with individual items in your list. For document libraries, they act as metadata that gets associated with the respective documents. Just as with columns in an Excel worksheet, SharePoint lists and libraries let you specify the type of information these columns can hold. Similarly, you can sort, filter, and group information using columns in SharePoint.

SharePoint supports various types of columns, as shown in the following screenshot:

After you select a column type, you can choose to specify additional properties for that column. For example, for the **Single line of text** column type, you can specify the maximum number of characters that the users can enter (with an upper limit of 255 characters). In addition to such column-specific properties, SharePoint also lets you specify some common properties, such as whether or not this will be a required column. You can view detailed descriptions of the different types of columns and their properties through this support article: `https://m365book.page.link/Column-types`.

Once a column is created, you can view and edit any of its properties through the **List settings** page. This is also where you can delete the column if you no longer see the need for it. The **List settings** page also lets you specify the order of columns to be shown in the data entry form. The *Viewing and changing list settings* recipe later in this chapter covers the **List settings** page in greater detail.

There's more...

In this section, we will learn about a few more actions that you can perform with columns. We will also learn about how to make your columns reusable across various lists and libraries in your site through the use of Site Columns.

Editing or deleting a column

Once a column is created, you can easily make changes to it, or even completely delete it. To do so, simply click on the column name, then click **Column settings** and then **Edit** to view the column in **Edit** mode:

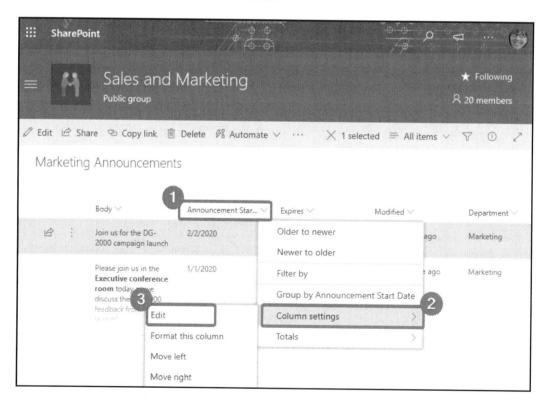

This will show you the **Edit column** screen, just like the one you saw when creating the columns. Here, you can make changes to the column and then click **Save** to save those changes. You can also delete the column by simply clicking the **Delete** button toward the bottom of the screen:

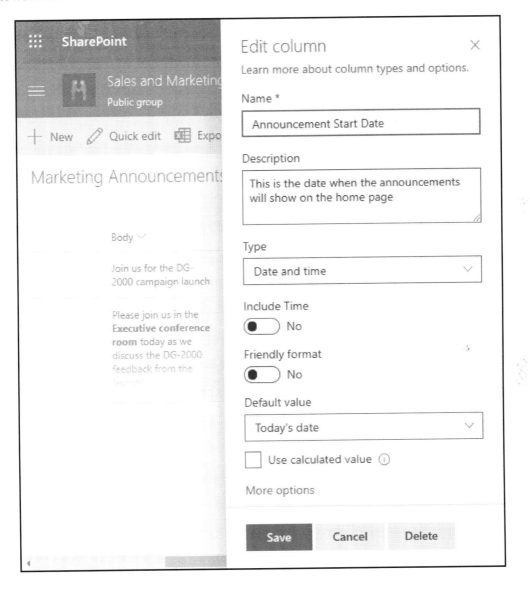

Clicking **More options** from the **Edit column** screen lets you set additional properties for the column:

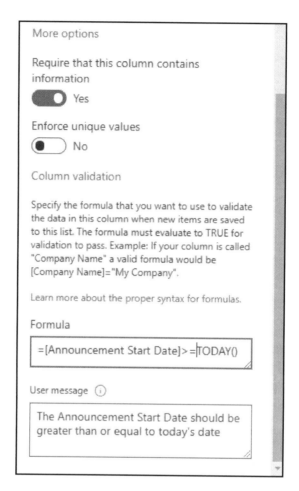

As shown in the preceding screenshot, in addition to specifying whether or not the column is mandatory and whether it should enforce unique values, you can also set validation for the values that the column would allow. In the example from this screenshot, we are validating for the start date to be greater than or equal to today's date (the date on which the item is being created or edited). We are also providing a message that SharePoint will display to users if the selected start date does not meet the validation criteria.

Other column settings

In addition to editing a column, clicking on **Column settings** lets you perform a couple of other actions with the column:

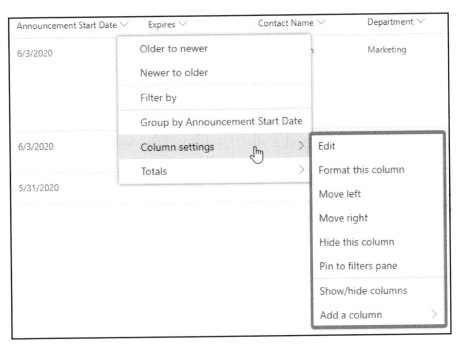

Here's a brief description of these settings:

- **Format this column**: Column formatting lets you customize the display of columns within the list or library. Column formatting is very similar to view formatting, which we have described in greater detail as part of the *Advanced view formatting* topic in the next recipe, *Creating a custom list view.* You can read more about column formatting here: `https://m365book.page.link/About-Column-formatting.` You can read more about using column formatting to customize SharePoint here: `https://m365book.page.link/use-column-formatting.`

- **Move left/Move right**: Moves the column toward the left or right in the view. You can also simply *drag* the column to reposition it within the view.
- **Hide this column**: Hides the column from the current view. The column can still be available through other views and/or forms.
- **Pin to filters pane**: This allows the column to be pinned to the filters pane for the view. We have discussed this in more detail through the *Filters pane* topic in the next recipe, *Creating a custom list view*.
- **Show/hide columns**: Clicking this option opens a list of all the columns from the list or library and enables you to select or deselect columns to be shown in the current view.
- **Add a column**: You can add a new column to the list using this option.

Site Columns

One disadvantage of creating columns the way we have created them previously is that they are local to that list or library. This means if someone else needs a similar column in another list or library in the site, they will have to create a similar column elsewhere. In addition to effort duplication, this also often leads to inconsistencies between columns that are similar to each other but have subtle differences because they were created independently of each other. These inconsistencies are further amplified in **Choice** type fields where users have to select one value from a list of predefined values. For example, one list could contain Human Resources as a department, while another list could contain HR as a choice for the department name. Furthermore, let's say you need to make modifications to such a column that is replicated across multiple lists or libraries. You will now need to do that in multiple places.

This is where **Site Columns** shine compared to individual list or library columns. Site Columns are similar to list or library columns, only that that they are defined and maintained at the site level. You will need **Design** or **Full Control** permissions on the site to be able to create Site Columns.

Creating a **Site Column** is almost always recommended instead of creating a column that is local to a list or library. Furthermore, it is usually recommended to create Site Columns at the site collection level versus just at the site level. That way, your Site Column can be used across multiple sites in your site collection. There is a chance that you might not have access to create a Site Column and that you might have to reach out to the appropriate site owner to do so. Even in such a situation, creating a Site Column is the recommended way to go where possible.

You can create Site Columns by browsing to the **Site Settings** page and then clicking the **Site Columns** link under the **Web Designer Galleries** heading. We discussed the **Site Settings** page as part of the *Viewing and changing site settings* recipe in Chapter 3, *Working with Modern Sites in SharePoint Online*. Once you are on the **Site Columns** page, you will see a list of the existing Site Columns for your site. You will also be able to click on the **Create** link on the top of the page to create a new Site Column:

From this point on, the steps to create the Site Column will be similar to those earlier in the recipe. The only difference will be that you will be prompted to choose a **Group** for your Site Column, as shown in the following screenshot:

Name and Type	Column name:
Type a name for this column, and select the type of information you want to store in the column.	
	The type of information in this column is:
	◉ Single line of text
	○ Multiple lines of text
	○ Choice (menu to choose from)
	○ Number (1, 1.0, 100)
	○ Currency ($, ¥, €)
	○ Date and Time
	○ Lookup (information already on this site)
	○ Yes/No (check box)
	○ Person or Group
	○ Hyperlink or Picture
	○ Calculated (calculation based on other columns)
	○ Task Outcome
	○ Full HTML content with formatting and constraints for publishing
	○ Image with formatting and constraints for publishing
	○ Hyperlink with formatting and constraints for publishing
	○ Summary Links data
	○ Rich media data for publishing
	○ Managed Metadata

Group	
Specify a site column group. Categorizing columns into groups will make it easier for users to find them.	Put this site column into:
	○ Existing group:
	Custom Columns ▼
	◉ New group:
	Contoso Marketing Site Columns

A **Group** is just a logical means of grouping Site Columns under one heading. It does not have any impact on the functionality of the Site Column. Once your Site Column is created, you can go back to your list and add it to the list through the **Add from existing Site Columns** link on the **List settings** page. We will discuss the **List settings** page in more detail in the *Viewing and changing list settings* recipe later in this chapter.

See also

- The *Creating a list* recipe in `Chapter 2`, *Introduction to SharePoint Online*
- The *Viewing and changing site settings* recipe in `Chapter 3`, *Working with Modern Sites in SharePoint Online*
- The *Viewing and changing list settings* recipe in this chapter
- The *Creating a Managed Metadata Site Column* recipe in `Chapter 6`, *Term Store and Content Types in SharePoint Online*

Creating a custom list view

Views in SharePoint enable you to organize and show list or library items that are the most relevant for you and your users. Through views, you can select which columns to show to users, filter data in the view based on various criteria, and select the order in which to show your data. Every list or library in SharePoint comes with an inbuilt view called **All Items**. Unless a list admin or a site admin changes it to something else, this view is shown by default anytime that a user browses to a list or library. For this reason, it is also sometimes known as the *default view* for that list or library. We can create additional *custom views* for our list to meet our data display needs. We can then show or hide columns in this view, change the sort and/or filter criteria, group by one or more fields, and add formatting to a view.

In this recipe, we will see how to create a custom view for the `Marketing Announcements` list that we just created. We will then save the view as the default view so that anyone who browses to the list will see the new view that we created.

Getting ready

You will need **Edit**, **Design**, or **Full Control** permissions to the list to be able to create public views for it.

You can create a personal view on a list for which you have **Contribute** access.

How to do it...

To create a new view for your list, follow these steps:

1. Browse to the list for which you would like to create a new view.

 SharePoint automatically saves changes to your views. So, unless we want to modify the existing view, we will first want to save the current view under a different view name.

2. Click **All items** and then **Save view as** toward the top-right corner of the page, as shown in the following screenshot:

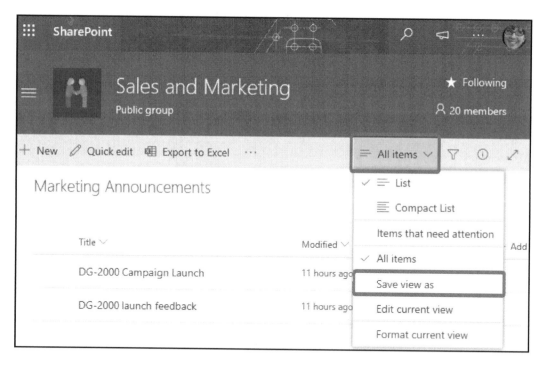

3. Give your view a name (for example, **Current Announcements**) and click **Save**. This will create a new view. Next, we will add columns to it.

4. Click **Add column** and then **Show/hide columns**, as shown in the following screenshot:

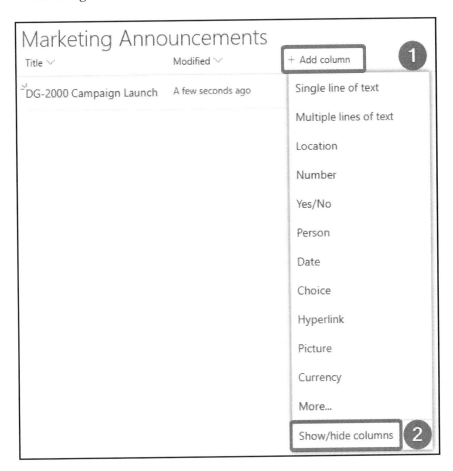

5. Select the columns you would like to show on the new view, and deselect the columns you would like to hide. For the `Marketing Announcements` list that we created earlier, we will deselect the **Modified** column, then select the **Body**, **Expires**, and **Announcement Start Date** columns. Then, we will click the **Apply** button on the top. This is shown in the following screenshot:

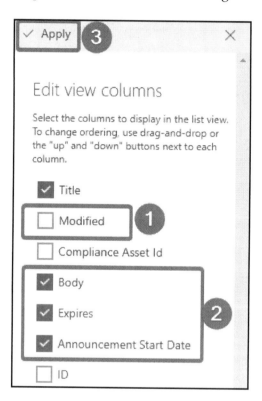

6. Then, drag the **Expires** column toward the extreme right from the main view itself, as shown in the following screenshot:

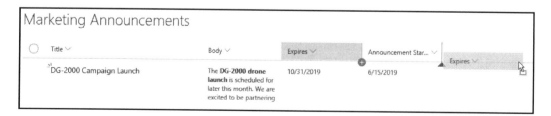

7. Next, we will add a filter to the view so that we only see current announcements. Click **Current Announcements** and then **Edit current view**, as shown in the following screenshot:

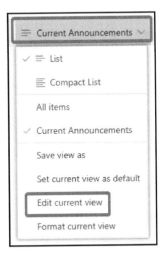

8. Scroll down on the **Edit View** page to the **Sort** section, and change the value in the **First sort by the column** drop-down option to **Announcement Start Date**. Then, select the **Show items in ascending order** option to sort the announcements in ascending order of the **Announcement Start Date**.

9. Scroll down further to the **Filter** section and change the filter values to the ones shown in the following screenshot:

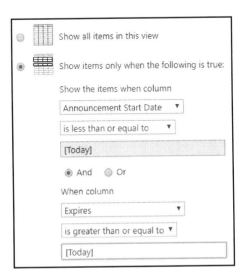

10. Scroll to the bottom of the page and click **OK** to save your changes.

11. Finally, click on the **Current Announcements** view and then click **Set current view as default**. Doing so will make this new view the default view for the list:

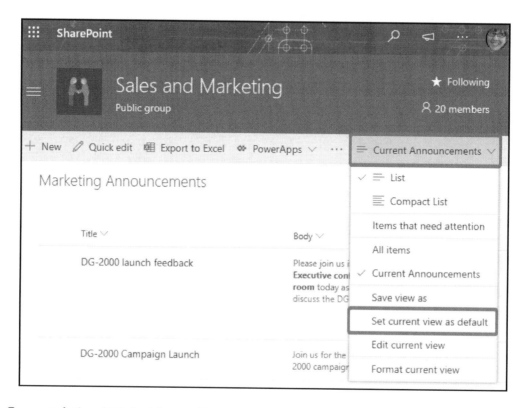

Congratulations! We just learned how to create a new view and then modify it for basic column ordering and sorting. We then saw how to edit the view, create a filter, and sort the items in that view. Specifically, for the Marketing Announcements list, the **Current Announcements** view only shows announcements where today's date lies between the **Announcement Start Date** and the date indicated by the **Expires** column. Finally, we set the new **Current Announcements** view as the default view so that users browsing this list will always see the **Current Announcements** by default. They will be able to change the view to the **All items** option if they want to see past announcements or others that happened to be filtered due to the criteria specified in the new view.

How it works...

Views are the presentation layer for information stored in lists and libraries. You can create multiple views to easily organize this information. You can create public views that are visible to anyone who has access to the list, or you can create personal views that are only visible to you.

Views *per se* don't have permissions associated with them. You can create filters on views to hide certain items. However, users can still get to such items through direct links, creating/modifying views, and through a search, as long as they have permissions to these items.

In this recipe, we saw how to edit a view to filter and sort information in it. There are a few additional actions you can carry out when editing a view from the **Edit View** page, as shown in the following screenshot:

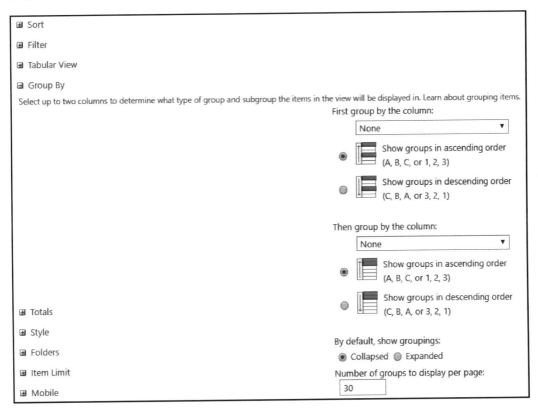

Some of the more prominent actions are as follows:

- Select or deselect the columns that get shown in the view and specify the order of those columns from left to right
- Specify a multi-column filter and sort criteria (we saw this earlier in this recipe)
- Group the items up to two group levels
- Specify some basic styles for the view
- Specify whether to show items in folders or to show them without the folders
- Specify a limit on the number of items shown per page or, optionally, a limit on the total number of items that get shown in the view
- Specify whether or not to show a separate view for mobile requests and basic settings for the mobile view

Finally, you can also delete a view from this page. To do so, simply click the **Delete** button in the top- or bottom-right corner of the page:

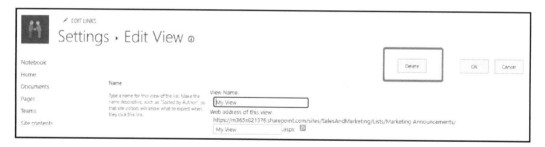

Note that you can only delete the view if it's not currently set up as the default view for the selected list or library.

There's more...

In this section, we will see the additional things that you can do with list views.

The Items that need attention view

SharePoint will provide you various indicators if you have items in your list or library that are missing the required information. As shown by (**A**), (**B**), and (**C**) in the following screenshot, it will show this through different means:

- (**A**): By showing a *missing metadata* icon next to the **Title** field
- (**B**): By clearly showing the missing information
- (**C**): By showing a red dot against the view name:

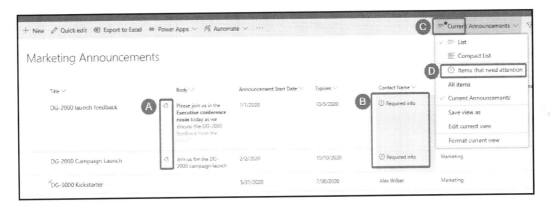

However, sometimes, a view may contain many items, or, for a document library, it may contain items nested within folders, making it difficult to find and work with just the items that are missing values. You can use the **Items that need attention** view, shown by (**D**) in the preceding screenshot, in such situations.

In document libraries, this view is called **Files that need attention**.

Switching to this view will only show you those items that are missing values. You can then easily work with such items in either the regular or the **Quick Edit** view that we discuss in the next recipe.

Bulk-editing properties

SharePoint lets you select multiple items and bulk-edit their properties. This is particularly useful when you need to backfill the property values after these items have been created. To bulk-edit multiple items, simply select the checkboxes next to them to open the details pane, as shown in the following screenshot:

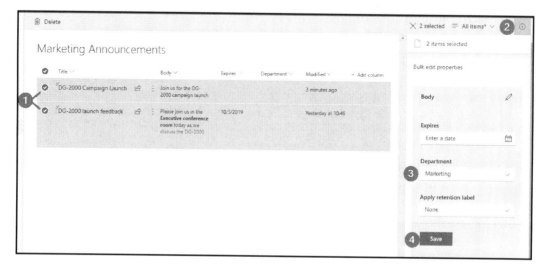

Then, simply enter or select values for the properties that you'd like to change, and click the **Save** button toward the bottom.

Exporting to Excel

SharePoint also lets you export the list items from the current view if you'd like to work with them in Excel. To do that, simply click **Export to Excel** from the top of your view and open the downloaded .iqy file, as shown in the following screenshot:

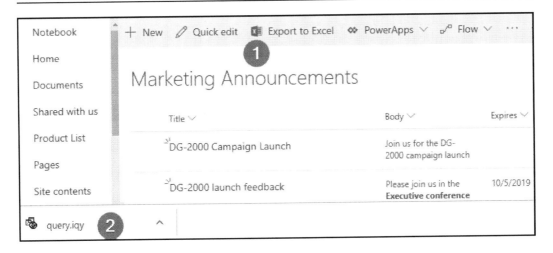

This will open the items from the view in an Excel workbook, as shown in the following screenshot:

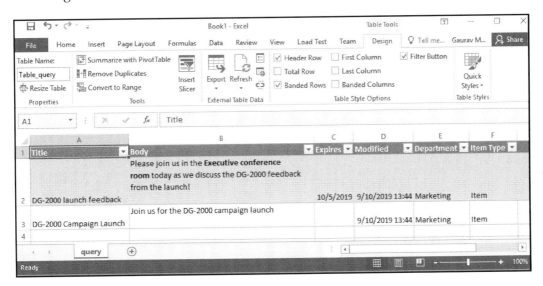

You can now work with this information just as you would with any other spreadsheet. Note that this is not a connected spreadsheet, in that the changes that you make here will not be published back to the corresponding list in SharePoint Online.

Advanced view formatting

Modern lists enable you to easily and significantly enhance the visual display of your views. A very common use of such formatting is when your list has a **Status** column and you'd like to highlight the items in the view based on the status values or other similar criteria. The following screenshot shows an example where we have highlighted the **Announcement Start Date** column of the `Marketing Announcements` list, based on the start month:

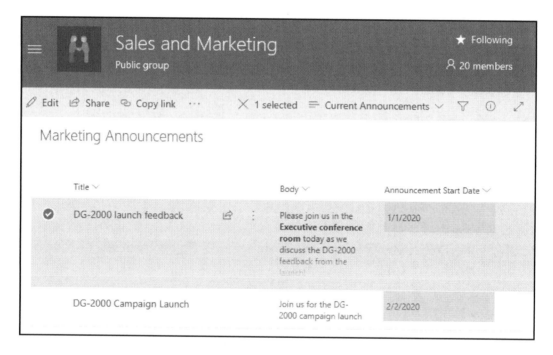

To format your view, simply click on your view name and then click **Format current view**, as shown in the following screenshot:

Then, select whether you would like the formatting to be applied to one of the columns or the entire row. Selecting an entire row will let you either specify alternating row styles or rule-based conditional styling to be applied to the entire row, as shown in the following screenshot:

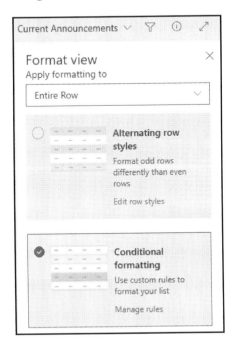

If you choose to apply the formatting to just a single column, SharePoint will show you options based on the type of column that you selected. In the following example, we are seeing the two different options that can be specified for date columns:

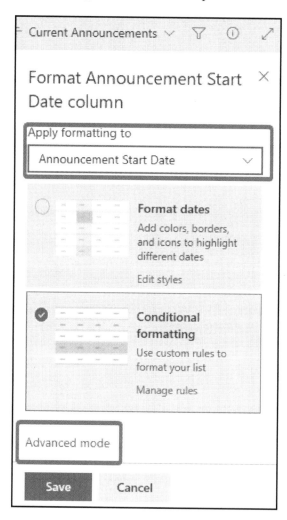

You can then specify formatting such as that in the rule shown in the following screenshot:

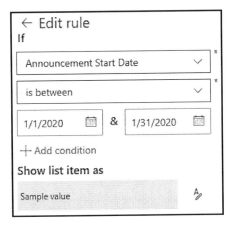

You can also click the **Advanced mode** link toward the bottom of the **Format view** pane to define more complex formatting for the view. An example of such advanced view formatting is shown in the following screenshot, where you can use basic code to convert the view display from this native, unformatted view:

The code will convert the display to a nicer-looking view, such as this:

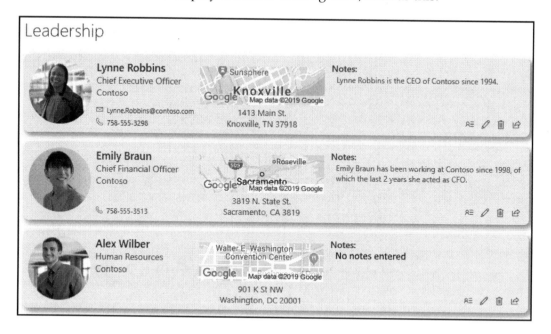

Advanced view formatting involves writing a little bit of code (**JavaScript Object Notation (JSON)**), and hence is beyond the purview of this chapter. You can learn more about JSON view formatting through these Microsoft support articles:

- Formatting list views: `https://m365book.page.link/Formatting-list-views`
- Use column formatting to customize SharePoint: `https://m365book.page.link/use-column-formatting`
- PnP list view formatting samples: `https://m365book.page.link/pnp-list-formatting-samples`

In-place view filtering, sorting, and grouping

The steps in the *Creating a custom list view* recipe showed you how to filter and sort your view using the view settings page. SharePoint also lets you filter and sort the current view of your list by columns from within the view itself. To sort a view by a particular column order, simply click the column name and then select a sort order. The sort options that you see will depend on the type of column that you are sorting on. These are shown by (**A**) in the screenshot that follows. You can only sort your view by one column at a time using this option.

To filter the view based on a column, click the column name and then click **Filter by** to reveal the values that you can filter on. This is shown by **(B)** in the screenshot that follows. Unlike sorting, you can filter by multiple columns. You can also use the filters pane, discussed in the next topic, for advanced filtering.

To group by a column, select the **Group by Column name** option, shown by **(C)** in the screenshot that follows. You can only group by one column using this approach. You can use the view settings page described in the preceding *How it works...* section to group by an additional column. Further, you can also show group totals and an overall total by clicking the **Totals** option, shown by **(D)**, **(E)**, and **(F)** in the following screenshot:

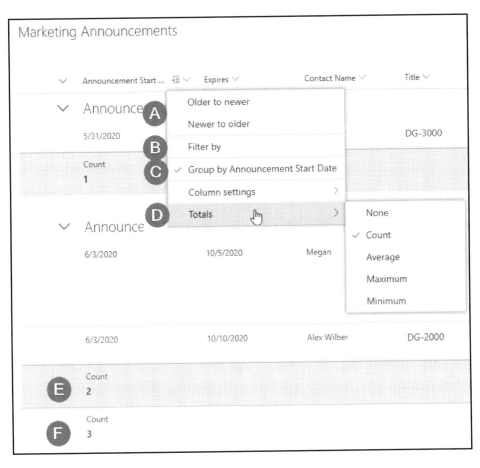

Further, the aggregation options that you will see under the **Totals** menu will depend on the type of column. The options shown in the preceding screenshot are those for a date column. A text column would only have shown **Count** as the aggregation option.

Filters pane

As we saw in the *Creating a custom list view* recipe, you can apply some basic filters on individual columns to create a filtered view. In addition to that, you can also create advanced filters on multiple columns in the view. As shown by (**A**) in the following screenshot, you can click the *filter* icon toward the right of your list or library menu to open the filters pane:

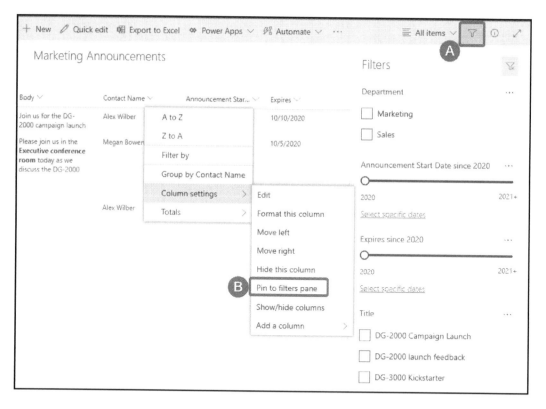

Here, you will see a list of columns with values that you can filter on. Only columns from your view will be shown here. You can add columns to the filters pane by clicking on the corresponding column name, then clicking **Column settings**, and then **Pin to filters pane**. Once the column is added to the filters pane, you can choose to filter your view using the values from this column in combination with the others already present in this pane. To make your filters permanent, simply save the view by selecting the view name, and then click **Save view as**, as described earlier in the recipe.

The following support articles provide additional details regarding the features and limitations of the filters pane:

- What is the list and library filters pane?: `https://m365book.page.link/ Filters-Pane`
- Use filtering to modify a SharePoint view: `https://m365book.page.link/ Use-Filters`

Working with large lists and libraries

You can store millions of items in a SharePoint list or library (30 million items, to be precise, at the time of writing). However, due to technical reasons beyond the scope of this book, there are special considerations to keep in mind when the number of items grows beyond 5,000. When that happens, you will be restricted from carrying out certain tasks in the list or library, including the following:

- Being able to show more than 5,000 items in a single view
- Programmatically retrieving more than 5,000 items through a single request
- Adding columns

There are multiple ways to overcome these limitations, including organizing documents within folders in a document library, but the most recommended approach is to create one or more *indexed columns* on your list. You will need to create the indexed column(s) before the items in your list or library exceed the 5,000-item limit. It is recommended that you index all columns that are being used or are anticipated to be used for filtering or sorting items in your list or library. As a list or library owner, you will, therefore, want to put in thought and planning upfront when you are expecting the information in your lists or libraries to grow beyond the 5,000-item limit.

You can read more about this important topic through these Microsoft support articles:

- Manage large lists and libraries in SharePoint: `https://m365book.page.link/Large-Lists`
- Add an index to a SharePoint column: `https://m365book.page.link/Add-Column-Index`

Using Quick Edit to bulk-edit list items

The **Quick Edit** view is a special view that is similar to Excel worksheets. In this recipe, we will see how to use **Quick Edit** to modify multiple list items. We will use the previously created `Marketing Announcements` list as an illustration for this recipe.

Getting ready

You will need **Contribute**, **Edit**, **Design**, or **Full Control** permissions to the list to be able to bulk-edit items in it.

How to do it...

1. Browse to the list for which you would like to bulk-edit the items.
2. Click **Quick Edit** in the navigation bar.

 If you are viewing a classic (and not a modern) list or if you are viewing a modern list in the classic view, you will see the **Edit this list** menu option instead of the **Quick Edit** option. Both options eventually work the same way.

3. Doing this reveals the *datasheet* view of the list. You can now directly enter and edit items in the list through this view, just like you would in an Excel spreadsheet.
4. Point to the first cell in the last row and simply start typing, or double-click the cell to make it editable.

You can use the *Tab* key, the arrow keys on the keyboard, or the mouse to move to the next cell in the row.

You can also use the arrow keys to navigate to other rows in the list. Doing so saves the current row, as long as you have entered all required information for that row.

5. Enter values for the other cells in the row, as shown in the following screenshot for the `Marketing Announcements` list:

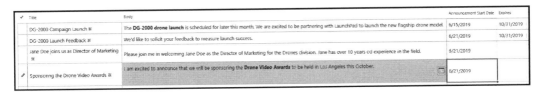

✓	Title	Body	Announcement Start Date	Expires
	DG-2000 Campaign Launch	The **DG-2000 drone launch** is scheduled for later this month. We are excited to be partnering with LaunchPad to launch the new flagship drone model.	6/15/2019	10/31/2019
	DG-2000 Launch Feedback	We'd like to solicit your feedback to measure launch success.	6/21/2019	10/31/2019
	Jane Doe joins us as Director of Marketing	Please join me in welcoming Jane Doe as the Director of Marketing for the Drones division. Jane has over 10 years of experience in the field.	6/21/2019	
✎	Sponsoring the Drone Video Awards	I am excited to announce that we will be sponsoring the **Drone Video Awards** to be held in Los Angeles this October.	6/21/2019	

6. Click the cell in the **Expires** column in the second row of the list shown in the preceding screenshot. Then, use the *Ctrl + C* keys to copy the date value from the selected cell.

7. Select the two empty cells under the **Expires** column for the last two rows and paste the copied value, as shown in the following screenshot:

✓	Title	Body	Announcement Start Date	Expires
	DG-2000 Campaign Launch	The **DG-2000 drone launch** is scheduled for later this month. We are excited to be partnering with LaunchPad to launch the new flagship drone model.	6/15/2019	10/31/2019
	DG-2000 Launch Feedback	We'd like to solicit your feedback to measure launch success.	6/21/2019	10/31/2019
	Jane Doe joins us as Director of Marketing	Please join me in welcoming Jane Doe as the Director of Marketing for the Drones division. Jane has over 10 years od experience in the field.	6/21/2019	10/31/2019
	Sponsoring the Drone Video Awards	I am excited to announce that we will be sponsoring the **Drone Video Awards** to be held in Los Angeles this October.	6/21/2019	10/31/2019

Just as with Excel, the **Quick Edit** view in SharePoint also lets you drag the corners of a cell or multiple cells to bulk-copy the cell values.

That's it! You just learned how to use the **Quick Edit** view to bulk-edit your list items.

How it works...

Working with lists is somewhat identical to working with database tables and Excel worksheets. The **Quick Edit** view lets you work with list items just as you would work with information in an Excel worksheet. Just like in Excel, you can click individual cells in a list to edit the items in those cells. Just as with Excel, you can carry bulk copy-paste operations in these cells. You can even add new columns through the datasheet view by clicking the + sign toward the top-right corner of the datasheet view. Clicking the + symbol opens a menu for you to select the column type:

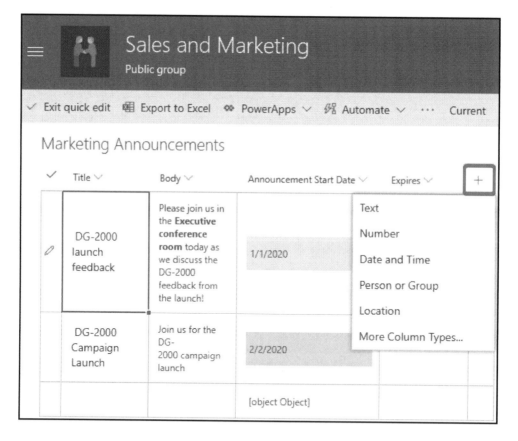

Clicking the column type will create a column and then let you enter a name for it, as shown in the following screenshot:

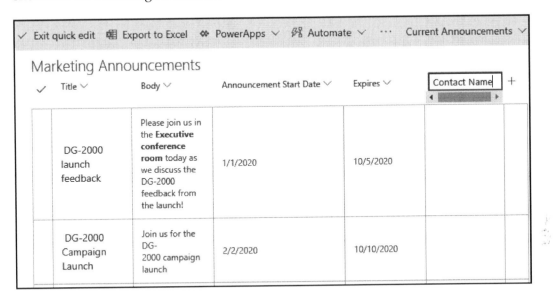

TIP

Every time you create a column in SharePoint, it creates two names for it: an *internal* name and a *display* name. It uses the *internal name* to internally reference the column. The internal name of a column does not have spaces, and never changes once the column is created. The *display name*, on the other hand, is the name of the column as you see it. It can have spaces, and you can change it even after you create the column. Both the internal and display names have to be unique within the list or library for columns created locally within that list or library. They need to be unique within the site for Site Columns.

When you create a column using the **Add column** functionality in a regular view, SharePoint will automatically create the internal name by removing spaces from within the column display name. For example, it will generate `ContactName` as the internal name for the `Contact Name` column shown in the preceding screenshot, when created through a regular list view. However, when you create a column using the **Quick Edit** view described in this recipe, it will give the column a randomly generated internal name. This is usually not a problem for most use cases but it might become a minor annoyance for some scenarios, especially those related to development surrounding such lists.

Viewing and changing list settings

SharePoint lets you view and change a variety of settings for your list.

In this recipe, we will use the `Marketing Announcements` list that we created earlier to add validation rules for the information that users can add to your list. We will add validation rules to ensure the following:

- The **Announcement Start Date** value is greater than the current date
- The **Expires** date entered by the users is greater than the **Announcement Start Date** value

Getting ready

You will need **Edit**, **Design**, or **Full Control** access permissions to the list for which you'd like to view or change settings.

How to do it...

1. Browse to the list for which you would like to view or change the settings.
2. Click the settings gear icon in the top-right corner.
3. Click **List settings**, as shown in the following screenshot:

4. On the **Settings** page, click the **Validation settings** link under **General Settings**.

5. Enter the desired validation formula in the **Formula** textbox. We are going to add the following formula for our example:

```
=AND([Announcement Start Date]>=TODAY(),
[Expires]>=[Announcement Start Date])
```

 SharePoint provides a ton of formulas for you to work with. You can find a list of all such formulas via this support article: `https://m365book.page.link/List-Formulas`.

6. Enter text in the **User Message** textbox to indicate details about the validation error. We are going to enter the following message for our example:

```
One or more of the following validation errors occurred:
  1. The announcement start date should be greater than or
equal to today's date.
  2. The Expiration date should be greater than or equal to the
Announcement Start Date.
  Please fix these errors and try submitting the form again.
```

7. The **Validation Settings** screen should then look like this:

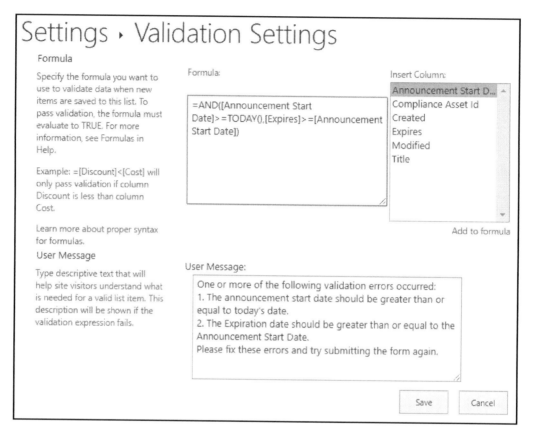

Settings ▸ Validation Settings

Formula

Specify the formula you want to use to validate data when new items are saved to this list. To pass validation, the formula must evaluate to TRUE. For more information, see Formulas in Help.

Example: =[Discount]<[Cost] will only pass validation if column Discount is less than column Cost.

Learn more about proper syntax for formulas.

User Message

Type descriptive text that will help site visitors understand what is needed for a valid list item. This description will be shown if the validation expression fails.

Formula:

```
=AND([Announcement Start
Date]>=TODAY(),[Expires]>=[Announcement
Start Date])
```

Insert Column:

Announcement Start D...
Compliance Asset Id
Created
Expires
Modified
Title

Add to formula

User Message:

One or more of the following validation errors occurred:
1. The announcement start date should be greater than or equal to today's date.
2. The Expiration date should be greater than or equal to the Announcement Start Date.
Please fix these errors and try submitting the form again.

[Save]   [Cancel]

8. Click the **Save** button to save the changes.

Note that you can only perform one validation and show a single validation message for the entire form. This means you will need to perform an AND operation if you'd like to validate multiple fields, as we did in the preceding example. As also shown in our example, you will want to make the information in the **User Message** textbox detailed enough to list all the possible causes that may result in a validation error.

9. Browse to your list again.

10. Click the **New** menu option to add a new item to your list.

11. Enter information in the list so that it satisfies the error condition. For our example, we are going to enter a past date for the **Announcement Start Date** field.

12. Click the **Save** button.

13. Notice the validation error message toward the top of the form, as shown in the following screenshot for our example:

New item

> Error: One or more of the following validation errors occurred: 1. The announcement start date should be greater than or equal to today's date. 2. The Expiration date should be greater than or equal to the Announcement Start Date. Please fix these errors and try submitting the form again.

Title *

This is a past announcement and should not be allowed to pass validation

Body

Announcement Start Date

6/11/2010

This is the date when announcements will start showing on the home page

Expires

6/28/2019

 Note that this validation also works when editing items and also in the **Quick Edit** view that we saw in an earlier recipe.

Congratulations! You just saw how to view and modify settings for a SharePoint list. You further saw how to set up validation for your list.

How it works...

SharePoint lets you manage your lists and libraries through various settings. We've already seen a couple of these important list settings through some of our previous recipes. Here are a few other more common list settings that we have not discussed so far:

- **List name, description, and navigation**: This is where you can change the title and description for your list. Note that the list URL remains the same even after you change the list name. This is where you can also specify whether or not to show the list in the site's **Quick Launch** (refer to the *Modifying the left navigation* recipe in `Chapter 3`, *Working with Modern Sites in SharePoint Online*).
- **Versioning settings**: This allows us to control whether or not to keep a version history of the changes to the list items. We will look at versioning in greater detail in a subsequent chapter.
- **Advanced Settings** (the more commonly used ones):
    - **Content types**: We will learn about content types in a subsequent chapter but at this point, it is sufficient to be aware that this setting is part of the list's/library's **Advanced Settings**.
    - **Item-level Permissions**: This setting allows you to define individual permissions for each item in the list. This setting is only applicable to lists (and not to libraries). We will discuss item-level permissions as part of the next recipe.
    - **Attachments**: Whether or not to allow attachment uploads for the lists. It is a good governance practice to consider enabling or disabling this setting every time a list is created. This setting is also available only for lists (and not document libraries).
    - **Folders**: Whether or not folder creation should be enabled for the list. Again, you should make a conscious decision as to whether or not to enable this setting for every list or library that gets created.

- **Search**: This option defines whether or not items from this list should show up in the search results. For most use cases, you will set this option to **Yes**. Instead of excluding items from just the search results, you should instead update the list or item permissions if you would like to hide items from other users. Once you change the list permissions, items from this list will also not show up in search results for users that don't have access to them. If, however, you have a compelling case to not show the list items in search results but still allow users to be able to access them, you simply change this setting to **No**. Doing so will hide the items from this list in the search results, while still allowing them to have direct access to them when they browse to the list or access them through shared links. Please refer to the *Viewing and changing list permissions* recipe later in this chapter for details on how to modify list and item permissions.

- **Reindex List**: Microsoft Search should automatically pick up new items from this list as part of the search results. Also, items that get deleted from this list should get dropped from the search results. If, however, for any reason you are not seeing appropriate items from this list in the search results, and you have waited sufficiently long enough for the search crawler to crawl and index this list, you can click the **Reindex List** button to completely delete and recreate the index as a way to fix the search results. Please refer to `Chapter 8`, *Search in Microsoft 365*, for more details on the different components of Microsoft Search and how it works in general.

- **List experience**: This lets you deviate from the default list experience setting for the site. Here, you can choose to explicitly use the classic list experience or the new modern experience for your list or library. Please see the next section in this recipe for the details of the modern versus classic list experience.

- **Delete this list**: Clicking on this link deletes the list and sends it to the **Recycle Bin** of that site. Deleting a list or library sends it to the recycle bin, where it stays for a couple of days until it gets moved to the second-stage recycle bin or gets permanently deleted. You can restore deleted lists or libraries, as long as they are still in the recycle bin and have not been permanently deleted. Please refer to the *Viewing site contents* recipe in Chapter 2, *Introduction to SharePoint Online,* to read more about the site recycle bin.

- **Workflow settings**: This allows us to specify workflow settings for the lists and libraries. Workflows are being replaced by **Microsoft Flow**. We have covered Microsoft Flow as part of a subsequent chapter. We will discuss workflows as part of the *Appendix*.

- **Columns**: This section lists the different columns for the list or library. You can click on the column names to view and change column settings.

- **Create column**: This link allows you to create a new column for the list.

- **Add from existing Site Columns**: Click this link to add a previously created Site Column to this list or library. We discussed **Site Columns** as part of the *Adding a column* recipe earlier in this chapter.

- **Column ordering**: Click this link to specify or change the order of the columns as shown from top to bottom in the **Details** pane or the add/edit forms for this list or library.

- **Index columns**: Specifying column indexes improves list performance when using filtered views. These are especially useful for large lists. You can use this link to specify indexes for your list or library.

- **Views**: This section shows the views currently configured for the list or library. You can edit existing views or create new views from this section.

The following support article provides a comprehensive listing of all the settings that are available for lists in SharePoint: https://m365book.page.link/List-Settings.

There's more...

SharePoint is an ever-evolving platform. Microsoft recently introduced a more modern, flexible, and mobile-friendly user experience for SharePoint. Modern lists and libraries are part of this new experience.

Modern versus classic list and library experience

Modern lists are faster, easier to use, less *SharePoint,* and mobile friendly. Some of the key benefits of modern lists and libraries are as follows:

- Easier to create and upload files and folders
- Easily add, sort, filter, and organize columns and views
- Easy access to file previews and information
- A better search experiences
- Easy customizations to the view display using column and list view formatting
- Ability to pin important documents to the top of the screen
- Ability to add files as links instead of having to copy them across sites
- A responsive experience

The classic experience is now deprecated and the modern experience is the default for newly created lists or libraries. To switch to the classic list experience, click **Return to classic SharePoint** from the bottom-left corner of the view page of your list or library. Note that while Microsoft lets you switch to the classic list experience, it is recommended that you continue to use the enhanced modern list and library experience unless there's a compelling and well-thought-out reason not to do so.

See also

- The *Adding an item to a list* recipe in Chapter 2, *Introduction to SharePoint Online*
- The *Viewing site contents* recipe in Chapter 2, *Introduction to SharePoint Online*
- The *Adding a column* recipe in this chapter

- The *Creating a custom list view* recipe in this chapter
- The *Viewing and changing list permissions* recipe in this chapter
- The *Adding a content type to a list or library* recipe in Chapter 6, *Term Store and Content Types in SharePoint Online*
- Chapter 8, *Search in Microsoft 365*

Viewing and changing list permissions

Just as in a site, you can adjust permissions on a list in a manner that allows control over who can view the list or edit items in it.

In this recipe, we will see how to view and change permissions in a SharePoint list.

Getting ready

You will need **Full Control** access to the list for which you'd like to view or change the permissions.

How to do it...

To modify list permissions, follow these steps:

1. Browse to the list for which you would like to view or change the settings.

 Libraries in SharePoint are a special type of list, hence a lot of settings that you can configure for lists are also relevant for the various types of libraries. This includes permission settings discussed in this recipe.

2. Click the settings gear icon in the top-right corner.

3. Click **List settings**, as shown in the following screenshot:

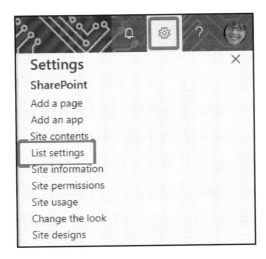

4. On the **Settings** page, click the **Permissions for this list** link under **Permissions and Management**. You can now view the current permissions for that list on this screen.

5. Click **Stop Inheriting Permissions** from the **PERMISSIONS** tab in the top navigation menu, as shown in the following screenshot:

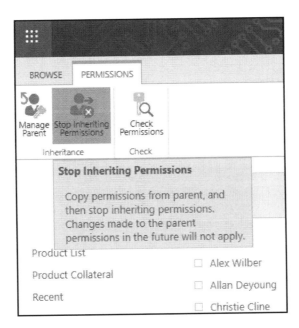

6. Click **OK** on the confirmation message.

As with the message states, by choosing to stop inheriting the permissions, you will have created unique permissions for your list. This means that the permissions on the list will have to be managed independently of the permissions on the site. Changes made to the permissions at the site level will not automatically be reflected in the permissions on the list. You can always reverse this setting and turn inheritance back on by clicking the **Delete unique permissions** menu option on the **Permissions** tab. Note that this option shows only if you are not inheriting permissions on the selected object.

7. You can now independently adjust the permissions on this list by carrying out one or more of the following actions:
    - Granting permissions to additional users or groups
    - Changing permissions for selected users or groups that already have access
    - Completely revoking access for existing users or groups that have access to the list

8. Select one or more existing users and click the **Edit User Permissions** menu option, as shown in the following screenshot:

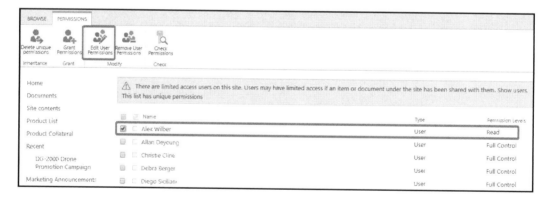

9. Change the permissions for the user and click the **OK** button, as shown in the following screenshot:

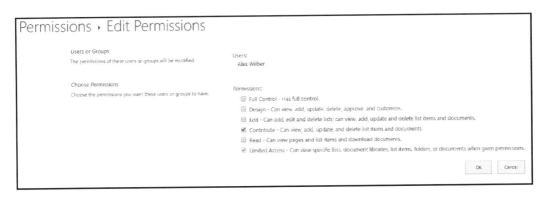

Congratulations! You just set up permissions for your list in a way that is different from the parent site.

How it works...

We saw permissions management in great detail in the *Determining and revoking permissions in a site* recipe in `Chapter 3`, *Working with Modern Sites in SharePoint Online*. We encourage you to review the recipe and related notes for more details on permissions in SharePoint, but to summarize, we covered the following:

- We reviewed permission levels in SharePoint.
- We saw how these permission levels relate to things that you are allowed to do and not allowed to do in SharePoint.
- We learned how to configure and adjust SharePoint permissions using these permission levels.

Permissions management in **Lists** and **Library** works similarly to permissions management on a site. When new lists and libraries are created, they *inherit* the security settings from the site, meaning that whatever access users have to your site, they will have the same level of access to the list. If, for example, a user has **Read** access to your site, they will by default have **Read** access to the list. After the **List** or **Library** is created, however, you can alter these permissions using the steps mentioned in this recipe.

A word of caution: While you can change permissions for each list and library, it is generally not recommended to do so for many lists and libraries in your site. Creating and managing individual permissions can very soon become a governance nightmare. Each situation differs, but you will likely be better off segregating audiences by way of creating different sites targeted toward solving the needs of those audiences.

There's more...

The permission hierarchy explained previously and subsequent management of this further trickles down to the item level, meaning that every item in a list and every document in a library by default *inherits* its permissions from the parent list or library. You can, however, break away from the inherited permissions and define distinct permissions for individual items. We discuss this and other related areas in the topics to follow.

Item permissions

Just as lists and libraries inherit permissions from their sites, items in lists and documents in libraries by default inherit permissions from the corresponding lists or libraries. SharePoint, however, lets you deviate from the norm and specify unique permissions for individual list items or documents. There are essentially two unique scenarios where you might want distinct permissions on individual items or documents within lists and libraries:

- The first scenario is where for all items in a list, you may want users to be able to only see their submissions to that list. An example of such a scenario could be a time-off request form, where individual department employees would submit their time off requests and department managers would approve or deny them. Such a scenario in SharePoint is easily handled by simply enabling item-level permissions through the list settings. To enable item-level permissions in your list, browse to the **List settings** page, as described in the previous recipe. Then, click **Advanced settings** link under the **General Settings** section. You will then see the **Item-level Permissions** section, as shown in the following screenshot:

Settings ‣ Advanced Settings

Content Types

Specify whether to allow the management of content types on this list. Each content type will appear on the new button and can have a unique set of columns, workflows and other behaviors.

Allow management of content types?

☐ Yes   ◉ No

Item-level Permissions

Specify which items users can read and edit.

Note: Users with the Cancel Checkout permission can read and edit all items. Learn about managing permission settings.

Read access: Specify which items users are allowed to read

◉ Read all items
○ Read items that were created by the user

Create and Edit access: Specify which items users are allowed to create and edit

◉ Create and edit all items
○ Create items and edit items that were created by the user
○ None

You can specify the following settings in this section:

- **Read access**: You can specify whether individual items can be read by everyone or can only be read by the users who created them.
- **Create and Edit access**: This is where you specify whether or not users can edit items created by others.

Please note that you will need **Design** or **Full Control** access to be able to update these settings. Also, worth noting is the fact that users with certain access levels, such as those having **Design** and **Full Control** access, will be able to view and edit all items in the list, irrespective of these settings. Also, these settings are only available for lists. You cannot configure item-level permissions for document libraries such as this. We'll cover how to apply unique permissions to documents in the next scenario.

- The second scenario is where you may want to deviate from the permissions norm for a single list item or for one or more documents in a library (since the item-level permissions described previously are not applicable to document libraries). Let's say that you'd like to get internal reviews done on a presentation before sharing it with a wider audience that has access to it via the parent container library. Until then, you would like to only share it with a few fellow colleagues for their review. For such scenarios, SharePoint lets you stop inheriting permissions from the parent library and specify custom permissions for the document in question. To do so, follow these steps:

  1. You would click the ellipsis next to the document and then click **Manage access**, as shown in the following screenshot:

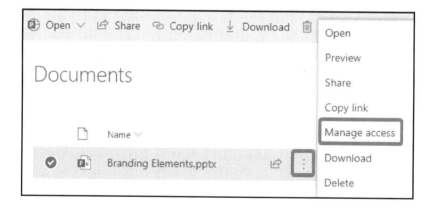

2. Then, click **Advanced**, all the way at the bottom of the **Manage Access** panel, as shown in the following screenshot:

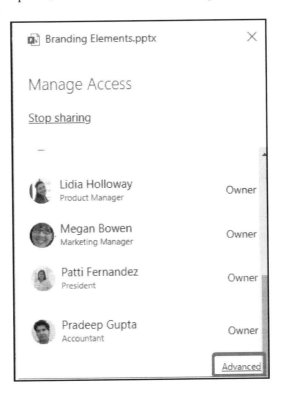

3. This will take you to the **Permissions** screen for that document. Here, you can view the existing permissions and also modify the permissions for this document as needed.

The steps to modify document permissions from this point on are the same as the steps to modify the list permissions, which we've described earlier in this recipe.

Navigation and search visibility

Modifying the permissions on lists or libraries and corresponding items or documents within them automatically ensures that the corresponding objects are not visible anywhere in the quick launch or global navigation. Furthermore, a search in SharePoint is also security trimmed to only show items that users have at least read access to. Any time that permissions on a document get updated, whether or not the document shows up in the search results for a user will depend on whether the user still has permissions to access the document.

See also

- The *Viewing and changing list settings* recipe in this chapter
- The *Determining and revoking permissions in a site* recipe in Chapter 3, *Working with Modern Sites in SharePoint Online*
- The *Searching content* recipe in Chapter 2, *Introduction to SharePoint Online*

Adding alerts

SharePoint notifies you by email when items are added, edited, or deleted in lists or libraries.

In this recipe, we will see how to create email alerts for SharePoint lists and libraries.

Getting ready

You will need at least **Read** access on the list or library for which you'd like to get alerted.

How to do it...

1. Browse to the list for which you would like to view or change the settings.

2. Click **Alert me**, as shown in the following screenshot:

3. This shows the **Alert me** dialog box. Here, you can specify various properties and settings for the alert to be created:

   - **Alert Title**: Specify a title for the alert that is descriptive of what the alert is for. The title will be shown in the subject line of the email alert that the selected users will receive.

   - **Send Alerts To:** Users with **Full Control** access to the list, such as the list owners, see this additional option. This option enables you to subscribe other users to receive these alerts. Note that only users that have at least **Read** access to the list will be able to receive alerts from it.

   - **Delivery Method**: The alert delivery method defaults to email. Note that even though the screen shows a **Text message (SMS)** option, that option is no longer enabled for SharePoint Online (at least, at the time of writing).

   - **Change Type**: This is where you can specify what kind of change triggers the alert—that is, would you like to get alerted if anything changes in that list or would you like to get alerted only if items are either added, modified, or deleted?

   - **Send Alerts for These Changes**: This lets you specify filters for when you would want to get alerted. You can select to be alerted when anything changes or when items that you have created or modified have changed. You can also restrict your alerts to trigger only when items in a particular view are changed by someone.

- **When to Send Alerts**: This final option lets you select the alert frequency. You can choose to receive an immediate alert or schedule a daily or weekly summary alert. If you opt to receive a daily or weekly summary alert, you can also choose the time at which you receive the summary notification email.

How it works...

Alerts in SharePoint are a very handy way to get notified about changes in a list or library. **Announcements**, **Contacts**, **Issue Tracking/ Tasks** lists, and **Calendar** are examples of where you might want to get notified of such changes. In addition to setting up alerts on entire lists and libraries, SharePoint also lets you set alerts on individual list items and/or documents, as shown in the following screenshot:

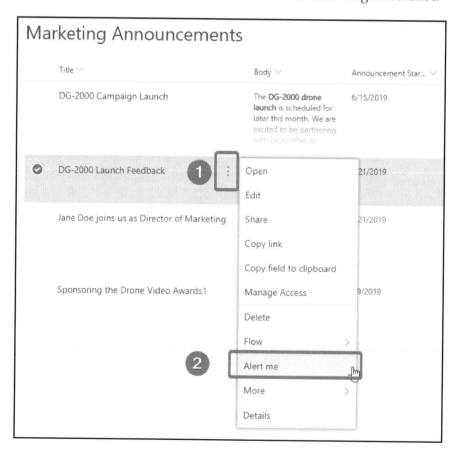

This can be handy when, for example, you are collaborating with your team on important documents and would like to stay up to date on any changes made to them.

Once you've created a list- or item-level alert, you can modify and/or delete it through the **Manage my alerts** menu option, as shown in the following screenshot:

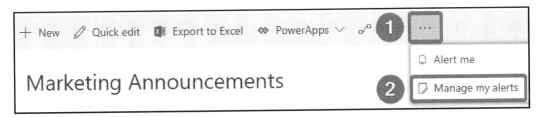

Clicking **Manage my alerts** will take you to the following screen, which will show you your alerts for all the lists, libraries, items, and documents across the entire site:

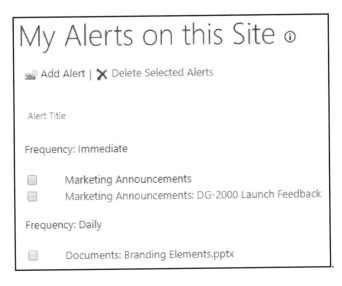

Clicking the alert name will enable you to make changes to it. Selecting one or more alert(s) and clicking **Delete Selected Alerts** will delete the alert(s). Note that unlike various other information types in SharePoint, deleted alerts don't go to the recycle bin, and hence cannot be recovered.

There's more...

When you sign up for alerts in SharePoint, you receive detailed email notifications every time that the alert is triggered. These emails contain various details about the item itself and metadata surrounding the triggering event. In the next section, we will look at these emails in more detail. We will then see how, as a site administrator, you can view and manage alerts that other site users may have subscribed to.

Notification emails

SharePoint sends two types of emails for alerts:

- **An email notifying you that the alert has successfully been created**: When you sign up for alerts on a list or library, SharePoint sends a confirmation email letting you know that an alert has been created. The following screenshot shows an example of such an email:

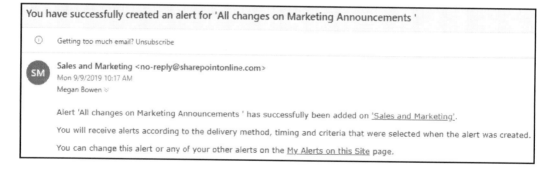

> You have successfully created an alert for 'All changes on Marketing Announcements '
>
> ⓘ   Getting too much email? Unsubscribe
>
> SM   Sales and Marketing <no-reply@sharepointonline.com>
>   Mon 9/9/2019 10:17 AM
>   Megan Bowen ⌄
>
> Alert 'All changes on Marketing Announcements ' has successfully been added on 'Sales and Marketing'.
>
> You will receive alerts according to the delivery method, timing and criteria that were selected when the alert was created.
>
> You can change this alert or any of your other alerts on the My Alerts on this Site page.

As you can see from the preceding example, the notification email contains the following information:

- The name of the list or library that the alert is for
- A link to the site that contains the list or library
- A link to the view/manage alerts page that we discussed in the preceding section

- **The actual alert email**: SharePoint sends an alert email when an activity occurs that matches your specified criteria. The following screenshot shows an example of an alert notification email:

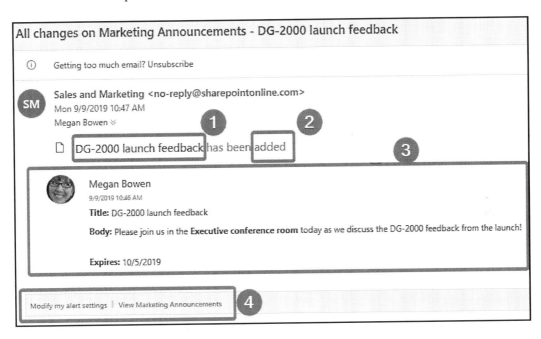

As you can see from the preceding example, the notification email contains the following information:

- Name of the item that the alert is for—the name hyperlinks to the corresponding item in the list
- The type of change that triggered the alert
- Details of the item, including who triggered the action and when
- A hyperlink to modify the alert settings
- A hyperlink to view the corresponding list

Finding and deleting other users' alerts

As a site administrator, you can not only view and manage your alerts but you can also view and delete alerts for other users of your site. To do so, browse to the **Site Settings** page of your site, as described in the *Viewing and changing site settings* recipe in Chapter 3, *Working with Modern Sites in SharePoint Online*. Then, click **User Alerts** under the **Site Administration** heading. This will take you to the **User Alerts** page, as shown in the following screenshot:

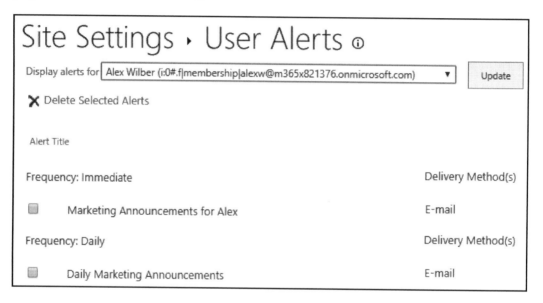

Here, you can select a user from the **Display alerts for** drop-down option, and click **Update** to view alerts that they are subscribed to. You can then select appropriate alerts and delete them by clicking **Delete Selected Alerts**.

See also

- The *Viewing and changing site settings* recipe, Chapter 3, *Working with Modern Sites in SharePoint Online*

5
Document Management in SharePoint Online

A **library** in SharePoint is a special list built specifically for managing files and the metadata around them. Libraries are similar to lists in that:

- Just like list *items* in SharePoint lists, libraries contain individual files that you can work with.
- Just as *columns* in lists define the information that gets stored as part of each list item, columns in libraries define the metadata that you can associate with each file. Once the columns for a library are defined, you can tag individual files with appropriate metadata.
- Similar to how you manage information in lists individually or together as a group of items, you can manage metadata in libraries individually or as part of groups of items.
- Just like list items, you can also individually manage permissions for these files.

From these perspectives (and in a lot of other ways), lists and libraries are similar to each other. One main difference between lists and libraries is that the library features are focused on files. A few notable examples of such capabilities are as follows:

- The file editing and sharing experience
- In-place file previews
- Copying and moving files
- Ability to pin important files to the top
- **Check in/Check out**, versioning, and approval experience

Libraries typically contain documents, but they can also contain various other file types. SharePoint provides a few pre-built libraries with different file types and associated capabilities in mind. We saw a listing of such library types in the *Builtin list and library templates* topic in the *Creating a list using a built-in list template* recipe of Chapter 4, *Working with Lists and Libraries in SharePoint Online*. Some notable examples of such pre-built libraries are as follows:

- **Site Pages library**: The purpose of this library is to store pages within a site.
- **Picture library**: The functionality of this library is centered around images.
- **Site Assets library**: This library is used to store reusable assets for your site (such as page images, stylesheets, and OneNote notebooks).

As the name suggests, a **Document library** is a type of library that is centered around documents. That said, there is no restriction at all on the types of files that you can upload to a **Document library**. We got some insight into working with document libraries and documents as part of Chapter 2, *Introduction to SharePoint Online*.

Also, Chapter 4, *Working with Lists and Libraries in SharePoint Online*, walked us through lists in great detail. We saw how to add columns, modify views, and modify other settings in a list. Since libraries are special types of lists, almost all of the guidance applicable to lists also applies to libraries. Before proceeding with the recipes in this chapter, it is highly recommended to review that chapter if you have not already done so. In this chapter, we will discuss recipes that we haven't discussed before since they are unique to libraries.

In this chapter, we will discuss the following recipes:

- Creating a new document
- Associating a document template
- Viewing and editing documents in the browser
- Viewing and editing documents in the client
- Downloading documents
- Moving and copying documents
- Viewing and changing document library settings
- Versioning settings, content approval, and document checkout

Creating a new document

In Chapter 2, *Introduction to SharePoint Online*, we saw how to upload existing documents and folders to a document library. In addition to uploading existing documents, you can create new documents from scratch within a document library.

There are two ways to create new documents within a library:

- Create it using the **New** menu in the library
- Create it using the local Microsoft Office app

This recipe will show you how to create a new **Word** document using either approach.

Getting ready

You will need **Contribute** permissions or higher to the library to be able to create a new document within it.

How to do it...

To create a document using the **New** menu in a document library, follow these steps:

1. Browse to the library where you would like to create the new document.

2. Click the **New** menu from the navigation bar on top of the library:

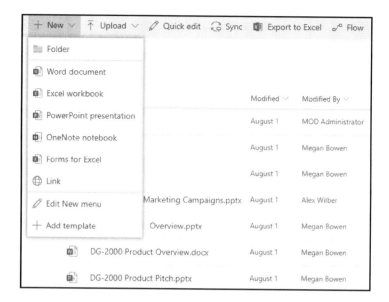

Selecting a document in the library replaces the top menu bar with the document actions menu. So if you have the required permissions for the library and are still not seeing the **New** menu, make sure you have not accidentally selected a document from the list of documents below.

3. Click on the type of new document you would like to create. We will choose a **Word document** for our example. Doing so will create a blank word document in the library and will open it for editing in a new browser window.

4. Click on the **Document - Saved** text at the top of the screen (above the ribbon menu):

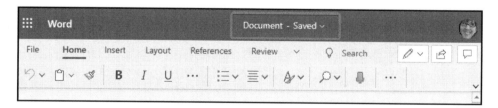

5. Give a name for your document and then press the *Enter* key or click anywhere outside the text box to save the change:

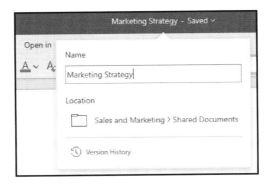

To create a new document using the Microsoft Office app on your computer, follow these steps:

1. Open the Office desktop application locally. We will open **Microsoft Word** since we are creating a Word document in this example.

2. Create or edit content in it like you typically would.

3. Click the **File** menu and then click **Save** or **Save As**. You will now be shown a list of your recent locations. These recent locations could be your online SharePoint and OneDrive libraries, or local folders on your computer:

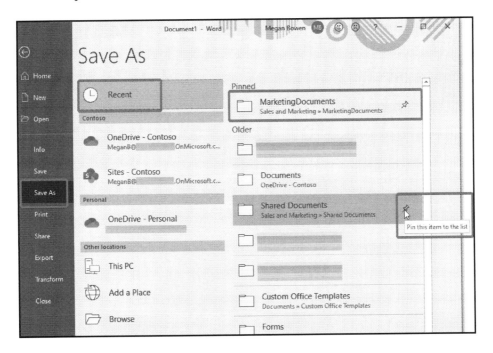

4. If you see your SharePoint Online library here, you can select it, enter a name for your file, and then save it here, as shown in the following screenshot:

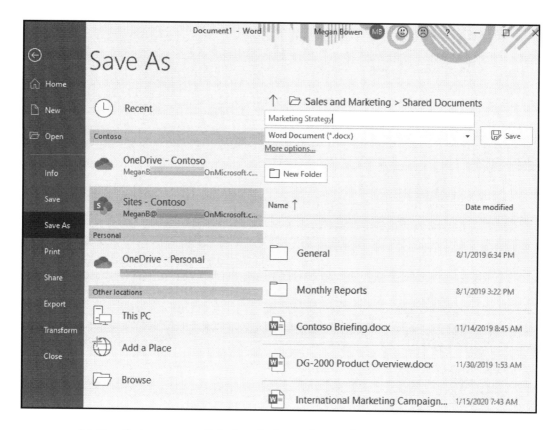

Notice that you can click the pin icon alongside your frequently used locations so they are pinned to the top of the list.

5. If you did not find your library in the list of recent libraries, you can click the **Sites - <YourOrganizationName>** option to view a list of your frequently accessed or followed sites:

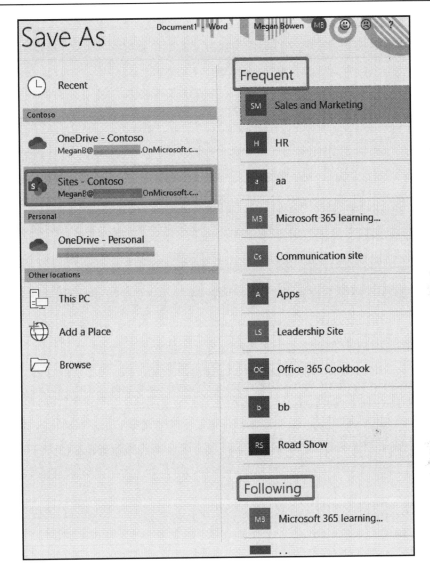

6. Clicking a site name then shows you the document libraries in those sites. You can then select a library and then save your document there, similar to the image shown in *step 4*.

7. Finally, if you do not see your site on this list, you can click the **Browse** button to open the **Save as** dialog. Then enter the URL of the library (without the trailing `Forms/AllItems.aspx`) and click **Save**, as shown in the following screenshot:

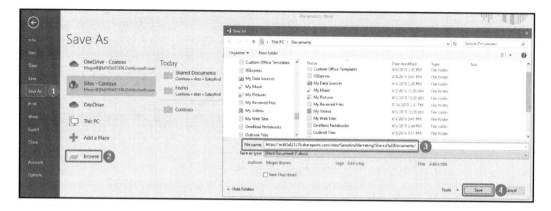

8. This takes you to the default view of the library (just like you would see it in the browser).

 Note that you may be prompted for credentials at this point, especially if you are doing this for the first time or not using your work computer. Please be careful to not save/remember the credentials if you are using a public computer to do this.

9. Enter a filename and click **Save** again to save the document to the library.

10. If your library contained mandatory columns for additional metadata, you will be prompted to enter values for those columns before you can save the document. If that happens, you will need to select or enter the required metadata and then click the **Retry Save** button:

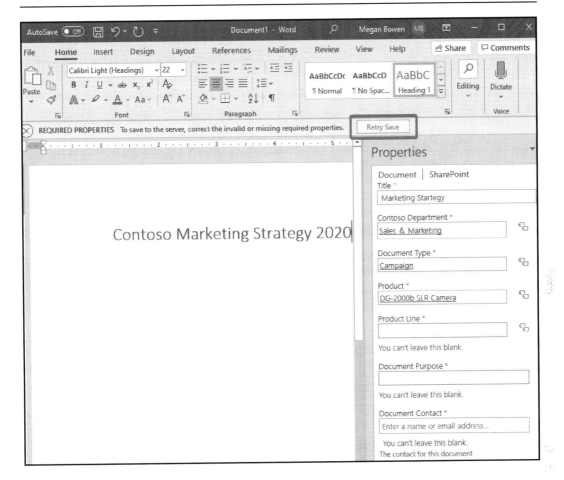

11. Doing so will save the document to the location that you had previously selected.

Congratulations! You just created a new document in the library. You learned how to do so by using the **New** menu from within the library or by using the corresponding Microsoft Office app from your local device.

How it works...

The one big difference between creating a document in SharePoint Online versus creating it locally is that when you create a new document in a SharePoint document library, it automatically becomes available to anyone else who has access to that library. Other users that have access can also collaborate on this document. Among other benefits, creating online documents also makes it easy to share them with others by merely emailing them links to those documents using the **Share** or **Copy link** functionality in SharePoint Online.

Governance and information architecture

Depending on their permissions, members of your site can create lists and libraries within it. They can further create columns within the libraries, create folders, customize library views, and change other settings for these libraries. This can quickly lead to lists and libraries all over your site, and along with that, multiple columns, views, and folders within those libraries.

For this reason, if you are a site owner or owner of a library, you should put some upfront thought into planning the permissions for your site and/or lists and libraries within the site. Also, you will want to plan the structure and organization of content that will be hosted within these sites. You should ideally do this before users start creating or uploading files in the library. As a site owner, you should think about whether content should be hosted in one library or multiple libraries. As a library owner, you should think about the following:

- The columns (a.k.a. metadata) that should be captured for the documents in the library
- The views that should be created for the library
- Whether you need to create folders to organize the files
- Versioning, Check out, and other settings for the library

In addition to this, you should think about the different audiences for the library and subsequently the permission settings for it.

See also

- *Uploading documents to a library* in `Chapter 2`, *Introduction to SharePoint Online*
- *Associating a document template* in this chapter
- *Adding alerts* in `Chapter 4`, *Working with Lists, Libraries in SharePoint Online*
- The *Creating a content type* recipe in `Chapter 6`, *Term Store and Content Types in SharePoint Online*

Associating a document template

The **New** menu in a library lets you create documents using the standard inbuilt document types:

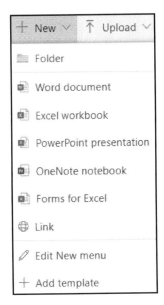

Clicking any of these document types will result in a blank document being created for you. There are times, however, when you would want your users to create documents using standard document templates defined by your organization. These templates might contain pre-defined branding, standard cover pages, footers, and headers as an example. You can modify the **New** menu to enable document creation using such templates and also optionally hide the default templates.

This recipe will show you how to associate such a pre-created document template with the **New** menu in your library. We will also see how to show this template at the top and then disable the inbuilt **Word document** option.

Getting ready

You will need the **Edit** permission or higher to be able to edit the **New** menu for a library.

How to do it...

To add a new template to the list of options in the **New** menu:

1. Click the **New** option in the menu bar.
2. Click **Add template** toward the bottom of the menu:

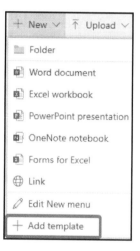

3. This opens the usual file selection dialog box for your computer.
4. Browse to the appropriate document template and then select it.
5. This will add the new document template to this menu, as shown in the following screenshot:

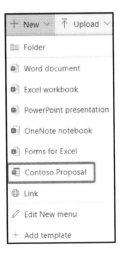

To modify the order of the different document types that the users see in the **New** menu, or to completely hide them:

1. Click the **New** option from the menu bar.
2. Click **Edit New menu** toward the bottom of the menu.
3. This brings up the **Edit New menu** screen. Here, you can hide the existing menu options, reorder them, or completely delete any custom options by clicking the ellipses to the right of the option:

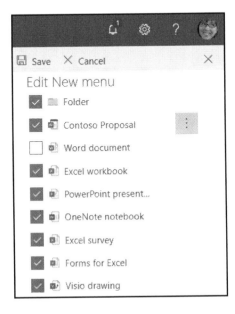

4. You can then click the **Save** button to save your changes to the **New** menu.

Congratulations, you just learned how to associate a document template with the **New** menu in your library. You then learned how to rearrange the order of the various menu options and then to hide the options that are not needed.

How it works

It is usually a good idea to associate document templates with your document libraries instead of your site users creating documents using the native blank templates. This further ties into the governance and information architecture discussion from the previous recipe in this chapter. Doing so where possible helps to further improve the quality of content and consistency within your site. Please note that your users can still upload documents to the library that may not be based on the template that you have defined. SharePoint cannot validate if the documents uploaded by the users of your library were created using a specific template.

See also

- The *Creating a new document* recipe in this chapter

Viewing and editing documents in the browser

Microsoft 365 conveniently enables you to view and edit files directly in the browser, without even having to download a local copy. This recipe will show you how to do that.

Getting ready

You will need **Read** permissions or higher on the document that you'd like to view and **Contribute** permissions or higher on it if you'd like to edit it.

How to do it...

To open a document in the browser, follow these steps:

1. Browse to the library that contains the document that you'd like to view or edit.
2. Click on the document you'd like to view or edit. This will open the document in a new browser window.

It may be that clicking the document will prompt you to open the corresponding desktop app for it. This can happen if the library owner has changed the default open behavior for documents in that library. To open a document in the browser for such a library, click the ellipses next to it, then click **Open**, and then **Open in browser**.

If you are the owner of such a library, we will discuss how you can change this behavior in a subsequent recipe in this chapter.

3. Depending on your permissions to the document, you will directly be able to view it or edit it in place in the browser.

That's it! You just learned how to view and edit documents from a SharePoint library in the browser.

How it works...

Office Online (now simply called **Office** and previously known as **Office Web Apps**) is the online Office suite that enables viewing and editing files in the browser. It supports hundreds of file types for viewing in the browser. This link provides a list of all such file types: `https://m365book.page.link/Preview-File-Types`.

In addition to the ability to view files within the browser, Office Online also enables you to edit a subset of these file types right from your browser. At the time of writing, the ability to edit documents in the browser was available for most Microsoft Office file types, such as `.docx`, `.pptx`, and `.xlsx`, and most text file types, such as `.txt`, `.css`, `.html`, and `.js`.

Please note that even though there is a limit on the file types that can be viewed or edited in the browser, there's practically no limit on the file types that can be uploaded to it. However, the browser viewing and editing experiences slightly vary depending on the type of file. Further, if SharePoint is unable to render a file type in the browser, clicking such a file will prompt you to download it to your computer. You can then open the file as you usually would on your computer.

Some of the advantages of browser editing are as follows:

- No additional licensing or software is required: Office Online is included with your Microsoft 365 subscription without an additional cost (a.k.a. free!). Further, it does not require any software to be installed (not even the Microsoft Office desktop software) and simply works out of the box with most commonly used browsers.
- Quick and convenient: It is certainly very convenient to be able to edit the documents from within the browser, instead of having to first download them. You can not only view and edit these documents on your desktop browser but also with a variety of mobile browsers and office mobile apps on a variety of other devices as well. Also, your changes are automatically saved so you don't need to manually save them.

The one main limitation of using Office Online to view or edit your documents in the browser is that not all features that are available in the corresponding desktop apps are available in Office Online. For example, not all transitions and animations are available in PowerPoint Online. Having said that, the capabilities available in Office Online still cover the most common usage scenarios. This article provides a detailed comparison of features that are available in the client apps versus those available in the corresponding web apps: `https://m365book.page.link/office-online-service-description`.

There's more...

We will discuss the co-authoring experience in SharePoint online in the next topic.

Co-authoring documents in the browser

Co-authoring is two or more people working on a document at the same time. Co-authoring in Office not only enables multiple people to simultaneously work on the same document but also lets them see each other's changes in real time. You can co-author MS Word, PowerPoint, Excel, or OneNote files that are stored in SharePoint Online or OneDrive. The following screenshot shows an example of co-authoring:

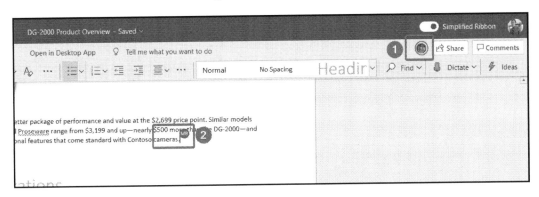

In the example shown in the preceding screenshot, a user, Alex, is making changes to a Word document. As shown in the screenshot, another user, Megan Bowen, is simultaneously editing the same document. Alex can see that Megan is editing the document by way of her image showing up in the top right corner of the document (illustrated by the rectangle marked number 1). Further, Alex can also see the changes that Megan is currently making in real time by way of a cursor that shows the initials of her name -MB (illustrated by the rectangle marked number 2).

Office provides various indicators when multiple people are co-authoring a document. In addition to the preceding indicators mentioned, Office will explicitly notify you when someone else starts editing a document that you already are presently editing. It will also notify you when they exit that editing experience. Please note that you do **not** get notified when others open the document to view it (you only get notified when they open the document to edit it).

Similar to this, Megan will also see the changes that Alex is making in real time through a presence indicator along with a cursor showing the initials of his name. If more than two users were editing this document, Word would similarly indicate their presence along with the real-time updates that they are making to the documents.

This support article provides more details on co-authoring: `https://m365book.page.link/co-authoring`.

See also

- The *Viewing and editing documents in the client* recipe in this chapter
- The *Adding alerts* recipe in `Chapter 4`, *Working with Lists and Libraries in SharePoint Online*

Viewing and editing documents in the client

Besides being able to view and edit documents in the browser, SharePoint also lets you view and edit online documents in the corresponding desktop applications. There are two ways to open an online document in the desktop app:

- Browse to the library and then open the document from there.
- Directly open an online document from the app.

In this recipe, we will see how to use both methods to view and edit a document that was uploaded to a SharePoint library in the corresponding desktop application.

Getting ready

You will need **Read** permissions or higher on the document that you'd like to view and **Contribute** permissions or higher on it if you'd like to edit it.

How to do it...

To open the online document from the library, follow these steps:

1. Browse to the library that contains the document that you would like to view or edit.
2. Click the ellipses next to the document (**1**).
3. Click or mouse-over the **Open** submenu option (**2**).
4. Click **Open in app**, as shown in the following screenshot (**3**):

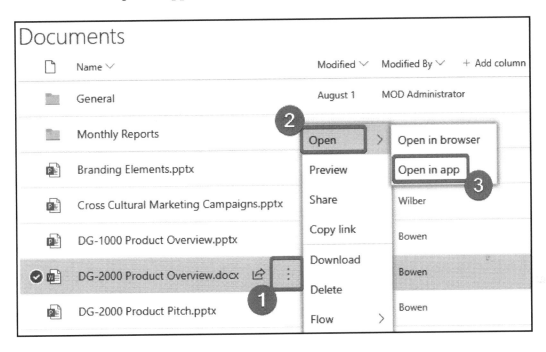

5. If you are opening a Word document, like we are in the preceding screenshot, click **Open Word** on the prompt that appears to confirm that you'd like to open the document in Word.

Anything you do in SharePoint, and Microsoft 365 in general, requires you to be authenticated and have appropriate access configured through permissions. This is true for documents that you are opening in the client as well. You will be prompted for credentials the first time you open any document in a client app (or if your credentials have changed since the last time). Your credentials will then be remembered from thereon, provided you were able to successfully authenticate yourself. From that point on, SharePoint will use the saved credentials every time you try to open a document (even though it will still check to make sure you have permissions to it).

6. The selected document will now open in the Word app. If you have the right to edit the document, you can start making changes to it and your changes will automatically be saved to the document library in SharePoint.

To open the document directly from the client app, follow these steps:

1. Open the corresponding desktop app, like you usually would.

2. Once you open the app, you will be shown the **Home** tab. Here, you can see all your recently opened documents, which include documents from Office Online. Click on the document to open it if you see it here. Otherwise, we can move on to the next step.

3. Click the **Open** tab or **File** | **Open** – the option you see will depend on the type of document that you are trying to open.

4. Here, you will again see a list of your recent files. If you have previously connected your Microsoft 365 account through the desktop client, you will also see a list of organizations that you have recently accessed.

5. Clicking on the organization name will show you your frequent and followed sites from the organization:

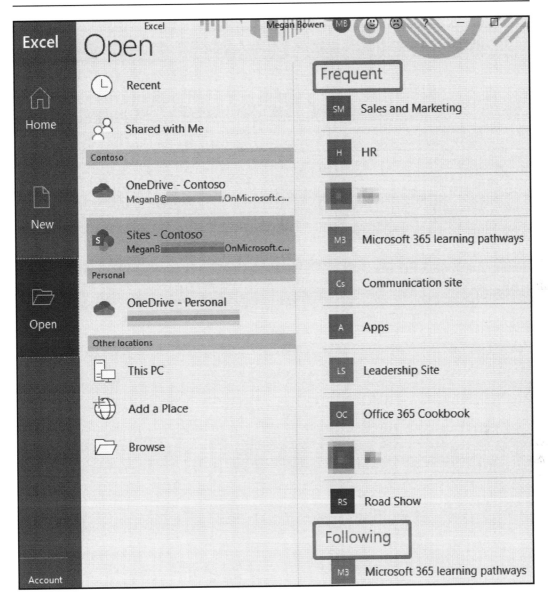

6. You can then click on the site and then the library to view all the folders and documents in that library.
7. You can click on the document to open it if you found your document here. If not, we will move on to the next step.

8. Click the **Browse** button to open the usual file selection dialog box.

9. Enter the URL of your site and then click **Open** to see a list of the libraries in that site.

   You will need to ensure that the URL points to the file and not any libraries or pages underneath it. For example, a URL like this will result in an error because it points to a page (and not a site): `https://<OrganizationName>.sharepoint.com/sites/S alesAndMarketing/SitePages/Home.aspx`.

   Consequently, the correct URL to enter in the file dialog for this site is `https://<OrganizationName>.sharepoint.com/sites/Sal esAndMarketing/`.

10. Select the library that contains your document and then click **Open** to view a list of documents in that library.

11. Select the document you'd like to open, and then click **Open**, as shown in the following screenshot:

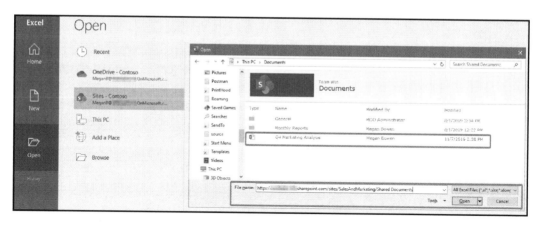

12. Doing so will directly open that document in the desktop client.

Congratulations! You just learned how to directly view and edit documents from a SharePoint library in a client app. Please note that you can currently only open Microsoft Office documents this way.

How it works...

Being able to edit documents online is very convenient. However, it lacks the advanced editing controls that the Microsoft Office desktop apps provide. The client editing capability brings together the best of both worlds. It lets you store and share your documents on the cloud, where they are easily accessible to everyone. Also, you can use the rich client capabilities to make modifications to your documents. As of now, you can only edit Microsoft Office documents connected to the cloud this way. All other file types that you would like to edit using the client applications will first need to be downloaded, edited, and then uploaded back to the library.

In addition to directly opening online documents in a desktop app, you can also use the **Open in Desktop App** option to open, in the corresponding desktop app, any online documents that you may be viewing or editing in your browser.

The Open in Desktop App option

When editing documents in the browser, SharePoint Online presents an **Open in Desktop App** menu option, as shown in the following screenshot. Clicking this option also opens the document in the corresponding desktop app:

There's more...

We discussed co-authoring as part of the last recipe. The discussion was focused on a browser-based co-authoring experience in that all users were using their browser to work with the documents. In the context of the current recipe, it is also possible to use the corresponding Microsoft Office desktop apps to co-author documents.

Co-authoring documents in the client app

While you edit the document in a desktop app, your co-workers could either be using the browser or a desktop app to view and edit the same document. The Office desktop app would provide you similar notifications and indicators to not only show you who else is editing the document but will also show their edits in real time.

The editing experience differs depending on the type of document that you are editing and the type of app that you are using. At the time of writing, the co-authoring experience in **Excel** desktop, for example, only works with certain installations of the app – specifically only if it's installed using the Microsoft 365 click-to-run installer. For apps installed using the Windows installer, the Excel file will open as read-only if another user is already editing it. This support article provides a good reference to troubleshoot any issues that you may be seeing with the co-authoring experience: `https://m365book.page.link/Troubleshoot-Coauthoring`.

One added benefit of using the desktop app for co-authoring is that clicking a person's presence indicator in the app lets you perform the following additional actions:

- Go to the location that the person is at in the document.
- Email the person.
- View their contact information.

Document metadata

When the document library containing the document is configured with columns to store additional metadata/information for the document, Microsoft Office lets you edit that metadata from within the client application. Further, if any of those columns are mandatory, the client application will require you to enter that information before you can save the document. It shows these columns through a properties pane, as shown in the following screenshot:

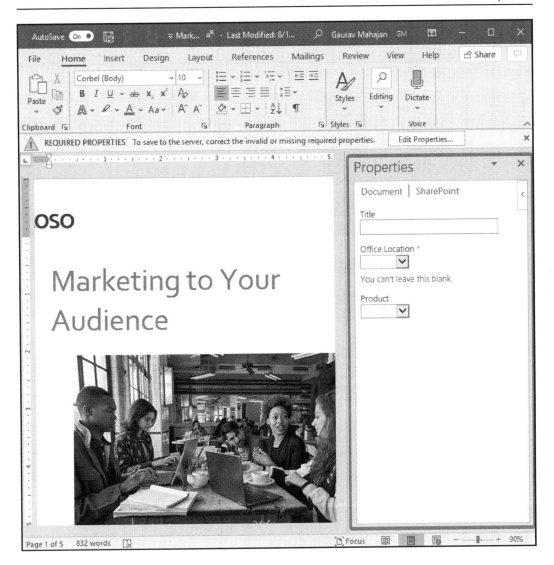

This property pane is also sometimes referred to as the **Document Information Panel**. The Office client will save your document to SharePoint once you update its properties through this panel. This experience is similar to the desktop app authoring experience that we discussed in the *Creating a new document* recipe earlier in this chapter.

See also

- The *Viewing and editing documents in the browser* recipe in this chapter
- The *Adding alerts* recipe in `Chapter 4`, *Working with Lists and Libraries in SharePoint Online*
- The *Versioning settings, content approval, and document checkout* recipe in this chapter

Downloading documents

In addition to viewing and editing documents in browsers or client apps, you can also download them for offline viewing. This recipe shows you how to do that.

Getting ready

You will need **Read** permissions or higher on the document that you'd like to download.

How to do it...

To download a document, follow these steps:

1. Browse to the library that contains the document that you would like to download and select the document that you would like to download.
2. Click the **Download** option from the menu at the top:

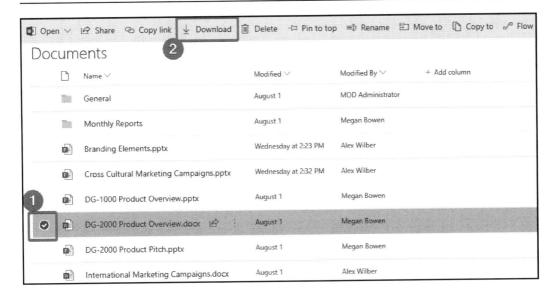

When you select a document, the options that you see in the top menu bar are also available to you when you click the ellipses next to the document. In this case, for example, you can also click the ellipses to reveal the **Download** menu option.

That's it! You just downloaded a copy of the document for offline use.

How it works...

You can download any file for offline viewing and editing. For file types that you can view in the browser, Office for web provides two different ways of downloading the files, depending on the file type:

- For Microsoft Office documents, once you have the document open in your browser window, you can click the **File** menu, then **Save As**, and then **Download a Copy**. You will also see some additional options depending on the type of Office document that you are viewing (Word, Excel, or PowerPoint). Word, for example, additionally presents a **Download as PDF** option:

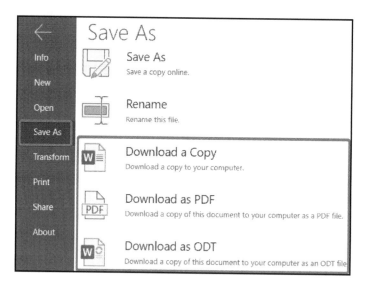

- For all other file types, you will be able to download the file by clicking the **Download** option in the top menu bar, which appears when viewing those files in the browser, as shown in the following screenshot for an image file:

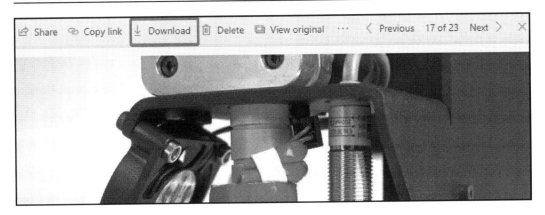

When you download and edit files this way, they are not connected to SharePoint online, meaning that your local edits to the documents will be saved locally and not to the cloud. Downloading files this way should, therefore, be avoided unless you have a very specific need that requires you to use an offline and disconnected copy of the file. For Microsoft Office file types, you can use the connected browser and desktop editing experience that we previously discussed. For viewing and editing non-Office file types, it is recommended that you use the **Sync** menu option to locally sync the documents from your library. Once you do that, any changes you make to the local files will continuously be synchronized with the online document. We will discuss **OneDrive** and how the sync works in more detail in a subsequent chapter.

See also

- Chapter 7, *OneDrive for Business*

Moving and copying documents

You can copy or move your documents from one site to another site in your tenant. In this recipe, we will see how to copy a document to a different library in another site.

Getting ready

To *copy* a document, you will need **Read** access to the library from which you are copying the document. If you are *moving* a document, you will need **Contribute** permissions or higher from where you are moving the document.

In addition, you will need **Contribute** access to the library where you are moving or copying the documents to.

How to do it...

To copy or move one or more documents, follow these steps:

1. Browse to the library that contains the documents that you'd like to copy or move.

You would follow the same steps if you'd like to copy files over from your OneDrive to a library in SharePoint.

2. Select the documents that you'd like to move or copy and click the **Move to** or **Copy to** options in the menu at the top, as shown in the following screenshot:

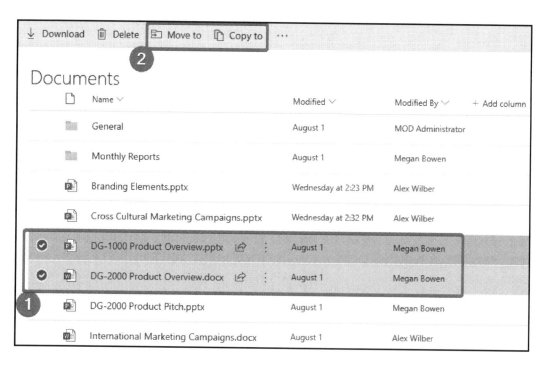

3. Choose a destination to move or copy your file to. You can choose from the following options, as shown in the following screenshot:

    1. Create a copy of the file within the same library

    2. Move or copy the file over to a folder in your OneDrive

    3. Choose a library from a list of recently used sites

    4. Browse to a site not shown in the list of recently used sites:

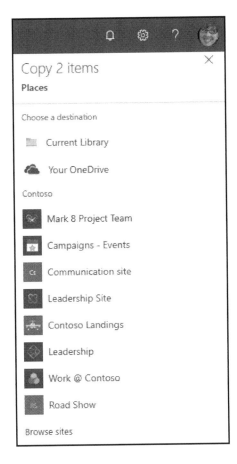

We will select the **Road Show** site for this example.

4. We will then select a library on this site.

5. If needed, we can further create new folders, or select existing subfolders, and then click **Move here** or **Copy here** to move or copy the files over to the selected library:

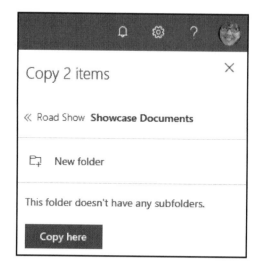

 The copied files will automatically inherit permissions from the destination library, even if the source library or documents had a different set of permissions.

That's it! You just learned how to copy or move files in SharePoint to another destination within SharePoint or OneDrive.

How it works...

Copying or moving files in SharePoint Online is quite similar to copying or moving files on your computer. If you are moving a file, the source file is deleted. If you are copying a file, the source file is maintained and a new copy of the file is created in the destination. Similar to when you are copying or moving files locally, SharePoint provides appropriate indicators when the file operation starts and once it succeeds or fails. The one difference between the copy and move operations in SharePoint is that since copying effectively creates a new file in the destination, certain properties of the file such as the version history do not carry over. Moving the file, on the other hand, results in the version history also being brought over to the destination file.

Please refer to the *Versioning settings, content approval, and document checkout* recipe later in the chapter to find out more about versioning and version history.

Also, if you have custom metadata associated with the document being copied or moved, that metadata is copied over along with it as long as the destination library has the same column as the source to store that information.

Finally, please note that at the time of writing, SharePoint restricts the maximum size of a copy or move operation to 100 GB, when the operation is across two sites. You can read more about this here: `https://m365book.page.link/Move-Copy-Limits`.

Viewing and changing document library settings

We saw several list settings as part of the *Viewing and changing list settings* recipe in `Chapter 4`, *Working with Lists and Libraries in SharePoint Online*. As mentioned earlier, libraries are an extension of lists, and hence these settings also inherently apply to libraries. They, however, also have a few additional settings of their own that are relevant to the way you work with files and documents.

We will look at some of these settings as part of this recipe. As an example, we will see how to change the default way that browser-enabled documents open. When you click on a document in a library, the default setting results in SharePoint opening the document in the browser. However, as described in the 'Viewing and editing documents in the browser' recipe, earlier in this chapter, the browser editing experience has its limitations. You may, therefore, require the documents in a particular library to open in the corresponding office clients so you can get that rich editing experience. This recipe will show you how to do that.

Getting ready

You will need **Edit**, **Design**, or **Full Control** access to the library that you'd like to view or change the settings of.

How to do it...

To change the default open behavior for documents in a library, follow these steps:

1. Browse to the library for which you would like to change this behavior.
2. Click the settings gear icon in the top-right corner.
3. Click **Library settings**, as shown in the following screenshot:

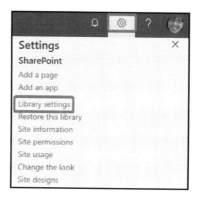

4. This takes you to the **Settings** page for the library. Here you can view and modify various settings for the list.
5. Click the **Advanced settings** link and scroll down to the **Opening Documents in the Browser** setting.
6. Select the **Open in the client application** option.
7. Click the **OK** button the bottom of the screen.

You just changed the default open behavior for browser-enabled documents. Clicking a document in the library will now prompt you to directly open it in the corresponding client app.

How it works...

As we saw in earlier recipes, working in the client has its advantages as well as drawbacks. This means you will want to carefully choose the default open behavior based on the specific needs of your team. Also note that since you can edit only Microsoft Office documents directly in the client, this setting will only impact those file types. Other files will continue to open in the browser (for file types that support browser viewing) or will get downloaded, based on the file type.

Some of the other settings relevant to documents are as follows:

- **General Settings – Advanced settings – Offline client availability**: This setting prevents documents in this library being synced locally using the OneDrive sync. Note that users can still download these documents – it's just that they will not be synced through the OneDrive sync client.

> We will learn more about OneDrive and the sync client in Chapter 7, *OneDrive for Business*.

- **General Settings – Column default value settings**: This is one of the more useful but overlooked settings in SharePoint Online. This settings page helps you to define default metadata values for your library, based on the folder that the documents are being saved to. As an example, let's assume there's a Policies library in your intranet site that is used to share the policies across various departments in your organization. The library has department-based folders (such as Communications, Finance, and H.R.) and then sub-folders to hold relevant policy documents. Let's also assume the library has a metadata column called **Department** so you can tag each policy document by the department it belongs to. You can now define default values for this column so that any documents uploaded to the library get automatically tagged by the department name depending on the folder they are being uploaded to. An example of this is shown in the following screenshot:

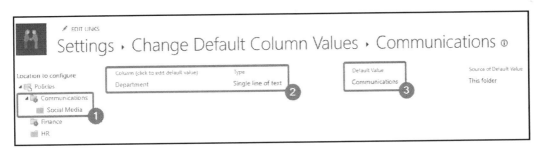

In the preceding screenshot, #1 represents the folder (and any subfolders) for which the default metadata is being defined, #2 represents the metadata column (and its type) for which the value is being configured, and #3 represents the default value that will be applied when documents are uploaded to the folder.

- **Permissions and Management – Manage files which have no checked-in version**: This page shows a list of all files that do not have a checked-in version. We will learn about this setting as part of the next recipe, *Versioning settings, content approval, and document checkout*.

See also

- The *Viewing and changing list settings* recipe in `Chapter 4`, *Working with Lists and Libraries in SharePoint Online*
- The *Viewing and editing documents in the browser* recipe in this chapter
- The *Viewing and editing documents in the client* recipe in this chapter
- The *Enabling versioning and requiring checkout* recipe in this chapter
- The *Adding a Content Type to list or library* recipe in `Chapter 6`, *Term Store and Content Types in SharePoint Online*

Versioning settings, content approval, and document checkout

The **Versioning Settings** page lets you control various settings related to document life cycle management, such as document versioning, approval, Check out, and draft document visibility.

In this recipe, we will change the versioning settings to require document Check out. Enabling this option results in the users having to first *check out* the document before they can make changes to it. This essentially locks down the document exclusively for their editing use. Once a document is checked out, other users will not be able to edit that document unless it's checked in again by the user editing it. Anyone with **Read** access or higher can still view the document. However, the version of the document that they will see is the one that was last checked in. They will not show the edits that the user who checked out the document is currently making until after they **Check in** the document.

Getting ready

You will need **Edit**, **Design**, or **Full Control** access to the library for which you'd like to view or change the versioning settings.

How to do it...

To require Check out for the documents in a library, follow these steps:

1. Browse to the library settings page as described in the previous recipe.
2. Click **Versioning settings** in the **General Settings** section.
3. On the **Version Settings** page, scroll all the way down to the **Require Check Out** section.
4. Select **Yes** for **Require documents to be checked out before they can be edited?**.
5. Click **OK** to save your changes.
6. Go back to the library by clicking on the library name in the breadcrumb navigation, as shown in the following screenshot:

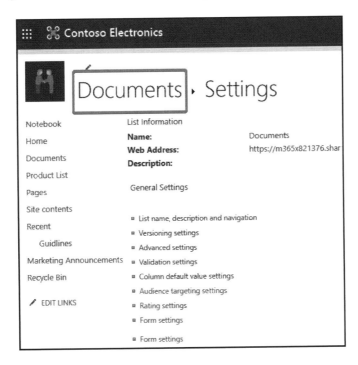

7. Click any document to open it.

8. If your document opened in the browser, you will notice a new **Edit Document** menu option in the top-right corner of the screen, as shown in the following screenshot:

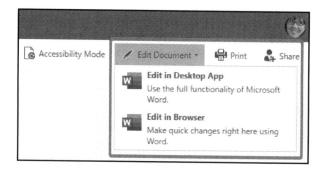

9. Click **Edit in Browser** and notice that Office Online now requires you to check out the document before editing it:

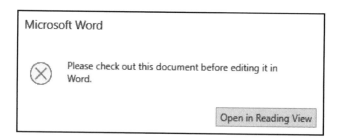

This prompt will look different in different types of Office documents. For example, at the time of writing, it looks like this for PowerPoint presentations:

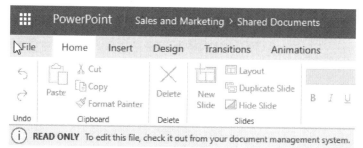

10. Close the browser tab containing the document and go back to the library.
11. Click the ellipses next to the document name.
12. Click **More** and then **Check out**, as shown in the following screenshot:

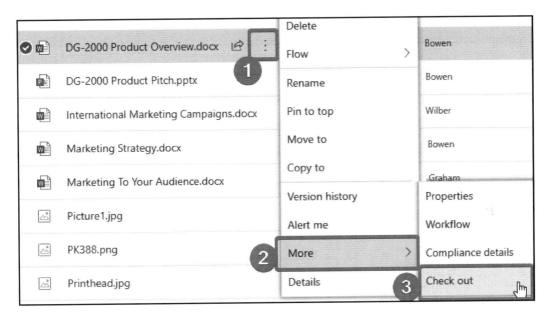

13. Click on the document to open it again in a new browser window.
14. Notice that the **Edit Document** option no longer appears and you are now able to directly make changes to it.
15. Close the browser tab to go back to the library once you have made the required changes to your document.
16. In the library view, click the ellipses next to the document name again and then click **More**.

17. You can now click **Discard check out** to undo your changes or click **Check in** to save your changes to the document, as shown in the following screenshot:

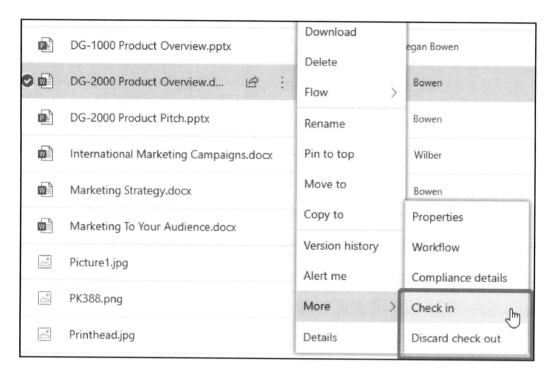

18. Clicking **Check in** opens a window that lets you enter comments for your **Check in**, as shown in the following screenshot:

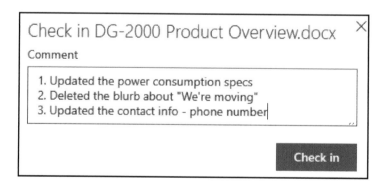

Check in comments are optional but are highly recommended. These comments should meaningfully describe the changes that you've made. Users with access to the document can then view these comments using the document version history and subsequently understand the changes that were made to the document throughout its life cycle.

19. Then click **Check in** again on the comments screen to Check in your changes and make them visible to others.

You just saw how to enable document **Check out** for your library. You also saw how to work with documents in a library that requires you to check them out before they can be edited in a browser. The process is a little different for documents that open in the client. We will look at that process as part of the next section.

How it works...

Requiring document Check out is not usually recommended due to the following reasons:

- **You cannot co-author**: Checking out a document locks it for your exclusive editing and no one else can make changes to it unless it's checked in again. For this reason, co-authoring is not possible on documents in a library that requires document checkout.
- **Additional steps are required to create and edit files**: For libraries that require **Check out**, additional steps, such as checking out the documents and then checking them back in, are needed for the documents to be created and for the changes to be visible to others. These additional steps are usually a deterrent to user adoption.
- **People forget to Check in**: It is not uncommon for users to forget to **Check in** their changes. At other times, users accidentally **Check out** the wrong documents for various reasons. This leaves stale checked out documents in such libraries. Someone with appropriate access then needs to go back and either discard these documents (which results in the users losing their changes) or contact individuals to **Check in** their documents. It can become cumbersome and time-consuming for the library owners to do that.

It makes sense to require checking out in these situations:

- **Large viewers and very few collaborators**: Requiring **Check out** inherently allows the document author to make and save changes to it without making those changes visible to rest of the viewers of the file. Others continue to see the previously checked-in document. This is useful in scenarios where you have very few people authoring the documents in that library but a large audience viewing them. Examples of such libraries are organization policy documents, guides, expense forms, and Excel templates.

- **Required metadata**: If you have libraries that require metadata to be entered, enforcing the **Check out/Check in** process ensures that the metadata is filled in. If **Check out** is not required and the users save the document without entering the mandatory metadata, SharePoint will provide an indicator that the metadata is missing but will still allow the users to save such documents. If however **Check out/Check in** is enabled on that library, SharePoint will prevent users from checking in the documents unless all required metadata is entered.

Other versioning settings

The **Versioning Settings** additionally let you control the following options for your SharePoint lists and libraries:

- **Content Approval**: This setting allows you to control whether new documents or revisions to existing documents in the library should undergo content approval or review before they become visible to other users. This is a useful feature if you would like your documents to be reviewed and/or approved before they are visible to a broader group of visitors to your site or library. An **Approval Status** column is added to the library once content approval is enabled for it. When a new document is uploaded or changes to an existing document are submitted for such a library, the status of the document is changed to **Pending**. Only users that have the authority to approve documents (typically users having the **Design** or **Full Control** permission to the actual document) can view such newly added documents or view changes to existing documents at that point. Such approvers can then approve or reject the changes and the **Approval Status** for the document is accordingly updated. Upon approval, the changes in the document become visible to regular users. You can read more about content approval in this support article here: https:// m365book.page.link/Require-Approval.

- **Document Version History**: The different options within this setting allow you to specify whether a copy of the document is maintained each time it is edited. Versioning is turned off for lists by default, but you can turn it on. For libraries, versioning is always on and cannot be turned off. In addition to enabling major versions (1, 2, 3...) you can also enable minor versions (1.0, 1.1, 1.2 ...). Minor versions are typically only used along with content approval and publishing scenarios where you would like to **Check in** your draft (minor) changes from time to time. This also allows content approvers to review the changes before they are published as a major version and become visible to everyone that has access to the item. In addition to enabling major versions (and optionally minor versions), you can also set a limit on the number of versions that SharePoint should keep.

> Limiting the number of versions is useful for older/on-premises versions of SharePoint. This was necessitated by the fact that SharePoint used to store duplicate copies of the document for every single version created, and this put a huge burden on the underlying on-premises infrastructure, depending on the number and size of the documents and libraries. SharePoint Online (and newer on-premises versions) however save the original document in its entirety and then only store the changes from that point on. This is much more efficient and, as a result, limiting document versions now is not as necessary.

Once versioning is enabled, SharePoint maintains an audit trail of all the edits that were made to your list item or document. You can use the ellipses next to a list item or a document to view all the changes that were previously made to that item by date and time. If **Check out** was required for the library, this screen will also show you any **Check in** comments that your co-workers might have entered to describe the changes made to the document as part of that **Check in**.

As shown in the following screenshot, you can also click on a particular date and time entry to view, restore, or delete a historical version of the item at that point in time:

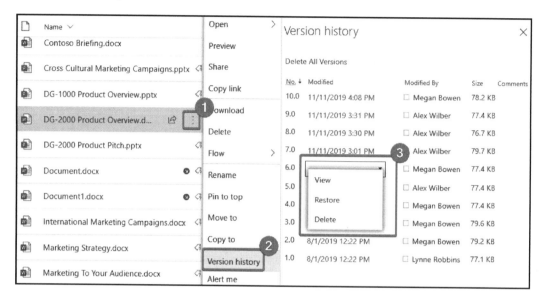

- **Draft Item Security**: This setting allows you to specify who can see document drafts in your library. This setting is only available if minor (draft) versions are enabled in your library or if you have required content approvals for items in your list or library. You would typically keep this option set to the default value, which allows only the document author, approvers, and the library owners to see the draft (minor) versions of the documents.

- **Require Check out**: You can use this setting to specify whether users need to **Check out** documents before they can make changes to them. We saw this setting in great detail in the preceding recipe.

There's more...

In this section, we will discuss the effect of requiring **Check out** and enabling versioning on co-authoring and opening documents in the client.

Checkout process for documents that open in the client

The preceding recipe described the steps to **Check out** and open documents in a browser. This experience is a little different when you open your documents directly in the desktop client or app. You will see a message toward the top of the client app if your library requires documents to be checked out, and you open a document from such a library in the corresponding client app:

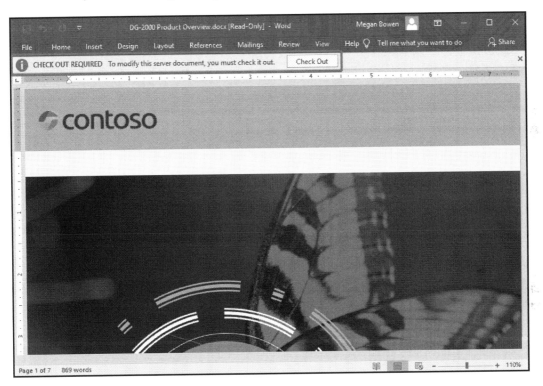

You can then click **Check Out** and make changes to your document as usual. Since the document was opened from a SharePoint online document library, your changes to it will automatically be saved to the library. You will, however, need to **Check in** the document for your changes to be visible to others. To do so, follow these steps:

1. Click the **File** menu and then **Info**.
2. Click **Check In** to initiate the **Check in** process.
3. Enter the **Check in** comments describing the changes you've made.

4. Click **OK** to **Check in** your changes to the document, as shown in the following screenshot:

This will then **Check in** the document and make your changes visible to others in the organization.

Co-authoring and versioning settings

When checkout is not required in a library and two or more users are working with the same document from that library, SharePoint will keep synchronizing and saving the changes being concurrently made by the users. This save operation occurs frequently (within a matter of seconds) and SharePoint will record the name of the last person to make the changes when this save operation occurs.

See also

- The *Viewing and editing documents in the browser* recipe in this chapter
- The *Viewing and editing documents in the client* recipe in this chapter
- The *Viewing and changing list settings* recipe in Chapter 4, *Working with Lists and Libraries in SharePoint Online*
- The *Viewing and changing list permissions* recipe in Chapter 4, *Working with Lists and Libraries in SharePoint Online*

6
Term Store and Content Types in SharePoint Online

Metadata is data about data, in the sense that it gives more information about other data. Examples of metadata for a document can be the document's author, creation date, size, or its security classification. SharePoint enables the following types of metadata:

- **Automatically generated metadata**: When you upload a document or create a list item in SharePoint, it automatically tracks who created the document or list item and when, who modified it and when, and accordingly adds the information to the document or list item.

- **Metadata that users can freely create in-place**: In addition to autogenerated metadata, users can also add information to each list item or document according to the columns created for the list or library that they are working with. They can enter this information in-place using various types of fields, such as the date field type, the single line of text field type, and so on.

- **Metadata that is maintained centrally for the entire organization**: The third type of metadata is one that is defined and managed centrally but is available for the entire organization to select and tag list items or documents with. Examples of such metadata could be an organization's office locations, departments, products, and so on. You will still need to create columns within various lists and libraries in order to tag them with this metadata but you would manage the metadata only from one central location called the **Term Store** in SharePoint.

Users with appropriate access can use the **Term Store management tool** to manage terms in the Term Store. Site or list and library owners can then create **Managed Metadata** columns that let users to accordingly tag information and documents with this centrally managed metadata. Doing so helps with the following benefits:

- **Consistent metadata definition across the organization**: Instead of the site, list, or library owner creating their own classification, users across the entire organization use the standard enterprise terms. This helps ensure uniformity and accuracy. For example, HR, H.R., H. R., and Human Resources all mean the same department. Allowing users to enter the department name through a *free flow* text field, even if it's defined at the site level, could lead to inconsistencies. On the other hand, if there was a single *selectable* department defined at the enterprise level, all documents and list items could then be tagged with the same department name.

- **Improved content organization and discovery**: Being able to tag documents using the same consistent terms leads to improved content discovery. As an example, you would be able to easily search for and discover all documents tagged with *Report* as the **Document Type** and *Finance* as the **Department**. The search would continue to return permission trimmed results so you only see what you have access to but you will not need to go to every single site, list, or library to discover this content. Also, **Managed Metadata** columns help you to better filter and sort information in the corresponding lists and libraries.

- **Central management of metadata:** The Term Store enables you to centrally manage metadata. You can add new terms or update the old ones as needed and the changes will be reflected throughout all sites, lists, and libraries across the enterprise. You can also define synonyms and multilingual terms centrally through the **Term Store**. So, for example, you can set up departments in the Term Store so that HR and Human Resources both point to the same term.

- **Navigation**: Metadata navigation for sites enables a site owner to create navigation based on metadata terms. This article describes the navigation options for SharePoint Online, including **managed navigation**, in more detail: https://m365book.page.link/navigation-options.
  Further, we discussed list views in the *Creating a custom list view* recipe in Chapter 4, *Working with Lists, Libraries in SharePoint Online*. There's a flavor of metadata navigation for lists and libraries that enables the creation of dynamic metadata-based views. This support article explains the steps to do so: https://m365book.page.link/list-metadata-navigation.

The recipes in this chapter will show you how to first create and manage **terms** in the **Term Store** and then use them to enrich the content within your site. We will also look at the concept of a **content type**, which is basically a reusable collection of pre-defined site columns that let you standardize the information that is captured in the lists and libraries within your site.

At the time of writing, Microsoft was rolling out updates to the **Managed Metadata** service, Term Store, and content types. You can read more about these updates here: `https://m365book.page.link/Modernizing-MMS`.

Even though these updates modernize the way these features are presented to you, the underlying concepts that we will discuss in this chapter continue to carry over to the newer UI.

In this chapter, we will cover the following:

- Creating a new group for term sets
- Creating term sets and terms
- Creating a Managed Metadata site column
- Creating a content type and adding columns to it
- Adding a content type to a list or library
- Tagging a document

Creating a new group for term sets

Terms in SharePoint are organized in **groups** and **term sets**. A Term Store group is a container for term sets, which in turn contain various terms. All term sets in a group follow a common security setup. Your organization could have defined multiple groups within the Term Store, with each group typically targeting a different set of owners and contributors.

In this recipe, we will see how to use the **Term Store management tool** to create a new group in the Term Store.

Getting ready

You will need the **Design** permission level or higher on your site to be able to browse to the **Term Store Management Tool**. You can alternately browse to it from the **Microsoft 365** admin center if you have **SharePoint admin** or higher permissions within your tenant.

You should additionally have been granted **Term Store administrator** rights within the Term Store to be able to create a new group once you browse to it.

How to do it...

To create a new group using the **Term Store management tool**, do the following:

1. Browse to the **Site Settings** page for the site where you would like to create the new group.

 Visit *Viewing and changing site settings,* in `Chapter 3`, *Working with Modern Sites in SharePoint Online,* if you are not familiar with how to browse to the **Site Settings** page.

2. Click on **Term store management** under the **Site Administration** heading, as shown in the following screenshot:

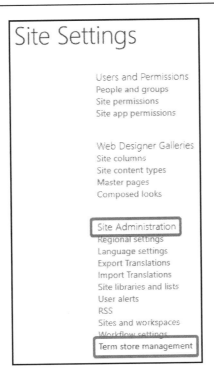

3. Click the down arrow next to the main node in the taxonomy tree on the left of the page and then click **New group**, as shown in the following screenshot:

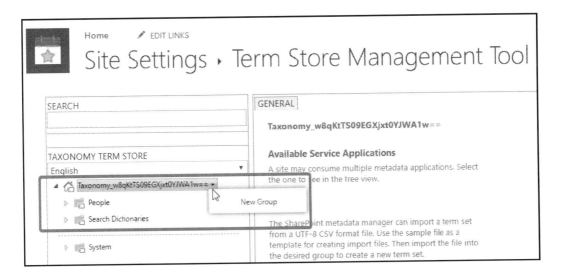

4. Enter a name for your group and then press *Enter* or click anywhere outside the box, as shown in the following screenshot. We will enter `Contoso Enterprise terms` for our example:

5. This will create the group and show you a screen that lets you edit various properties for the group. You can optionally enter a description for the group through this screen. You can also enter or select the managers as well as the contributors for the group. This is shown in the following screenshot:

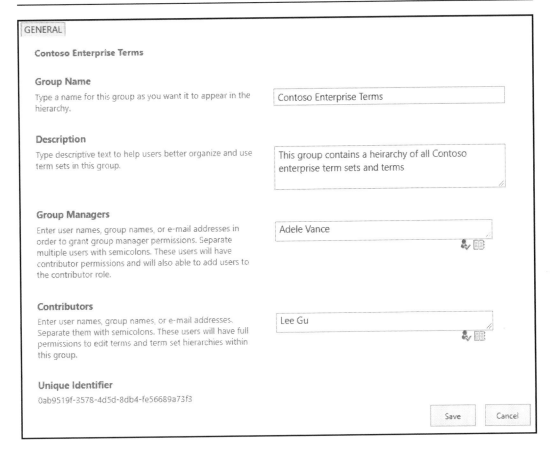

 The group **Contributors** can create and edit term sets and terms within the group. The **group Managers** have **Contributor** permissions and can additionally manage users in the **Contributors** role. The permissions that you grant to a group are applied to all the underlying term sets and terms for that group. You cannot set or alter permissions on individual term sets or terms within the group.

6. Click **Save** to save the updated properties for your new group.

Congratulations! You just created a new group in the SharePoint Term Store. Note that even though the group was created by navigating to the Term Store from within your site, it was created at an enterprise level. This means that anyone with appropriate access to the Term Store within your entire organization will be able to view/edit this group in the Term Store. Typically, this should only be a few users. Additionally, other users from across your organization will be able to tag items on their sites using the terms from within this group.

How it works...

The Term Store, at its core, is a way to organize and group a hierarchy of terms. The **Term Store management tool** lets you centrally manage this taxonomy for your organization.

Provided that you have appropriate permissions, you can access this tool directly from the **Site Settings** page from within the site that you are working on. Please refer to the *Viewing and changing site settings* recipe in `Chapter 3`, *Working with Modern Sites in SharePoint Online* for details on how to do this. Alternatively, you can access the Term Store through the SharePoint admin center if you have been granted one of the SharePoint admin or Global admin roles.

The highest node in the Term Store hierarchy is that of the service instance itself. As shown in the following screenshot, clicking this node enables you to view or manage the properties of the Term Store service instance for your tenant:

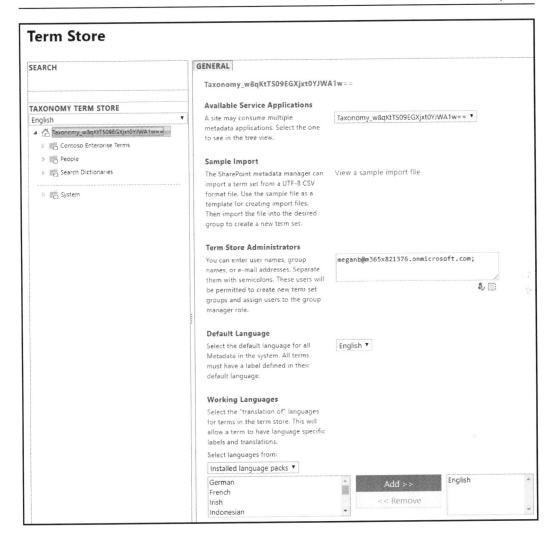

A few key things you can do through this screen are the following:

- View the **Sample Import** file: The Term Store lets you create entire term sets and their underlying terms by importing them from CSV files. Clicking the **View a sample import file** link downloads a sample CSV file that you can update and then use to import your term sets. We will see how to use this import file in the *Term Set properties* topic of the *Creating term sets and terms* recipe later in this chapter.
- Assign **Term Store Administrators**: This setting lets you specify users that can create and manage Term Set groups and the underlying term sets.

- Change the **Default Language**: The Term Store allows for terms to be defined in multiple languages. It also lets you choose the default language for all the terms in the Term Store. You can choose from a list of languages that have been enabled for your environment. As mentioned in the property description, every term will need to have a label defined in the default language.
- Edit the **Working Languages**: This setting enables you to select the languages allowed for the Term Store. For each term, you can then define a label in one of the allowed languages. As shown in the following screenshot, since **German** was one of the languages enabled in our tenant, we have defined an alternate label for **Engineering** in **German**:

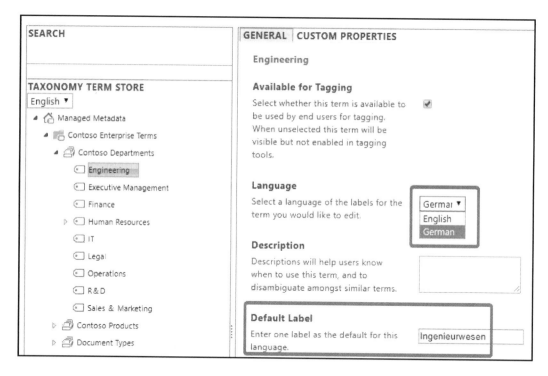

Note that you need to be in the **Term Store Administrators** group or be part of the tenant wide **Sharepoint admin** or **Global admin** roles to be able to manage the properties of this node.

A Term Store group comes next in the hierarchy, below/after the Term Store service instance. The group properties are self-explanatory and were also described as part of the preceding recipe.

See also

- The *Viewing and changing site settings* recipe in `Chapter 3`, *Working with Modern Sites in SharePoint Online*

Creating term sets and terms

A Term Set is a Grouping container for all the related terms. Some possible examples of term sets are a list of all products and/or services offered by your organization, a list of all office locations of your organization, a list of all departments, and so on.

There are two ways in which you can create a Term Set and underlying terms:

- You can use the **Term Store Management Tool** to manually create each Term Set and then create individual terms underneath it.
- You can use the CSV import functionality to import a Term Set along with the underlying terms.

This recipe shows you how to create **term sets** using both these approaches.

Getting ready

You will need **Contribute** access to the term group to be able to add and update term sets and terms within that group.

How to do it...

To create a new Term Set and terms from scratch, do the following:

1. Browse to the **Term Store Management Tool** from the **Site Settings** page on your site.

 Visit the *Creating a new group for term sets* recipe earlier in this chapter if you are not familiar with how to browse to the **Term Store Management Tool**.

2. Click the down arrow against the group under which you would like to create the new Term Set and then click **New Term Set**, as shown in the following screenshot:

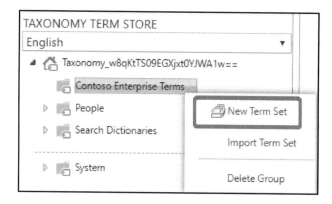

3. Enter a name for your Term Set and then press *Enter* or click anywhere outside the box, as shown in the following screenshot; we will enter Contoso Departments for our example:

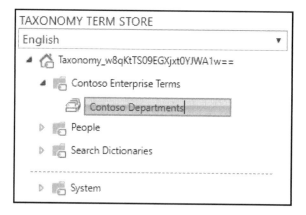

4. This will create the Term Set and show you a screen that lets you edit various properties. You can optionally edit various properties for this Term Set on this screen.

5. Click the down arrow next to the Term Set and then click **Create Term**, as shown in the following screenshot:

6. Enter a name for your term and then press *Enter* or click anywhere outside the box. We will enter Human Resources for our example.

7. This will create the term and show you a screen that lets you edit various properties for the term.

8. Next, we will add a child term to the term that we just created. To do that, click the down arrow next to the term and then click **Create Term**.

9. Enter a name for your Term Set and then press *Enter* or click anywhere outside the box. We will enter Compensation and Benefits for our example.

10. Like before, this will create the new term and then show you the properties screen for it. The entire structure is shown in the following screenshot:

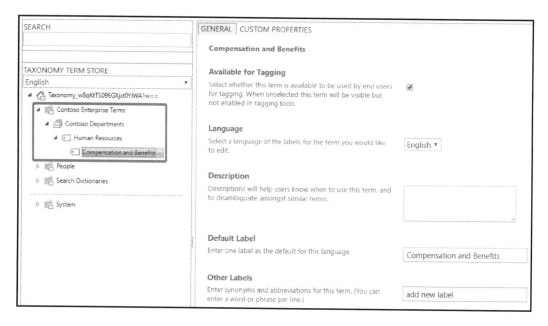

To import a new Term Set and underlying terms from a CSV file, do the following:

1. Browse to the Term Store and click on the topmost node within the taxonomy tree.
2. Click the **View a sample import file** link in the **Sample Import** section.
3. Open the downloaded file. This file contains columns in the format required by the Term Store to be able to create a new Term Set through the import feature. It also contains sample data that helps illustrate the file structure. We will populate this sample file with the details for the Term Set that we are going to create.
4. Replace the sample data with the Term Set and hierarchical terms, as shown in the following screenshot:

	A	B	C	D	E	F	G	H
1	Term Set Name	Term Set Description	LCID	Available for Tagging	Term Description	Level 1 Term	Level 2 Term	Level 3 Term
2	Contoso Departments	These are all the Contoso Departments		TRUE	The Engineering department and its sub-departments	Engineering		
3				TRUE	The HR department and its sub-departments	Human Resources		
4				TRUE		Human Resources	Compensatio n and	
5				TRUE		Human Resources	Recruiting	
6				TRUE		Human Resources	Training and Development	
7				TRUE	The IT department and its sub-	IT		
8				TRUE	The Legal department and its sub-departments	Legal		
9				TRUE	The Operations department and its sub-departments	Operations		
10				TRUE	The R&D department and its sub-departments	R&D		
11				TRUE	The Sales department and its sub-departments	Sales & Marketing		

5. Save the file. Make sure you save the file preserving the original `.csv` format.

6. Back in the Term Store, click the down arrow next to the Term group within which you would like to import the Term Set and then click **Import Term Set**, as shown in the following screenshot:

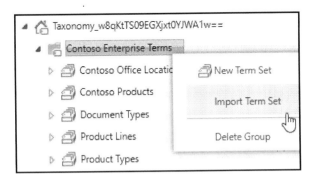

7. Click the **Choose File** button in the **Term Set import** pop-up box and then select the CSV file that you saved as part of the previous steps.
8. Clicking **OK** will import the contents of your file and show you the newly created Term Set under the selected group. This is shown in the following screenshot:

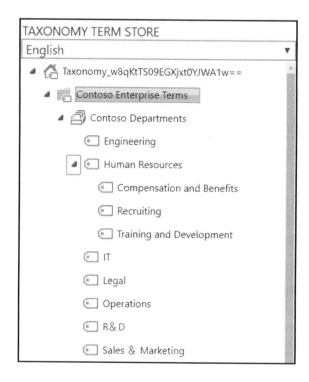

Congratulations! You just learned how to create a new Term Set and then add hierarchical terms to it.

How it works...

Term Sets help prevent the repetition of metadata definitions across multiple sites, thus ensuring consistency. By maintaining and managing this information in a central place, we also ensure additional governance for this metadata. Once created centrally through the Term Store, term sets and corresponding terms will be available for use across all sites in your organization.

Term Set properties

The Term Set property pages enable the management of various aspects of the Term Set. The following is a description of some of the notable properties:

- The **General** tab:
    - **Owner, Contact, and Stakeholders**: While SharePoint lets you specify an owner, contact, and stakeholders for a Term Set, these values do not grant any additional permissions to the Term Set and are just a way to track the business owners or stakeholders for a Term Set. The permissions for all term sets within a group are controlled through the group's properties. You can read more about **Term Store** permissions here: `https://m365book.page.link/termStore-Permissions`.
    - **Submission Policy**: This property specifies whether or not users using a Term Set can freely add **terms** to the Term Set. When it's set to **Closed**, only users who have access to the Term Set through permissions on the Term Store can add terms to it. When set to **Open**, users can add in-line terms while they are tagging content, and if the term that they are looking for is not present in the Term Set. The **Allow Fill-in** column level property will also need to be set along with this value to enable end users to add new inline tags. We will look at the **Allow Fill-in** property as part of the next recipe, *Creating a Managed Metadata site column*. Generally speaking, it is a good idea to keep the Term Set closed. This helps maintain consistency and control over your data. There may be scenarios where you would want your Term Set to be open, especially when the classification is more informal. This article discusses formal and informal classification in greater detail: `https://m365book.page.link/Folksonomy-Taxonomy`.
- The **Intended Use** tab:
    - **Available for Tagging**: Uncheck this option to disable the terms from this Term Set to be made available for tagging.

- **Use this Term Set for Site Navigation**: On-prem versions of SharePoint let you use term sets and their underlying terms to drive the global (top) navigation. In fact, at the time of writing, this is the preferred method for the on-prem installations of SharePoint. This method of managing global navigation is now deprecated in the modern version of SharePoint Online. You can refer to the following links to understand **managed navigation** and how to enable it for the on-prem versions of SharePoint:
  `https://m365book.page.link/Managed-Navigation` and `https://m365book.page.link/Managed-Navigation-SPO`.
  The following link explains how to plan navigation for the modern SharePoint Online experience:
  `https://m365book.page.link/Plan-Modern-Navigation`.

- **Use this Term Set for Faceted Navigation**: The term faceted navigation is used to describe filters or refiners that can be added to certain pages to make it easier to get to the content. Just like managed navigation, this feature is now deprecated in SharePoint Online and is only available for on-prem versions of SharePoint. You can read more about configuring faceted navigation and refiners here:
  `https://m365book.page.link/Faceted-Navigation`.

- The **Custom Sort** tab: By default, the terms in a Term Set are sorted alphabetically. If the need arises, however, you can specify a custom sort order for your terms. This can be useful in certain scenarios where you would like to have a non-standard sort, say, for example, a list of the products sorted by the newest product first.

Term properties

Some of the notable properties of a **term** are the following:

- The **General** tab:
  - **Available for Tagging**: If unchecked, the term will be visible but cannot be used by end users. An example use of this property is if you have hierarchical terms and you want the users to select only the child terms and not the parent terms. To achieve this, you would uncheck this value for the parent term and leave it checked for the children.
  - **Other Labels**: SharePoint lets you define synonyms for your term, as shown in the following screenshot:

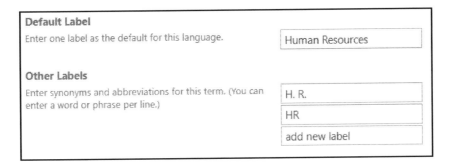

Your site users will then be able to select such terms either using the default label or one of the synonyms, as shown in the following screenshot:

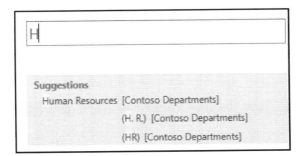

- The **Custom Properties** tab: You can add additional properties to your term and thus further define it through this screen. You can then utilize and display these properties through a custom-coded solution. You can also configure the SharePoint search to display one of these properties as part of the search results.

There's more...

If you click the down arrow next to a **Term Set** or a **term**, you will notice a few contextual actions that you can perform on them. We will discuss these actions in the following section.

Organizing the Term Store: Copy, reuse, and pin term sets and terms

The down arrow next to the Term Set shows the following actions in addition to the **Create Term** action that we saw as part of this recipe:

- **Copy Term Set**: Clicking this option creates a copy of the Term Set and its underlying terms. The underlying terms are *reused*. We will see in a bit what *reusing* a term means.
- **Reuse terms**: Enables you to select a term to *reuse* from a different Term Set. Reusing results in creating a linked copy of the selected term as a child of the selected Term Set. Additionally, if you make changes to the source term (such as renaming the term), the changes are also reflected in the destination term and vice versa.
- **Pin term with children**: Lets you select a term to *pin* from a different Term Set. Just like reusing a term, pinning a term results in a linked copy of the original term. The difference is that any changes made to the source are also reflected in the destination but the destination term is now read-only (you cannot make any changes to it).
- **Move Term Set**: Click this action to move the selected Term Set and its underlying terms to another group.
- **Delete Term Set**: Altogether delete the selected Term Set and its underlying terms. Note that unlike most other SharePoint information types, deleted term sets or terms are not stored in the Recycle Bin and hence cannot be recovered.

The down arrow next to a term shows the following actions in addition to the **Create Term** action that we saw as part of this recipe:

- **Copy term**: Clicking this option creates a copy of the term. The copied term can be independently managed from this point on.
- **Reuse terms**: This option works exactly like the **Reuse terms** option of a Term Set except that the term being reused is brought over as a child of the currently selected term.
- **Pin term with children**: This option works exactly like the corresponding option of a Term Set except that the term being pinned is brought over as a child of the currently selected term.
- **Merge terms**: Moves the selected source term as a label under the selected destination term.
- **Deprecate term**: This makes the selected term unavailable for tagging going forward. Existing items that use the term continue to remain tagged with the term. You should almost always deprecate terms instead of deleting them. This will prevent orphaned tags if the term is being used somewhere.
- **Move term**: Click this action to move the selected term and its underlying terms to another Term Set or term.
- **Delete term**: Altogether delete the selected term.

The following links provide more details regarding these actions:

- https://m365book.page.link/termSet-Actions.
- https://m365book.page.link/term-Actions.

Exporting and importing using PnP

In addition to creating a taxonomy from scratch, you can also import the entire taxonomy tree, just a few term groups within the taxonomy, or individual term sets within those groups. You can achieve this by creating a **comma-separated values (CSV)** file of your groups, term sets, and terms and then use the PnP commands to import them into the Term Store.

PnP short for (**Patterns and Practices**). You can read more about it in the *SharePoint PnP* sub-section of the *Office Development Frameworks* section in the *Appendix*.

Once you have the taxonomy changes defined in the `.csv` file, you can import them into your organization's Term Store using the `Import-PnPtermSet` command, as described here: `https://m365book.page.link/Import-PnPtermSet`.

Similarly, you can use the `Export-PnPTaxonomy` command to export the taxonomy tree to a CSV file of your choice, as documented here: `https://m365book.page.link/Export-PnPTaxonomy`.

See also

- The *Creating a new group for term sets* recipe in this chapter
- The *SharePoint PnP* topic in the *Office Development Frameworks* section of the *Appendix*

Creating a Managed Metadata site column

In the previous recipe, we saw how to create term sets and terms in the Term Store. In this recipe, we will see how to create a column that utilizes these terms and makes them available to end-users for tagging. We will create a managed metadata site column called **Contoso Department** for this recipe. The purpose of this column will be to enable users to tag documents with the department that authored it and is responsible for it.

Getting ready

You will need **Design** or **Full Control** permissions for the site within which you would like to create the new column.

How to do it...

To create a new site column that utilizes the taxonomy from the Term Store, do the following:

1. Browse to the **Site Settings** page for the site, as described in the *Viewing and changing site settings* recipe in `Chapter 3`, *Working with Modern Sites in SharePoint Online*.

2. Then click **Site columns** under the **Web Designer Galleries** heading.

3. Click **Create** to be taken to the **Create Column** screen. You can enter various details for your column on this screen.

4. We will begin by entering the column name and selecting **Managed Metadata** as the column type. We will use `Contoso Department` as the column name for our example.

5. We will then enter or select the following additional properties:

    - **Group**: This is just a way to group your custom columns. Select an existing group if you previously created one or create a new one by entering its name. For our example, we will create a new group called `Contoso Enterprise Columns`.

    - **Description**: Enter a meaningful description that explains the purpose of your column.

    - **Require that this column contains information**: Set this to **Yes** or **No** depending on whether or not this column will be mandatory.

    - **Multiple Value field**: If selected, this will enable users to enter or select multiple terms for this column. We will leave this unchecked for our example.

You will want to make sure that the column name reflects whether the column allows multiple values or not. For our example, we called the column `Contoso Department` because we anticipate that the users will only select a single department when tagging documents and list items with it. We would have called it `Contoso Department` if the business need was to allow documents and list items to be tagged with multiple departments. Either way, you should discuss business, governance, and information architecture requirements before selecting various properties for the column, including the **Multiple Value field** property for the **Managed Metadata** columns.

- **Display format**: This property specifies whether to display the entire hierarchy for the selected term. It is usually best to leave this value to the default setting, which only displays the term name, instead of the entire hierarchy, which can get lengthy and confusing for most scenarios.
- **Term Set Settings**: This is where we will select the Term Set to associate with the column. Users will then be able to tag list items and documents with the terms from the selected Term Set. To select the desired Term Set, expand `Taxonomy_` node to find the appropriate group. Then expand the group to view all the term sets in that group and select the Term Set:

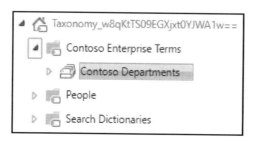

- **Allow Fill-in**: If your Term Set is an open Term Set, meaning it allows users to enter new values instead of just selecting existing ones, you can choose to disable or enable that feature specifically for your column.
- **Default Value**: You can enter or select a default term for this column. Selecting such defaults is a good idea in some scenarios. As an example, if this column is being added for an HR site, it may be a good idea to select **Human Resources** as the default value for this column. That way, all items added to a list or library containing this column, will automatically get tagged by the **Human Resources** term. Contributors to your list will still be able to change the default values if there are exceptions to this rule.

6. Click **OK** to create your new column with the preceding properties. After creating your column, SharePoint will take you to the **Site Columns** page and show the new column under the appropriate group, as shown in the following screenshot:

Contoso Enterprise Columns		
Contoso Department	Managed Metadata	Sales and Marketing

Congratulations! You just learned how to create a new **Managed Metadata** column and associate a Term Set with it.

How it works...

We discussed *Site Columns* in the *There's more* section of the *Adding a column* recipe in Chapter 4, *Working with Lists and Libraries in SharePoint Online*. The **Managed Metadata** column type is just like any other site column, except that it lets you connect the Term Store to associate a Term Set. Note that **Managed Metadata** columns will almost always get created as site columns versus lists or library columns. This is because they connect to the Term Store, which contains enterprise metadata, versus something that would be used just once.

See also

- The *Adding a column* recipe, Chapter 4, *Working with Lists, Libraries in SharePoint Online*
- The *Creating term sets and terms* recipe in this chapter

Creating a content type and adding columns to it

In the most simple terms, a **SharePoint content type** is a collection of columns for items or files in a list or library. More specifically, a content type is a blueprint for the properties that get associated with a type of list item or file within the corresponding list or library, thus making the information more meaningful. A content type ties an item or file to its properties. Further, content types are reusable and therefore offer the ability to standardize the type of information that gets collected across multiple lists and/or libraries within your site.

In this recipe, we will see how to create a new **content type** for your site and add columns to it.

Getting ready

You will need **Design** or **Full Control** permissions to the site where you would like to create the new content type.

How to do it...

To create a new content type, do the following:

1. Browse to the **Site Settings** page for the site, as described in the *Viewing and changing site settings* recipe in `Chapter 3`, *Working with Modern Sites in SharePoint Online*.

2. Then click **Site content types** under the **Web Designer Galleries** heading. This will take you to the **Site content types** screen.

3. Click **Create**, as shown in the following screenshot, to be taken to the **New Site content type** screen:

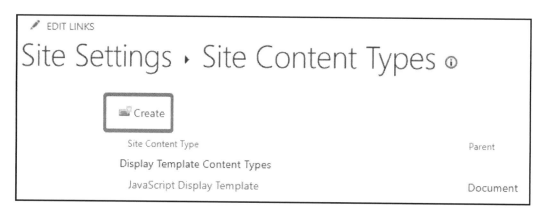

4. Here, we will enter the following properties for the content type being created:

   - **Name**: A descriptive name for the content type. This name will show up on the **New** menu for your list or library. We will use `Contoso Document` as the name of the content type for our example.

   - **Description**: Enter a description for this content type. This is just for your internal/tracking purposes and is not shown anywhere.

- **Group**: It is recommended to place custom content types in a separate group. You can select an existing group or create a new one. We will create a new group called `Contoso content types` as an example.

5. Click the **OK** button to create the new content type.

6. You will now be taken to a screen that displays information for the newly created content type, as shown in the following screenshot:

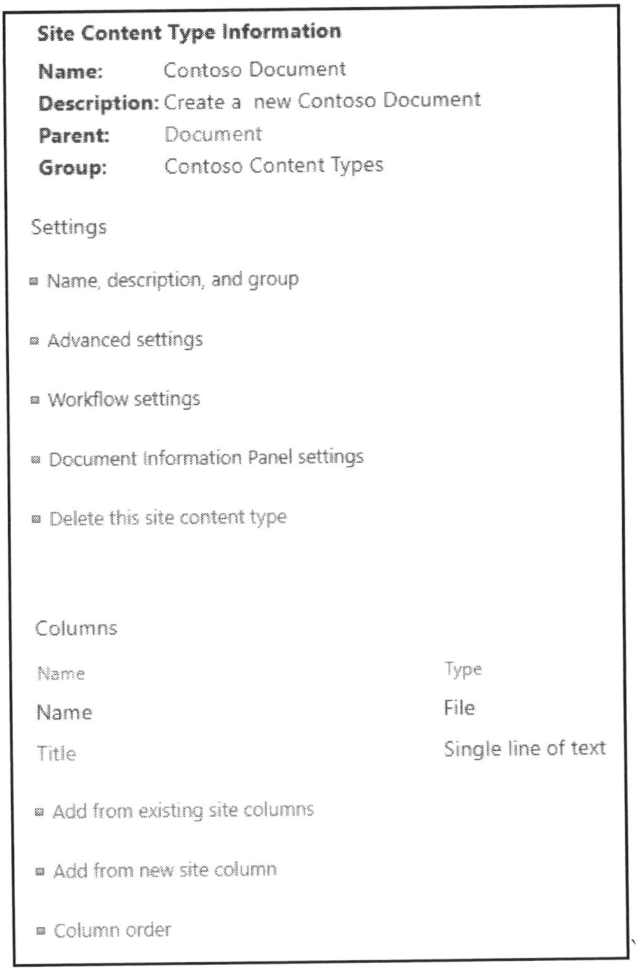

Site Content Type Information

Name: Contoso Document
Description: Create a new Contoso Document
Parent: Document
Group: Contoso Content Types

Settings

▫ Name, description, and group

▫ Advanced settings

▫ Workflow settings

▫ Document Information Panel settings

▫ Delete this site content type

Columns

Name	Type
Name	File
Title	Single line of text

▫ Add from existing site columns

▫ Add from new site column

▫ Column order

7. Notice the **Columns** section for this content type. Since this content type was created based on the **Document** site content type, it came with fields that let you edit the title of the uploaded documents. We will now add more columns to this content type.

8. Click **Add from existing site columns** to be taken to the **Add Columns** screen.

Since we created our site column in the *Creating a Managed Metadata site column* recipe earlier in this chapter, we will click the **Add from existing site columns** link for our example. You will click **Add from new site column** instead to create a new site column.

9. Select a group name from the **Select columns from** list to filter the column selection based on the group name or directly select columns from the **Available columns** list. As an example, we will add the following custom columns that we created on our example site:

- **Contoso Department**: This is a **Managed Metadata** column containing a list of all the departments for the organization. We created this column as part of a prior recipe in this chapter.
- **Document Type**: This **Managed Metadata** column contains a list of the various types of documents across the organization. Some examples are **Case Study**, **Product Overview**, **Campaign**, and so on.
- **Product**: This **Managed Metadata** column contains a list of all products across the organization.
- **Product Line**: This **Managed Metadata** column contains a list of all the organization-wide product lines. Examples are **Audio**, **Cameras**, **Gaming**, and so on.
- **Document Purpose**: A **Single line of text** column to describe the purpose of the document.
- **Document Contact**: A **Person or Group** column allowing the document author to select a point of contact for that document.

10. Click **Add >** to move them to the **Columns to add** list.

11. You will receive the following warning if even one of the columns that you are adding to the content type is a **Managed Metadata** column:

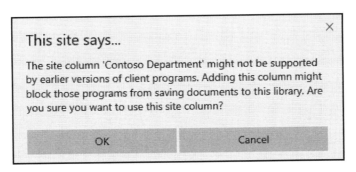

This message is for **Office 2007** or older versions of **Microsoft Office** and is shown because those versions of the **Office** client applications do not have the ability to edit **Managed Metadata** columns. Since **Office 2007** and earlier versions have been out of support for a long time, it is very likely that you are using one of the newer versions. Even if you are using an older version, you can always edit these properties directly in SharePoint. Either way, you can click **OK** to acknowledge this message. As a reminder, we discussed editing document properties in client applications as part of the *Viewing and editing documents in the browser* recipe in `Chapter 5`, *Document Management in SharePoint Online*.

12. Select **Yes** for **Update List and Site Content Types**. If you are editing a content type that is already being used in lists and/or libraries within your site, selecting this option will make sure that the new column is propagated to those lists and/or libraries.

The only time you might need to set this value to **No** is if this content type was being used in existing lists or libraries and someone made direct changes to the list or library content type. That is not a good practice anyway and beats the whole purpose of maintaining information consistency by using content types. Changing this setting to **No** would mean that the new column(s) will not be propagated to existing lists or libraries and will only show up in new lists and libraries using this content type.

13. Click **OK** to save your changes and add the columns to the content type. As shown in the following screenshot, you will now see the columns you've added in the list of columns against the content type:

Columns		
Name	Type	Status
Name	File	Required
Title	Single line of text	Required
Contoso Department	Managed Metadata	Required
Document Type	Managed Metadata	Required
Product	Managed Metadata	Required
Product Line	Managed Metadata	Required
Document Purpose	Single line of text	Required
Document Contact	Person or Group	Required

Congratulations! You just learned how to create a new content type for your site and add columns to it.

How it works...

As you saw in this recipe, a content type creates a schema or specification for the type of content that will eventually get associated with it. It does this by letting you define a set of columns or metadata that go together with it. content types exist at the site level and get reused across the different lists and libraries within the site and its sub-sites. Also, we can only add site columns to a content type. Because of these reasons, content types help to ensure data consistency whenever they are used in the various lists and libraries on your sites. Any changes to the columns within a content type or to its properties get reflected in all places that the content type is used (unless otherwise is desired).

Content Type properties

We saw some basic properties of content types in the previous recipe. We will look at some additional properties in this section:

- **Advanced settings**:
    - **Document template**: This is similar to the document templates that we saw in the *Associating a document template* recipe in `Chapter 5`, *Document Management in SharePoint Online*. Once you associate a document template with a Document content type, any new documents that get created in a library that uses this content type will follow the default structure and styling defined by this template. Please note that users can still directly upload other documents to the library instead of using the **New** menu to create them. It is not necessary then for those documents to use this template. Depending on the purpose of the Document content type, it may be a good idea to associate a document template with it.
    - **Read Only**: Setting this property value to **Yes** ensures that lists or libraries using the content type cannot freely change the columns or various properties when using the content type. Note that the list or library owners can still set this flag to **No** just for that list and/or library. That then gives them the ability to modify the content type for their list or library only. As a governance rule, you would typically want to set this value to **Yes** to help maintain consistency across all lists and libraries that use this content type.
    - **Update Sites and Lists**: This setting helps you control whether or not the changes you made on this screen should be propagated to the lists and libraries already using this content type. You will also see this setting on some of the other settings screens for the content type when making changes to it. For example, you will notice this setting in the add/edit column screens. You will typically want this flag set to **Yes** (which is the default). An example scenario, though, where you may want to set this flag to **No** is if you made a breaking change that could affect the existing lists and libraries that are already using this content type.

- **Document Information Panel settings**:
  - **Document Information Panel Template**: When you open a SharePoint Online document using a client application, you can directly edit its properties within it using the **Document Information Panel** in **Office 2013** or earlier versions and using the **Document Properties Panel** in **Office 2016** and above. Older versions also let you customize this panel. This is, however, now deprecated in newer versions and we will therefore not discuss it in detail here.
  - **Show Always**: Selecting this property ensures that the **Document Properties** panel always shows when you open a document that uses this content type. This will also force the panel to show up if you save a new document within the library for the first time and when using the client app:

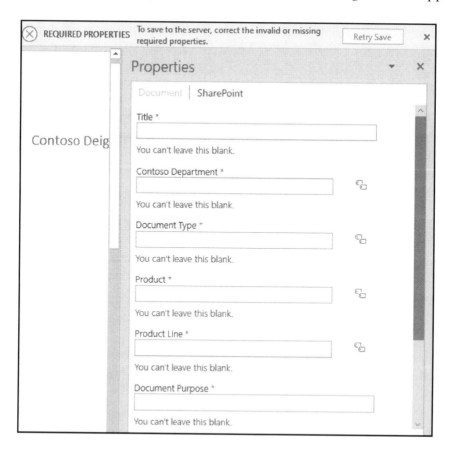

It is recommended to select this option so the users of your application can see and set those properties as desired.

- **Column order**: This screen lets you specify the order of the columns when they show up in the details pane for the list or library item. This order will also be used when displaying the columns in the new/edit forms for the list or library item. The following screenshot shows the column order for the example content type and the corresponding columns as they show up in the **Edit Properties** form for a document:

There's more...

In this section, we will see how to edit a column that is part of a content type or how to completely remove it. We will then briefly look at some advanced concepts related to content type inheritance and publishing.

Editing or removing a column from a content type

For your content type, you can select whether or not a particular column is required or optional. To do so, simply click on the column name to go to the **Change content type Column** screen and then change the corresponding setting. When doing this, you can also select the appropriate option to specify whether you would like the setting change to be propagated to the existing lists or libraries using this content type:

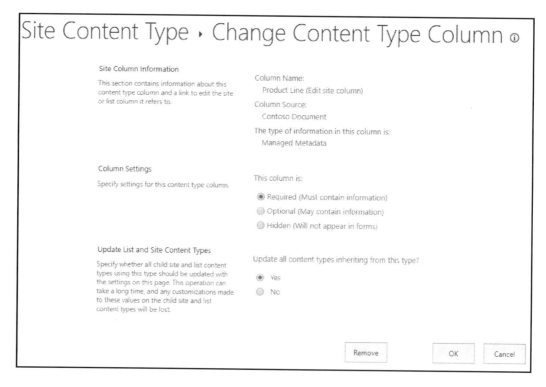

This screen also lets you disassociate the column from this content type. You can click the **Remove** button toward the bottom of the screen to do so. Note that since columns within a site exist independent of the content types, removing the column from this content type will not delete it from the site.

Content Type inheritance

Just like in real life, where children inherit certain behaviors and traits from their parents, in the software world, the term "inheritance" is used as a way to define the parent-child relationships of software objects. The child object acquires and then adds on to the traits and properties that it *inherits* from its parent. In the world of SharePoint, this concept applies to content types.

As an example, let's say we create a content type called **Contract** for the legal department. Also assume that this content type contains the following custom columns: **Product Line**, **Product**, **Company Contact**, **Contract Status**, and **Execution Date** (optional). We could potentially have the following content types inheriting from it:

- **Sale Contract**: This content type would potentially contain the following columns in addition to those in the *parent* **Contract** content type: **Sales Person**, **Client Name**, **Units**, **Sale Amount**, and so on.
- **Vendor Contract**: This content type would instead contain the following additional columns: **Vendor Name**, **Part Id**, **Part Name**, **Quantity**, and so on.

Both the **Sale Contract** and **Vendor Contract** content types would automatically inherit the columns that we defined earlier for the **Contract** content type. This lets us define the common columns and set various column properties only in one place (for the **Contract** content type), and then simply reuse them for one or more child content types. If it's required to add, change, or remove a common column, we make that change only in a single place and the change gets propagated to the children. This enables greater control, better governance, and the scalability of content types and the related information architecture for your sites.

Note that in SharePoint, you will always select one of the existing content types as a parent and never create a content type from scratch. The **Contract** custom content type that we used for our example would have inherited the built-in **Document** content type. The **Document content type**, in turn, inherits the built-in **Item** content type, as shown in the following screenshot:

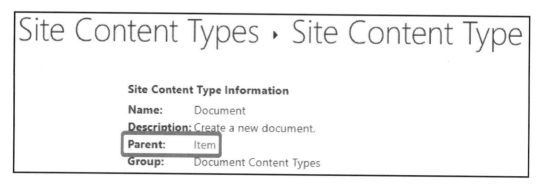

The **Item** content type is the *base* content type for all practical purposes (although it inherits from a hidden **System** content type). These links discuss the content type hierarchy and, specifically, content type inheritance in greater detail:

- **Content type Hierarchy**: https://m365book.page.link/Content-Type-Hierarchy
- **Creating content types**: https://m365book.page.link/Creating-Content-Types

Please note that even though these articles were written for SharePoint 2010, these concepts continue to apply to all modern versions of SharePoint.

Content type hub and content type publishing

As we saw earlier, content types exist at the **Site** level and are accessible to the underlying lists, libraries, and subsites within that site. Further, as mentioned in the *There's more* section of the *Creating a modern Team Site* recipe in Chapter 2, *Introduction to SharePoint Online*, all sites in SharePoint are part of one parent container site called a **Site Collection**. This means that the highest level where a content type can exist is at the root site or **Site Collection** level.

In a true enterprise scenario, however, you would want to be able to use content types across multiple site collections within the enterprise. This capability is accomplished in SharePoint using content type publishing and the **content type hub**. A content type syndication hub is a feature that can be enabled for any **Site Collection**. SharePoint Online, however, already has a specific site designated as the syndication hub. You can access this site by browsing to `https://<yourtenant>.sharepoint.com/sites/contenttypehub`.

When you create a content type in the designated hub, you see an additional link on the content type properties page, as shown in the following screenshot:

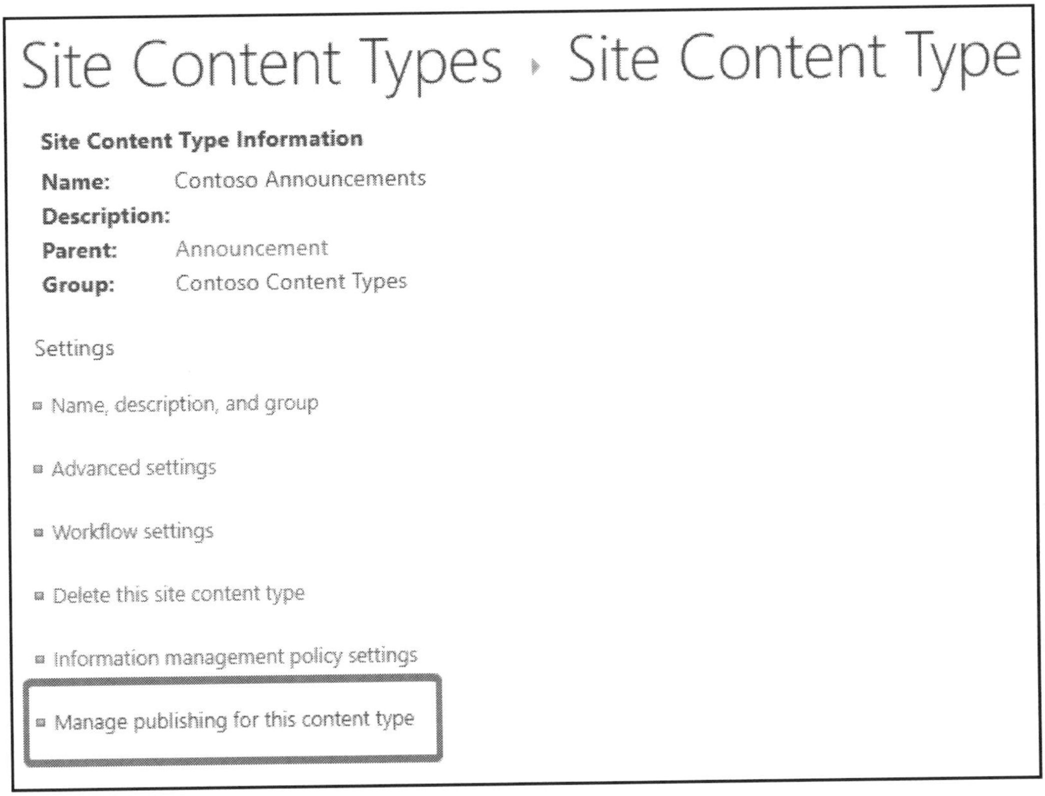

Site Content Types › Site Content Type

Site Content Type Information

Name: Contoso Announcements

Description:

Parent: Announcement

Group: Contoso Content Types

Settings

▫ Name, description, and group

▫ Advanced settings

▫ Workflow settings

▫ Delete this site content type

▫ Information management policy settings

▫ Manage publishing for this content type

Clicking this link takes you to the **content type Publishing** page, which lets you manage the publishing for this content type. As shown in the following screenshot, you will need to select the **Publish** button when you first create the content type:

Content Type Publishing: Contoso Announcements

Content Type Publishing

- ◉ Publish
  Make this content type available for download for

- ◌ Unpublish
  Make this content type unavailable for download fo
  this content type being used in other site collection

- ◌ Republish
  If you have made changes to this content type, the
  consuming content types from this location.

Publishing History

The date on which one or more service applications have successfully published this content type.

Once you do that, your published content type is now ready for consumption in all other site collections in your organization's tenant. To make any published content types available for your site collection, you will need to do the following:

1. Browse to the **Site Settings** page for that site collection.
2. Click **Content Type publishing** under the **Site Collection Administration** heading to be taken to the **Content Type Publishing Hubs** page.
3. Select the **Refresh All Published Content Types** option and click **OK** on this page.
4. After some time, you will start to see, on the **Site Content Types** page of the subscriber site collection, the published content types along with the site columns that they contained.

The content types are pushed from the *hub* to the *subscriber* sites through timer jobs that run every few hours. You might, therefore, see a delay before the content types start appearing in your subscriber site collections.

You can read more about content type publishing at these links:

- **Content Type publishing**: `https://m365book.page.link/Content-type-publishing`.
- **Publish a content type from a content publishing hub**: `https://m365book.page.link/publish-content-type`.

Content type publishing, coupled with site columns, provides a great way to ensure consistency and governance for the content in your organization's SharePoint environment. It is, therefore, highly recommended to consider this feature when planning your organization's information architecture and SharePoint implementation strategy.

See also

- The *Creating a new document* recipe, in `Chapter 5`, *Document Management in SharePoint Online*
- The *Creating a Managed Metadata site column* recipe earlier in this chapter
- The *Viewing and editing documents in the client* recipe, in `Chapter 5`, *Document Management in SharePoint Online*
- The *Creating a modern Team Site* recipe, in `Chapter 2`, *Introduction to SharePoint Online*

Adding a content type to a list or library

content types coupled with site columns drive consistency across the lists and libraries on your site. In the previous recipe, we saw how to create a content type and added site columns to it.

This recipe will show you how to associate the content type we created earlier to a library so that the content in the library adheres to the metadata requirements defined by the content type. Note that even though this recipe uses a library as an example, the concepts and outlined steps work equally well with lists.

Getting ready

You will need **Edit**, **Design**, or **Full Control** access to the library for which you would like to add the content type.

How to do it...

To add your content type to a library, do the following:

1. Browse to the *Library Settings* page, as described in the *Viewing and changing document library settings* recipe in `Chapter 5`, *Document Management in SharePoint Online*.

2. Click **Advanced settings** under the **General Settings** heading.

3. Change the **Allow management of Content Types?** setting to **Yes** and click the **OK** button toward the bottom of the screen. Doing so will take you back to the library settings page.

4. Scroll down to the **Content Types** section on this page and click the **Add from existing site content types** link, as shown in the following screenshot:

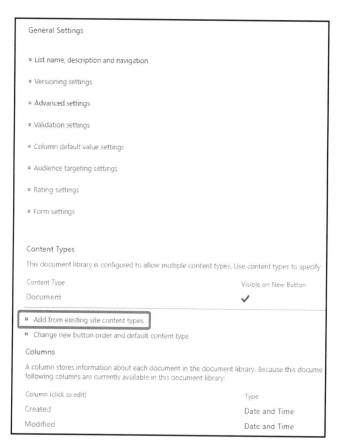

Like the preceding screenshot shows, the library already has a content type called **Document** associated with it. This is the default content type for document libraries. Every library that gets created uses the **Document content type** by default. Once we associate our new content type to the library, we will disassociate this default content type from it.

5. Select the content type you would like to add from the **Available Site Content Types** list and click the **Add >** button to add it to the **Content Types to add** list, as shown in the following screenshot:

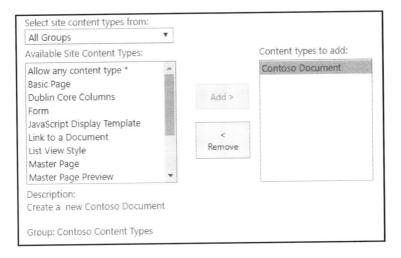

Since we are working with a library, the only content types that you will see in the **Select site content types from** list are the library content types. You will not see content types that derive from the **Item** base content type. Conversely, if you were working with a SharePoint list (instead of a library), you would only see content types that are based on the **Item** content type. We discussed content type inheritance in more detail in the *Adding columns to a content type* recipe, earlier in this chapter.

6. Click the **OK** button toward the bottom of the screen to save your changes and be taken back to the library settings screen. You will now see the new content type in the list of content types for this library. Notice that the columns from our new content type also show up in the list of columns for this library. This is shown in the following screenshot:

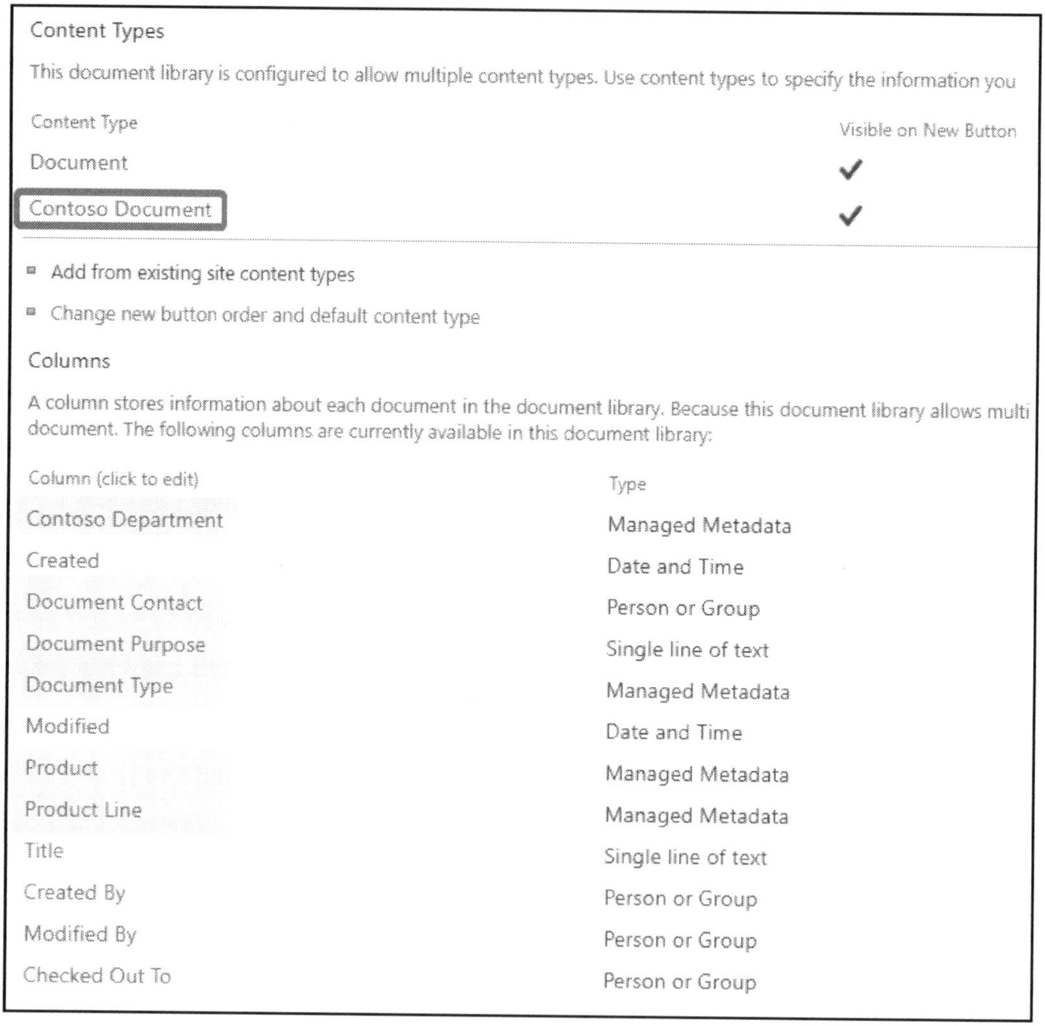

Content Types

This document library is configured to allow multiple content types. Use content types to specify the information you

Content Type	Visible on New Button
Document	✔
Contoso Document	✔

▫ Add from existing site content types

▫ Change new button order and default content type

Columns

A column stores information about each document in the document library. Because this document library allows multi document. The following columns are currently available in this document library:

Column (click to edit)	Type
Contoso Department	Managed Metadata
Created	Date and Time
Document Contact	Person or Group
Document Purpose	Single line of text
Document Type	Managed Metadata
Modified	Date and Time
Product	Managed Metadata
Product Line	Managed Metadata
Title	Single line of text
Created By	Person or Group
Modified By	Person or Group
Checked Out To	Person or Group

---

7. Now that we have added our content type, we will now remove the default **Document** content type from this library. To do so, simply click on the **Document content type** and then click **Delete this content type** from the next screen, as shown in the following screenshot:

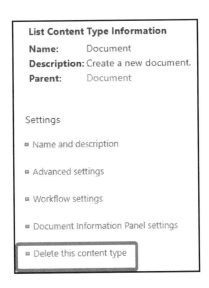

8. You should now see the new content type that we just added as the only one associated with your library.

Congratulations! You just configured your library to use a new content type.

How it works...

As you saw in this recipe, a content type groups a list item, or in this case, a document with its metadata. Every list or library in SharePoint has at least one content type associated with it by default. This default content type often varies depending on the type of list or library. For example, as we saw in this recipe, the **Document** content type is the default content type for a SharePoint document library. On the other hand, the **Announcements** list in SharePoint has the **Announcement** content type as its default. This means that any time you create an item in a list or a document in a library, you are actually associating that item with the columns defined by that default content type.

You can associate more than one content type with a list or library. We will discuss this next.

Multiple content types

SharePoint lets you associate multiple content types with your list or library. For such libraries, users will need to consciously choose the content type that they would like to associate with the item being created. A classic example of such a scenario is the **Site Pages** library. You will notice the following content types if you browse to the settings page of a **Site Pages** library:

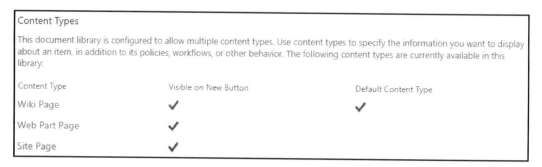

Now if you go back to a view in the library, and if you have permission to add items to this library, you will notice that clicking the **New** menu option enables you to create items from one of these content types:

Also, you will notice in the earlier screenshot that **Wiki Page** is selected as the **Default content type** for the library. This setting is not as relevant for the **Site Page** library since it does not let you upload files, but for any other document library, uploading a document to it automatically associates the document with the selected default content type, and will prompt you to enter the necessary metadata for that content type. You can then change the content type through the details pane for that library. Note that changing the content type associated with the item will also mean that you will now need to enter information for the newly selected content type.

Multiple content types sometimes make it difficult to work with lists and libraries, especially for the not so savvy end user. It is therefore not recommended to use this option too frequently. If you have a need for two different content types, you are almost always better off creating separate lists or libraries that contain items for the separate content types.

There's more...

SharePoint enables you to interface with a variety of external systems and read from or write to these systems using the familiar list interface.

External content type and external list

The first step toward achieving this is to create an **external content type** to connect to the external data source. You would then create an **external list** and associate the **external content type** with it to be able to interact with this external data.

A more detailed discussion of this topic is beyond the scope of this book but here are a few links that can help you understand the capability in more detail:

- **External content types in SharePoint**: `https://m365book.page.link/External-Content-Type`
- **Make an external list**: `https://m365book.page.link/External-List`

Please note, however, that the methods to create external content types described in these links are now somewhat deprecated. It is recommended to use some of the newer tools (such as PowerApps, Power Automate, and Power BI) from the **Microsoft 365** ecosystem to address such scenarios that require interaction with external data. We extensively discuss these tools and apps in subsequent chapters of this book.

See also

- The *Viewing and changing list settings* recipe in `Chapter 4`, *Working with Lists, Libraries in SharePoint Online*
- The *Viewing and changing document library settings* recipe in `Chapter 5`, *Document Management in SharePoint Online*

- Chapter 13, *Power Automate (Microsoft Flow)*
- Chapter 14, *PowerApps*
- Chapter 15, *Power BI*

Tagging a document

We have seen two different ways of adding columns to a library so far:

- *Adding a column* recipe in Chapter 4, *Working with Lists, Libraries in SharePoint Online*, showed you how to directly add columns to lists and libraries.
- *Adding a content type to a list or library* recipe, earlier in this chapter showed you how to associate **content types** with a library, thereby also associating the corresponding columns from such content types.

Adding a **Managed Metadata** column to a list or library is just like adding any other column type in SharePoint. Once you have added **Managed Metadata** columns to a library, you can tag documents with the terms from those columns. The steps to do this are no different than carrying out similar steps for other column types in SharePoint.

This recipe will show you specifically how to tag your documents with terms from **Managed Metadata** columns. Note that the steps for updating items in lists containing the **Managed Metadata** columns are also going to be the same. For the purposes of illustration in this recipe, we will use the **Contoso Department** column that we created earlier.

Getting ready

You will need **Contribute** access or higher to the corresponding list or library.

How to do it...

Follow these steps to tag a document with terms from the **Managed Metadata** columns in your library:

1. Select the row containing the document by clicking anywhere on it.
2. Click the information icon in the right-hand corner of the library menu to open the details pane, as shown in the following screenshot:

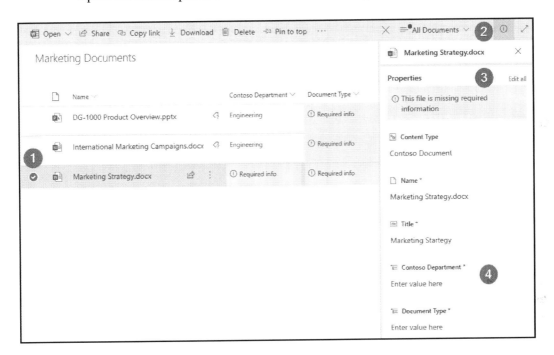

3. You can now edit the properties directly in this pane or click **Edit all** in the **Properties** section to edit the properties in an expanded view.

4. Click within one of the **Managed Metadata** fields and start typing a value for that field. SharePoint will autocomplete it for you with the term name if it finds a match. This is shown in the following screenshot:

5. Next, we will click inside another (**Document Type**) **Managed Metadata** field. This time, however, we will click the tag image next to the field:

6. This opens a dialog for you to select your term.

7. Here, you can select the appropriate term by first clicking the term, then the Select > > button, and then **OK**, as shown in steps **1** through **3** in the following screenshot:

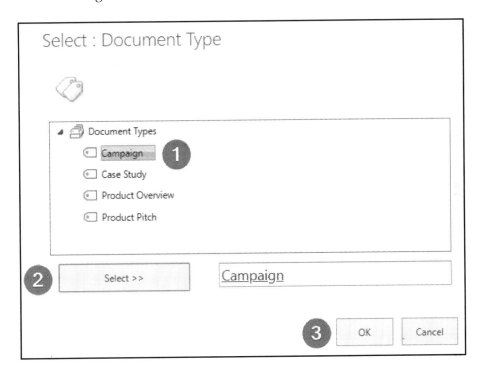

8. You can then similarly enter or select the rest of the properties for the document and then click the **Save** button:

9. This will update the document with the selected or entered properties, including any metadata tags that you may have applied. Depending on how the view for the library is configured, you will now see these properties as part of the view columns for the document, as shown in the following screenshot:

Congratulations – you just learned how to tag your documents with **Managed Metadata** by using terms that were created as a standard across the enterprise.

How it works...

Entering information in **Managed Metadata** columns is quite similar to entering or selecting information in some of the other column types. The one big difference for the **Managed Metadata** columns is that instead of entering or selecting information that is just used one time, you would typically enter or select terms that are maintained at the enterprise level. Just doing this opens up various additional scenarios. One of the biggest benefits of doing this is the ability to use SharePoint search to pull information globally from across multiple sites. To illustrate the point, let's refer to the document we just tagged in this recipe. We are going to see how tagging it with a particular product helps users easily search for it. Let's assume a user is looking for marketing *campaigns* related to the "Action Camera 1000s" **Product**.

The following is the result set that SharePoint brings back if I just search for the word `campaigns`:

However, since we tagged our campaign document with the appropriate product, users will be able to significantly narrow down the search to get to what they were looking for just by typing the name of the product against the search term. The following is the result set that SharePoint returns if they search for the following term (which includes the product name in the search) – `campaigns Action camera 1000s`:

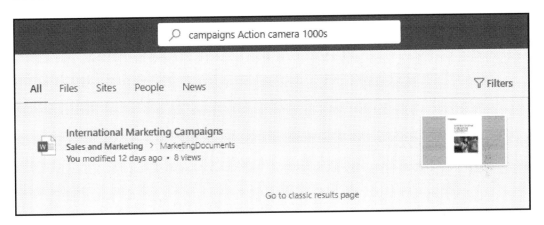

As you can see, just the fact that we tagged the document with the product name helped us considerably narrow down the search results from potentially hundreds of documents to exactly what we were looking for.

Planning information architecture and the content structure along with the correct governance policies goes a long way in making sure that users can quickly get to what they are looking for. In the preceding example, we not only created the required term sets and corresponding **Managed Metadata** columns but also enforced the selection of the appropriate tags by marking these columns as required within our content type.

In addition to improved search, using **Managed Metadata** columns for the content in your library also enables you to set up better-organized information in it. The use of Managed Metadata columns enables you to use them to better filter, sort, and group information in your lists or libraries. The following screenshot shows how the library view was changed to show documents grouped by the **Document Type Managed Metadata** field that was previously created for our example:

See also

- The *Adding a column* recipe in `Chapter 4`, *Working with Lists, Libraries in SharePoint Online*
- `Chapter 8`, *Search in Microsoft 365*

OneDrive for Business

7

OneDrive for Business is a cloud-based storage solution for your personal files. In a way similar to using a SharePoint document library to store and share files that your team is co-working on, OneDrive for Business lets you store and work on files that are private to you. It is your personal space for files that belong just to you and/or are not yet ready to be shared with a wider team. In that sense, your OneDrive area is like any other library on SharePoint Online. However, there are a few key differences between the two, which we will cover in later sections of this chapter, but for the most part, your OneDrive area is a simplified document library that you are the owner of and have full access to. You can add, update, and delete files or folders in your OneDrive area as you would in any other document library. You can then share these files with others in your organization as well as those external to your organization, and in the process of doing so, grant them viewing or editing rights to these files.

You would typically use OneDrive for files that you are working on by yourself. This could be files that you don't intend to share with others or that need some work before you can share them with a wider group. This could also be files that are only meant to be shared with a colleague on a one-off occasion. If you are working on files that are intended for a wider audience, you would typically store them on a SharePoint site or in Teams. If you started with a file in OneDrive that is now ready to be shared with a wider audience, you can easily move it to a library on a SharePoint site or to Teams using the **Move to** feature.

As with any other file on a SharePoint Online library, you can view and edit your OneDrive files from a multitude of mobile and desktop devices. OneDrive for Business also comes with a client app that you can install on your devices. This app (also referred to as the Sync client) then helps you maintain on-demand copies of your files for offline viewing and editing. It also ensures that any updates you make to these files from one device are replicated to your online OneDrive storage area and to any other devices that run the app. The app also lets you share files with your co-workers from any device without you having to visit OneDrive for Business online on Microsoft 365.

OneDrive comes in two different forms:

- **OneDrive**: This is your personal (**non-work**) online storage area, which you can access when you set up a free or paid Microsoft home or personal account. You can use your personal OneDrive area to store documents, photos, videos, and other files in the cloud and share them with your friends and family. You can get started with a free account, which gives you a limited amount of free space. It lets you and your family or friends to view and edit various file types on the cloud, which includes co-authoring capabilities for Microsoft Office documents. You can also install the OneDrive sync app to sync your files and work with them on your favorite devices.

- **OneDrive for Business**: This is an online storage area offered through your **work or school account**. You get 1 TB of storage (or more) for individual use. Your account and certain account policies, such as external sharing, are managed by your organization. Additionally, you can install the OneDrive for Business app to sync your files on your favorite devices and work with them, if permitted by your organization.

You can, potentially, have access to both versions of OneDrive—through your work or school and through your personal Microsoft account. You can install both versions of the sync client in parallel on the same device and also concurrently work with the files in either type of client app.

The recipes in this chapter will show you how to work with the files in **OneDrive for Business** through your school or work account, although most of the recipes will also apply to your personal OneDrive account. We will also learn how to use the OneDrive for Business app to locally sync your files and how to share them with others within and outside your organization.

In this chapter, we will cover the following recipes:

- Uploading a file to OneDrive for Business
- Syncing files and folders
- Sharing a file

Uploading a file to OneDrive for Business

Saving files in OneDrive and, in broader terms, saving them to the cloud, lets you access them from anywhere on various devices. As we saw in earlier chapters, saving files to the cloud also makes sharing easier as it lets us share just the links to files, rather than having to send over copies of files each time. This enables you to maintain a single version of a file. You can continue to make changes to your copy of that file, and others who have access to it can easily see these changes as they happen.

In this recipe, you will learn how to browse your OneDrive for Business account and upload a file to it.

Getting ready

There are no special requirements for accessing OneDrive for Business. As long as you have access to SharePoint Online, you will also have access to OneDrive for Business.

How to do it...

To upload a file to OneDrive for Business, take the following steps:

1. Browse to any page in your organization's Microsoft 365 tenant. You may be asked to sign in with your work credentials if you are not already signed in.

2. Click the app launcher in the top left-hand corner of the page and then click **OneDrive**. The following screenshot shows you what this looks like from the SharePoint Online home page:

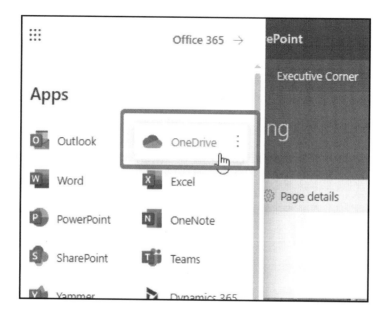

You will then be taken to your OneDrive home page, which shows you all your files.

The OneDrive home page is just a view on top of an underlying SharePoint library that only you are the owner of. All of the content on this site, as well as in this library, is secured so that only you have access to it, unless you chose to share it with others.

3. Click **Upload** and then **Files** from the navigation menu at the top of the page:

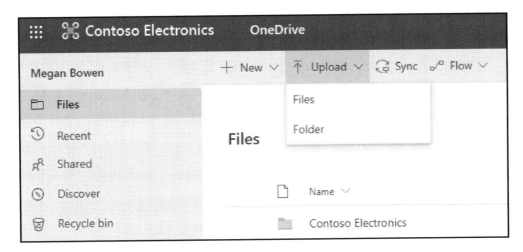

This is the same navigation menu that you previously saw in the *Uploading an existing document to the library* recipe in Chapter 2, *Introduction to SharePoint Online*.

Just like in a regular document library in SharePoint, you can simultaneously select and upload multiple files to your OneDrive area with this option. As with any other library in SharePoint, you can also drag and drop one or more files to upload them to your OneDrive area. You can also choose the **Folder** option under the **Upload** menu to upload an entire folder and its contents.

4. As the following screenshot shows, the document will upload to your OneDrive area. You will also receive a notification confirming this. The notification message will also give you the option to share the document with others. We will look at sharing documents in more detail in the *Sharing a file* recipe in this chapter:

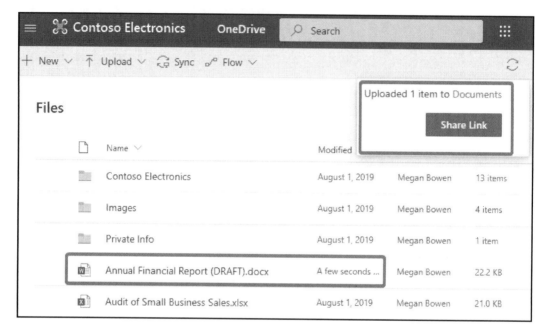

That's it! You have just learned how to browse your OneDrive for Business account and upload a file to it.

How it works...

Saving your files to the cloud enables you to access them from anywhere and through your favorite devices. Doing so also makes it easy for you to share these files with your colleagues by just sending them a link to the file instead of sending copies of the file itself. In addition, you can work on these files offline using the OneDrive for Business app, which we will see how to do in the *Syncing files and folders* recipe in this chapter.

File and folder operations

Since your OneDrive area is a simplified document library, most of the actions that you can perform in a document library can also be performed here, too. We discussed most of these actions in the following chapters:

- Chapter 2, *Introduction to SharePoint Online*
- Chapter 5, *Document Management in SharePoint Online*

As well as these actions that were described in the recipes of previous chapters, you can perform the following actions in your OneDrive area:

- Create new files or folders
- Upload existing files or folders
- Save Microsoft Office documents and other supported document types directly to Microsoft 365 using **Save As**:

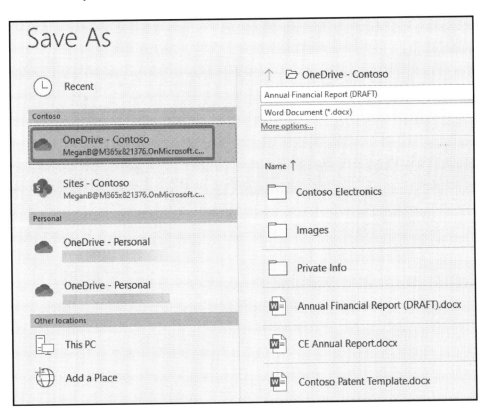

- View and edit existing files in your OneDrive
- Delete files or folders
- Move or copy files and folders between OneDrive and SharePoint
- Share files or folders with others

In addition to using the online browser-based interface, you can also perform these actions using the OneDrive for Business app. We will describe this in more detail in the *Syncing files and folders* and *Sharing a file* recipes later in this chapter.

You can upload any file type to OneDrive for Business, but the maximum file size should not exceed 100 GB. You can also preview hundreds of file types in the browser. The *Viewing and editing documents in the browser* recipe in `Chapter 5`, *Document Management in SharePoint Online*, discussed the file types that are supported for viewing and editing in Microsoft 365.

If you are using a mobile device, you can use the OneDrive app to scan a document, whiteboard, or business card directly to your OneDrive for Business account, as well as upload existing photos, videos, or files from it. Go to `https://m365book.page.link/OneDrive-Mobile` to find out how to do that.

There's more...

While the primary function of OneDrive for Business is to help you with your private files, it truly is more than just a single library. Your OneDrive for Business account is actually a single SharePoint site collection area that you are the owner of. Refer to the *Creating a modern team site* recipe in `Chapter 2`, *Introduction to SharePoint Online*, if you would like to understand more about what site collections are. Your OneDrive home page, which lets you interact with all your OneDrive files, is just one of the pages on your OneDrive site.

Other pages on OneDrive for Business online

The following screenshot shows some of the additional functionalities that your OneDrive account has to offer:

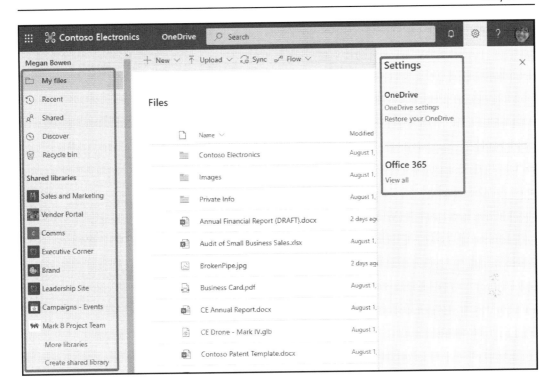

Let's discuss these features further:

- **My files**: The **My files** page is the home page for your OneDrive for Business account. We saw this page in the *How to do it...* section of this recipe. This page enables you to interact and work with your private files.
- **Recent**: This page shows you the recent files that you have worked on across all connected sites.
- **Shared**: Here, you can view the OneDrive files that others have shared with you or that you have shared with others.
- **Discover**: This section uses artificial intelligence and machine learning to understand your work patterns and then shows you content that is relevant to you. Refer to Chapter 9, *Office Delve*, to understand how this feature works.

- **Recycle bin**: Click this tab to show your recently deleted OneDrive files. From here, you can select a file and permanently delete it or restore it back to your OneDrive area. Files stay in the recycle bin for 90 days, after which they are moved to a second-stage recycle bin, where they stay for another 90 days before they are permanently deleted. Usually (on SharePoint sites), the second-stage recycle bin is only available to certain admins. However, since you are the owner of your OneDrive site collection, you have access to the second-stage recycle bin as well. This, therefore, gives you a total of 180 days to recover any files or folders that you may have accidentally deleted. Refer to the *Site recycle bin* section of the *Viewing site contents* recipe in Chapter 2, *Introduction to SharePoint Online*.

- **Shared libraries**: Here, you will see a listing of the top eight SharePoint document libraries that you have access to and that you use the most. Clicking on **More libraries** toward the bottom of the list will take you to a page where you can see an expanded list of your most frequented libraries. On this page, you will also see a list of the sites that you are following. Refer to the *Getting to the SharePoint home page* recipe in Chapter 2, *Introduction to SharePoint Online*, to learn how to follow a site. Clicking the name of a site on this page will show you the document libraries for that site.

- **Create shared library**: Clicking on this link will let you create a new team site connected to Microsoft 365 Groups. The default document library that comes with the team site will then be shown in the **Shared libraries** section mentioned in the previous point.

- **OneDrive settings**: This page lets you view and change your notification settings, as well as other settings for your OneDrive account. The notifications you can manage from here are self-explanatory, so we will not cover them in more detail. Similarly, the settings are either legacy settings or far too advanced for the scope of this book. There is, however, one setting that's worth mentioning here:

  - **Run sharing report**: Clicking on this link generates a report that lists all of the files or folders that you have shared, as well as who you have shared them with and what permissions they have on each file or folder. It then places a copy of this report in a folder of your choice in your OneDrive area. The following screenshot shows an example of the information that is generated in this report:

Resource Path	Item Type	Permission	User Name	User Email	User Or Group Type	Link ID	Link Type
personal/meganb_m365x821376_onmicrosoft_com/Documents/Annual Financial Report (DRAFT).docx	docx	Read	SharingLink		SharePointGroup	984c7765-ca3	Anyone
personal/meganb_m365x821376_onmicrosoft_com/Documents/Annual Financial Report (DRAFT).docx	docx	Read	SharingLink		SharePointGroup	92139652-a2!	Organization
personal/meganb_m365x821376_onmicrosoft_com/Documents/Annual Financial Report (DRAFT).docx	docx	Contribute	SharingLink		SharePointGroup	d38c0d08-21!	Organization
personal/meganb_m365x821376_onmicrosoft_com/Documents/Audit of Small Business Sales.xlsx	xlsx	Read	Alex Wilber	AlexW@M365x821376.OnMicrosoft.com	Internal		
personal/meganb_m365x821376_onmicrosoft_com/Documents/Audit of Small Business Sales.xlsx	xlsx	Read	Patti Fernandez	PattiF@M365x821376.OnMicrosoft.com	Internal		
personal/meganb_m365x821376_onmicrosoft_com/Documents/Audit of Small Business Sales.xlsx	xlsx	Read	Isaiah Langer	IsaiahL@M365x821376.OnMicrosoft.com	Internal		
personal/meganb_m365x821376_onmicrosoft_com/Documents/Audit of Small Business Sales.xlsx	xlsx	Read	Miriam Graham	MiriamG@M365x821376.OnMicrosoft.com	Internal		
personal/meganb_m365x821376_onmicrosoft_com/Documents/BrokenPipe.jpg	jpg	Read	Everyone except external users		SecurityGroup		

- **Restore your OneDrive**: The OneDrive app synchronizes files from your devices to OneDrive online (and vice versa). If the files on your device become corrupted—for example, by malware or a virus—you can use this feature to restore your OneDrive files. You can read more about this feature at `https://m365book.page.link/OneDrive-Restore`.

See also

- The *Creating a modern team site* recipe in `Chapter 2`, *Introduction to SharePoint Online*
- The *Uploading an existing document to the library* recipe in `Chapter 2`, *Introduction to SharePoint Online*
- The *Site recycle bin* section of the *Viewing site contents* recipe in `Chapter 2`, *Introduction to SharePoint Online*
- The *Viewing and editing documents in the browser* recipe in `Chapter 5`, *Document Management in SharePoint Online*
- The *Moving and copying documents* recipe in `Chapter 5`, *Document Management in SharePoint Online*
- `Chapter 9`, *Office Delve*
- The *Sharing a file* recipe in this chapter

Syncing files and folders

OneDrive for Business comes with the OneDrive sync app, which can be installed on a multitude of devices. The OneDrive app lets you work with your files locally, as you would with any other file on your computer or mobile.

In this recipe, we will look at how to sync your OneDrive online files to your local computer.

Getting ready

You should have the OneDrive sync client installed on your machine or have appropriate permissions to be able to install it. The following steps assume that you are using Windows as your OS. While the underlying concepts are the same, the installation steps for OneDrive are different for macOS. Refer to `https://m365book.page.link/OneDrive-Mac` for the installation and configuration steps for macOS.

How to do it...

You can use the OneDrive sync app to sync either your OneDrive for Business files and/or your SharePoint files locally to your computer.

To sync files from your OneDrive for Business account, take the following steps:

1. Browse to your OneDrive account in the Microsoft 365 portal.
2. Click the **Sync** option in the header menu, as shown here:

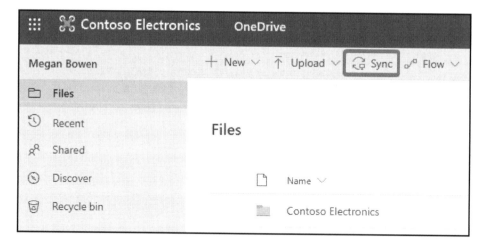

3. At this point, you will be prompted to launch OneDrive on your computer. You will also receive the following message indicating that OneDrive is launching on your computer. The message also provides a link to download OneDrive if you haven't already done so:

4. If this is your first time signing in, follow these steps:

    1. You will be prompted to log in to the client app:

2. You will also be prompted to select a location for OneDrive to store synced files. You can keep the default location suggested by OneDrive or change it if needed.

3. Next, the setup wizard will take you through a few information screens and will also prompt you to get the mobile app. It is highly recommended that you download the mobile app so that you can access your OneDrive files on the go on your mobile devices.

4. Upon completing the wizard, you will be prompted to open the newly installed OneDrive app.

5. OneDrive will now create a local sync folder and will start to sync your files.

5. Once the app is installed, clicking the **Sync** option from OneDrive in your browser will start the OneDrive app, if it isn't already running, and will also give you the option to open the local OneDrive sync folder.

Unless you disable it, the OneDrive app will automatically start when your computer starts. This ensures that your local files always stay synced with the online files.

6. The OneDrive icon will now show up in the Windows taskbar. You can right-click on this icon to see the status of the current sync operation, as shown in the following screenshot:

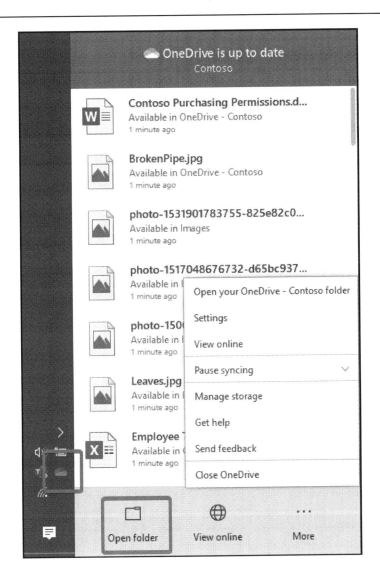

7. From here, you can also click on **Open folder** to open your OneDrive folder in Windows File Explorer. As the following screenshot shows, this folder shows all the files in your online OneDrive library:

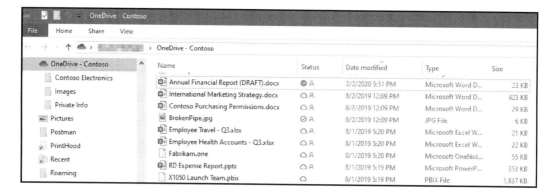

To sync the files and folders from a SharePoint library, take the following steps:

1. Browse to your SharePoint library.
2. Click the **Sync** option from the library's menu bar, as shown here:

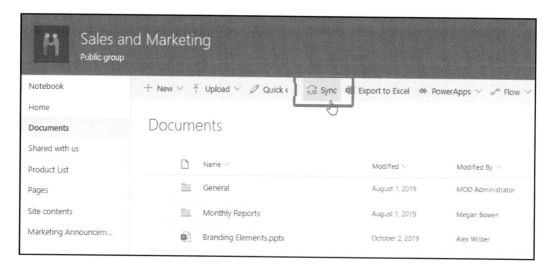

3. Follow the steps similar to those described for syncing files from OneDrive to set up the sync (steps *3*, *4* and *5* described previously).
4. You will see the following notification in your notification center once the sync is successfully set up:

5. OneDrive will now create a folder with the name of your organization under the `C:\Users\<YourLoginName>\` folder, as shown here:

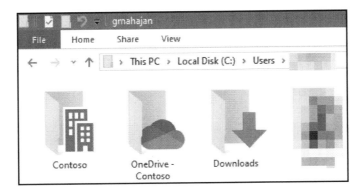

6. As the following screenshot shows, it will then create a folder for each library that you sync:

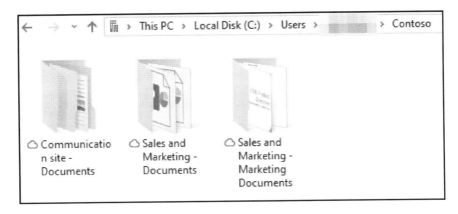

7. Opening or expanding the libraries in Windows Explorer will then show you a local representation of the online files and folders from that library:

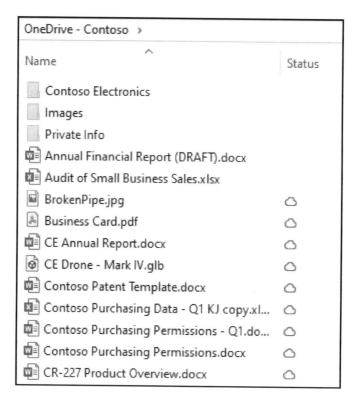

Congratulations! You have just learned how to set up and configure the OneDrive sync locally. From this point on, you can work with the files locally on your computer.

How it works...

Once the OneDrive sync is set up, you can work on files in your local OneDrive folder, just as you would with files in any other folder on your computer. Any updates that you make to the files in your local OneDrive folder will also be automatically synced to your online OneDrive, and vice versa. You can add, view, edit, and delete files or folders locally as you normally would. If you are connected to the internet, your changes will be copied over immediately to your online OneDrive and to other devices where you have OneDrive installed. If you are not connected to the internet while making these changes, OneDrive will cache your changes and sync them as soon as you are next online. In the meantime, OneDrive will still let you work on the file, as long as a local copy of the file was previously synced to the device that you are working on.

 Once you have set up the sync client, you can easily move existing files from your computer over to OneDrive. To do so, simply right-click on the file(s) and then click **Move to OneDrive**. Doing so will move the files over to your local OneDrive folder and then automatically sync them over to OneDrive online.

The OneDrive app has various settings that enable you to control and manage your sync options.

OneDrive app settings

We are going to review some key OneDrive settings in this section.

- Clicking the OneDrive icon and then clicking on **More** shows the following options:

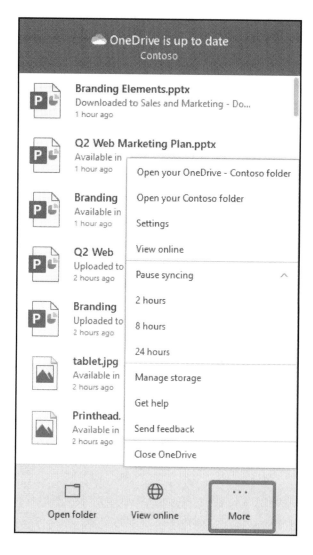

- **Open your OneDrive - [Organization Name] folder**:
  Clicking this option opens your local OneDrive sync folder in
  the file explorer.
- **Open your [Organization Name] folder**: Clicking this option
  opens your local profile folder, which contains all the
  SharePoint libraries that you are synchronizing with
  SharePoint Online.
- **Settings**: This option opens the advanced settings for the
  OneDrive app. We will look at these settings shortly.
- **View online**: Clicking this option opens your online
  OneDrive area.
- **Pause syncing**: This enables you to pause the sync for **2**, **8**, or
  24 hours. You can always resume the sync whenever you
  need to.
- **Close OneDrive**: This closes the OneDrive sync client. This
  option is generally not recommended as this may cause your
  local OneDrive and SharePoint files to be out of sync with the
  online files.

- Clicking the **Settings** option from the preceding menu options opens the
  advanced settings dialog, which has the following tabs:
    - **Settings**: Most settings on this page are self-explanatory and
      you should leave them at their default selections. The most
      important setting that you should know about is the **Files
      On-Demand** setting. If you uncheck this setting, OneDrive
      will restart and then download all files from OneDrive
      online, as well as any SharePoint Online libraries that you
      might be syncing. Depending on the files stored on your
      OneDrive online and the SharePoint Online libraries that you
      are syncing, this may cause significant local storage to be
      used on your device. It's generally not recommended to
      deselect this setting. Also, note that the **Always keep on this
      device** and **Free up space** options that we had discussed
      earlier will only show up when **Files On-Demand** is
      enabled.

- **Account**: If you work for multiple organizations, you can manage your accounts from this tab. This is also where, for each library that you are synchronizing, you can manage which folders to sync for which library. You can also stop syncing individual libraries from this page:

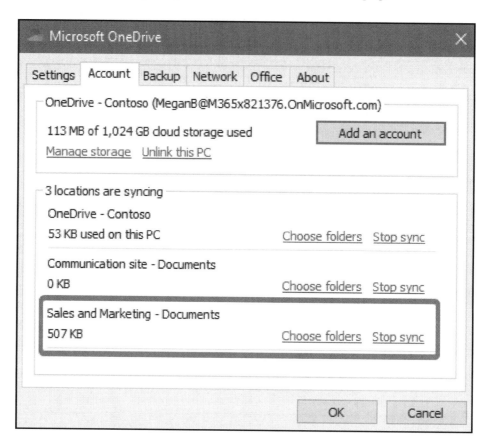

- **Backup**: This tab lets you enable a continuous backup of files from the `Desktop`, `Documents`, and `Pictures` folders on your computer. It is recommended that you turn on this option so that your local files are always backed up and available to you through the cloud. One important thing to note here is that if you turn off the backup after enabling it, OneDrive will end up deleting all the content from your local `Desktop`, `Documents`, and `Pictures` folders. This content is, however, still available on your OneDrive. You should, therefore, only turn on the **Backup** option if you don't intend to cancel it.

- **Network**: You can throttle the bandwidth that your OneDrive app uses to sync files to OneDrive and SharePoint Online. You would generally leave these settings at the default values. You can read more about them at `https://m365book.page.link/OneDrive-Network`.

- **Office**: You can use this tab to manage how your Office files are synced online. You can read more about the settings on this tab at `https://m365book.page.link/OneDrive-OfficeApps-Sync`.

There's more...

Instead of downloading all the files and folders from your OneDrive area or from a Sharepoint library at once, the OneDrive app lets you download these files on-demand as you need them. We will review this feature in more detail in the next section. Then we will look at why the sync app can sometimes fail to sync the files, how to identify and fix such sync issues.

Files on demand

You can enable or disable the files on-demand feature through the **Settings** tab in the OneDrive sync client settings.

You might not have the latest OneDrive app or the latest Windows 10 updates if you are unable to see the files on-demand feature. Please review the instructions at `https://m365book.page.link/OneDrive-OnDemand` to ensure you have the latest updates.

When you first set up the OneDrive sync from a library, OneDrive will only replicate the folders in that library or those from your OneDrive online area. It will not download the actual files and will only create placeholders for them. By not downloading all the files from your online library, it helps save space on your computer, while still allowing you to work on those files locally, just as if this was another local file on your device. These files and folders are indicated by a cloud icon, as shown in all the following screenshot:

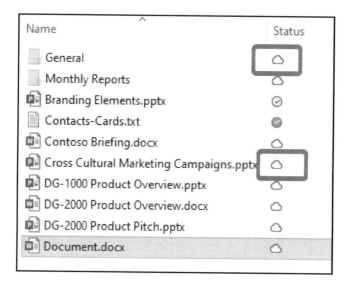

These files are only available when you are connected to the internet and so don't take up space on your computer. If you are working offline (that is, you are not connected to the internet), trying to open these files will result in the following error:

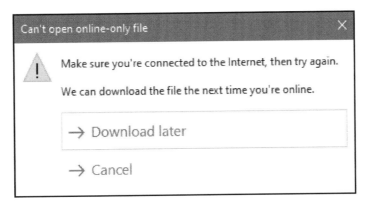

Clicking **Download later** will download the file to your computer once you are online (and connected to the internet) again.

Once you open an online-only file from your device, the OneDrive app automatically downloads it before opening it locally. These files are indicated by a blank circle with a checkmark in it:

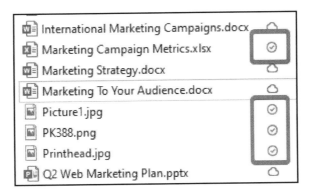

You can open these files at any time, even if you are not connected to the internet. OneDrive will then sync your changes to your online OneDrive area or to the corresponding SharePoint library when you next connect to the internet. Once you are done with your changes and you don't need to access the file locally—or if you'd like to remove the files from your local storage altogether—you can right-click on the local OneDrive file or folder in question and then click **Free up space.** As the following screenshot shows, doing so will remove these local files and change their status to online-only, indicated by the cloud icon. Compare the icons in this screenshot to the status icons for these files shown earlier:

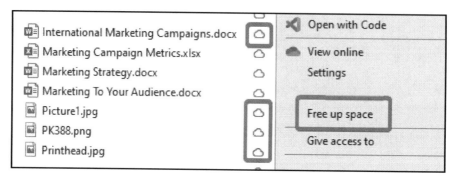

Finally, you can make sure that a file (or all the files in a folder) is always available on your computer, even when you are offline. To do so, right-click on the file or folder and then click **Always keep on this device**. Doing so will change the status icon to a green circle with a checkmark in it, as shown in the following screenshot:

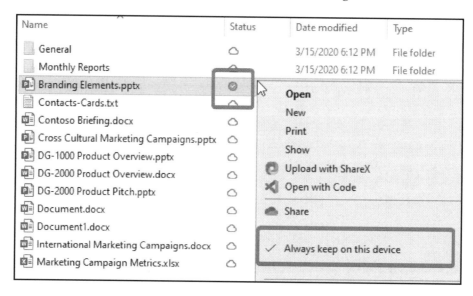

As mentioned earlier, you can always click **Free up space** to remove the local copies of these files or folders.

Note that the status icons and the OneDrive context menu shown in the previous screenshot will only appear in the OneDrive folders on your local device. Also, they will only show up when the OneDrive sync client is running.

Sync issues

The OneDrive sync app is very robust and has come a long way from when it was first introduced. One of the key gotchas of the sync client concerns filenames and invalid characters. Also, you may run into file lock issues and sync conflicts due to the nature of what the sync client does. You may find the following articles useful if you run into issues like this or you would like to read more about the file naming conventions and restrictions:

- Invalid file names and file types in OneDrive and SharePoint: `https://m365book.page.link/OneDrive-InvalidFiles`
- Fix OneDrive sync problems: `https://m365book.page.link/OneDrive-SyncIssues`

Sharing a file

We saw how to share documents in the *Sharing a document* recipe in `Chapter 2`, *Introduction to SharePoint Online*. Sharing files or folders from OneDrive works in the same way. The one minor exception is that your organization can set up different sharing restrictions on the files stored in OneDrive for Business versus those stored in SharePoint Online. For example, your organization may have turned off anonymous link sharing (signing in is not required to view a shared document) for your SharePoint sites, but might have enabled it for OneDrive.

In this recipe, we will use the OneDrive client to share a document from a local `OneDrive` folder on our computer.

Getting ready

There are no special requirements for sharing a file through OneDrive for Business online. As long as you have access to SharePoint Online, you will also have access to OneDrive for Business and you can share any files from there.

You should have the OneDrive sync client installed on your machine or the appropriate permissions to install it in order to share files directly from your computer.

How to do it...

To share a file or folder from your computer, take the following steps:

1. Make sure the OneDrive sync client is running and then go to your local `OneDrive` folder.

2. Right-click on the file or folder that you would like to share and then click **Share**, as shown in the following screenshot:

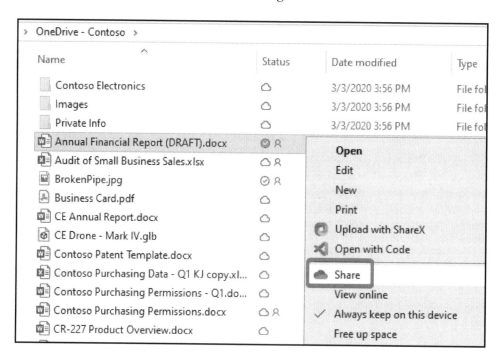

3. This will open the OneDrive sharing dialog box with the default sharing option selected. As the following screenshot shows, the **People you specify can edit** option was shown for me, by default:

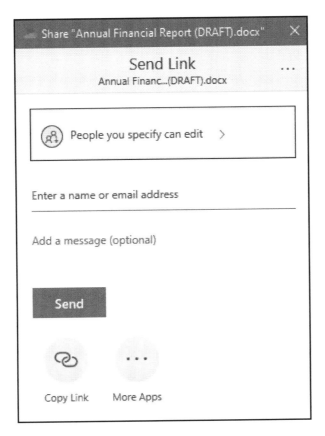

 Note that the default sharing option that is presented to you is controlled by your organization. In the *Sharing a document* recipe in Chapter 2, *Introduction to SharePoint Online*, we saw the various other sharing options and how to switch to one of the other options.

4. As we saw in the *Sharing a document* recipe in Chapter 2, *Introduction to SharePoint Online*, we can select the people we want to share the document with. There is also an option to enter a message. After this, click **Send** to share the document with them. The person will receive an email containing a link to the document.

That's it! You have just learned how to directly share a link to a document stored on your OneDrive for Business area from the `OneDrive` synced folder on your local machine.

How it works...

The sharing options that you will see when sharing from the OneDrive client will be the same as those that you will see from OneDrive online. The one added functionality you will notice, however, when you share using the OneDrive app on your device is the **More Apps** widget toward the bottom of the **Share** screen:

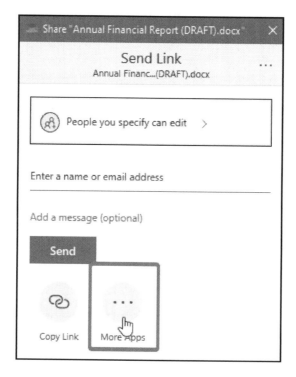

Clicking **More Apps** will enable you to share a link through other apps installed on your device. For example, on a mobile device, it will let you text a link to the document or send it via a Teams message, as shown in the following screenshot:

You can also similarly share a document that's in your OneDrive area right from within the document editing app that you are working on:

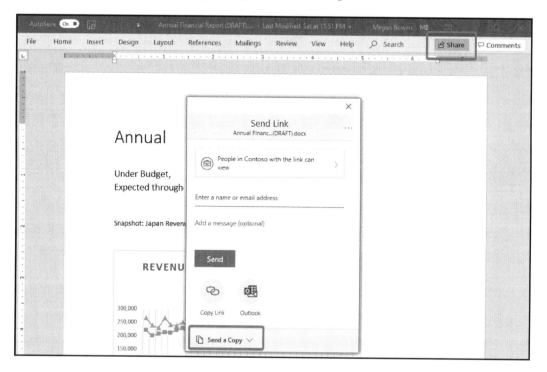

Note the **Send a Copy** option toward the bottom of this sharing screen. Clicking this option will open a new email and attach a Word or a PDF copy of the document to it.

There's more...

We saw how to check document permissions in SharePoint Online in the *View existing permissions* section in the *Sharing a document* recipe of Chapter 2, *Introduction to SharePoint Online*. When you do that, the document information pane will also show you all the links that you can use to grant access to the document to other people and who they provide access to. You can use these steps to view existing permissions on a file stored on your OneDrive for Business account.

If you are working on a OneDrive or SharePoint Online document from your local `OneDrive` synced folder, you can still view the links for providing access right from the **Share** screen we discussed in the previous section.

Links granting access

To view the existing links that grant access to other individuals, click the three dots at the top-right corner of the **Share** screen and then click **Manage Access**:

Doing so will show you all the links to grant others access to the document and who they will provide access to. If a link has an expiration date set on it, you can also view that here, as shown in the following screenshot:

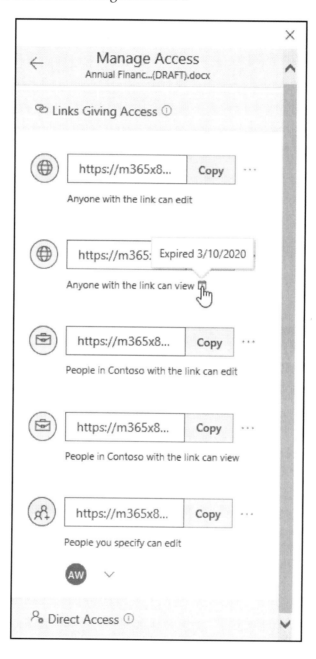

Please note that this screen will not show you any users that have access to the document through inherited permissions (if the document inherits permissions from the parent library). You will need to view the permissions of that document by browsing to the corresponding library in SharePoint Online. You can then view the permissions that users may have on a document by accessing the parent library. Please refer to the *Permission inheritance* topic in the *Determining and revoking permissions in a site* recipe of `Chapter 3`, *Working with Modern Sites in SharePoint Online.*

See also

- The *Syncing files and folders* recipe in this chapter
- The *Sharing a document* recipe in `Chapter 2`, *Introduction to SharePoint Online*
- The *Determining and revoking permissions in a site* recipe in `Chapter 3`, *Working with Modern Sites in SharePoint Online*
- The *Changing list permissions* recipe in `Chapter 4`, *Working with Lists and Libraries in SharePoint Online*

Search in Microsoft 365 **8**

Microsoft Search lets you effortlessly find and discover content that you need in order to complete your everyday tasks. It then presents this content back to you through a modern and easy-to-navigate user experience. The content that Microsoft Search returns is highly personalized to your work patterns and what's trending around you—things you've been working on (based on your activity in Microsoft 365), who you work with, activity in the content shared with you and with them, and so on. This personalization experience, coupled with advanced analytics and machine learning algorithms, brings the relevant content back to you even without you having to specifically search for it. If you have been working with a particular set of files, interacting with certain people, or working within the context of certain sites, Microsoft Search will automatically show this content to you even without you having to search for it. This content is presented to you through various means:

- You will see results by just clicking anywhere inside the search box, even before you start typing text, as shown in the following screenshot:

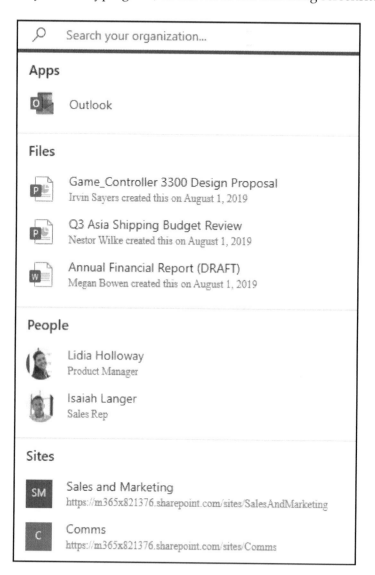

- Through the **Recommended** and **Discover** sections on the **Microsoft 365** home page, as shown in the following screenshot:

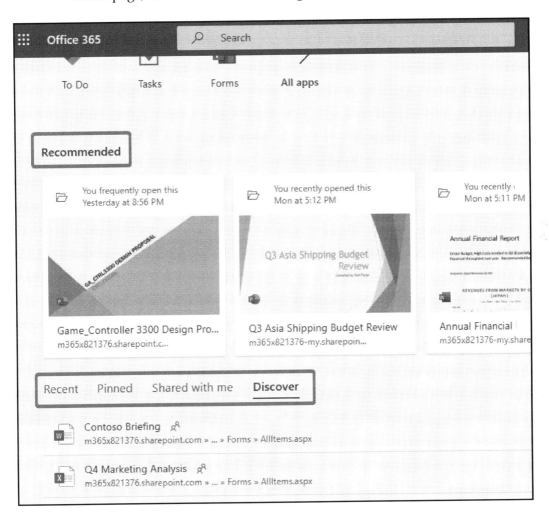

- Through various pages and sections in Delve, as shown in the following screenshot. Note that the list of people shown in the following screenshot is again based on your behavioral and environment patterns in Microsoft 365:

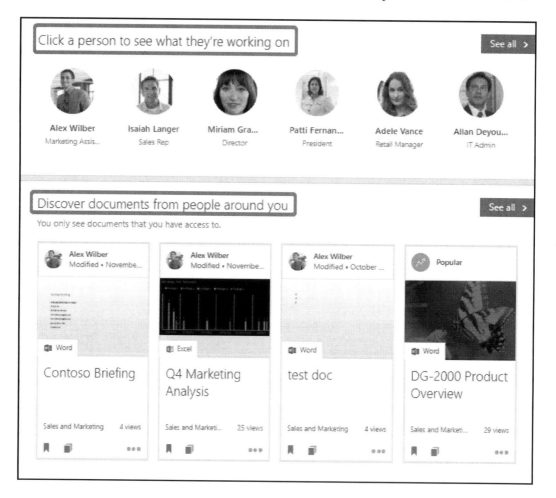

- Various web parts on SharePoint, such as the **Highlighted content**, **News**, and **Site activity** web parts.

Microsoft Search is available everywhere via the search box in the header area of all the Microsoft 365 apps, as shown in the following image:

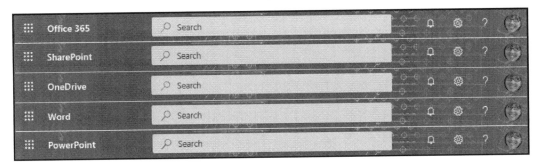

This makes it very easy to get to the content you are looking for. Let's say that you are working on a PowerPoint presentation and need to look up content from the corresponding Word document. You can simply search for the Word document right from within the search box in PowerPoint.

Additionally, Microsoft Search is aware of the context of the app you are searching from. So, if you are searching from within a SharePoint list or library, it will scope the search to that list or library. Searching from a SharePoint site will first return you results from that site, but will also let you easily switch the context to the corresponding hub or the entire organization.

Your site administrator has the ability to change the scope of the site search so that you see results from the entire organization or the corresponding hub by default instead of just the results from that particular site (this is a work in progress at the time of writing).

Some other examples of contextual searches are when you perform a search from the following workloads (at the time of writing):

- **Outlook**: Searching from Outlook will return results from within Outlook.
- **Yammer**: Searching from Yammer will return files and conversations from within Yammer.
- **Teams**: While files shared through Teams are stored in SharePoint and/ or OneDrive, the conversations are not. You can therefore only search for any Teams conversations from within Microsoft Teams.

Furthermore, SharePoint online offers two flavors of search:

- **The more modern, personalized, and intelligent search experience**: The **modern** SharePoint search utilizes Microsoft Search for a more modern search experience. As previously described, this experience is consistent across most workloads of Microsoft 365.
- **The classic search experience**: The **classic** search experience is what you will see in the classic SharePoint sites. This experience is slowly being deprecated.

Both of these experiences utilize the same underlying search **index**, meaning that the underlying source of truth for both search experiences is the same, however, the modern search applies machine learning coupled with usage analytics to this index to bring back what's more relevant to you. It then uses a more modern user experience to display these results back to you. We will see the modern search experience in this book. Please go to `https://m365book.page.link/Search-Classic-Modern` if you would like to understand the differences between classic and modern search experiences in SharePoint.

Finally, we learned how to perform a basic search as part of the *Searching Content* recipe in `Chapter 2`, *Introduction to SharePoint Online*. In this chapter, we will look at the more advanced capabilities and some specific use cases of Microsoft Search.

In this chapter, we will cover the following recipes:

- Performing an advanced search
- Finding experts and people
- Searching with Bing Search

Performing an advanced search

Just like any other search engine, Microsoft Search supports advanced search queries. You can build these advanced queries by adding various operators and property filters to the search keywords. This recipe will show you how to do that.

For our scenario, let's say that, as a product design engineer, I am working on a design proposal for a new product. I remember that a similar proposal was presented by one of my colleagues, Irvin Sayers, in the not so recent past. I liked the proposal and would like to use it as a template for my presentation. In this recipe, we will see how I can use an advanced search to narrow down the results to quickly find this proposal.

Getting ready

You can access Microsoft Search from any workload in your Microsoft 365 tenant. You can also search from within the apps that are installed locally on your computer, as long as they are connected to the Microsoft 365 tenant. Search will only return results from the content to which you have at least *read* access.

How to do it...

To perform an advanced search, we will begin with a routine search and then start narrowing down the results through advanced parameters to find exactly what we are looking for. To do so, go through the following steps:

1. Browse to the Microsoft 365 home page for your tenant.

Since you know that you are looking for a file in SharePoint, you can also perform this search from the SharePoint home page. In general, however, it is a good idea to start your search from the Microsoft 365 home page since it has a wider reach compared to just using SharePoint.

2. Based on what I am looking for, I will begin my search by typing `design` in the search box at the top of the page.

3. As shown in the following screenshot, this returns a lot of results. Along with the people that these results return, some of these results are related to branding and visual design:

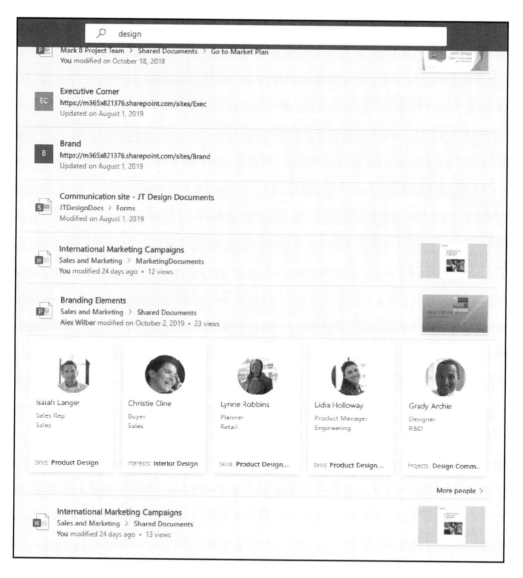

4. To remove these unwanted results, I will go ahead and add the following advanced filters to my search text:
   - I will add the text `-visual` to it since I am not looking for visual design.

- Also, since I am specifically looking for presentations, I will add the text `FileExtension:pptx`.

5. Entering the preceding filters as text in the search box further narrows down the search results to just presentations surrounding product design and overviews, as shown in the following screenshot:

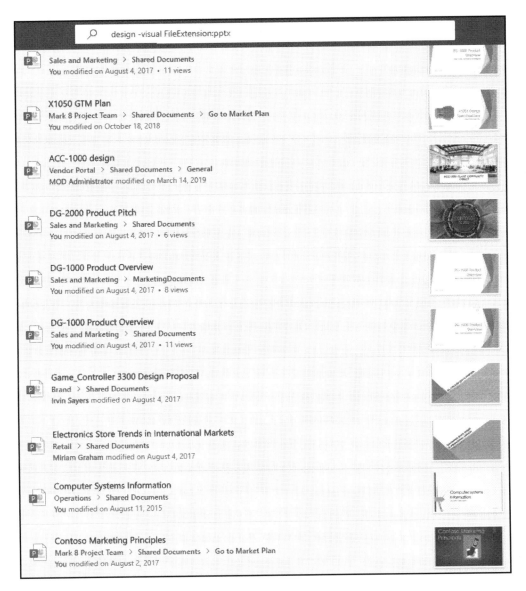

6. Finally, since I know that the design proposal was presented by my colleague, Irvin, I am going to add a filter that shows only the documents authored by him. To do so, I will add `Author:irvin` to my search text:

7. This narrows down the search results to exactly what I was looking for. This is shown in the following screenshot:

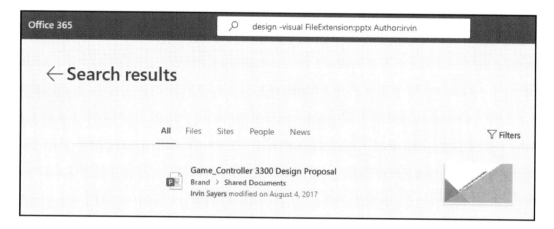

Congratulations! We just learned how to use advanced search in SharePoint Online to narrow down the search results and find exactly what we were looking for.

How it works...

Microsoft Search, just like any other search, has the following components to it:

- **Crawler**: This is the part of the search engine that scours the content in your tenant and then uses a content processing engine to transform it into a suitable format for the indexer to use.

- **Indexer**: This part of the search engine organizes and *indexes* the content in a format that is easily searchable.

- **Query component**: This part of the search engine is responsible for processing the user search queries, filtering the results, ranking them, and sending them back to the user.

- **UI**: The UI is the part of the search engine that lets the users submit queries, send them to the query component, and eventually render the results.

Microsoft Search not only *crawls* and *indexes* the content, but also the underlying properties and column names. For each SharePoint column that the crawler encounters, it creates a corresponding property within its crawl database.

This additionally enables you to *query* and *filter* the content by easily specifying the property or column names. We saw this earlier in this recipe when we specifically filtered the results by the **Author** column.

In search terminology, such properties that get created within the search database are called **crawled properties**; however, not all crawled content or metadata is useful to have in the search index. So the search schema maintains a separate list of useful metadata columns, called **managed properties**. The search index only includes content and metadata from the managed properties. The **Author** property is an example of such a managed property.

Please also note that Microsoft Search will create managed properties only for the corresponding site columns. Any columns that directly get added to lists or libraries will not get a corresponding crawled property. This means that you will still be able to search for content in such columns, but will not have the ability to specifically filter the search results by specifying these column names, as we did in this recipe.

This capability, coupled with a proper information architecture that uses consistent column names, goes a long way in helping users quickly find the right content. We discussed the concept of content types and the content type hub in *Creating a content type and adding columns to it* recipe of `Chapter 6`, *Term Store and Content Types in SharePoint Online*. Imagine the following scenario, keeping the concepts from that recipe in mind:

- You have defined a base content type and published it through the content type hub, for use in all the libraries in your organization.
- This content type contains a managed metadata site column called **Department**.
- The content type and the corresponding site column then gets replicated to every department site.
- You then optionally update the site column for each such department site and set its default value to represent the particular department name.
- Now, any documents uploaded to libraries using this content type will automatically get tagged by the name of the corresponding department (or users will need to manually select the department name if the defaults are not specified).
- Because these columns were created as site columns, the search crawler will create crawled and managed properties for this column.

- Users across the organization will now easily be able to filter the search results by the department name and quickly narrow them down to the exact content that the user is looking for.

Such an arrangement involves more upfront planning and setting up time, but helps achieve better user satisfaction and increased productivity.

 For advanced users and administrators, the information at `https://m365book.page.link/Search-Schema` provides more insight into the SharePoint Online search schema.

Certain columns, such as the managed metadata column, require some additional handling before they can be used in filters. The following articles describe these steps in more detail. Note that even though they are written for SharePoint Server, the steps are equally valid for SharePoint Online:

- **From site column to managed property – What's up with that**: `https://m365book.page.link/Managed-Properties`
- **Mapping crawled properties to pre-defined managed properties**: `https://m365book.page.link/Map-SearchProperties`

Fine-tuning search and keyword query language

Microsoft Search presents a very simple user interface along with a very powerful underlying search engine. This engine will return results for most of your queries, but if you are not getting the expected results back, then you can implement the following measures:

- Ensure that sufficient time has elapsed since the content was created. Referring to the search components described earlier, the crawler component needs to first crawl the content, process it, and submit it to the index before it can be searched. This usually happens at scheduled intervals, which means that there's a slight lag between the time the content gets created and the time it shows up in the search results. Usually, this process is almost instantaneous, but sometimes it can take up to 4 hours or more before you or other site users get the newly created content back as part of the search results.

- Unlike some public search engines, Microsoft Search is currently susceptible to spelling errors and does not provide a *'Did you mean...?'* functionality for incorrect spellings. This means that if the text is misspelled in the content of your query, then Microsoft Search will (currently) not be able to find it.
- As mentioned previously, Microsoft Search may return different results for the same search depending on who is searching for content. The result ranking in a modern search is based on complicated machine learning algorithms that take into account your activity, patterns, and environment. So, it might be that others may see a result higher up in the results list while you see it a little lower. You can always refine your queries to get more focused results if needed.
- Everything in Search is permission-based. This means that you will only see results that you have at least *read* access to. If you have tried refining the queries and are still not seeing results that others are seeing, then there's a possibility that you may not have access to that content.
- SharePoint understands an advanced query syntax called the **keyword query language (KQL)**. KQL helps you build highly focused and complex queries. The information at `https://m365book.page.link/Search-KQL` explains the various elements of a KQL in more detail.

The article at `https://m365book.page.link/Search-Tuning` discusses more details as to how to fine-tune your search if you are getting too few or too many results.

There's more...

Microsoft Search comes with quite a few admin settings that can be used to significantly alter the search experience. The following section provides an outline of such admin settings.

Owner and admin controls

You can apply admin settings at various levels to control what shows up in the search results and how:

- As a list or library owner, you can choose to exclude your list, library, or content from the search results. This setting is available from within the **Advanced settings** page for your list or library.
- As a site owner, you can similarly specify various settings for the site. Most of these settings are geared toward the classic search experience; however, some settings apply to both the classic and modern experiences. The ability to exclude the site and its contents from showing up in search results is one such setting. This can be accessed from the **Search and offline availability** page under **Site Settings**. This page also lets a site owner view and make limited changes to the search schema.

Finally, as a global admin or a tenant search admin, I can control various aspects of the organization-wide search experience. In addition to managing the search schema, the following are some settings related to the modern experience that you can manage through the Microsoft Search admin center:

- View organization-wide search usage reports, as described at `https://m365book.page.link/Search-Usage`.
- Help create predefined search results, such as acronyms, bookmarks, Q and A's, locations, and floor plans. These predefined results are based on the most commonly used scenarios for your user experience and show up before the other results do. Note that these result types show up only when the search is being done across the organization, and not when the search is narrowly scoped (such as when searching in a list, library, or site). You can read more about these in the *Provide answers* section (in the navigation towards the left of the page) at `https://m365book.page.link/Provide-Answers`.
- Create and configure connectors to search and bring back results from external data sources. You can read more about this at `https://m365book.page.link/Search-Connectors`.

- Make additional configuration changes to the search. You can read more about these configuration changes in the *Customize and configure* section (in the navigation towards the left of the page) at `https://m365book.page.link/Search-Customize`.

Some examples of these configuration changes are as follows:

  - Creating search verticals
  - Changing the search result layouts
  - Managing the classic versus modern search experience in SharePoint
  - Turning Bing Search on or off (see the *Searching with Bing Search*, recipe later in this chapter)

Please note that some of these features were in preview at the time of writing this book and may or may not be available in your organization's Microsoft 365 tenant.

See also

- The *Searching content* recipe in, Chapter 2, *Introduction to SharePoint Online*
- The *Creating a content type and adding columns to it* recipe in, Chapter 6, *Term Store and Content Types in SharePoint Online*
- The *Viewing and changing list settings* recipe in, Chapter 4, *Working with Lists and Libraries in SharePoint Online*
- The *Viewing and changing site settings* recipe in, Chapter 3, *Working with Modern Sites in SharePoint Online*

Finding experts and people

Microsoft Search in SharePoint not only helps you find documents but also helps you find people. You can search for people based on who they are, where they work, or what role they fulfill in the organization.

Continuing the example from the previous recipe, let's say that I am looking for help with creating the product *design* proposal. This recipe will show you how you can use Microsoft Search to search your organization for an expert to help with it. It will then show you how you can also reach out to them through your favorite communication tools from within that interface.

Getting ready

Unless your organization disables it, people search is enabled by default and is available to anyone in the organization who has access to Microsoft 365.

How to do it...

To look for someone with design skills, go through the following steps:

1. Browse to the Microsoft 365 home page for your tenant.
2. Type the text `designer` in the search box at the top.
3. You should see *person results* after the first few document results. You can also click the **People** tab to just view the people-only results, as shown in the following screenshot:

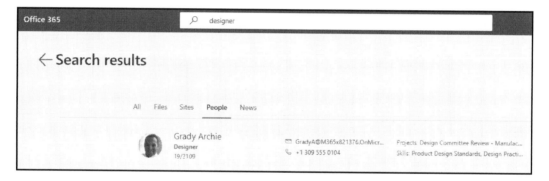

4. In this example, I can see that the first result that was returned was **Grady Archie**, who has the word **Designer** in his job title. I can then click on Grady's name to see more details about him. Doing so opens his **Profile card** (also known as the **Contact card**), as shown in the following screenshot:

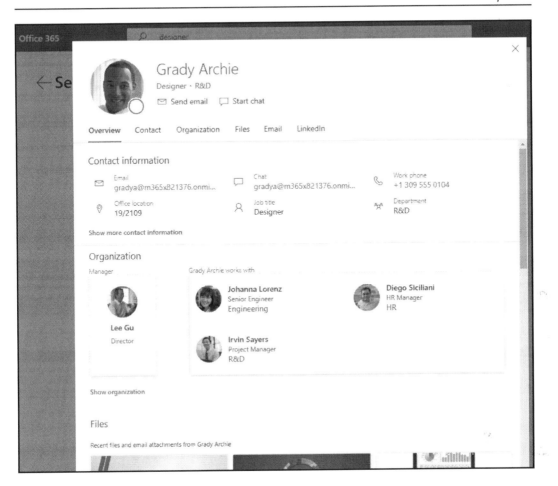

5. In the **Overview** tab of his profile card, I can view various aspects of his profile, such as his contact information, his manager and colleagues, files he has shared, my recent email conversations with him, and his **LinkedIn** profile.

6. Clicking a different tab from the profile card shows further details surrounding these areas in that tab. Clicking the **Contact** tab, as an example, shows additional details about Grady, such as his skills, education, and the projects that he has worked on, as shown in the following screenshot:

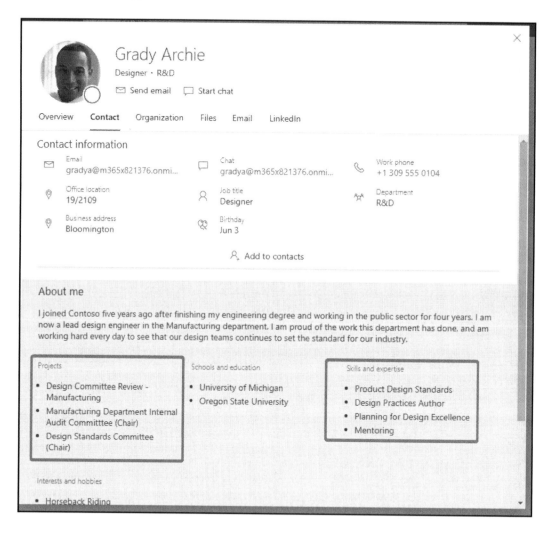

The properties shown in the **Contact information** and **About me** sections need to be populated first before they are searchable or even show up in the profile card. Your organization can maintain and then sync over some of these properties to Microsoft 365 so that they are maintained in a central place, usually through HR or IT management systems. They can also optionally make these properties editable for you so that you can maintain them on your own through your profile page in *Delve*, which we will see in the next chapter.

7. Going by his profile summary, I can see that this matches exactly with who I am looking for. Hence, I can click **Start chat** to open Grady's profile in Teams (or Skype for Business), as shown in the following screenshot:

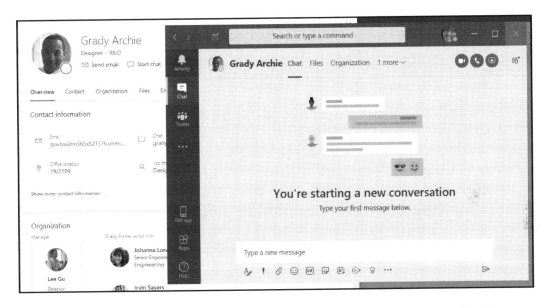

8. From here, I can call him or start a chat with him using the familiar Teams interface.

Congratulations! You just learned how to perform a people search in Microsoft 365 and then learned how to contact them directly using a familiar tool of your choice.

How it works...

An enhanced people search lets you identify the right people in your organization by using attributes, such as *designer*, and assists in obtaining answers or help quickly. In the preceding example, with one attribute, Microsoft Search identified *Grady* as a *design* subject matter expert.

From that point on, the deep contextual information returned by Microsoft Search through the user profile card created efficiencies for us, improving productivity by reducing the friction of switching between apps and browser tabs. We can quickly send an email to or chat with the identified expert without having to leave the browser. We can also see other details about them, such as their location, in case we'd like to get in touch with them.

In addition to performing a generic search, as we did in this recipe, you can also use pre-configured managed properties (see the previous recipe to understand managed properties in more detail) to perform a highly targeted search. Some examples are as follows:

- `jobtitle: *design*`: This will return all profiles where the job title partially or fully matches the word *design*. Following the example from the recipe, this will bring back Grady's profile, since his job title is **Designer**.
- `schools: Michigan`: This search will bring back all profiles where the person's school name contains *Michigan*.
- `skills: *design*`: This search will bring back all profiles where the person's skill partially matches the word *design*. An example of this search is shown in the following screenshot:

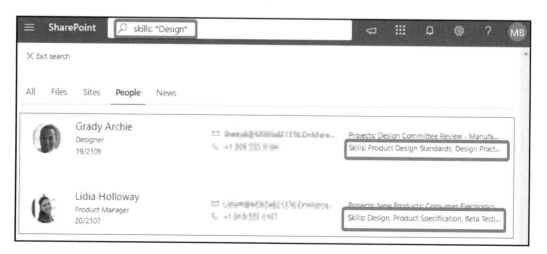

Please note that the targeted search mentioned previously, as well as the information being returned through Microsoft search and profile cards, is contingent on it being maintained in the first place. The HR department in your organization is typically the one that would solicit the creation and maintenance of such employee profile information. The IT department then helps set up the synchronization of this information to Microsoft 365. These departments will subsequently need to work hand in hand so that this profile information is regularly maintained. It's highly recommended that you expend some time upfront to plan and set up the backend processes (either manual or automated) so that this information stays up to date. More often than not, stale information being presented through the search experience or through other workloads in Microsoft 365 can discourage users from effectively utilizing the platform.

See also

- The *Performing an advanced search* recipe, earlier in this chapter

Searching with Bing Search

Bing is a web search engine that is owned and operated by Microsoft. If you have a Microsoft 365 work account and you perform a search from within Bing, you can also get results from your organization in addition to the usual web results that are returned by the search engine. Of course, all of this is available to you in a multitude of browsers across a variety of device types.

This recipe will show you how to use Bing as your one-stop search engine for not only bringing back public results from the web but also the results from within your organization's Microsoft 365 environment. For illustration purposes, we will use the same scenario that we did in the *Advanced Search in SharePoint Online* recipe, earlier in this chapter. As a product design engineer, I am working on a design proposal for a new product. In the recent past, I remember that a similar proposal was presented by one of my colleagues, Irvin Sayers. I liked the proposal and would like to use it as a template for my proposal. In this recipe, we will see how I can use Bing Search to quickly find this proposal.

Getting ready

Your organization should have enabled Microsoft Search for Bing. Also, to view your work results alongside the web search results, you will need to log in to Bing using your work credentials; this recipe will also show you how to do this. Other than that, the requirements for viewing your work results in Bing are the same as those for the regular Microsoft 365 search, in that it will only return results for which you at least have read access.

How to do it...

To view your company's Microsoft 365 results in Bing Search, perform the following steps:

1. Open your favorite browser and browse to `https://www.bing.com/`.
2. Click the **Sign in** link in the top-right corner of the Bing search page, as shown in the following screenshot:

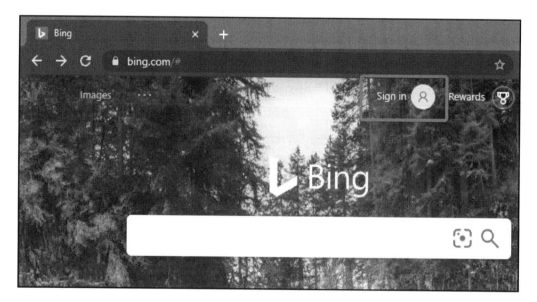

3. Doing so will take you to a familiar Microsoft sign-in experience, where you can enter your Microsoft 365 credentials to sign in.
4. Once signed in, you will be brought back to the Bing home page, with the sign-in button and corresponding image replaced by your details from your organization's Microsoft 365 environment.

It is recommended that you sign in to Bing only on personal/private computers. Signing in on a public device or a device that does not belong to you will leave your organization's information susceptible to being stolen and misused. If you do have a critical or urgent need to sign in on a public device, you should remember to sign out and completely close the browser session after you are done.

5. Since I am looking for a design proposal that was presented by Irvin Sayers, I am going to search Bing for any files that were authored or modified by him. To do so, I will enter the text `Irvin Sayers files` in the search box and press the *Enter* key.

6. This will bring back the file search results from my organization that is centered around Irvin. As shown in the following screenshot, the design proposal I was searching for shows as the first result. This is likely because there's current activity trending around that file and/or the machine learning algorithm identified this file to be of greater relevance to me compared to the other file results:

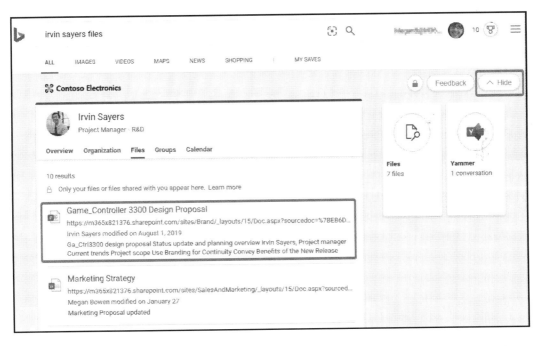

7. Clicking the **Hide** button in the top-right corner, as shown in the preceding screenshot, will hide the organization results and just show you the web results.

That's it! You just learned how to use Bing as the one-stop search engine to bring back not only internet results but also results from your organization.

How it works...

We discussed the different components of Search as part of the *Performing an advanced search* recipe earlier in this chapter. Bing's search works by securely tapping into your organization's search index and using its own query and UI components. This enables Bing search to serve some advanced queries, in addition to the more common and simplistic queries that it can also return search results for. Some examples of such advanced queries include the following:

- Searching for `my files` or `my documents` returns the most recent documents that you worked on:

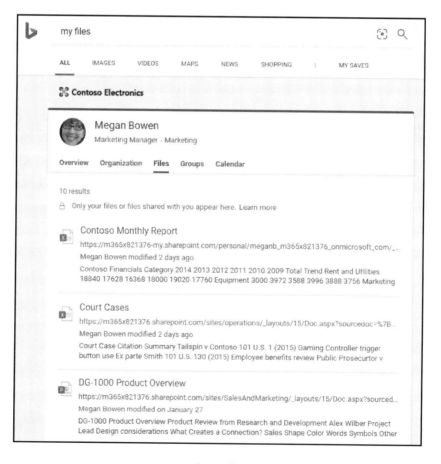

- Searching for `<employee name> org`, `<employee name> direct reports`, or `<employee name> manager` returns the organization chart for the employee:

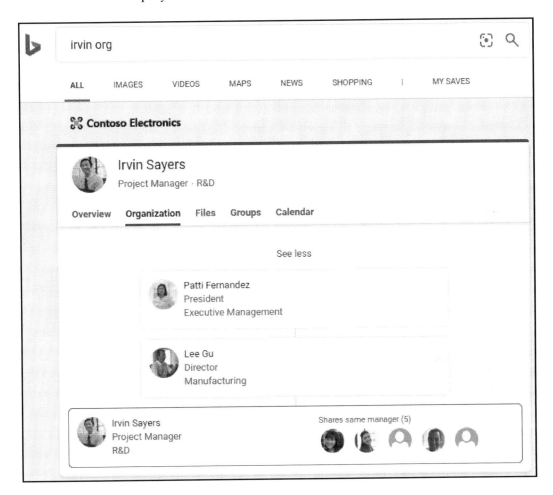

- Searching for `Conversations about <topic>` returns conversations from Teams and Yammer:

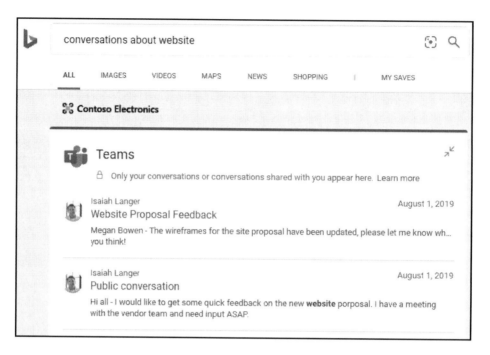

You can also perform some of the other regular kinds of search through the Bing organization search, such as searching for people:

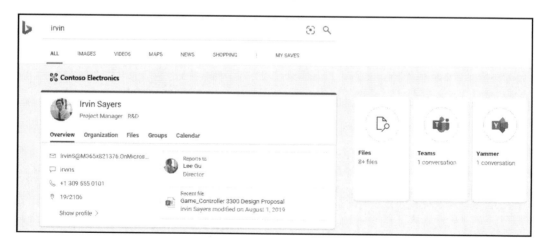

This returns not only the person's contact details but also their files and conversations. Furthermore, you can also click the **Show profile** link to view the familiar people profile card.

Remember that, irrespective of where you perform the search from or what search you perform, you will always only see content that you have access to through security and permissions. In the preceding screenshot, I see those files and conversations only because they were individually shared with me, one of the groups that I am a member of, or with the entire organization.

See also

- The *Performing an advanced search* recipe, earlier in this chapter
- The *Finding experts and people* recipe, earlier in this chapter

9
Office Delve

Delve is the workload of Microsoft 365, which lets users easily view all their relevant content in one place. Delve will not only show you your content but also content that your colleagues have been working on and have shared with you. This content includes OneDrive for Business documents, SharePoint Online documents, and documents that were shared with you through email attachments. Delve automatically surfaces all this content without even needing for the users to search for it.

Delve is powered by **Microsoft Graph**, the same AI-based tool that powers **Microsoft Search**.

You can read more about Microsoft Graph in the section on *Office development frameworks* in the *Appendix*

Office Graph plays three critical roles in Delve in particular and Microsoft 365 in general:

- First, it monitors your interaction with content and people across multiple Microsoft 365 workloads, such as (but not limited to) SharePoint, Teams, OneDrive for Business, and Outlook.
- Based on these interactions, it uses machine learning to understand the connections between you, those people, and the crawled content.
- It then uses the developed understanding to automatically surface content in the order of relevance for you.

Things like what you've been working on, who you've been work with, what they've been working with, who your manager is, who else has the same manager as you – all of these impacts the relevance of the content that you see in Delve. This helps you find and discover the most relevant and fresh content first, instead of having to go through a list of search results, or for that matter, even having to perform a search in the first place!

In this chapter, we will cover the following topics:

- Navigating to your Delve profile page
- Changing your profile photo
- Updating your profile information
- Grouping documents through boards

Navigating to your Delve profile page

Delve essentially has two landing pages:

- Your Delve profile landing page
- The Delve home page

In this recipe, you will see how you can get to your profile page in Delve. We will then discuss, in subsequent sections, the difference between these two pages and also how you can get to the Delve home page.

Getting ready

The only requirement for you to be able to access Delve is that your administrator should have enabled it for your organization.

How to do it...

To get to your Delve profile page, follow these steps:

1. Browse to the Microsoft 365 home page or the home page of any app in your Microsoft 365 tenant.
2. Click your profile image in the top-right corner.
3. Click on **My Office profile**, as shown in the following screenshot:

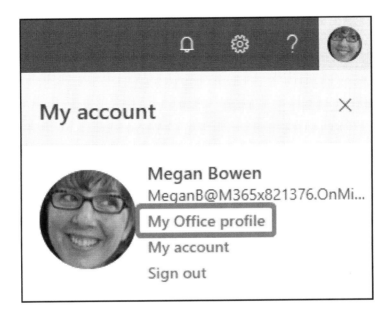

4. You will now be taken to your **Delve** profile page. Here, you will see documents and people's profiles that are most relevant to you.

Congratulations! You just learned how to browse to your Delve profile page. In the next sections, we will learn about the various sections on this page in greater detail.

How it works...

The Delve profile page is a great way to quickly get back to what you were working on and also discover relevant content around you:

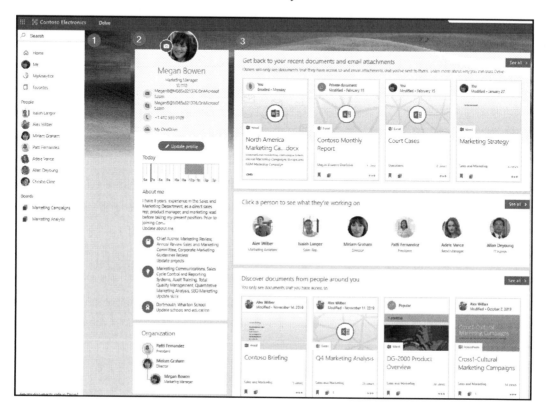

As shown in the preceding screenshot, the content on the page is subdivided into these three sections:

- **Search and left navigation**: You can perform the following actions from this section:
  - **Search**: You can perform an organization-wide search from the search box in this section. Note that this search is slightly different from the usual Microsoft 365 search:
    - When bringing back search results, it gives more weight to what's relevant for you and shows that content first.

- It will only show you people results, documents, and Delve boards (we will learn more about boards in a subsequent recipe in this chapter) in the search results.
- You cannot use the advanced search filters when searching from Delve.

- **Home**: Click this link to go to the Delve home page.
- **Me**: Click this to view your profile page.
- **MyAnalytics**: This is a Microsoft 365 app that provides insights into your work patterns within Microsoft 365. You can read more about it at: `https://m365book.page.link/MyAnalytics`.
- **Favorites**: You can mark documents as favorites and then view all your favorites in one place from here.
- **People**: This section shows a list of people that you've been working with most or whose profiles are the most relevant to you. You can click a person's name or picture to see their profile page.
- **Boards**: This section shows you your favorite boards. We will learn more about boards in the *Grouping documents through boards* recipe, later in this chapter.

- **Your profile information section**: This section lets you do the following:
  - **Add or change your profile photo**: This is where you change your profile photo. We have covered this in more detail in the *Changing your profile photo* recipe, later in this chapter.
  - **View a snapshot of today's calendar**: This is a quick snapshot of your Outlook calendar for the day. If you are viewing someone else's profile, you will see their Outlook calendar here.
  - **View or update profile information**: You can view a snapshot of your profile information in the **About me** section. You can also click the **Update profile** button to make changes to it. This is covered in more detail in the *Updating your profile information* recipe, later in this chapter. If you are viewing someone else's profile, you will see a **View profile** button below the **About me** section. Clicking this button will show you detailed contact and profile information for that person.

- **View the organization hierarchy**: This section shows a limited graphical view of the organizational hierarchy for the person whose Delve profile you are viewing.

- **Relevant content and profiles (driven by Office Graph)**:
  - **View the recent documents and email attachments**: This sub-section shows you the recent documents that you've been working on. This includes documents in any emails that you may have exchanged with others. Documents within Delve are presented in the form of **document cards**. Document cards are unique to Delve, and we will see in a little bit all the things that you can do with a document card. You can also click **See all** to get an expanded view showing more documents that you recently worked on. This view also provides a few additional filtering capabilities.
  - **View the Delve profile page of people that you most work with**: This sub-section shows you a list of people that are most relevant to you based on your interactions in Microsoft 365. Clicking on a person's image will take you to their profile page, which is similar in structure to yours but shows content that is centered around them, and that you have access to via permissions.
  - **Discover relevant documents from people around you**: This section shows you relevant documents from the people around you. Remember that the relevance is based on a multitude of factors, including but not limited to things that you've been working on, who you report to, who you work with, and what's most popular among them. Also, remember that these documents are shown using the document cards described previously.

Delve home page

Similar to the profile page, the Delve home page also surfaces relevant content for you and helps you stay in touch with the documents that are popular and relevant for you. You can browse to the Delve home page by clicking on the Delve app in the Microsoft 365 app launcher, as shown in the following screenshot:

You can also click the **Home** hyperlink from anywhere in Delve to be taken to the Delve home page.

There's more...

Document cards provide a nice way to view information related to a document. We will look at document cards in the next section. We will then discuss how Delve only shows you content that you have access to. We will finally look at how to completely turn off Delve if you need to do so for any reason.

Document cards

The following screenshot shows a preview of document cards in Delve:

For an Outlook attachment, clicking anywhere in the document card opens a preview of the document in Outlook. For SharePoint and OneDrive documents, you can perform the following additional actions through a document card:

- Click the document name to open it in a new browser window.
- View the document within the original library: You can see a hyperlinked name of the parent SharePoint site or the OneDrive for Business folder toward the bottom left of the card. Clicking this link takes you to the site and specifically the corresponding library containing the document within that site.

- Click the bookmark/favorites icon toward the bottom left to add or remove the document from your favorites list. As mentioned earlier, all your favorite documents can be accessed in one place through the **Favorites** option in the navigation menu on the left of the page.
- Click the **Manage boards** icon to manage the boards for this document.
- Click on the three dots toward the bottom right corner of the card to do any of the following:
- Copy and/or directly email a link to the document using **Copy link** or **Send a link**.
- View the permissions (who has access to it) for the document by clicking **Who can see this?**. We will cover this in more detail in the next section, *Delve and security*.

- See the number of times the document has been viewed.

Delve and security

Delve always only brings back relevant content based on what you have access to, and never changes any permissions on it. This means the following:

- Only you can see content that is private to you, and others do not see any documents that you have not shared with them.
- Others will only see their private content or content that they were given access to through permissions.
- Similarly, you will only see content from others that you have been granted access to.

Who sees a document is ultimately determined by the respective document permissions in the corresponding library in SharePoint or OneDrive for Business. You can view who has access to a particular document by clicking on the three dots toward the bottom of the respective document card and then clicking **Who can see this?**:

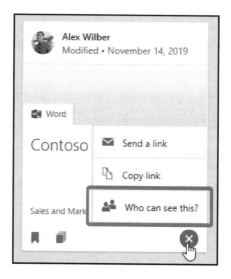

Clicking this link will open the corresponding library in a new browser tab or window and shows you the current permissions on that document:

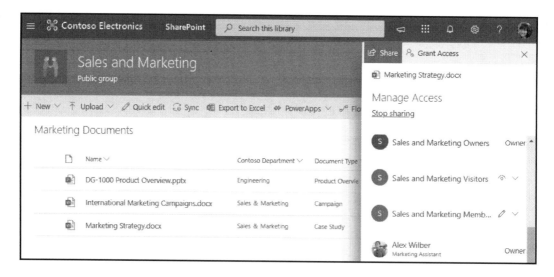

Turning off Delve

Delve can help you quickly get to the relevant content and people. If your organization has enabled Delve, you cannot completely turn it off. You may, however, turn it off just for yourself so that when others view your profile, they will not see your documents. Once you do that, you too will not be able to view documents on their profile page. They will still be able to visit your profile page and view your profile details and organization chart. To turn off Delve for your profile, click the gear settings icon in the top-right corner of your profile page, click **Feature settings**, and then turn the toggle under the **Documents** heading from **On** to **Off** and click the **OK** button, as shown in the following screenshot:

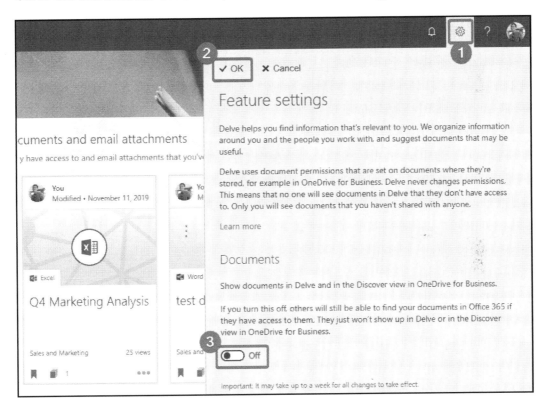

From that point on, you will start seeing a message on the Delve profile page indicating the fact that you've turned off documents in Delve. This is shown in the following screenshot:

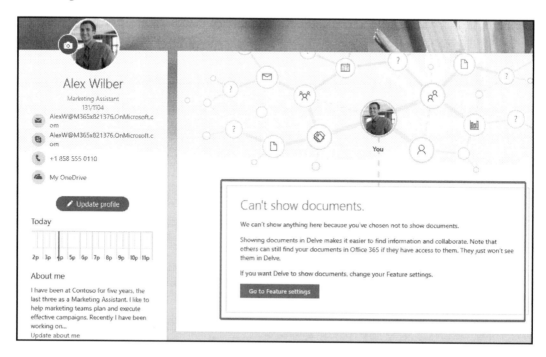

In addition to completely turning off Delve on your profile, you can also prevent individual documents from showing up at all in Delve. This page describes the steps to do that in detail: `https://m365book.page.link/Hide-From-Delve`. `You will need to be an admin on the site that contains the document(s) that you'd like to hide from Delve.`

See also

- The *Determining and revoking permissions in a site* recipe in `Chapter 3`, *Working with Modern Sites in SharePoint Online*
- The *Changing list permissions* recipe in `Chapter 4`, *Working with Lists, Libraries in SharePoint Online*

Changing your profile photo

Your profile photo shows across various Microsoft 365 workloads. It shows up in the navigation bar in the top-right corner for most workloads. In Teams, it shows against the conversations that you participate in. In SharePoint, it shows against the documents that you have modified and various other places.

You can change this profile photo from your Delve profile page. At the time of writing this book, **Teams** is the only other workload of Microsoft 365 that also lets you change your profile photo.

This recipe shows you how to change your profile photo from the Delve home page as well as using Teams.

Getting ready

Delve should have been enabled by your organization for you to be able to change your profile photo from there. Your organization should also have allowed changes to the profile photo in Delve.

Similarly, for you to be able to change the profile photo from Teams, your organization should have assigned a Teams license to you and they should have allowed making changes to the profile photo.

How to do it...

To change your profile photo in Microsoft 365 using Delve, follow these steps:

1. Browse to your profile page in Delve, as described in the previous recipe in this chapter, *Navigating to your Delve profile page*.

2. Click on the camera next to your profile image, as shown in the following screenshot:

3. Click **Upload a new photo** on the next screen to select a photo from your computer.

4. Once you select the photo, you can pan or zoom using the controls on this screen, as shown in the following screenshot:

5. Click **Apply** to save your changes.

6. Your new photo should immediately show up on the **Delve** home page. It might take a couple of hours though for the photo to be reflected in other Microsoft 365 workloads.

That's it! You just saw how to change your profile photo in Microsoft 365 from the Delve profile page.

To change your profile photo in Teams, follow these steps:

1. Open Teams in the desktop app or the browser.
2. Click your profile photo in the top-right corner.
3. Click the **Change picture** link under your profile name.
4. Click **Upload picture**, as shown in the following screenshot:

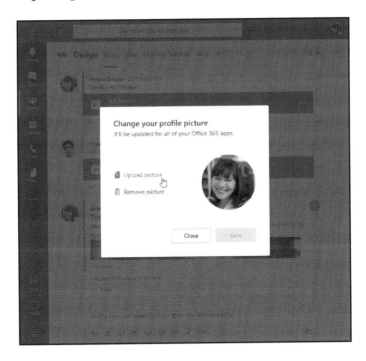

5. Select the new photo.
6. Click **Save**.

That's it! This will update your profile photo in Teams. Just like Delve, changes made to the profile photo from within Teams also sync across the other Microsoft 365 workloads.

How it works...

Both Delve and Teams let you change the profile photo in one single place and then sync it across all workloads. Note that once you change your profile photo from these workloads, it may take up to 24 hours for it to reflect across other workloads. Until the new picture is synchronized, you will continue to see the old photo in these workloads.

See also

- Chapter 11, *Microsoft Teams*

Updating your profile information

Your profile properties help you to showcase your credentials, skills, and interests to others in your organization. Besides, they help others to easily find you through search. In this recipe, we will see how you can keep your profile information up to date. As an example, we will add the **SEO Marketing** skill to our existing profile.

Getting ready

Delve should have been enabled by your organization for you to be able to make these changes. Also, some organizations like to control the profile properties that are allowed to be directly updated by the users. For you to be able to make updates to your profile properties, your organization should have not locked these properties from being edited.

How to do it...

To update your skills in Delve, follow these steps:

1. Browse to your profile page in Delve, as described in an earlier recipe in this chapter, *Navigating to your Delve profile page*.
2. Click the **Update profile** button located below the profile picture.

When you are viewing the Delve profile page for someone else in your organization, you will see a **View profile** button instead of the **Update profile** button that you see on your Delve profile page.

3. Click the **Skills and expertise** link, as shown in the following screenshot:

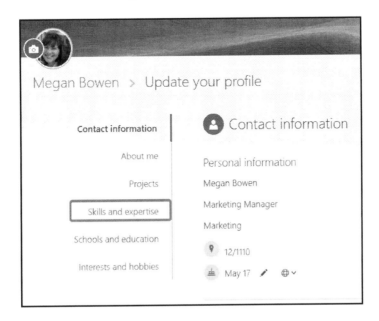

4. Type your skill and click **Add skill**:

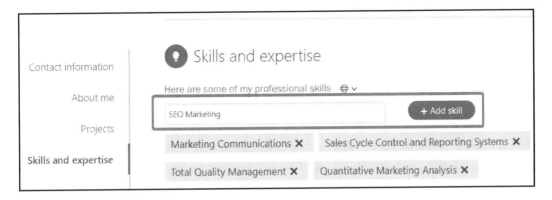

5. That's it! The newly added skill will now show up along with the existing skills. As long as the privacy setting for this section is public, anyone viewing your profile will also see this newly added skill right away:

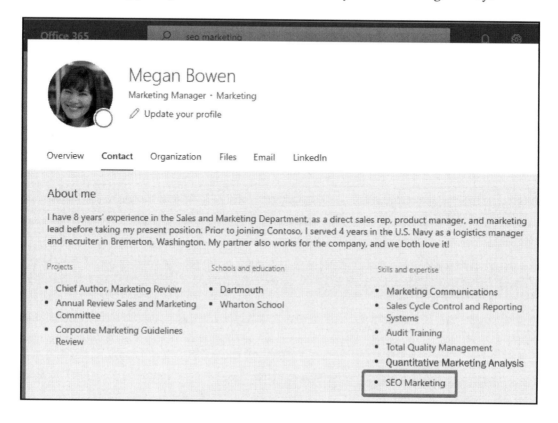

6. A Microsoft 365 search for `SEO Marketing` will now also bring back your profile in the search results. This is depicted in the following screenshot. Please note, however, that it might take a little bit of time before the search crawler re-crawls your profile and updates the search index. Please refer to the *How it works...* section of the *Advanced Search in SharePoint Online* recipe in `Chapter 8`, *Search in Microsoft 365,* for details on how the search crawler works:

Congratulations! You just learned how to update your profile. Among other benefits, keeping your profile updated helps others in your organization to easily find you.

How it works...

The **Delve** profile page contains the following sections that let you view and/or edit various aspects of your contact and profile information:

- **Contact information**: This section contains information such as your name, title, department, location, email, and phone number. Most of this information is usually maintained by your organization's IT/HR departments through external systems and is not editable from here. As shown in the following screenshot, you will see a small pencil icon next to the properties that you are allowed to edit. For each property, Delve will also show you whether that property is visible only to you or if it's also visible to others who view your profile from your organization. There are some properties, such as your birthday, for which you can change the privacy. As also shown in the following screenshot, for properties where you can edit the privacy, you will be able to specify whether this property is private or if it's visible to others:

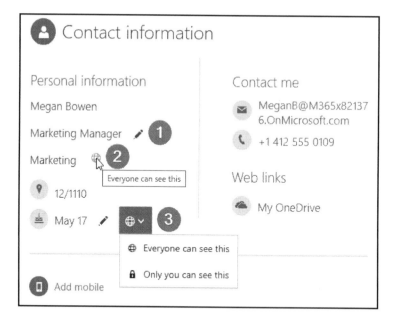

- **About me**: This is a short blurb about you.
- **Projects**: This is where you can enter the names of various projects that you have worked on in the past. You can choose whether your projects should only be visible to you or visible to others in your organization.

- **Skills and expertise**: This is where you can mention your professional skills and things that others can reach out to you for.
- **Schools and education**: You can mention the schools you've attended here.
- **Interests and hobbies**: Here, you can mention the things that you like to do in your leisure time. Again, you can set the privacy of this section.

Remember also that properties from your profile are only searchable if their privacy is set to public. If you set a property to be visible only to you, it will not be indexed and will therefore not be brought back as part of the search results.

Also, for each profile property, your organization can control the following:

- Whether or not it is displayed on the Delve profile page
- Whether or not it is changeable by you
- The default privacy setting for it
- Whether or not you can change that privacy setting

See also

- The *Advanced Search in SharePoint Online* recipe in Chapter 8, *Search in Microsoft 365*
- The *Finding experts and people* recipe in Chapter 8, *Search in Microsoft 365*

Grouping documents through boards

As mentioned earlier in this chapter, Delve uses **Office Graph** to surface content for you from all over Microsoft 365. **Boards** in Delve help you to better organize related content and share it with others in your organization.

This recipe will show you how to create a board in Delve and thus share related content from that board with others. For our scenario, we will create a new board to organize the marketing campaigns within our organization.

Getting ready

The only requirement for you to be able to create boards is that your organization should have enabled Delve for you.

How to do it...

To create a board in Delve, follow these steps:

1. Browse to your Delve profile page or the Delve home page to view a list of relevant documents.

2. Click on the manage boards icon for the document that you would like to add to the board, as shown in the following screenshot:

3. This opens the **Manage boards** screen with a text box toward the bottom to enter the name of your board:

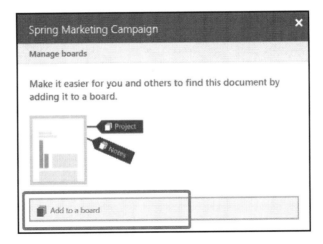

4. As shown in the following screenshot, you will see a list of existing boards as you start typing the name in this text box:

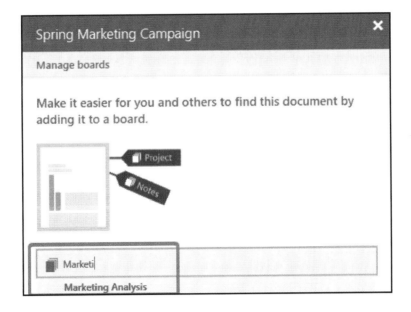

5. You can then select an existing board to add the document to it or create a new one if you did not find a match. Since we did not find a match for **Marketing Campaigns**, we will continue typing the board name and then press the *Enter* key when done. This creates the new board and adds the document to it.

6. This will also add it to your Delve favorites list so the new board appears in the **Boards** section toward the bottom of the left menu, as shown in the following screenshot:

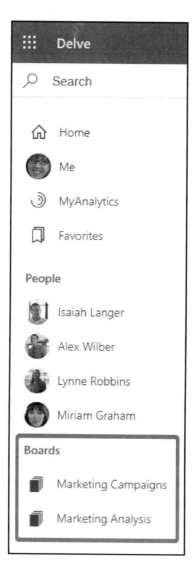

7. From within Delve, we can also search for other relevant documents and add them to the board we just created, as shown in the following screenshot:

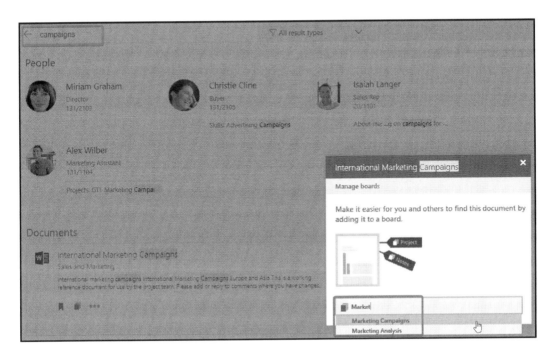

 Note that Delve will also return, as part of the search results, any boards whose names match the search term. In the preceding screenshot, since we searched for the term `campaigns`, the results will also return our newly created Marketing Campaigns board. While at the time of writing, boards are specific to Delve, Microsoft is working toward integrating boards with other workloads in Microsoft 365 with support of additional content types.

8. If you now click on the board in the **Boards** section in the left menu, you will see all related content in one place as part of the new board that you just created. The following screenshot shows the Marketing Campaigns board that we just created:

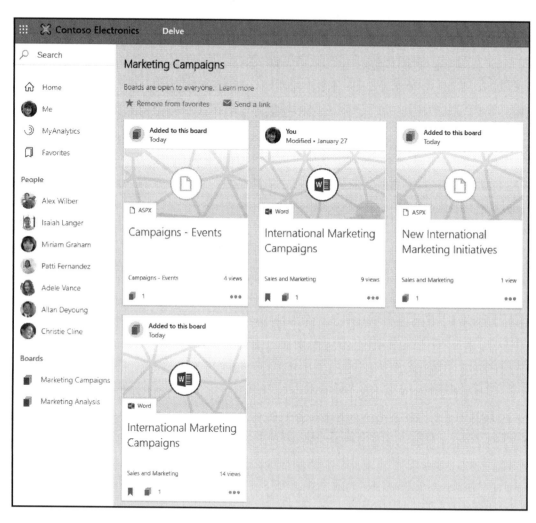

9. Boards are viewable by everyone in your organization. This means that anyone in your organization can search for boards and view related content that is part of the board. You can also directly share boards with others by clicking the **Send a link** option from the top of your board. Doing so will open an email with a link to the board. You can also copy a link to the board from the browser address bar and then share it with others in your organization.

Congratulations! You just learned how to create a board in Delve so you can organize all related content in one single place and share it with others in your organization.

How it works...

Boards are a great way to group related content and then share it with others. Remember that boards are public, in that as soon as you create them, anyone in the organization can view them via the following means:

- Through search results in Delve
- By clicking **Manage boards** on a document card for a document that's already part of a board
- Through the auto-complete results on the **Manage boards** screen, when trying to add a document to a board
- Through a direct link to the board that could have been emailed to them

Once they find a board, they can permanently add it to their favorites. Doing so will start showing the board under the **Boards** heading in the left-hand navigation menu in their Delve.

It is important to note that even though boards are public, documents within those boards are governed by permissions defined for them. This means that once you click on a board to view the documents within it, whether or not you will see a specific document from within that board will depend on your permissions for that document itself. Even though your co-workers may have added various documents to that board, you will only see the documents that you have access to via individual permissions for each of them. For this reason, different viewers of a board may see different documents on it, depending on which documents from that board they have access to.

Microsoft 365 Groups 10

The core objective of Microsoft 365 is to enable collaboration between teams and team members. This common theme can be seen across all Microsoft 365 tools. Every Microsoft 365 service offers a unique capability.

The beauty of a Microsoft 365 group is that it takes the best elements of each service and provides a collaborative area for a group of people or a team. So, when you create a Microsoft 365 group, you get the following:

- A shared conversation space where team conversations are stored
- A shared calendar where team members can book their meetings
- File storage to save and share all team documents, spreadsheets, and so on
- A notebook to capture and share meeting agendas and notes
- A new workspace to share group reports

It also means that you do not have to create separate instances of these services for your team, nor do you have to go through the pain of granting each member access to these separate service instances.

Creating a Microsoft 365 group creates these service instances automatically and once you add members to the group, they are automatically added to each of these services.

Microsoft 365 groups can be created in several ways. You can create a group *directly* via Outlook, as described in *Creating a group recipe* in this chapter.

Microsoft 365 groups are created *indirectly* when you do the following:

1. Create a planner in Microsoft 365—for more info, go to `https://m365book.page.link/groups-planner`.

2. Create a group in Yammer—for more info, go to `https://m365book.page.link/groups-yammer`.

3. Create a group in Power BI—for more info, go to `https://m365book.page.link/groups-powerbi`.

4. Create a group in Microsoft Dynamics 365—for more info, go to `https://m365book.page.link/groups-dynamics`.

5. Create a team in Microsoft Teams—for more info, go to `https://m365book.page.link/groups-teams`.

6. Create a modern team site in SharePoint Online—for more info, go to `https://m365book.page.link/groups-sharepoint`.

Technically speaking, we can, therefore, say that Microsoft 365 Group is a cross-application membership service in Microsoft 365 that has other inbuilt workloads associated with it, such as a SharePoint team site, a Yammer group, a shared Exchange mailbox, Planner, Power BI, and OneNote.

 Any Microsoft 365 subscription that has **Exchange Online** and **SharePoint Online** will support groups. To find out more about Microsoft 365 plans, go to `https://m365book.page.link/m365-plans`.

In this chapter, you will learn about the following:

- Creating a group
- Deleting a group
- Joining a group
- Leaving a group
- Adding members to a group
- Removing members from a group
- Having conversations
- Booking meetings
- Sharing files
- Collaborating on a notebook

Creating a group

A group in Microsoft 365 refers to an entity in **Azure Active Directory** that grants shared resources to a set of people (known as members). Members get access to common resources, such as a group mailbox, a group calendar, shared file storage, permissions, and so on, as soon as they are added to the group. Groups make collaboration easy.

In the old days, you had to request the IT department to create a distribution list (which lets you email several people by using a single recipient address) or a security group (to manage permissions to resources). A Microsoft 365 group provides you with the benefits of both distribution lists and a security group. In fact, it provides you with more features than distribution lists and security groups combined. On top of that, end users can create and manage Microsoft 365 groups themselves without needing the IT department's support.

In this recipe, you will learn how to create a group.

Getting ready

The ability to create Microsoft 365 groups depends on the model adopted by the organization, as shown here:

Model	Advantages
Open (default)	Users can create their own groups.
IT-led	Users request the Microsoft 365 administrator (usually part of the IT department) to create one for them.
Controlled	Group creation is restricted to specific people, teams, or services.

A Microsoft 365 group can be created directly via the Outlook client, Outlook Web Access, or the Outlook mobile app. We will demonstrate the steps that you need to follow using Outlook Web Access. There are also indirect ways of provisioning Microsoft 365 groups, which we will learn about in the coming chapters.

How to do it...

Microsoft 365 groups appear at the lower left-hand corner of your Outlook profile. Here, it will list all the Microsoft 365 groups you are a member of. To create a new group, perform the following steps:

1. In the **Groups** section on the left, and click on **New group** as shown:

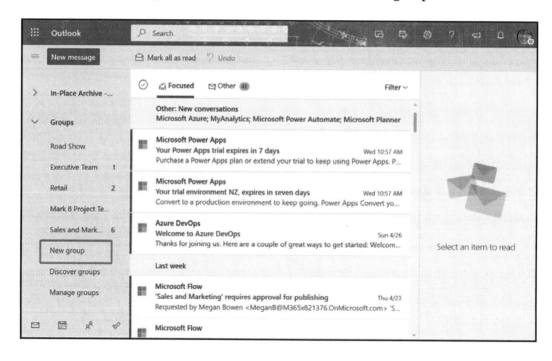

2. Provide a **Group name** and **Description**:

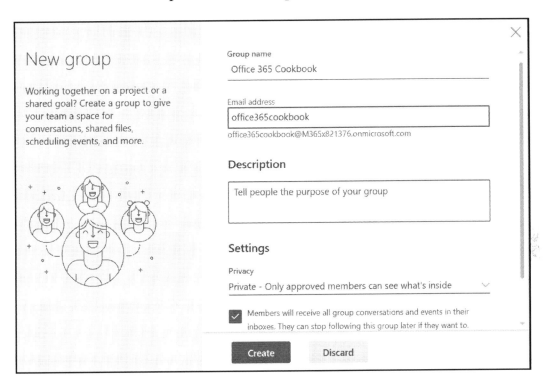

3. Microsoft 365 creates a group email address based on the group name. You can change the email address if you like.

4. Next, specify the **Privacy** option.

"Public" groups will let anyone in the organization join your group. Users can see the group members and also contribute to the group files. "Private" groups will require the group owner's approval in order for someone to join the group. The creator of the group becomes the group owner by default.

5. Once you have filled in all the sections, click **Create**.

6. Your group is now ready to be shared with members. You can add other colleagues or even other groups. You should be able to invite people from outside your organization (if your organization allows this). You can add up to 1,000 members in one group. The following screenshot shows you how to do this:

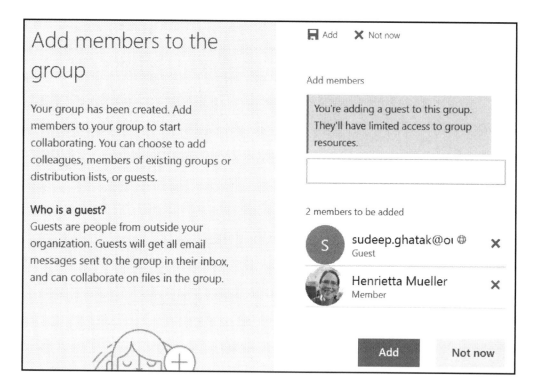

Now, your group is ready. The new group should start appearing under the **Groups** section. At this point, members will receive a welcome email with links to common group tasks.

How it works...

When a new group is created, the group gets an email address assigned to it. You can send a single email to the group email address and all the group members will receive it.

As mentioned previously, when a member is added to the group, they receive a welcome email. The welcome email looks as in the following screenshot:

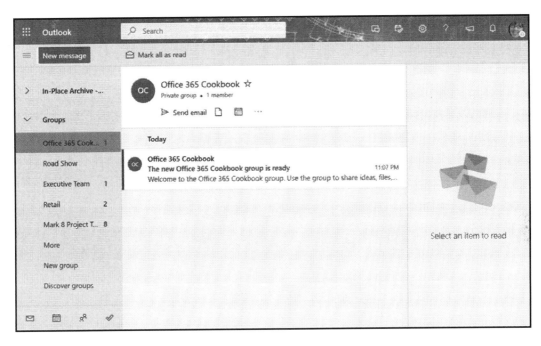

The email basically contains four links, each taking you to a specific group feature. Let's see what these four features are.

Group Emails

The Microsoft 365 group reserves a conversation area for the group where all group conversations are saved. All emails sent to the group email address will appear in the Group mailbox. These conversations remain in the group, even if the participants leave the group at some stage. Having conversations in one place is useful because new group members get access to all past conversations.

Group team site

The Microsoft 365 group provisions a SharePoint site for the group, where all the group files can be saved. The members of the group are granted access to the site. SharePoint offers additional capabilities, such as news articles, content pages, and so on. The following screenshot shows the landing page of the SharePoint site that is provisioned for the group:

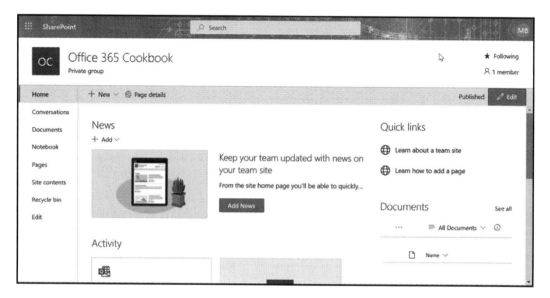

Sharing files

The SharePoint site that is provisioned with each Microsoft 365 group, comes with a default document library called Documents. The group files can be stored in this library, or in additional libraries. Lists can be provisioned by the group members. Staff outside the group will not have access to these files.

A group member can invite someone outside the group or even outside the organization (if adding users outside the organization is enabled).

Connecting your apps

The Microsoft 365 group lets you connect to a host of other apps from the Microsoft 365 store, as shown:

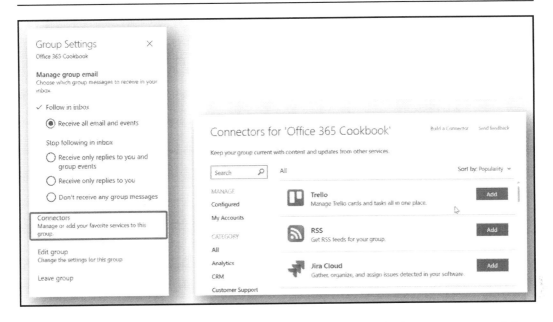

These apps can be used to facilitate tasks within the group. For instance, you could add the **Twitter** connector to receive tweets from an account or track certain hashtags.

See also

- The *Creating a group using Teams* recipe in Chapter 11, *Microsoft Teams*
- The *Creating a Yammer group* recipe in Chapter 12, *Yammer – The Enterprise Social Network*
- The Creating a group using Planner recipe in Chapter 17, *Planner*

Deleting a group

Groups are created with a specific objective in mind. Once the objective is achieved, the group can be deleted to free up system resources. It is recommended that you move any documents that you might need in the future to another location before deleting the group.

In this recipe, we will learn how to delete a group.

Getting ready

Microsoft 365 users can only delete groups created by them. You can do this via the Outlook client, Outlook Web Access, or the Outlook mobile app.

How to do it...

On Outlook Web Access, you can see all the Microsoft 365 groups that you are part of in the lower left-hand side navigation section. Follow these steps to delete a Microsoft 365 group:

1. Select the group you want to delete and click on the **Settings** symbol next to the group members:

2. This should bring up the **Group Settings** pane. Click on **Edit group**, as shown:

3. Click on the **Delete group** link at the bottom of the pane.

After completing this step, you have now deleted a group.

How it works...

Deleting a group is a permanent action. It deletes all conversations, files, notebooks, and tasks. There is no concept of a group recycle bin, where you can go to restore the group. However, the administrator has the option of restoring the deleted group within 30 days.

If you want to restore a Microsoft 365 group that got deleted, follow the instructions provided in this article:

```
https://m365book.page.link/m365-restore
```

See also

- The *Leaving* a group recipe in this chapter

Joining a group

Before creating a new group, it is worth checking whether another group has already been created for the same purpose. If a group already exists and is public, you can join it straight away or ask the owner to add you if the group is private. This recipe will show you how to join a group.

Getting ready

You can join groups that are not created by you. On Outlook Web Access, if you right-click on **Groups** and click **Discover**, it lists all the groups in the organization. Some of these groups might be private, while others will be public.

How to do it...

To join a group, do the following:

1. Right-click on **Groups** and click **Discover**. This will bring up the **Discover** pane with a search box. Start typing the group name you would like to join, as shown here:

 Public groups will let you join immediately. **Private groups** will require the group owner's approval.

2. Click on **Request to join** or **Join**. If you are joining a private group, you will need to provide the reason for making the request, as shown here:

By clicking **Send**, your request to join the group will be logged and the group owner will take the appropriate action.

How it works...

If you wish to join a public group, you simply click **Join** and become a member of the group. You can then participate in group conversations and have access to group files.

In the case of a private group, the owner of the group receives an email informing them about your interest. They can then choose to grant you access or ignore your request. The email will look something like this:

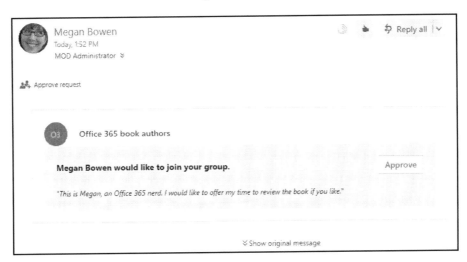

If the owner approves your request, you will receive a group welcome email.

See also

- The *Creating a group* recipe in this chapter

Leaving a group

If you think you do not need to contribute any more to the group, or you find that the group is not relevant to your work, you can leave it by following the instructions in this recipe.

Getting ready

You can leave a group at any time. You do not need any special permission to leave the group.

How to do it...

On Outlook Web Access, you can see all the Microsoft 365 groups that you are part of in the lower left-hand side navigation section. To leave a group, do the following:

1. Select the group you want to leave and click on the **Settings** symbol next to the group members
2. Click on **Leave group.**

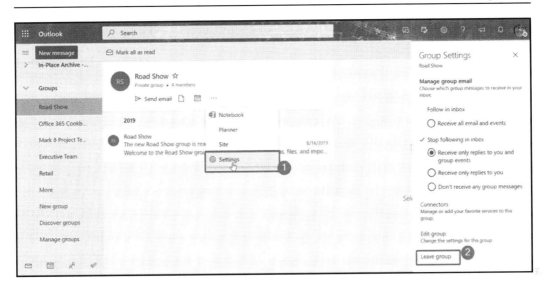

How it works...

When you click the **Leave group** option, all your permissions to the group resources are revoked. If you want to retain access to the group but just do not want to receive notifications about the group activities, you could update your **email preferences** in the group settings page, as shown in the following screenshot:

See also

- The *Deleting a group* recipe in this chapter

Adding members to a group

You can add members while creating a group or after the group is created. The members will gain access to all the group resources as soon as they are added. At times, you might need to invite members from outside your organization. Say you are organizing the staff Christmas party and you need to get input from a food vendor; you can invite them to the "Christmas Party" group so that they can participate in the conversations in the group. To add new members to the group, follow the instructions in this recipe.

Getting ready

If you are a group owner, you can add additional members to the group. You can also invite people from outside your organization (if your organization permits this).

How to do it...

You can add new members to the group while you are creating a new group. If the group has already been created, take the following steps:

1. Select the group and click on the number of members, as shown here:

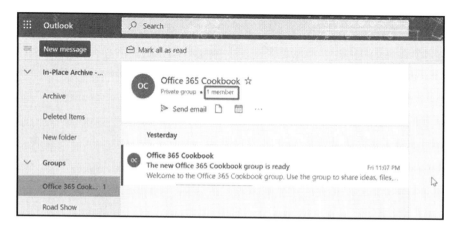

2. The new screen lets you add new members by searching for them in the company directory, as in the following screenshot:

3. Clicking on **Add members** brings up a text box that lets you type in the email address of the team member.
4. When you start typing the email address, the text box displays suggestions from the company's active directory. To invite external users, type in their email addresses:

5. When you select a member from the list, they get added to the group.

How it works...

Adding members grants them access to all the group resources. Microsoft 365 manages the permissions automatically for you.

 If you are adding external users, they receive an email at the email address that you provided. In order to log in to Microsoft 365, the user needs a Microsoft account. If the email address provided is a Microsoft account, the user can simply log in to Microsoft 365. If not, then the user is prompted to create a Microsft account using the email.

See also

- Creating a group recipe in this chapter
- *Removing members from a group* recipe in this chapter

Removing members from a group

As a group owner, if you think you do not need any input from any of your group members, you can remove them from the group. To remove one or more members from a group, perform the following steps.

Getting ready

If you are a group owner, you can add or remove members from the group. This will revoke their access from the group resources.

How to do it...

On Outlook Web Access, you can see all the Microsoft 365 groups that you are part of in the lower left-hand side navigation section. You can remove members from the group by following these steps:

1. Select the group and click on the number of members:

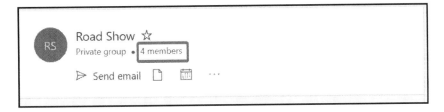

2. Remove the user from the group by clicking the **X** icon, as shown here:

How it works...

Removing a member (which includes external users) revokes their access from all the group resources. Microsoft 365 manages the permissions automatically.

See also

- The *Adding members to a group* recipe in this chapter

Having conversations

The conversation feature is powered by Exchange. All your group emails arrive in the group mailbox, which can be accessed by everyone in the group. The conversation area displays all the group emails in one place and lets you respond from within the group interface.

Getting ready

You will have access to the conversation space if you are a group member. Users who are not members of the group can, however, send an email to the group's email address.

How to do it...

On Outlook Web Access, you can see all the Microsoft 365 groups that you are part of in the lower left-hand side navigation section. To initiate a conversation, do the following:

1. Select the group, click **Send email**:

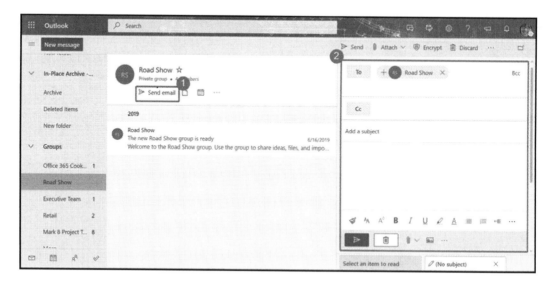

2. Type your message and press the **Send** icon.

How it works...

The conversation space is like a group mailbox, where everybody in the group can view all the conversations. All recent conversations appear at the top.

Conversations in a public group can be read and responded to by anyone in the organization. In the case of private groups, only group members can participate in conversations.

Conversations can include attachments, emojis, and rich text content. They also support @mentions to notify specific people of a message.

By default, conversations appear in the group's conversation area, but you can choose to receive conversations in your personal inbox by following the group by clicking on the **Follow** icon in the group team site, as you can see in the following screenshot:

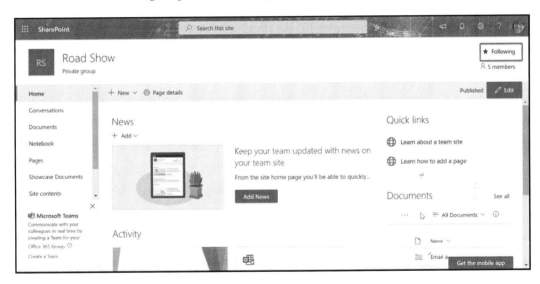

See also

- The *Booking meetings* recipe in this chapter
- The *Sharing files* recipe in this chapter
- The *Collaborating on a notebook* recipe in this chapter

Booking meetings

Sometimes, a situation requires all group members to come together to discuss their ideas. Meetings provide you with that platform. The meetings that you set appear in your calendar as a group meeting, alongside your personal meetings. The following are the instructions for how to book a group meeting.

Getting ready

You will have access to the group calendar if you are a group member. You can book group-specific meetings or group events using the group calendar.

How to do it...

On Outlook Web Access, you can see all the Microsoft 365 groups that you are part of in the lower left-hand side navigation section. To book a meeting, follow these steps:

1. Select the group and click on the **Calendar** icon:

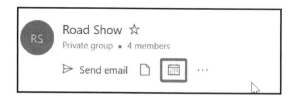

2. The screen will look as shown in the following screenshot:

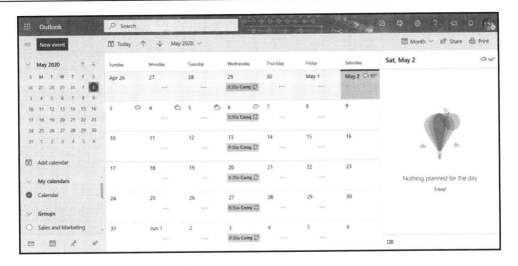

3. To book a new meeting, click on **New event**. Specify the event information, including the following:

- A title for the event
- The event location
- Participants
- The start time
- The end time
- Recurrence
- The meeting agenda

You can see these fields in the following screenshot:

4. Once the fields have been filled in, click **Send** to send the invite.

How it works...

The meeting created in the group's calendar appears when you select the group from the navigation pane:

The meetings from all the selected groups are superimposed on top of each other but coded in different colors:

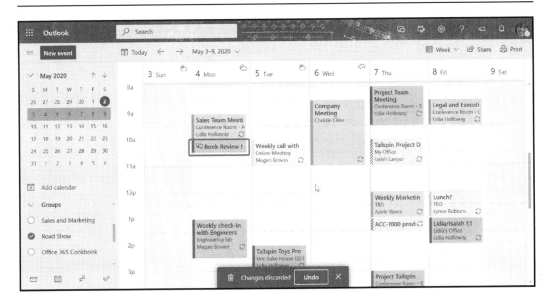

You can change the view to take a wider or closer look at your schedule:

See also

- The *Having conversations* recipe in this chapter
- The *Sharing files* recipe in this chapter
- The *Collaborating on a notebook* recipe in this chapter

Sharing files

Every group needs to collaborate by sharing digital assets. These can be images, documents, spreadsheets, or presentations. Uploading files to your group is always better than adding attachments in an email. In a group, you can share files and maintain versions of the files when they are edited. You can also restore files if they are deleted by a member.

Getting ready

Every Microsoft 365 group has a SharePoint site associated with it. All the group files are saved in the SharePoint database in one or more document libraries. Every group member has "contribute" access to the files.

How to do it...

On Outlook Web Access, you can see all the Microsoft 365 groups that you are part of in the lower left-hand side navigation section. To share files, do the following:

1. Select the group and click on the **Files** icon. This displays all the files stored in SharePoint's default **Documents** library:

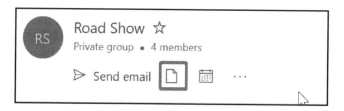

2. To add a new Office document (Word, Excel, or PowerPoint), click on **New**:

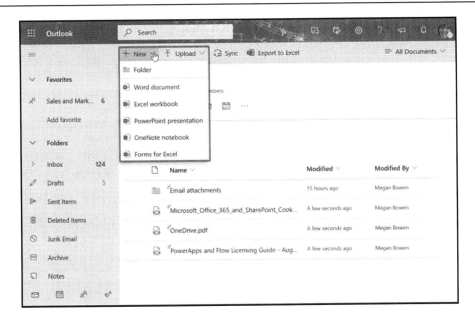

3. The new file will be created in the library.

4. You can also upload an existing document by clicking on the **Upload** option.

5. To download the file, click on it and then click on the **Download** option from the ribbon or the context menu:

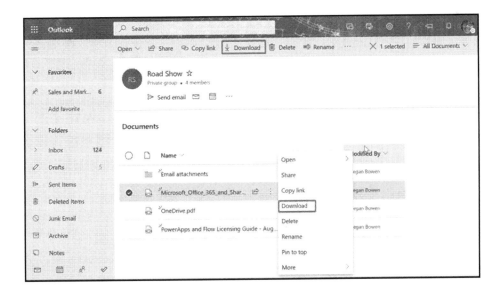

Note that you cannot delete files using the **Files** tab from within a Microsoft 365 group. These files can be deleted from SharePoint. The process is explained in the next section.

How it works...

The **Files** management in Groups is limited when accessed from within the Microsoft 365 group. But the same files can also be accessed by going to the SharePoint site associated with the group. You can navigate to the SharePoint site by clicking on the **Site** menu option:

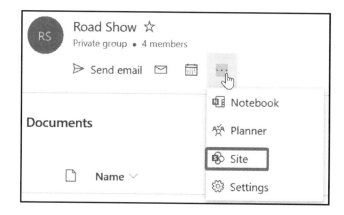

By navigating to SharePoint, you will not only have access to the default documents library but you can also create additional libraries, not to mention the other benefits it brings along, including the following:

- Versioning
- Metadata
- The recycle bin, and so on

The following is a screenshot of a SharePoint landing page provisioned for the group:

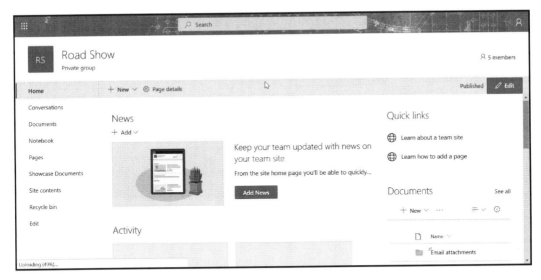

See also

- The *Viewing and editing documents in the browser* recipe in `Chapter 5`, *Document Management in SharePoint Online*

- The *Having conversations* recipe in this chapter

- The *Booking meetings* recipe in this chapter

- The *Collaborating on a notebook* recipe in this chapter

Collaborating on a notebook

Microsoft 365 provides a note-taking application to capture notes during meetings. OneNote lets you capture ideas in any form, including typed text, a link, an image, an embedded video, or even handwritten text. To collaborate on a writeup, follow the instructions in the next section.

Getting ready

Microsoft OneNote is primarily a note-taking application. Its simple user interface allows it to be used as a canvas or a notebook. It supports both handwriting and typed text. In OneNote, users can create notes that include text, tables, pictures, and drawings. You can add links to your notes with a web page, a link to Office documents, and more. Your work is automatically saved as you go along.

OneNote offers a very good platform for channeling your creativity. As a member of the Microsoft 365 group, you get access to a team notebook, which lets you create and share team notes and capture team meeting minutes.

How to do it...

The notes in OneNote can be organized in pages and sections. You can think of sections as chapters in a book. Each section can contain several pages. You get a blank notebook, to begin with:

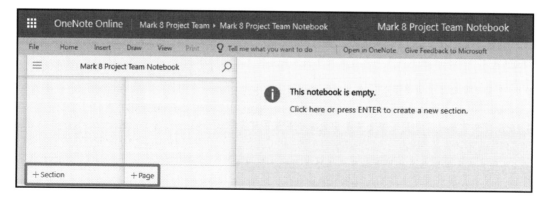

1. To create a section, click on **+ Section** and give it a name.
2. To create a page, click on **+ Page** and give it a name.
3. To draw a picture, go to the **Draw** tab and select **Pen**. Use your mouse or a pen (for touch screen devices) to draw.
4. Switch to the text mode by selecting **Text** and capture your notes.
5. Use formatting options, such as bullet points or to-do controls, accordingly:

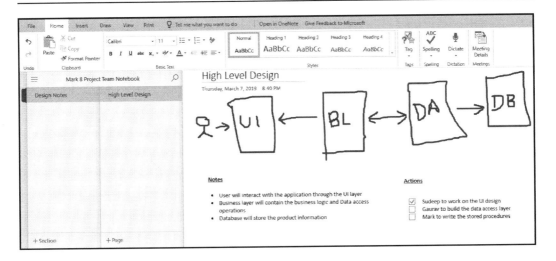

How it works...

OneNote lets you share your notebook with others. Anyone who has access to the notebook can see all the sections and pages. The Microsoft 365 group creates a notebook that the entire team can access. You can use this to capture, compile, and share minutes, thoughts, and ideas with your teammates. You can switch between your notebooks by clicking on the three lines as shown in the following screenshot:

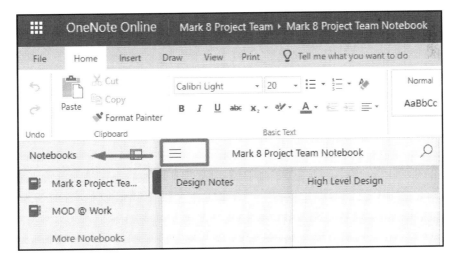

See also

- The *Having conversations* recipe in this chapter
- The *Booking meetings* recipe in this chapter
- The *Sharing files* recipe in this chapter

11
Microsoft Teams

Microsoft Teams is your hub for collaboration in Microsoft 365. While it provides a chat-based workspace that lets you have instant threaded communication, video chats, and meetings with your peers, it also provides a collaboration space to work together and share information. Teams' deep integration with SharePoint and Microsoft 365 groups can change the way your team members communicate, collaborate, and interact with others. The collaboration experience is further enriched by the integration capabilities that Teams provides with other applications.

Those of you who are familiar with Skype for Business (Microsoft's instant communication application) might wonder what's the difference between Skype for Business and Teams. One of the key aspects of Teams is that, unlike Skype for Business, conversations within Teams are threaded around a specific topic. So, conversations always have a context. Besides conversations, Teams also brings together other Microsoft 365 collaboration services, such as groups, Planner, OneDrive, and SharePoint. Teams also supports connectors to numerous third-party applications, such as Trello, GitHub, Evernote, SurveyMonkey, and so on.

In this chapter, you will learn about the following:

- Installing Teams
- Creating a new team
- Adding a member
- Joining a team
- Leaving a team
- Deleting a team
- Creating channels and tabs
- Initiating conversations via posts

- Scheduling a meeting
- Sharing files
- Searching within Teams
- Adding a connector

Installing Teams

Teams can be accessed from both the web browser (which doesn't require any installation) and the Windows app (which requires an installation). There are some benefits to installing the Windows client as some of the features are not supported on the web (although the web client is catching up fast with its app counterpart). One key difference between the two versions is that the web version requires you to be logged in to your Office account in order to receive notifications. The Teams client, on the other hand, runs in the background, even while you are working on a different application. So, the user receives notifications about team activities and individual messages. Once installed, new updates are applied automatically to the Teams client. It checks for updates every time the client is launched.

In this section, we will learn how to install the Teams app.

Getting ready

To access the Teams app, you need the appropriate Microsoft 365 license plan as described in Chapter 1, *Overview of Microsoft 365*

Microsoft also provides a Commercial Cloud Trial offer for existing Microsoft 365 users in your organization. They can try the product for 1 year without being licensed for Teams.

How to do it...

To install Teams, follow these instructions:

1. Go to www.office.com.
2. Sign in with your work account as described in Chapter 1.

3. Click on **Teams** (shown in the following screenshot):

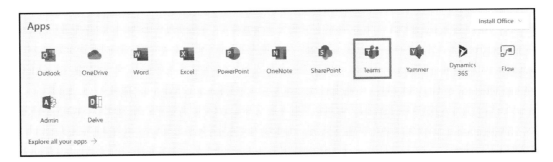

4. You will be prompted to download the desktop version by a pop-up screen, as in the following screenshot:

5. Click the **Get the Windows app** button to get the client version of Teams.

This will download the client application installer for you. Running the installer will guide you through the installation process and install Teams for you. You can then sign in to the Teams desktop app by using your organization credentials.

 If you choose to stay on the web app, you can download the app later by clicking on the **Get App** icon in the lower left-hand pane of your Teams web application interface.

How it works...

Although Teams has a web and client version, the user experience on the web and desktop applications is strikingly similar. The ability to join video calls and share your screen is supported on both the desktop app and the web version (only Edge and Chrome are supported at the moment). However, some features, such as the ability to host "live events," are only available on the desktop version:

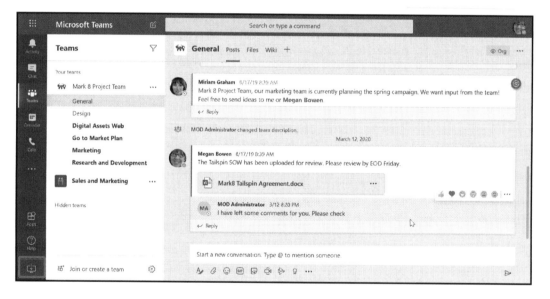

Teams Top Panel

The Top panel in the Teams interface provides the following options:

1. Allows you to navigate back and forth between Team views.
2. Allows you to compose a new chat message (explained in the Chat section that follows).
3. Allows you to perform a search and invoke commands (explained in the *Searching within Teams* recipe in this chapter).
4. Allows you to change organization: you will see other organizations in this section if you are invited to collaborate with external teams outside of your organization.
5. Clicking the profile picture provides additional settings, such as:
   - **Setting availability** (Available, Busy, so on)
   - **Setting a status message** (for example, I am working from home today)
   - **Accessing Saved messages** (discussed in the *Initiating conversations via posts* recipe in this chapter
   - Updating **General Settings** such as:
     - Choosing a Teams skin color
     - Setting default audio devices for Team calls
     - Managing notifications (discussed in the *Creating channels and tabs* recipe in this chapter
     - Setting keyboard shortcuts for common Teams tasks

Teams Left Panel

The panel on the left lets you navigate through various features within Teams. Please note that some feature icons might be hidden under ... icon. Let's look at some of these features in more detail.

Activity

Clicking on the **Activity** tab takes you to the activity feed. This feed rolls up notifications related to all your team channels and team conversations and one-on-one chats or calls. A notification appears in your activity feed when someone does the following:

- Mentions you
- Mentions a team you are part of
- Mentions the channel of the team you are part of
- Replies to your post
- Likes your post
- Adds you to a team
- Makes you a team owner
- Leaves you a chat message
- Calls you (and you missed the call)

If you have any unread notifications and you are not in your activity feed, a red circle with a number appears next to the **Activity** icon:

Under **Activity | Feed | My Activity,** you will see all the messages that **you** posted on any of your Team channels

Clicking the **filter** icon next to the Feed icon displays a text box that lets you type free text, thereby filtering the search results:

You can also click on the **...** icon to filter the search results by a certain type:

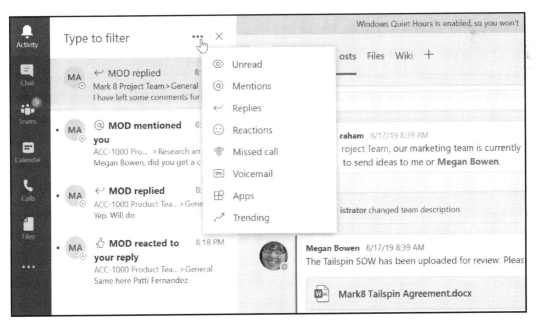

Clicking the *gear* icon next to the *filter* icon takes you to Team settings page, as described

Chat

The **Chat** tab lets you initiate a chat with an individual or a group. You can have threaded conversations with one or more people. You can also share files by uploading the files in the chat window or just by dragging them to the conversation text window. The files are automatically uploaded to OneDrive and participants receive a link to access them:

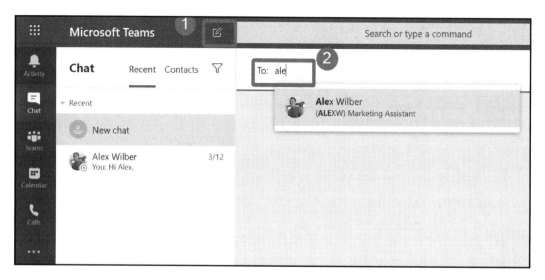

Teams

The **Teams** tab displays all the teams that you are part of. It also lets you join or create a team:

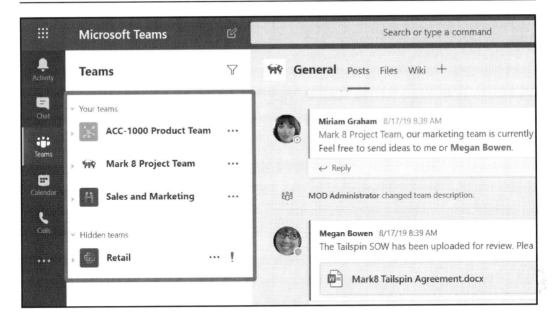

Every team that you create has a default **General** channel to start with. Channels let you create focus areas, such as a specific topic, department, or project. We'll learn about channels shortly.

If you are a team owner, you can add more channels:

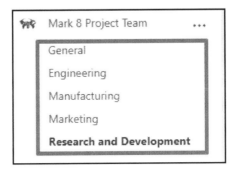

Each channel gets its own area for posts and a storage place for channel-specific files in SharePoint:

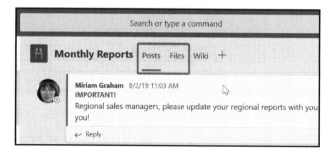

We will learn about channels in the *Creating channels and tabs* recipe in this chapter.

Calendar

The **Calendar** option lets you schedule team meetings or audio/video calls with an individual or team. Read more about the **Calendar** in the *Scheduling a meeting* recipe

Calls

The **Call** option lets you make audio/video calls with an individual or team. Clicking on this tab, takes you to the **Speed dial** page where you can see people you frequently interact with. You can add people to your speed dial for quicker access:

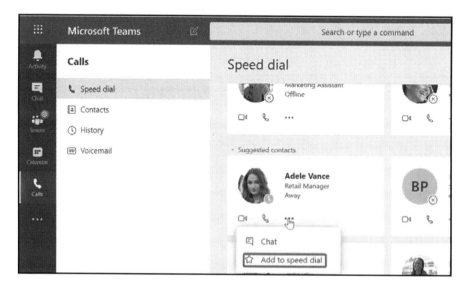

You can also create a group to logically club them based on your interactions with them as shown in the following screenshot. To add people into a group, you need to create the group first (**1**) and then add people (**3**) into the group (**2**):

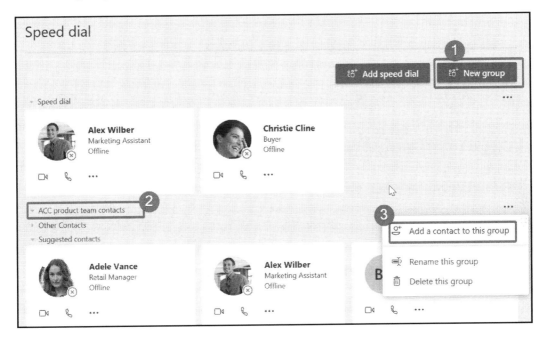

You can access your contact list by selecting **Contacts**. You can add internal or external contacts from this screen:

You can check the history of calls that you placed or received using the **History** link.

Teams also support **voicemails**. People can leave a voicemail for you if you are unable to attend the call. The good thing about voicemails is that it even generates a transcript of the message. So, you can choose to read the message instead of listening to it. This is especially handy when someone leaves you a voicemail while you are in a meeting. Instead of attending the call, you can glance through the transcript of the voicemail.

Read more about **Calls** in the *Scheduling a meeting* recipe.

Files

Finally, the **Files** option displays all the files that you have access to or files that have been shared with you in Teams, OneDrive for Business, or SharePoint. The **Location** column displays where the file actually resides (including other cloud locations like dropbox, google drive, etc.)

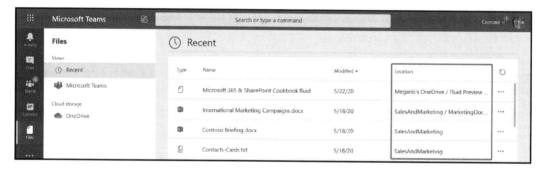

You can access your OneDrive files by clicking on the OneDrive link on the left. You can move or copy your files from OneDrive to Teams using the context menu.

There's more...

Microsoft Teams also comes with a free version that can be used for chats, file sharing, and video calling. The features that it offers have been listed on the Office website. You can access this at `https://m365book.page.link/teams-free`.

Microsoft Teams supports keyboard shortcuts and might be handy for those who prefer the keyboard. You can find Teams keyboard shortcuts for Windows and Mac listed in the following link: `https://m365book.page.link/teams-shortcuts`.

Creating a new team

Microsoft Teams is your one-stop-shop for accessing all your Microsoft 365 applications. Teams enables collaboration; team members achieve more together when all their chats, meetings, files, and apps reside in a single workspace. Creating a team does a lot in the background. It provisions a SharePoint site for you, along with a Microsoft 365 group for the team. Teams lets you connect with other services within Microsoft 365, as well as with third-party apps (via connectors).

In this recipe, we will learn how to create a new team.

Getting ready

You should be able to create a new team as long as your organization has assigned you a valid Teams license and has enabled Team creation.

How to do it...

Follow these steps to create a new team:

1. Click on the **Join or create a team** option:

2. Clicking **Join or create a team** actually takes you to the Join or create a team screen where you can join one of the existing teams, join a team with a code, search for an existing team to join or, create a new team.

3. If you Create a new team, you can choose to create a new team (which creates a Microsoft 365 group in the background) or connect the team to an existing Microsoft 365 group. Those of you who are already using Microsoft 365 groups can use the latter option to connect your existing group to Teams:

 Creating a Microsoft 365 group does not create a team; however, creating a team creates a group. The Microsoft 365 group created as a result of a team doesn't appear in Outlook by default. Administrators will need to run a script if this feature is required.

4. You will then be asked whether you want to create a private, public, or organization-wide team.
5. Give your team a name.

Now, you have created your own team.

How it works...

We just learned how to create a new Team from scratch. The other option lets you convert an existing Microsoft 365 group into a team. As it turns out, Microsoft 365 groups were released before Microsoft Teams. So, this option allows you to upgrade to Teams, any such groups that were created before Teams was released. We will discuss this more in the next section.

Based on its privacy, a Team can be of the following types:

- A private **team**: This is a restricted area that is only accessible to the team members.
- A public team: This Team is available to join for everyone in the organization.
- An **organization-wide team**: This adds all of the organization's staff to a team. Only global administrators can create organization-wide teams. You will automatically be added to an organization-wide team unless your administrator has explicitly disabled your Teams account.

There's more...

The following key considerations should be kept in mind while creating teams:

When you specify the team name while creating a Team, Microsoft 365 doesn't validate whether a Team with the same name already exists. It will instead let you create another one with the same name, as shown in the following screenshot:

The new team with the same name then appears in the Teams interface.

This poses a challenge because a SharePoint site is created for each Team and you cannot have two SharePoint sites with the same URL. In order to assign a separate storage space, Microsoft 365 adds a random number next to the Team name when provisioning the SharePoint site, which can then result in a lot of confusion. As an example, it created the following site for the second Team from the illustration above, `https://m365x263078.sharepoint.com/sites/`**`Sales774`**`/Shared%20Documents`.

It is, therefore, recommended that you check for an existing team before creating one using the search option on the team creation page, as shown here:

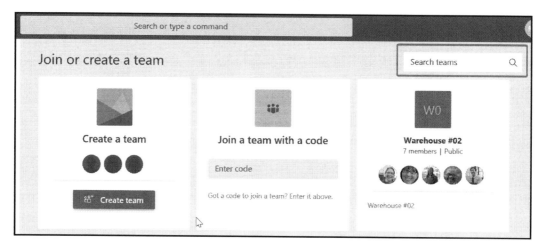

Team owners can assign an email address to each team channel. The email address cannot be changed or modified. The email address assigned is random and appears in your organization's global address list. This feature has some benefits, which we will see later.

See also

- The *Joining a team* recipe in this chapter
- The *Leaving a team* recipe in this chapter
- The *Adding a member* recipe in this chapter
- The *Removing a member* recipe in this chapter
- `Chapter 10,` Microsoft 365 Groups

Adding a member

You can add new members to an existing team. They can belong to the same organization or can be added as a guest from another organization. A team can hold up to 5,000 people.

Member of a team can have one of the following roles:

- **Owner**: The team owner manages the settings for the team. The owner can do the following:
    - Add and remove members.
    - Add guests.
    - Change team settings.
    - Restore deleted files or older versions.

 A team can have multiple owners.

- **Member**: Members are added to a team by the owner. Members can do the following:
    - Post messages.
    - View, upload, and change files.
    - Schedule team meetings.
- **Guest**: Guests are people outside your organization. They can only be invited by the team owner. They can post messages and share files with the team.

Follow the instructions provided in the next section to add a member to a team.

Getting ready

Members can be added to a team by the team owner. Only an owner can promote another member to the **Owner** role.

How to do it...

To add a new member:

1. Select **Teams** from the left-hand side pane.
2. Click on the **...** link next to the team name.
3. This brings up a context menu with an **Add member** option.
4. Type the name of the person you would like to add.
5. Change the role of the member to **Owner** (if you have owner privileges).

The team members section will look as follows:

How it works...

The new member automatically gets access to all the related Microsoft 365 services, such as SharePoint, Planner, and Microsoft 365 groups. The new member receives an introductory email after being added.

You, and other members of your Team, are notified via the **General** tab about new members being added to your team:

What a member or a guest can or cannot do is set by the team owner through the **Teams** settings:

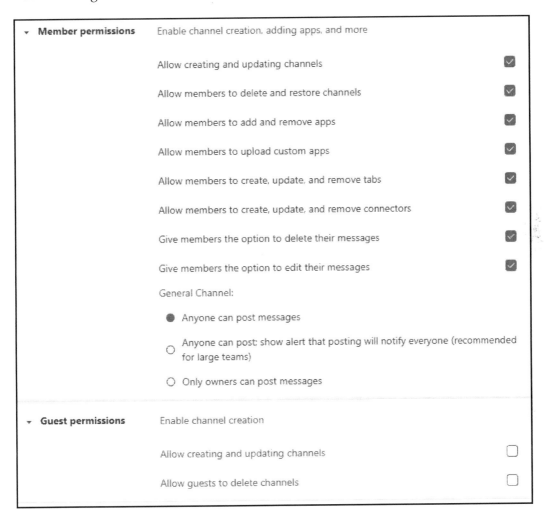

You can request to **Join** a Team even if you were not specifically added to it by an owner. We'll see how to join a team in the next topic.

See also

- The *Joining a team* recipe in this chapter
- The *Leaving a team* recipe in this chapter
- The *Removing a member* recipe in this chapter

Joining a team

You can join an existing team by either using the **Join** option (in the case of public teams) or asking the owner to add you as a member (in the case of private teams). This recipe will show you how to join a new team.

Getting ready

You are added to an organization-wide team as soon as you are added to your organization's Microsoft 365 tenant. For public and private teams, you need to take the following steps.

How to do it...

To join a team, do the following:

1. Select **Teams** from the left-hand side pane.
2. To join a public team, click on the **Join or create a team** option.
3. You should see all the publicly available teams.
4. Click on the **Join team** option to join the team.
5. To join private teams, the team owner will have to either add you as a member or send you a team code. A team code can be generated by going to **Team | Settings | Team code**.
6. Click the 3 dots next to the team name -> **Manage team | Settings | Expand Team code | Generate**

Guest users won't be able to join a private team using a code. They need to be added explicitly by the owner.

How it works...

After joining a team, you can participate in team conversations. You can also view conversations that have taken place in the past. When you are part of a team, you can access all the channels within that team. Once you have joined it, the team starts to appear in the left-hand side navigation pane along with the other teams you are part of.

See also

- The *Leaving a team* recipe in this chapter
- The *Adding a member* recipe in this chapter
- The *Removing a member* recipe in this chapter

Leaving a team

If you think you no longer need to contribute to a team or you find that a team is no longer relevant to you, you can leave the team. To leave a team, follow the steps provided in the next section.

Getting ready

You do not need special permission to leave a private or public team.

 You cannot leave an organization-wide team on your own. You will need to ask the administrator to remove you.

How to do it...

To leave a team:

1. Select **Teams** from the left-hand side pane.
2. Click on **...** next to the name of the team you want to leave.

3. Select the **Leave the team** option from the context menu, as shown here:

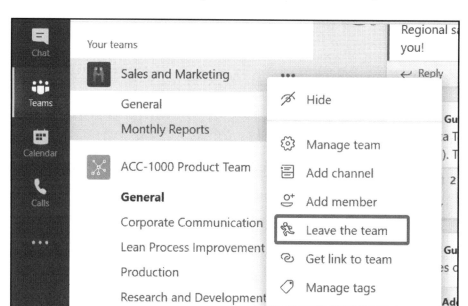

How it works...

When you click **Leave the team**, all the permissions associated with that team and its channels are revoked. You also lose access to the underlying SharePoint site and all the content within it.

See also

- The *Deleting a team* recipe in this chapter
- The *Joining a team* recipe in this chapter

Deleting a team

You need to be the owner in order to delete a team. In addition to deleting a Team from the Teams app, you can also delete it via the Outlook client, Outlook Web Access, or the Outlook mobile app.

Getting ready

You need to be the owner in order to delete a team. You can delete a team via the Outlook client, Outlook Web Access, or the Outlook mobile app.

How to do it...

1. To delete a team, do the following:
2. Click on **...** next to the name of the team you want to delete.
3. Select the **Delete the team** option from the context menu, as shown:

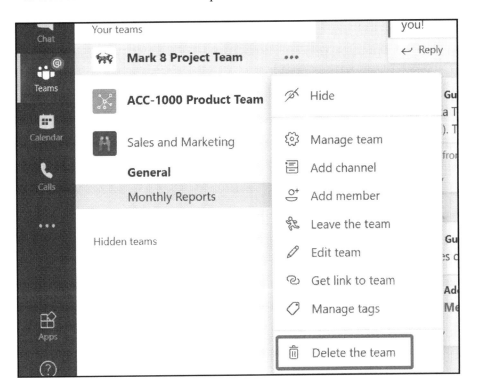

How it works...

By deleting a team, you lose all of its associated components, such as the team mailbox, calendar, SharePoint site, notebook, Planner tasks, and so on.

 The team owner or administrator can restore a deleted team within 30 days.

See also

- The *Leaving a team* recipe in this chapter
- The *Joining a team* recipe in this chapter

Creating channels and tabs

Channels are dedicated spaces that keep conversations and files around a topic together. Every team comes with a default channel named **General** but additional channels can be added. Every team supports up to 200 channels. All team conversations happen within a specific channel. The following section explains how you can create new channels and tabs.

Getting ready

Team owner can create new channels. The owner decides if members can create channels and tabs.

How to do it...

To add a channel:

1. Select **Teams** from the left-hand side pane.
2. Click on **...** next to the name of the team you want to add a channel to.
3. Select the **Add channel** option from the context menu, as shown:

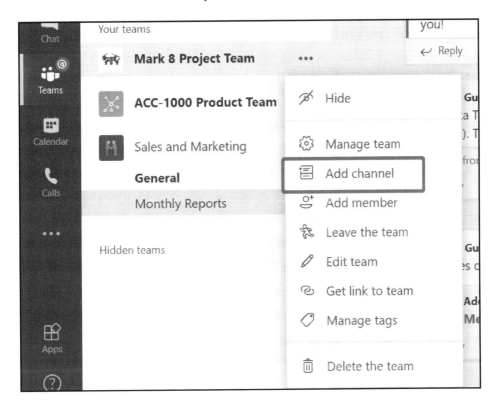

4. Provide a channel name and set the **Privacy** option:

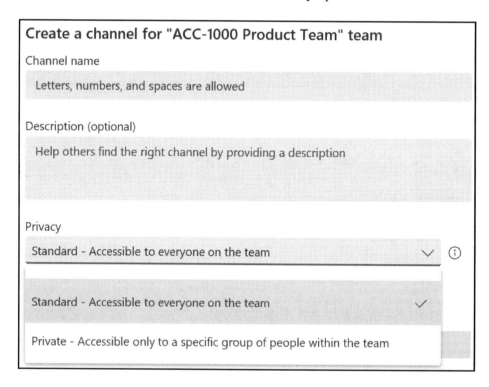

Adding a channel adds two tabs to the channel—one for conversations and the other for shared files.

Besides the standard apps, a channel lets you enhance the Teams experience by connecting other Microsoft 365 or third-party applications. You can use connectors for scenarios that include the following:

- Managing team backlog items in Trello
- Posting messages in your team channel using Microsoft Flow
- Enhancing team conversations using actionable cards

To add additional tabs, do the following:

1. Click on the + symbol next to the **Files** tab.
2. Choose an app from the list or search for it, as shown here:

3. Provide the details required for the specific app and click **Save**.

How it works...

Creating a channel provides you with a dedicated conversation area and a place to store all your files. Channels are public or private. All public channels in a team share a common SharePoint document library in a team site.

However, creating a private channel assigns you with a separate SharePoint site collection altogether. Owners or members of the private channel are the only ones who can access the channel.

Private channels appear with a lock icon (🔒) in front of the channel name.

Tabs in the channel let you connect to both Microsoft 365 as well as to connect to other third-party apps to your team. There are two types of tabs:

Static tabs provide a personalized experience to each individual (such as a tab for your personal notes in the channel).

Configurable tabs need you to provide additional configuration information while adding the app, such as the following:

- In order to add a Power BI dashboard, you need to specify the workspace name.
- In order to add an Excel app, you need to provide the worksheet name.

Tabs offer interactive web content to the user without them having to leave the team's interface.

Showing or hiding teams and channels

Keep your list of teams and channels tidy and relevant by hiding any teams or channels you don't want to see. Just click on the three dots (**...**) beside the team/channel name and select **Show** or **Hide**:

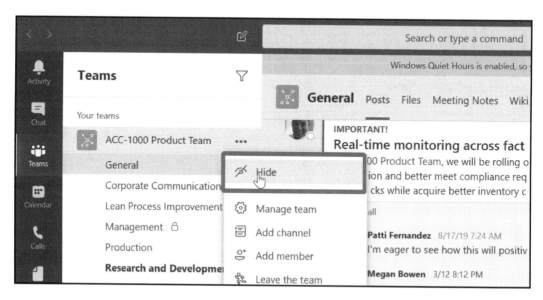

Hiding a team will remove it from your list of teams, but you can always access or show it again by expanding the **Hidden teams** section towards the bottom of the teams list. If you know you're a member of a team but you can't see it, you can scroll down to this section, locate your team, click the three dots next to it and then click Show to move it to the **Your teams** section:

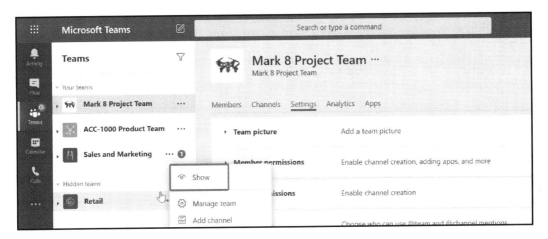

Managing notifications

There are, broadly, three types of notifications that you receive in teams.

A banner: This alert pops up on your device (on desktop, your web browser, or mobile) even when you are using another application:

In the feed: A badge notification appears on the icon:

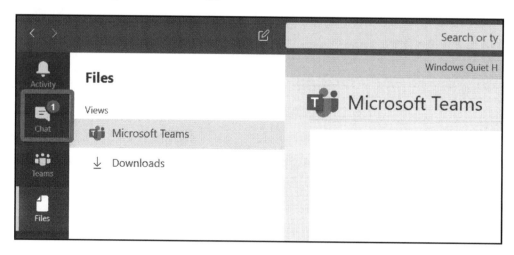

An email: A notification arrives in your inbox:

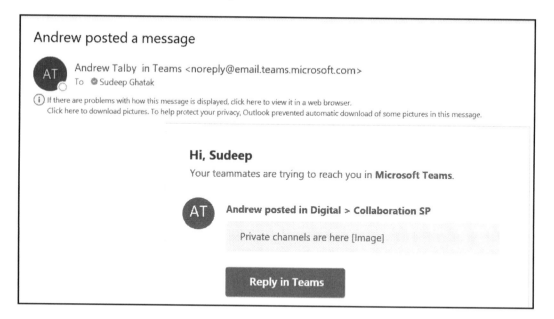

There are lots of different ways to access and manage these notifications in Teams.

A good place to start is via the notification settings—click your profile picture at the top-right of the screen (or initials if you don't have a profile picture), then go to **Settings** | **Notifications**. This is where you can turn your notifications (and their associated sounds) on and off and select how you would like them to display. There are lots of things you can turn on and off, so you can either set it up to your liking or just stick with the default:

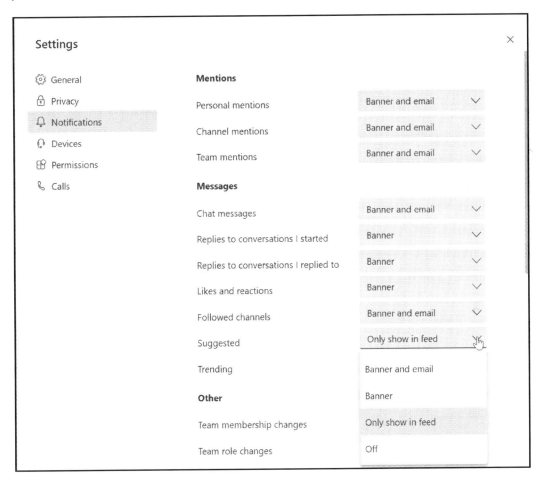

If you receive too many notifications, you can also reduce them by hiding a channel. Hidden channels will only show up in your list if a message is marked important or when someone @mentions you or the channel.

See also

- The *Initiating conversations via posts* recipe in this chapter
- The *Sharing files* recipe in this chapter

Initiating conversations via posts

Posts or conversations can be described as group chats where everyone in the team participates. Conversations are located in a team channel. They can be viewed by all members of the team. Teams attempts to reduce reliance on the more formal and conventional mode of communication—email. The following section provides steps for how to initiate a conversation.

Teams is great for conversations with your teammates:

- Conversations are persistent—your conversation history sticks around and you can go back to it later.
- You can share files with offline participants.
- You can add GIFs and memes.
- The conversations are searchable—search for files, content, or people.

Getting ready

We mentioned earlier that every team can have one or more channels. The **Posts** tab in the channel displays team conversations and other channel activity. All team members can view channel conversations and participate in them.

How to do it...

To initiate a conversation:

1. Select **Teams** from the left-hand side pane.
2. Click on **...** next to the name of the team that you want to post in.
3. Select a channel. You will see all the channel activity in the conversation area.

4. To participate in conversations, use the text box provided at the bottom, as shown in the following screenshot:

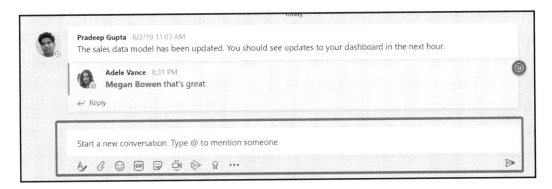

Conversations support @mentions, emojis, attachments, and video calling.

5. Press *Enter* or the ▷ symbol.
6. To edit a message, click on the **...** symbol and choose the **Edit** option.

The ⎄ option lets you save a message. You can search for saved messages later.

You can upvote a conversation by clicking on the like button, as shown:

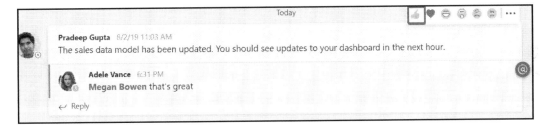

How it works...

The options available under the text box are configurable and can be switched on or off by your administrator. This can be done through the team's admin center.

Using @mentions is a way of notifying an individual or team of a message (shown in the following screenshot). When mentioned, the individual or team will receive a notification in their Microsoft Teams client. Using the **Reply** button will keep messages in the same conversation thread:

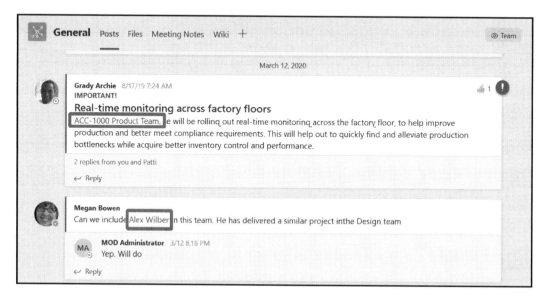

A channel appears in bold if there are new, unread conversations in the channel:

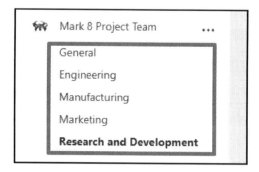

There's more...

Besides conversations, Teams also supports one-to-one and group chats. These chats can be initiated from the chat icon in the top pane (see **1** in the following screenshot). You can type the name of the individual(s) you would like to chat with (see **2** in the following screenshot). Your conversations are only seen by the participants of the chat. Any files that you share in these chats will be saved in OneDrive and shared with the participants:

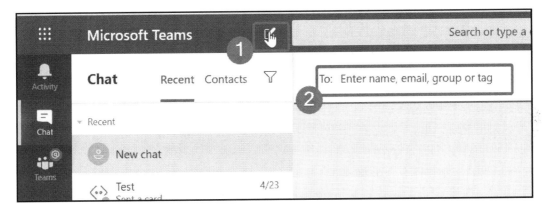

See also

- The *Sharing files* recipe in this chapter
- The *Adding a connector* recipe in this chapter

Scheduling a meeting

Microsoft Teams lets you organize team meetings or have one-off audio/video calls with your colleagues.

There are four meeting types that you can use with Teams based on the context:

- **Scheduled meetings**: When you want to schedule meeting at a future date with an individual or colleagues.
- **Meet in a channel**: when you need to hold an open meeting in your team, create a meeting in a channel.
- **Instant meetings**: when you want to convert your ongoing conversation into a desktop sharing session
- **Teams live events**: when you want to broadcast video and meeting content to a large online audience.

To schedule a meeting in Teams, follow the steps in the next section.

Getting ready

You do not need any special permission to schedule or join a team meeting.

How to do it...

You can set up the various meeting types in the following ways:

Scheduled meetings

1. Select **Meetings** from the left-hand side pane.
2. Click on **+ New meeting**:

3. Provide the required details (such as a title, the participants, and so on), as shown in the following screenshot:

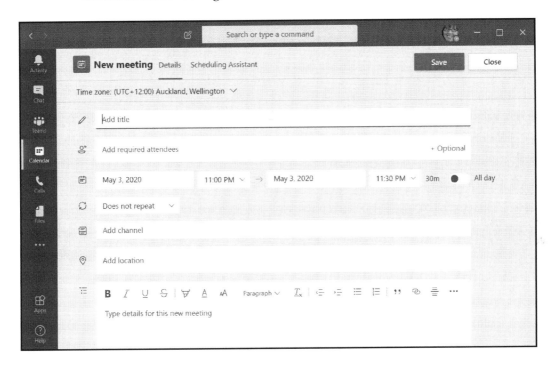

4. Click **Schedule**.

You have now scheduled a meeting.

Meet in a channel

1. Select **Meetings** from the left-hand side pane.
2. Click on **+ New meeting**.
3. Provide the required details.

4. Select a channel as shown in the following screenshot:

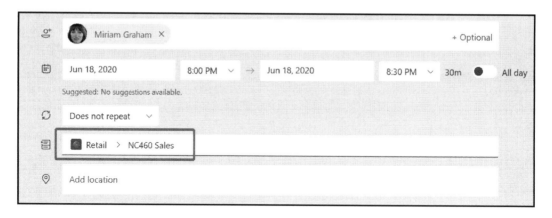

5. Click **Schedule**.

Meet Now

1. Go to your team's channel (**1**)
2. Go to your team's channel post (**2**)
3. Click on Reply (**3**) and then click on the **video camera** (**4**) icon:

4. Specify the **Title** of the meeting, turn video **on** or **off** and click **Meet now**:

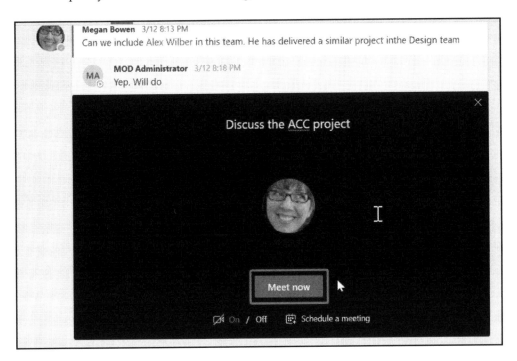

Live Events

1. Select **Meetings** from the left-hand side pane.
2. Click on **Live event**:

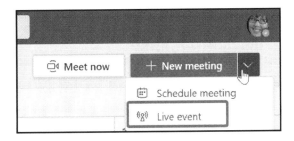

3. Add presenters, and assign them a **producer** or **presenter** role:

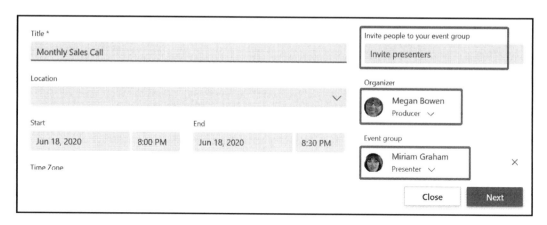

4. Define the scope of the live event, you can run it across the company or within a selected group:

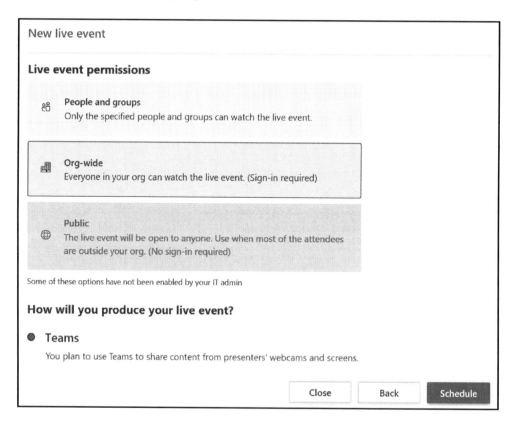

5. Click **Schedule**.

How it works...

All meeting types (except live meetings) provide an interactive experience to the attendees. The team's meeting interface displays a control pane when you move your mouse in the meeting interface:

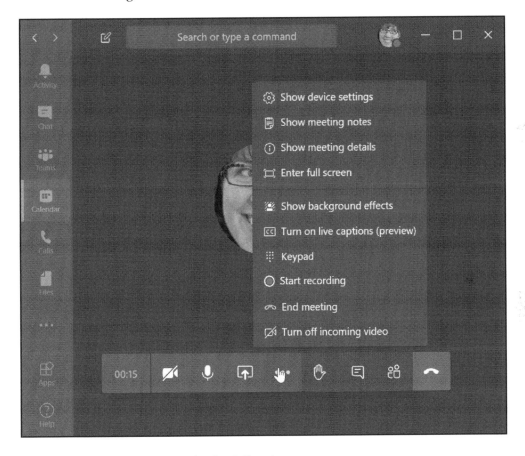

This panel contains options to do the following:

- Turn your video camera on or off.
- Mute the microphone.
- Share your screen or application.
- Raise your hand to ask a question or to request to be unmuted.

- Send a message.
- Share a file.
- Invite more participants.
- Choose your speaker and microphone.
- Bring up the meeting notes pane.
- Reveal meeting information (such as conference bridge details).
- Make the window fullscreen.
- Add background effects (discussed later).
- Launch the keypad.
- Share files.
- Record the meeting.
- End the meeting.

If you record a meeting, they automatically appear in **Microsoft Stream** and can be shared with others who missed the meeting. A searchable transcript of the recording is also generated:

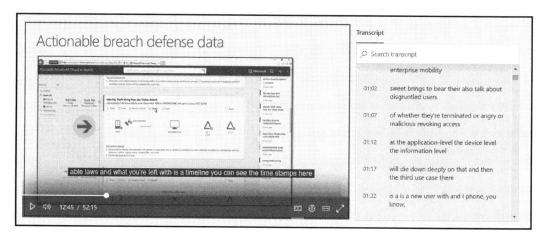

Teams has various capabilities to enhance the calling experience in meetings.

Live captions

The live captions feature adds real-time captions to a conversation for anyone who wants to use them, which helps make meetings more inclusive and effective. The feature is useful for people with a hearing impairment or differing language proficiencies:

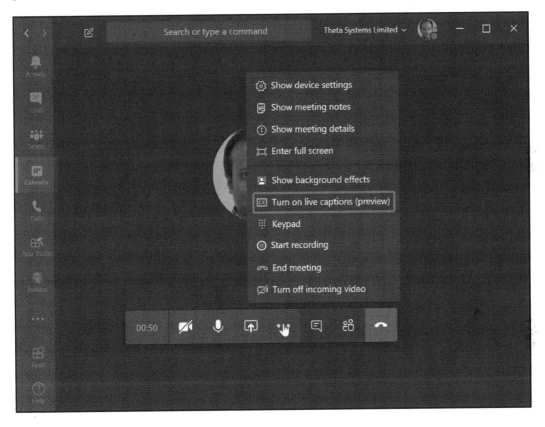

Once it is turned on, the function will transcribe what anyone says and display it as a live caption at the lower-left side of the meeting screen.

Custom backgrounds

This feature lets you add a custom background while keeping your face in focus. It is a useful feature to use when you are in a public place or working from home. There are many custom background images provided by default.

The one highlighted in the following screenshot lets you blur your background:

You can take this even further by using a photo of your office with your company branding or simply use an image to add some humor:

There's more...

Those of you who prefer using Outlook to schedule meetings can use the Teams add-in:

This option lets you leverage Outlook's familiar **Scheduling** window. A link to the Teams meeting is inserted automatically in the invite and the meeting location is set to **Microsoft Teams Meeting**:

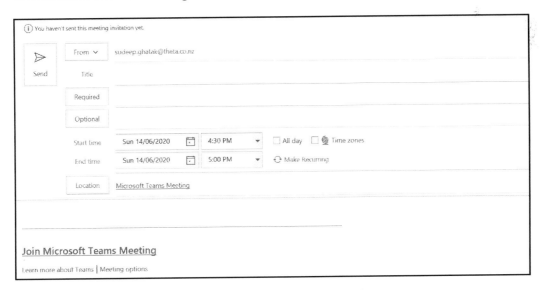

Microsoft Teams also comes with a special meeting type called **Live event** that lets you stream a video or content to a large audience. You can schedule and run a live event using the Teams client.

When you schedule a live event, you are assigned the role of producer. You can add additional event presenters or co-producers. Besides the meeting time, meeting venue, and meeting agenda, you can choose some other special options:

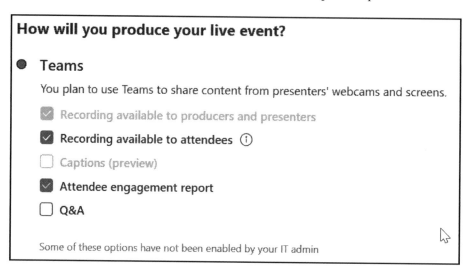

The **Q&A** feature is very useful when you are running a webinar and don't want to get distracted by attendees talking in the background. Attendees are all muted; they can ask questions, which appear on the producer's dashboard.

The questions that are asked are not visible to others until the producer chooses to publish them. The producer can publish or delete a question:

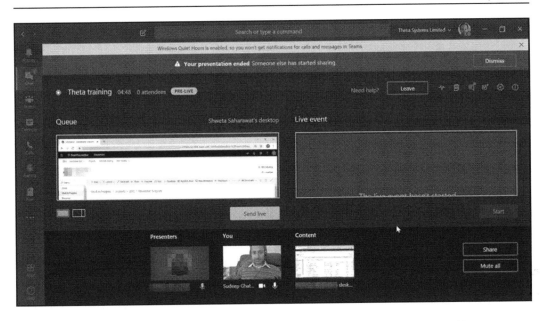

The producer controls the streaming content that appears on the screen of live attendees. You can share your desktop, application, or a video feed with the attendees. You can even live stream a video or YouTube clip by turning on the option to share system audio:

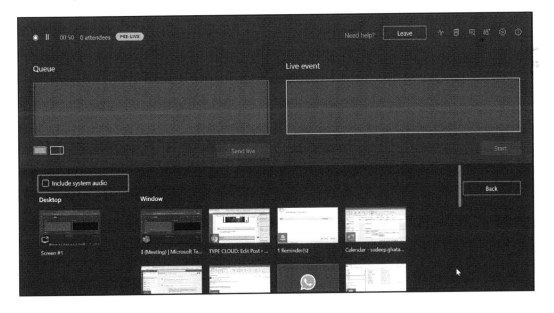

You can run a live event from Microsoft Stream as well. You can turn on captions for the event and share a video with subtitles later:

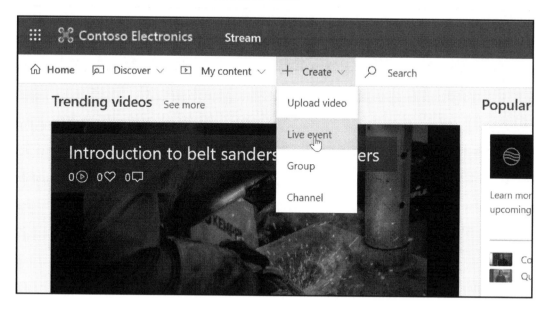

See also

- The *Initiating conversations via posts* recipe in this chapter
- The *Sharing files* recipe in this chapter

Sharing files

Teams provides an extremely simple collaboration platform to exchange files with colleagues and teams. Files in public teams can be accessed by everyone. Private teams only provide access to team members. Teams lets you share files within each channel.

The next section explains the different ways that files can be uploaded to Teams.

Getting ready

All members of a team can upload files to any channel they wish to.

How to do it...

There are multiple ways of adding files to your team channel, which we will explore in detail.

Sharing files via the Upload button

To upload files within teams:

1. Select **Teams** from the left-hand side pane.
2. Click on a channel.
3. Go to the **Files** tab (as shown):

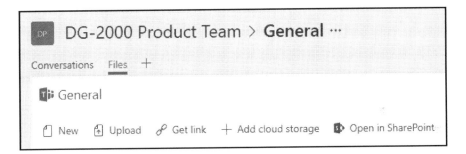

4. Click on **Upload**.

Select the file you want to upload.

Sharing files via conversations

To share files with peers in a conversation:

1. Select **Teams** from the left-hand side pane.
2. Click on a channel.

3. Drag and drop a file into the conversation area, as shown in the following screenshot:

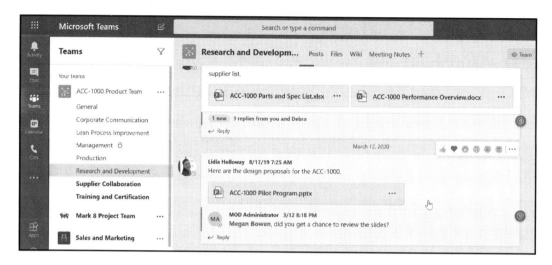

Also, note that if files are shared in the chat portion of the interface rather than in a channel post, they will be stored in and shared from the user's OneDrive for Business account.

Sharing files via SharePoint

To share files with peers from a SharePoint library, do the following:

1. Select **Teams** from the left-hand side pane.
2. Click on a channel.
3. Click on **...** next to the channel name and click **Open in SharePoint**.
4. Click on **Documents** in the left-hand side navigation panel.
5. Click on the folder with the channel name.
6. Drag and drop the file into the folder:

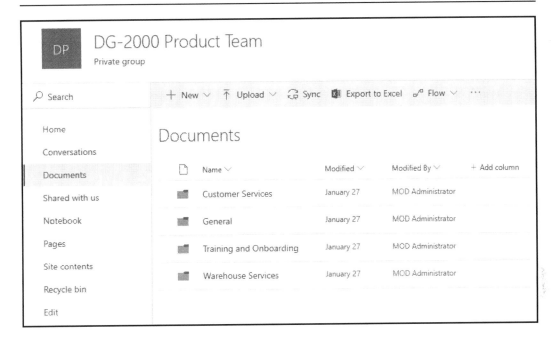

7. Once you are in SharePoint, you can add additional libraries to manage the team's files. However, only the files in the **Documents** library are visible through Teams.

 Note that if you create your own folder structure within a document library, **it does not appear** as a channel within Teams; for now, it only flows from Teams into SharePoint.

How it works...

Files are stored in the **Documents** library inside a folder with the same name as the channel name.

Files that are shared in the conversation area are uploaded to the **Documents** library automatically.

The uploaded files can be copied, moved, or even shared across multiple channels (instead of creating copies of the same files) by using the **Get link** option and then paste the link in another team or channel.

There is a **File** option in the left-hand side navigation panel, as shown in the following screenshot:

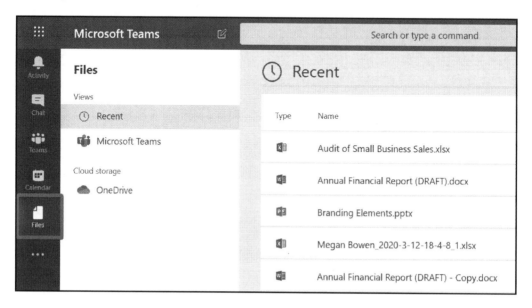

There is also a **File** option in each channel:

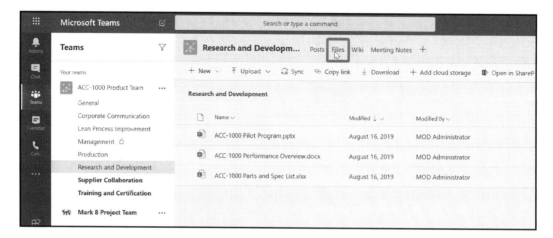

The difference is that the option in the left-hand side navigation panel displays all the files that you have access to or the ones that have been shared with you by a colleague from within SharePoint, OneDrive for Business, and Teams, whereas the option under the channel area displays only the files shared within that channel.

See also

- The *Initiating conversations via posts* recipe in this chapter
- The *Creating channels recipe* in this chapter
- The *Scheduling a meeting* recipe in this chapter

Searching within Teams

When you are a member of a vast number of teams, finding specific information you need can become a challenge. That is where the search functionality within Teams comes to the rescue. The search function lets you search for people, conversations/messages, and documents, as well as the contents of documents. The search box provided in Teams' interface serves as both a search and a command box.

To search for messages, people, or files, follow the instructions provided in the next section.

Getting ready

The search feature within Teams is available to everyone. However, you can only search for stuff you have access to.

How to do it...

To search for a message, person, or file:

1. Type the word or phrase you are searching for in the search box. In this example, we will search for the word everyone. The search results are grouped under three topics—**Messages**, **People**, and **Files**:

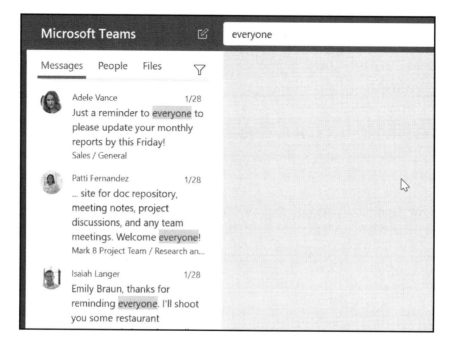

2. Clicking on a search result will reveal the contents of the result.
3. You can use the filter option to narrow down your search results:

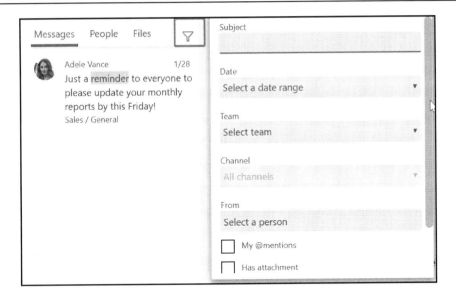

4. The search box also serves as a command box if you type / in the search box. The Microsoft Teams interface brings up a list of all the available commands and what each command does:

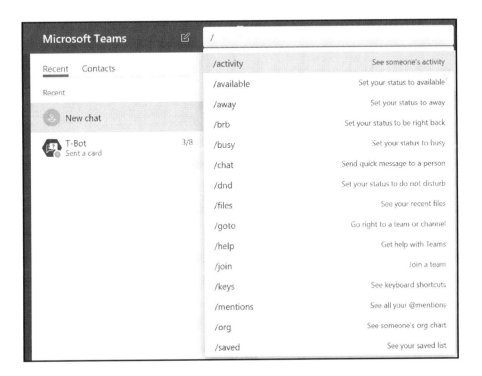

How it works...

Using Teams, you can search for messages, people, and files.

Searching for messages and conversations within teams

You can search for a keyword across all the channels and teams you have access to. The keyword you entered is highlighted in the search results, along with a preview of the message. Clicking on a preview reveals the entire thread in the main area. You can filter the search results further by specifying a start and end date or specifying a specific team or channel.

Searching for people in your Microsoft 365 tenant

You can search for your colleagues from within the Teams interface:

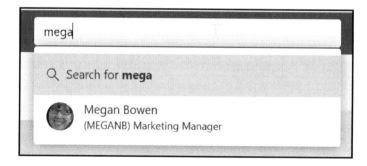

You can initiate a chat with your colleague using the Teams command box. Simply type /chat followed by the name of the person:

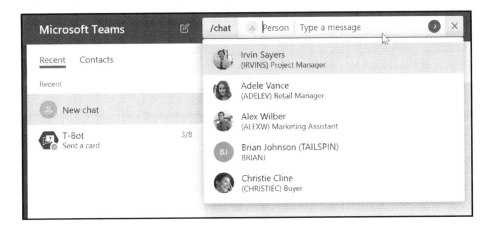

Searching for files within Teams and other Microsoft 365 locations

The `/files` search feature searches for files across Microsoft 365, including OneDrive and SharePoint. Just typing `/files` reveals all your recent files. The list is filtered as you type the filename:

See also

- The *Initiating conversations via posts* recipe in this chapter
- The *Scheduling a meeting* recipe in this chapter
- The *Sharing files* recipe in this chapter

Adding a connector

One of the highly effective features of Teams is the ability to add connectors to other applications inside a channel. Connectors let Teams communicate with an external application. So, you can do things such as manage your GitHub project from within Teams or track your team's progress within Trello.

 Trello is a popular web-based Kanban-style task management application.

This is different from adding a tab to a Teams channel. Adding a tab would just render the application within the Teams interface, but it would not actually talk to Teams specifically. However, adding a connector allows you to send or push information from one application to another.

The next section provides steps to integrate other applications with Teams.

Getting ready

You need to be a team owner in order to add a connector.

How to do it...

To add an external connector:

1. Select a team using the navigation bar on the left.
2. Select the channel you want to add the connector to.

3. Click on the **...** symbol, as shown, select **Connectors**:

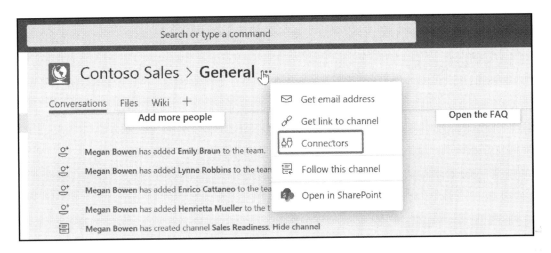

The next screen will display all the available applications that can be connected to Teams. You can use the filters on the left to narrow down the list:

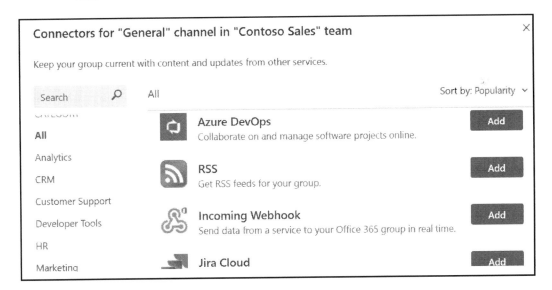

4. Click **Add** and follow the application-specific instructions.

How it works...

Depending on what app you add, you might see subsequent screens that take you through a setup process. For instance, if you add a connector to GitHub, it will ask you to log in with your GitHub credentials and then it will pull your GitHub information through:

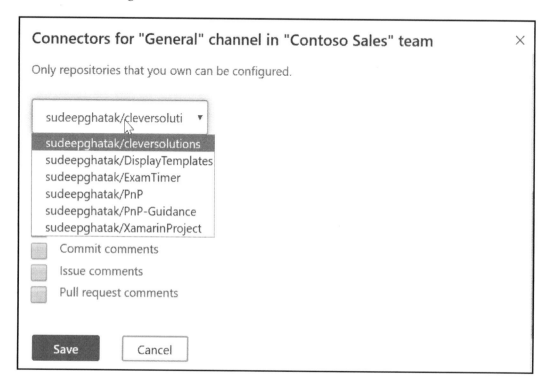

So, now, we don't need to have access to GitHub to track progress. We can track progress right from within a Teams channel conversation area:

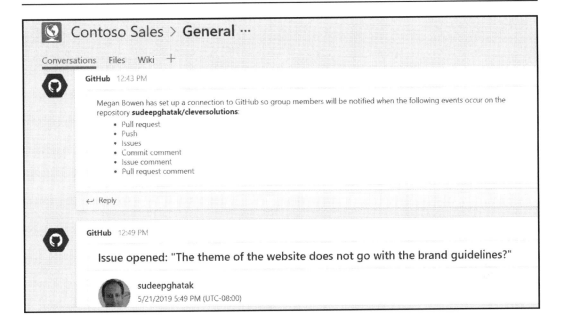

There's more...

You can use connectors to create actionable cards in Teams, which lets you perform actions in the external application without having to leave the Teams interface. You can read about actionable cards here `https://m365book.page.link/adaptive-cards`.

See also

- The *Creating channels and tabs* recipe in this chapter

12
Yammer - The Enterprise Social Network

Yammer is a social networking platform that keeps enterprise communication in mind. Yammer provides a common area for employees to interact in. Since its acquisition by Microsoft in 2012, Yammer has been used by close to 80% of the Fortune 500 companies.

Yammer brings social networking to the workplace. Is that a good thing? It definitely is. It provides a platform where people can get help solving problems through others in the organization that they might not even have met yet. Yammer thus lets you get answers from unexpected people.

The main uses of Yammer are to gather ideas, solve problems, share knowledge, and gather feedback. Additionally, Yammer makes the office a fun place. It allows people to create their own interest groups around shared topics, interests, or areas of practice.

In this chapter, we will learn about the following:

- Joining a Yammer network
- Creating a Yammer group
- Joining a Yammer group
- Using the activity feed
- Following people and topics
- Posting messages
- Tagging colleagues
- Inviting external members to your network

Joining a Yammer network

The Microsoft 365 sign-in options for Yammer let you access Yammer with your Microsoft 365 identity. This means when you visit www.yammer.com or when you choose Yammer from the Microsoft 365 waffle, you will be logged straight into Yammer (with your Microsoft 365 credentials). To join a Yammer network, use the following instructions.

Getting ready

Every Microsoft 365 user can access the organization's Yammer network and join groups of their choice. Users external to the company can only join if they receive an invitation. However, they can only view the external group they have been added to.

How to do it...

To join the Yammer network, follow these steps:

1. Go to www.yammer.com:

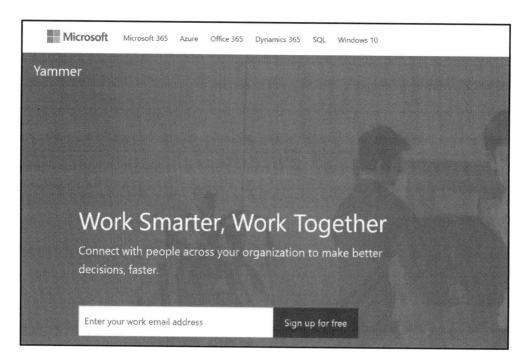

2. To join using your organization's account, Click on **Log In** and provide your **Email Address**:

3. If your organization has a Microsoft 365 tenant, you will be taken to your organization's sign-in page.
4. Enter your Microsoft 365 credentials.

You are in!

How it works...

When you log in to Yammer, this is how your homepage looks:

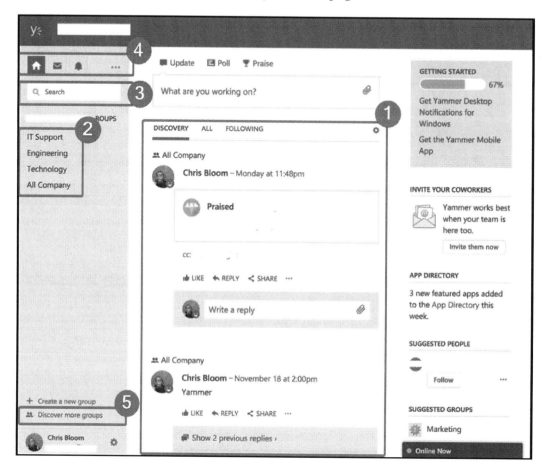

1. In the center, we have a discovery feed and conversations. This is where you create and consume content. The content here is gathered from the various groups that you have joined or the people you follow.

2. All the groups that you have subscribed to will appear in the left pane.

 Everyone in the organization is added to the **All Company** group by default. They can join other public groups based on their interests.

3. You can search for groups, posts, and people using the Yammer **Search** option in the left-hand side pane.

4. At the top-left corner, you can see the home, inbox, and notifications icons.

Inbox

The inbox is for focused messages that have been posted in your team or a post you decided to follow, as shown here:

The notifications just show activity around your group or post (such as new members, likes, and so on):

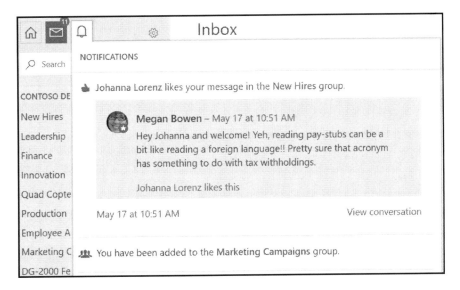

Underneath the search box , you can see a list of the groups you are part of. You can find more groups in your organization by using the **Discover more groups** link (number **5** in the preceding Yammer homepage screenshot).

 If you post a message, it is posted in the **All Company** group by default. So, if you want to post a message to a specific group, select the group first, then post your message.

There's more...

Before it was integrated with Microsoft 365, Yammer used to allow users to sign up using their organization's email address and a password of their choice (which was different from their Microsoft 365 password). This credential was termed a "Yammer identity."

If the user has Microsoft 365 identity enforced, they can log in to Yammer using their Microsoft 365 credentials.

If the user doesn't have Microsoft 365 identity enforced, but use their Microsoft 365 linked email address to sign up to Yammer, they are allowed to log in with their Microsoft 365 credentials.

If the user doesn't have Microsoft 365 identity enforced and the email to use to sign up to Yammer doesn't have a Microsoft 365 account associated, they are allowed to log in using their Yammer identity.

See also

- The *Joining a Yammer group* recipe in this chapter
- The *Inviting external members to your network* recipe in this chapter

Creating a Yammer group

Groups in Yammer make it easy for you to share ideas with other people within or outside your organization. It is recommended that you use the **Discover more groups** option to look for an existing group before creating one. If a group exists already and is also "public," you can join the group. If a group doesn't exist, proceed with creating one yourself. When you create a group, you are automatically made the owner of the group.

Getting ready

Anyone can create a Yammer group. When you create a group, you automatically become owner of that group.

How to do it...

To create a Yammer group, do the following:

1. Go to www.Office.com and select **Yammer**.
2. From the left pane, select **Create a group**.
3. Choose between the two group types:

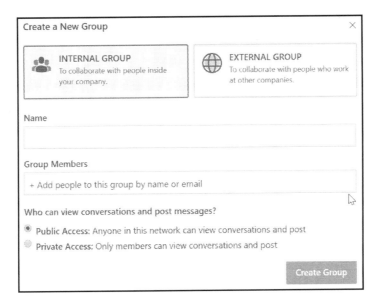

4. Provide a group name, add members, and specify the privacy settings—either public or private.
5. Click **Create Group**.

How it works...

Yammer groups can be created either to collaborate or socialize with internal staff or external vendors or partners. In some organizations, admins can turn off the ability to create external groups.

While creating a group, you can specify its privacy.

Public Access: This option lets anyone within the organization post messages, pictures, videos, and other content to the group.

Private Access: This option only lets members of the group post messages and other content to the group. Additionally, you can uncheck the box that says **List in our network's directory and search results**. If you uncheck this box, users in your organization can't find the group when they search for it by group name.

See also

- The *Joining a Yammer network* recipe in this chapter
- The *Inviting external members to your network* recipe in this chapter

Joining a Yammer group

The idea behind Yammer is that you can subscribe to subjects that you're interested in. You can do so by joining groups of your choice. Although you can see messages posted in all groups, you are only notified about messages posted in the groups that you have joined. The following steps will explain how you can join a group within your organization.

Getting ready

By default, you can join any group within your organization. However, certain groups may be "private," which limits the membership to a selected set of individuals. To join these groups, you need to send a request to the administrator.

How to do it...

To join a Yammer group, do the following:

1. Log in to the Yammer home page.
2. Use the search bar to look for a group or click **Discover more groups**:

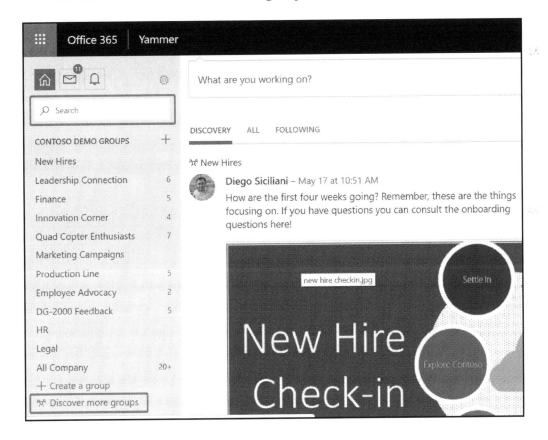

3. Yammer will suggest some groups that might interest you based on your connections and other groups you might have joined. Alternatively, you can choose to look at all the groups in your organization:

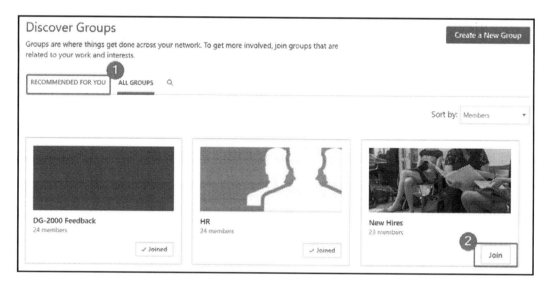

4. To join a specific group, click **Join**.

How it works...

When you join a group, you will start seeing posts from the members of that group on your Yammer home page.

Yammer is closely connected to Outlook, so you will keep getting notifications when there is any activity within your group. Sometimes, your Outlook inbox can get too busy if you have joined several groups. You can, in that case, customize your preferences to reduce the email clutter. You can update your preferences by clicking on the gear icon in the left-hand side pane and choose **Edit Settings**:

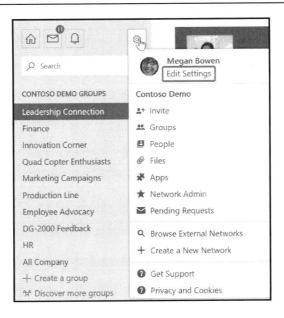

Click on the **NOTIFICATIONS** tab. You can personalize your settings by specifying what you want to get notifications for:

See also

- The *Joining a Yammer network* recipe in this chapter
- The *Inviting external members to your network* recipe in this chapter

Using the activity feed

The activity feed is the section where all the posts that are relevant to you will appear. This includes posts from your colleagues, any announcements, and content that is trending. Your activity feed is tailored to you depending on the groups and people you follow, as well as the posts you have shown interest in. The following section describes how you can use the activity feed.

Getting ready

All Microsoft 365 users that have joined Yammer network can access the Yammer home page.

How to do it...

To access the activity feed, do the following:

1. Go to www.office.com and click on **Yammer**:

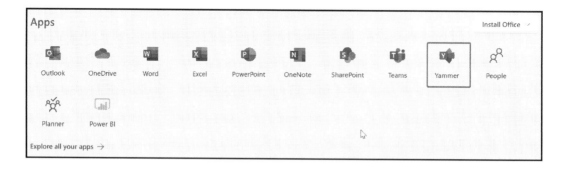

2. Click on the waffle icon and select **Yammer**:

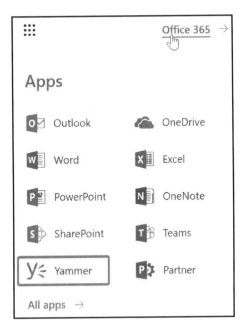

3. The activity feed appears on the center of the page. As the following
   screenshot shows, it is comprised of the following:
   - **DISCOVERY**: This tab displays the most recent, unread
     conversations relating to groups that you're connected to, people
     you work closely with, and the trending content across your
     company.
   - **ALL**: This tab displays all activity happening across the groups,
     including the ones you haven't subscribed to.

- **FOLLOWING**: This tab displays the content you have expressed an interest in, posts from people you are following, and the posts you have shown interest in by liking or commenting:

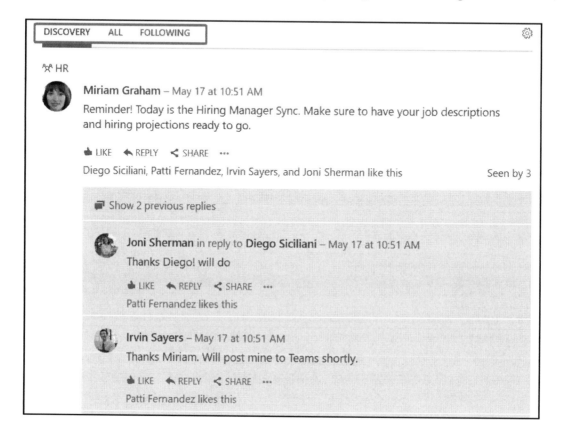

How it works...

Yammer's discovery feed uses AI to curate content just for you. It keeps getting smarter with time and learns from your choices. For example, if you follow a particular user, Alice, Yammer might occasionally show you a post from Alice's colleagues or her manager. It then monitors your reaction to find out whether these posts are of any value to you. If you like these posts or comment on them, it will start showing you other posts from those users in the future. Not just that, you will also notice that the discovery feed changes during the day, even though you haven't taken any action. This is because Yammer's algorithm arranges the feed in order of importance and relevance at that time of the day.

See also

- The *Following people and topics* recipe in this chapter
- The *Posting messages* recipe in this chapter
- The *Tagging colleagues* recipe in this chapter

Following people and topics

Yammer generally displays posts from the groups you have subscribed to. However, you can follow specific people or topics instead of joining a group. For example, you might be interested in what Kim, the marketing manager, has to say; however, you might not want to join Kim's "Marketing" group because there will be posts that the marketing team publishes that are of no interest to you. When you follow someone on Yammer, messages that they post will show up in your feed on your home page under **FOLLOWING**.

You can also follow specific topics. Topics are created in Yammer with hashtags, such as #hrupdate. In the next section, we'll explain how you can follow people and topics.

Getting ready

You can follow anyone within your company and you can follow any topic that has been hash tagged.

How to do it...

To follow a person, do the following:

1. Hover your cursor over the person's name and click **+ Follow**:

2. If the person does not appear in your activity feed, you can search for the person (see **1** in the following screenshot) and repeat the preceding step:

3. To follow a topic, search for the topic or click on the hashtag from within a post and then click **+ Follow** (see **2** in the preceding screenshot):

How it works...

By following a person or a topic, you are requesting to be notified about any activity they have been associated with. This is a good way of subscribing to a topic or specific people within the company that you are interested in without joining multiple groups. Companies can use hashtags to create specific topics, such as #shareprice or #employeeofthemonth, in order to keep staff informed about what's going on.

See also

- The *Using the activity feed* recipe in this chapter
- The *Posting messages* recipe in this chapter
- The *Tagging colleagues* recipe in this chapter

Posting messages

Yammer gives you the opportunity to share your ideas and opinions with the rest of the company. Yammer allows you to post messages, images, and announcements and run polls. If you want, you can associate your message with a topic. You'll learn more about posting messages in the next section.

Getting ready

Anyone in the company can post a message. They can post messages to **All Company** or any publicly available group.

How to do it...

To post a message, do the following:

1. Go to the Yammer home page.
2. Choose the group you want to post the message to.

If you post a message without selecting a group from the navigation bar, it is posted in the **All Company** group by default.

3. Type your message in the text box provided on the home page:

4. You can also upload an image or run a poll and post it in a group:

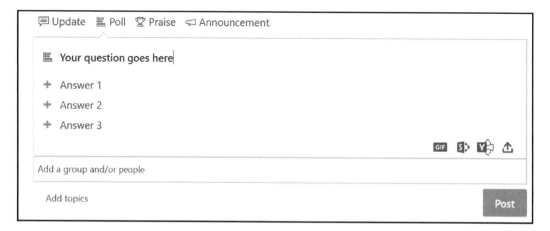

Only group administrators can post announcements in Yammer.

How it works...

The message posted appears on the home page of the group it was posted to. The section in the left-hand side panel of the home page displays the total unread posts in the group. This is how subscribers of the group know that new posts are available to read:

An announcement is a special type of message that only administrators of the group can post. It has the same features as messages, but announcements also send an email notification to all the group members. They also appear at the top of the group feed. Announcements are meant to be used to convey an important message or a key development.

You can share an existing post to other groups by using the **Share** option. This lets you preserve comments that were posted under the original conversation (shown in the following screenshot):

 Patti Fernandez – April 24 at 1:37 PM

We are getting closer to having open office spaces implemented. Here are some of our designers making plans at the main office.

 👍 LIKE   ↩ REPLY   ⟨ SHARE   •••

 The members can choose to respond to messages from the Yammer portal by just replying back to the Yammer notification in their mailbox.

You can also post a message in Yammer by simply replying back to the notification email. When you reply to the email, it is posted in the same conversation thread.

See also

- The *Using the activity feed* recipe in this chapter
- The *Following people and topics* recipe in this chapter
- The *Tagging colleagues* recipe in this chapter

Tagging colleagues

Tagging your co-workers is a good way of drawing their attention. When you tag a colleague, they receive an email notification and a notification in Yammer.

In the next section, I will explain how you can tag your colleagues to stay connected.

How to do it...

To tag someone, do the following:

1. Go to the Yammer home page.
2. Compose a message and mention the person you want to tag by typing @ followed by their name:

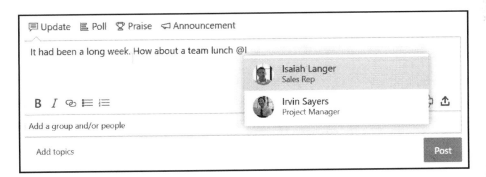

3. You can also mention an individual or an entire group in the area highlighted in the following screenshot:

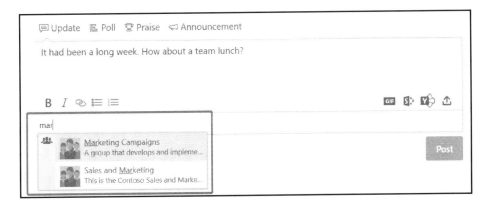

How it works...

Tagging an individual notifies that person through an email. If you tag an entire group, everyone in the group receives an email. You can invite people from outside the group you are posting the message to. This feature is really useful if you need to bring an expert into an existing conversation.

See also

- The *Using the activity feed* recipe in this chapter
- The *Following people and topics* recipe in this chapter
- The *Posting messages* recipe in this chapter

Inviting external members to your network

Yammer lets you invite external people to a conversation; so, you can get feedback from experts outside the organization as well. This feature is handy for inviting customers, vendors, and suppliers to a conversation. As a security measure, Yammer makes everyone in the group aware that an external member has been added to the conversation. The next section explains how you can invite people from outside your organization to your Yammer network.

Getting ready

You can invite anyone (with a valid email address) to a conversation.

How to do it...

To invite someone, do the following:

1. Go to the Yammer home page.
2. Compose a message and provide the email address of the person from outside your organization that you want to add:

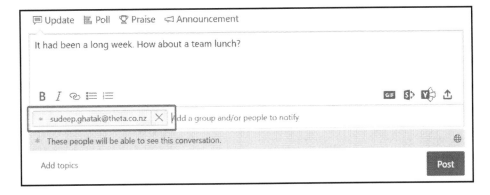

3. Post the message.

How it works...

When an external member is invited to a conversation, they can participate and view all the messages in the thread. If the thread is too long, other members of the group might not realize that someone outside the company is following their conversation. In order to circumvent the issue, Yammer adds a globe symbol, along with a note on all future responses making it clear that the reply will be visible to people outside the network:

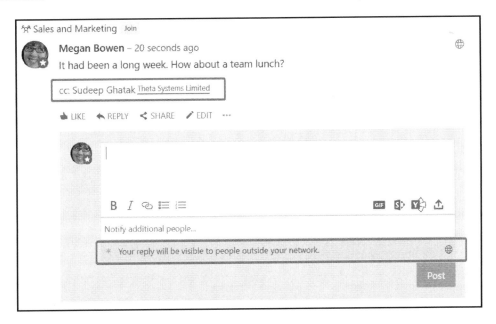

The external member receives an email notifying them that they were mentioned in a Yammer post:

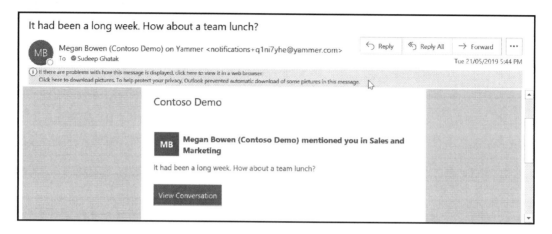

If they have a Yammer account, they will receive a notification on their Yammer home page as well:

They can respond back to the message by simply replying to the Yammer email or replying via the Yammer portal.

See also

- The *Joining a Yammer network* recipe in this chapter
- The *Joining a Yammer group* recipe in this chapter

13
Power Automate (Microsoft Flow)

Power Automate (formerly Microsoft Flow) has been launched as Microsoft's lightweight workflow engine for end-users, developers, and IT professionals. It lets you build personal automated workflows using a wide range of services, without having to learn any code. There are hundreds of templates available to build flows that talk to Dropbox, Twitter, Yammer, Facebook, Dynamics, and other services. This makes building flows quicker and easier. There are over 300 services available as of today. Some are shown in the following:

Power Automate provides a rich user interface that allows you to build a process map and configure your actions.

Every flow starts with a **trigger**. A trigger is an event that will initiate the flow (or the workflow). The following are some examples of triggers:

- When an email arrives in my mailbox
- When a file is created in my OneDrive

- When a new item is created in a SharePoint list
- When I tweet with a hashtag

After a flow is triggered, it can go through a series of steps that are laid out one after the other. Power Automate also lets you create parallel branches and add conditional logic, as shown in the following screenshot:

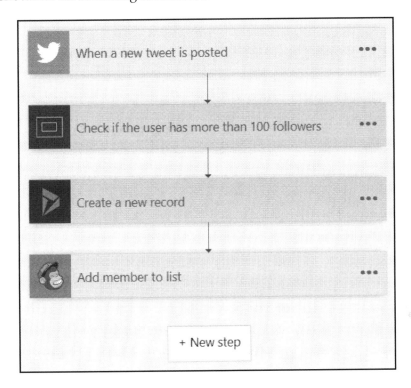

Power Automate is available in two plans:

- Per user per month
- Flows per month

You can check the pricing of these plans at https://m365book.page.link/flow-pricing.

In this chapter, we will learn about the following:

- Creating a flow using a template
- Editing a flow
- Importing a flow
- Exporting a flow
- Adding owners
- Testing your flow
- Creating a solution
- Creating a flow in a SharePoint library

Creating a flow using a template

If you have an idea in your head, someone probably had it before you. So, before building a new flow from scratch, you could look for an existing template. This will save you lots of time since the template will come with actions and a process flow that can then be modified or extended. It will also serve as a quick-start guide and a learning tool. Just as you can use flows created by others, you could submit your own flows to the Flow store. Your flow will appear on the gallery page if it successfully goes through the approval process.

Getting ready

You can sign up for a free Power Automate account at `https://flow.microsoft.com`. It has a free plan as well as business plans. Power Automate comes with most Microsoft 365 licensing plans. Refer to Microsoft Licensing guide for more details. You can download it from `https://m365book.page.link/flow-licensing`.

The free plan lets you run a limited number of flows until it expires.

How to do it...

1. Log in to `https://office.com` using your Microsoft 365 account.
2. Click on **Power Automate** from the list of apps

3. On the Power Automate landing page scroll to the end of the page to access starter templates. If you can't see what you are looking for, click on **See more templates** and use the search bar to find more templates:

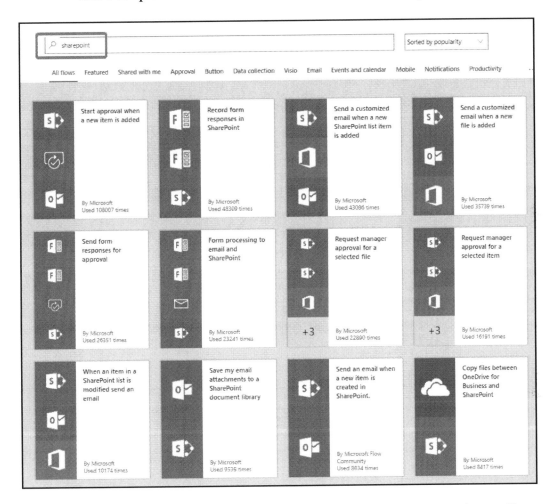

4. Select a template that looks the most like what you are looking for. We'll pick the first one in the preceding list.

5. The next job is to provide credentials for all these connectors, as shown in the following screenshot:

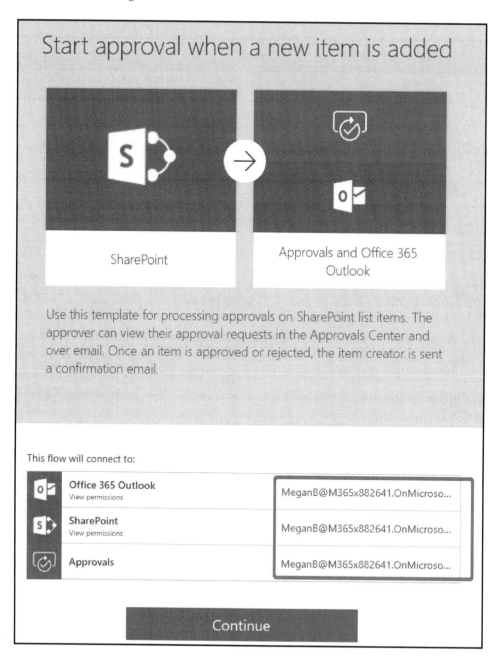

6. You will then be taken to the Power Automate designer screen, as shown in the following screenshot:

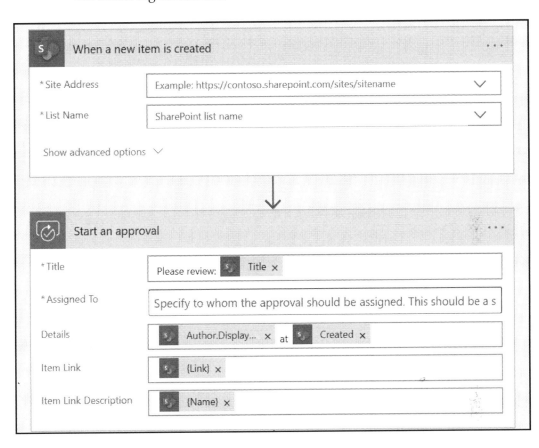

7. You can customize the flow as per your requirements at this stage and click on **Save** in the far-right corner once you are done:

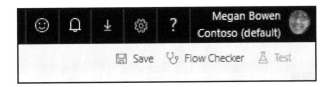

8. Click on the name field in the top left to change the name of the flow:

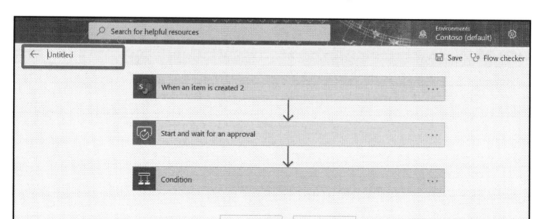

You just built your first flow.

How it works...

In order to understand the basics of a flow, you need to understand the following concepts.

Components of a flow

Trigger: Every flow starts with a trigger. A trigger is a condition that initiates the flow. In the preceding example, creating a list item in SharePoint acted as a trigger, which means that the flow will run every time a new item is created.

You can create three main types of triggers:

- **Automated**: A flow triggered automatically by an event, such as creating a new item in SharePoint or receiving an email in your inbox.
- **Instant**: A flow triggered manually by a button.
- **Scheduled**: A flow that runs once or as a recurring action at a specific time.

Triggers have a setting called **trigger conditions**, which let you specify one or more expressions that must be true for the trigger to fire—for example, if you have a trigger on an **item update** event, then the flow will run every time the item is updated. But if you want to refine the trigger condition so that the flow only gets triggered when a particular column (let's say **Status**) in the list has a specific value (for example, **In progress**), then you can achieve this by adding a trigger condition:

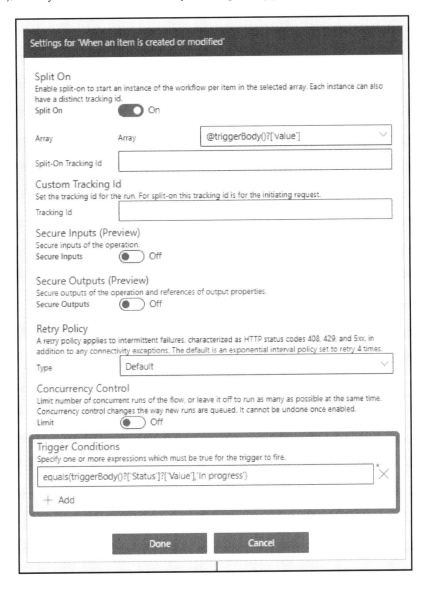

Action: A trigger is followed by one or more actions. An action could be a query, create, update, insert, or delete operation. The following are some examples of actions:

- Creating a new list item.
- Moving a file from OneDrive.
- Sending an email notification.

Connections: Connections let you interact with data from other systems. To establish a connection, you need to specify credentials to log in to the application you are connecting to.

Flow landing page

This section explains how the flow designer is structured. On your left, you have the following links:

- **Home**: The home page displays the featured flow templates available for you to use grouped by category. You can even search for flows by use case:

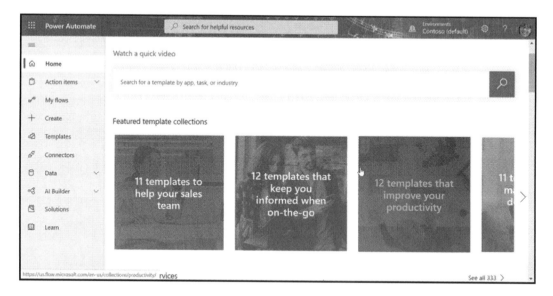

- **Action items**: All of your approval tasks (across every flow) are going to appear under the **Approvals** section. You can approve or reject them by providing comments. All your past approval actions can be seen under the **History** link:

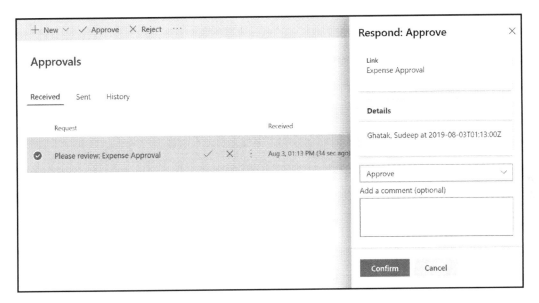

- **My flows**: The flows that you build appear under the **My flows** link. If you share these flows with a colleague, then the flows move under the **Teams flows** link. The banner on this page also lets you create a **New** flow or **Import** an existing one:

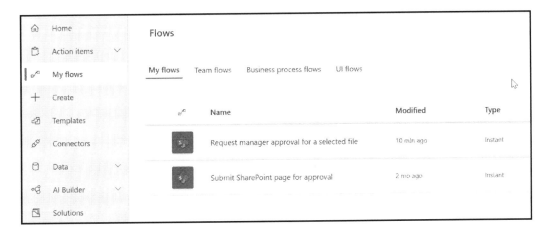

- **Business process flows**: There are flows that are built using **Common Data Service (CDS)**. You can think of CDS as a storage option for your business data. CDS stores data within entities, unlike databases, which store data in tables. CDS manages data as well as the entity schema, so you can focus only on the business process (which you can build using Power Automate).

- **UI flows**: These let you record and playback user interface actions (clicks, keyboard input, and so on) for applications that don't have APIs available. UI flows have a **record** feature that lets you perform your manual actions and save them as a part of the flow.

- **Templates**: As the name suggests, this page displays a list of flow templates to choose from.

- **Connectors**: The connectors in Power Automate provide you access to the functionality of other Microsoft 365 services (SharePoint, OneDrive for Business) or third-party services (Dropbox, MailChimp, and so on). A list of available connectors can be seen at `https://m365book.page.link/flow-connectors`.

- **Data**: The data link provides access to CDS entities as described previously. It also enables you to pull data from your on-premises environment through **gateways**.

- **AI Builder**: The AI builder lets you leverage Microsoft's artificial intelligence features, such as text recognition, outcome prediction, and so on, to build AI models.

- **Solutions**: Hosting flows in a solution makes it easier to move them and all their components from one environment to another. You can add multiple flows in a single solution.

Run history

A run history shows you each instance that the flow is executed, or you could also say every time the trigger condition is met:

If you click on a specific run, the flow expands and displays the actions that were executed, along with the time it took to run each action:

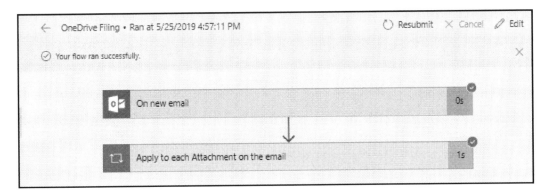

 The run history is maintained for 30 days. If you want to use this information for auditing purposes, save the information in SharePoint or another data store.

Flow properties

You can update the flow properties from the top-right side of the landing screen. The flow properties let you modify the properties of a flow, as shown in the following screenshot:

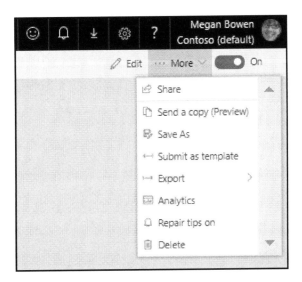

- **Edit**: Lets you open the flow in designer mode.
- The toggle switch next to **... More** lets you enable or disable a flow.
- **... More**: Opens up a drop-down menu containing the following elements:
  - **Share**: Add other owners to the flow.
  - **Send a copy**: Allows you to share a copy of this flow with others so that they can build their own version of the flow.
  - **Save as**: Lets you create a copy of the flow.
  - **Submit as template**: Lets you submit your flow to the gallery.
  - **Export**: Lets you save the flow as a package. It can then be imported to another tenant.
  - **Analytics**: Lets you see the metrics related to the flow.
  - **Delete**: Deletes your flow.

There's more

When you build a flow, you are added as the owner automatically. The flow then runs in the context of your user account. This isn't a bad practice. But you need to make the following considerations:

- If you have used **Send email** actions in your flow, recipients will receive emails from the user who published the flow.
- If your flow is updating SharePoint list items, the **Modified By** field will display the flow owner's name.
- Your flows will stop running if the user's account gets deleted or disabled.
- The flow will only be able to perform tasks that the user is authorized for.

User accounts can be used for simple scenarios but should be avoided for complex business processes. You should use a **service account** in such cases. A service account is just a regular Microsoft 365 account that is not associated with a staff member. However, you need to keep the following points in mind while using a service account:

- You need to assign a Flow license to the service account.
- The service account should be given the most limited access that it needs to perform its job.
- They shouldn't be added in privileged groups or other security groups.
- Set the password to **never expire**. If the password expires, your business process will error out.
- Do not set **Multi-Factor Authentication** on service accounts.

See also

- The *Editing a flow* recipe in this chapter
- The *Testing your flow* recipe in this chapter

Editing a flow

You can update the flows that you have created. These flows appear under the **My flows** tab in the flow landing screen. Other flows that have been shared with you can be seen in the **Team flows** area.

Getting ready

You need to be a flow owner in order to edit it.

How to do it...

1. Log in to https://office.com using your Microsoft 365 account.
2. Click on **Flow**. This takes you to the landing page.
3. Choose the flow you want to modify or click **Edit**:

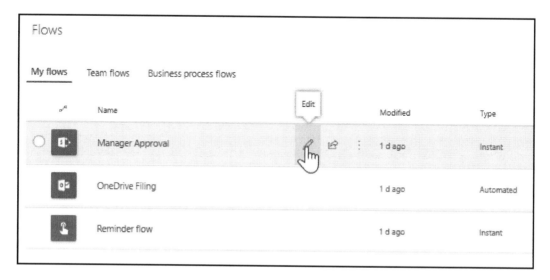

4. Edit the flow by clicking on the **Edit** link in the top right-hand corner.
5. Make changes to the flow and click **Save**.

How it works...

A newer version of the flow is created every time you make a change. Currently, there is no way of going back to an older version. If you would like to save multiple versions of the flow, then you can do so by exporting the flow before making a change and saving the package in a version control system, such as VSTS or GitHub.

See also

- The *Creating a flow using a template* recipe in this chapter
- The *Testing your flow* recipe in this chapter
- The *Creating a flow on a SharePoint library* recipe in this chapter

Exporting a flow

Exporting and importing a flow allows the reusability of the package and its deployment from one environment to another environment. A flow can be saved as a template, along with the dependencies used by the flow and all associated metadata, so that it can be reproduced in another Microsoft 365 tenant. This feature is useful in the absence of a version-control mechanism within a flow.

Flows can also be moved from one environment to another, using solutions, but we'll discuss solutions later in this chapter.

If you want to migrate a *single* flow, then the **Import/Export** options are useful features to employ.

Getting ready

You need to be a flow owner in order to save a flow as a template.

How to do it...

1. Log in to `https://office.com` using your Microsoft 365 account.
2. Choose the flow you want to export.
3. Go to **Export | Package (.zip)** under the **More** link in the top right-hand corner, as shown in the following screenshot:

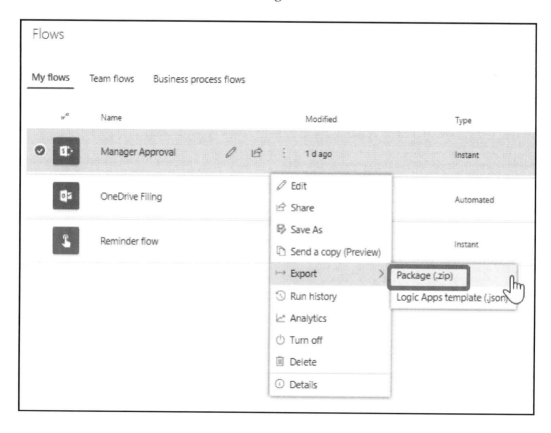

4. Give the package a name and click **Export Package**:

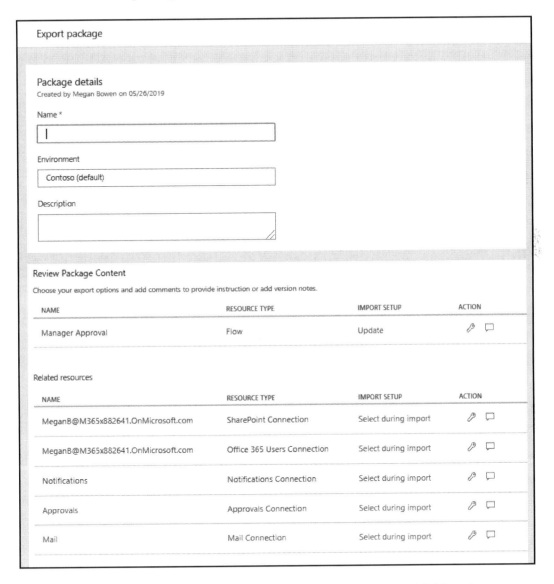

The flow will be downloaded as a ZIP file in the default download folder of your browser.

How it works...

The exported flow file can be saved in two formats: `.zip` and `.json`. A zipped version is perhaps the most widely used and user-friendly way to export flows. A JSON file is the coded version of the flow logic and is useful when migrating the flow logic into a separate platform, such as Logic Apps.

 JSON (short for **JavaScript Object Notation**). It is just another format (just like XML) that is universally accepted for representing data.

See also

- The *Importing a flow* recipe in this chapter
- The *Creating a flow on a SharePoint library* recipe in this chapter

Importing a flow

A flow package contains the logic of the flow as well as information about the connectors. It can therefore be imported into a new, completely separate environment, preserving the flow logic; however, the connection information needs to be updated according to the environment it is imported to.

Getting ready

Everyone within an organization can import a flow and publish it.

How to do it...

To import a flow, follow the following steps:

1. Go to the Power Automate landing page.
2. Click on **Import**, specify the location of the saved template, and click **Import**.
3. Specify whether you would like to update an existing flow by selecting **Update** or create a new flow:

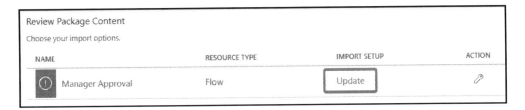

4. When the flow is imported into a new environment, the connections have to be reconfigured by clicking on the **Select during import** link:

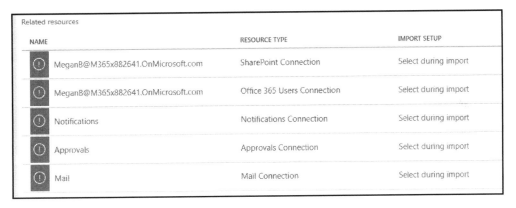

5. This brings up a panel on the right that lets you create a connection or choose an existing connection:

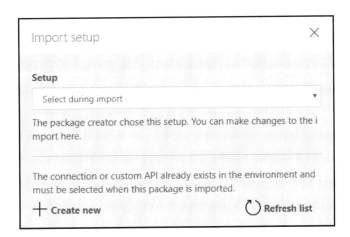

6. You can save the flow after the connections have been configured.

How it works...

Please ensure that you don't have another flow with the same name in your environment when choosing **Update** in the **Import** setup. This operation will overwrite your existing flow, which can't be retrieved once this is done.

 One of the limitations of the flow import process is that you cannot import a solution into an environment in which the solution already exists. You could use the **Save as** option if you want to clone a flow.

See also

- The *Creating a flow using a template* recipe in this chapter
- The *Exporting a flow* recipe in this chapter
- The *Creating a flow on a SharePoint library* recipe in this chapter

Adding owners

Owners can edit and save existing flows. By default, the creator of the flow is added as an owner.

While you could build personal flows to automate some of your personal work (such as monitoring your emails or OneDrive), it is always advisable to have more than one owner if you are designing the flow to achieve a common objective or business process. A flow that has more than one owner is called a **team flow**.

Besides editing the flow, an owner can also do the following:

- View the history of a given flow.
- Edit the properties of a flow.
- Modify an action or condition.
- Manage owners.
- Delete a flow.

Getting ready

Owners must have a Power Automate plan to create a team flow (you can look at the options at `https://flow.microsoft.com/pricing/`). Only an owner of the flow can add other owners.

How to do it...

1. Go to the Power Automate landing page.
2. Go to the **Owners** section on the bottom right-hand corner of the screen and click **Add an owner**.
3. You should be able to add any individual from the organization or user group.
4. A pop-up screen will appear, explaining the permissions that the owner will have regarding the connections inside the flow. Click OK.

The new owner is added!

How it works...

When you add a new person as an owner of the flow, they will receive a notification and the flow will start appearing on their landing page under **Team flows**:

As a co-owner, you can also add SharePoint lists to a flow so that everyone who has editing access to the list automatically gets editing access to the flow:

 Owners will be able to use services in a flow, but they won't be able to modify the credentials for a connection created by another owner.

Power Automate enables you to *share flows* with your colleagues either by adding them as co-owners or (for manual flows only) run-only users.

See also

- The *Creating a flow using a template* recipe in this chapter
- The *Editing a flow* recipe in this chapter
- The *Creating a flow on a SharePoint library* recipe in this chapter

Testing your flow

Every solution that is built needs to be validated against a set of test cases to ensure that it does what it was created to deliver. Power Automate offers a very good platform to test the flow logic. The testing process actually runs the business logic, and so you shouldn't test flows on your production (live) system. The flow user interface (as demonstrated in the *How to do it...* section) can be used to observe inputs and outputs, as well as investigate errors.

Presently, the feature only lets you test the last five flow runs.

Getting ready

Only the flow owner can test the flows, which means that you will need to be added as a co-owner if you want to test the flow.

How to do it...

1. Go to the Power Automate landing page.
2. Select the flow that you want to test and click **Edit**.
3. Click on the top right-hand corner to test the flow:

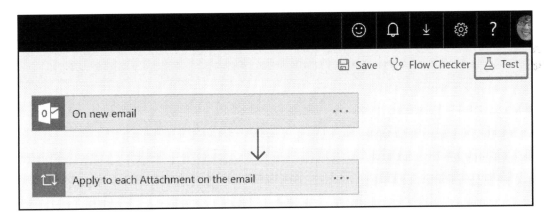

4. This will reveal a panel on the right with some options:

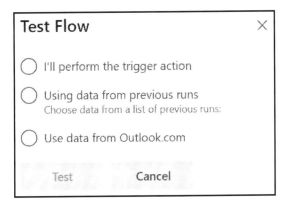

5. Choose the appropriate option from the list. This list might look different depending on the type of trigger that is chosen. In order to test the flow, do one of the following:
   - Manually satisfy the trigger condition.
   - Use data from previous runs to perform the test.
   - For certain triggers, you can provide a conditional logic that satisfies criteria—for example, for a SQL trigger, you could pass a query.

How it works...

To ensure that your flows run as expected, perform the trigger, and then review the inputs and outputs that each step in your flow generates.

After the flow has run, you can investigate the flow by looking at the flow output in the center of the page.

The actions that succeed have a green check, whereas the ones that fail have a red cross:

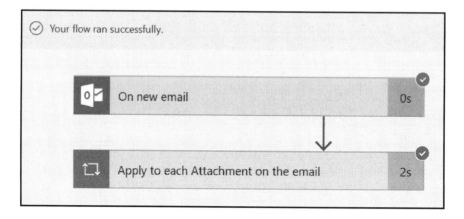

Clicking the action (or trigger) reveals more information:

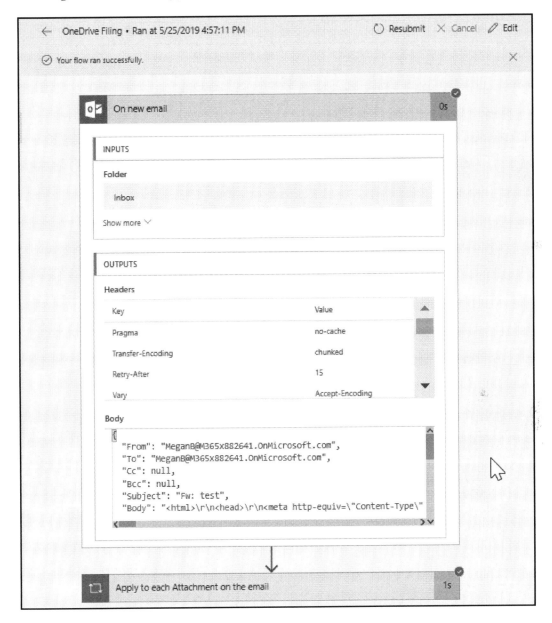

This view lets you investigate the input and output values. In the case of an error, the error information is displayed.

See also

- The *Creating a flow using a template* recipe in this chapter
- The *Editing a flow* recipe in this chapter

Creating a solution

Solutions provide the **Application Lifecycle Management (ALM)** capability for Power Apps and Power Automate. Solutions let you bundle related flows (and apps) within a single deployable unit and migrate them from one environment to another.

An environment is a place to store, manage, and share your organization's business data, Power Apps, and flows. They also act as secure spaces to separate apps that may have different roles, security requirements, or target audiences.

The following are some scenarios where you could consider different environments:

- Creating separate environments for test and production versions of your apps
- Isolating the apps and flows to specific teams or departments in your company
- Creating separate environments for different global branches of your company

Creating and managing environments for Power Platform is beyond the scope of this book. You can read more about creating environments for Power Platform at `https:/ /m365book.page.link/environments`.

As you might have noticed, when you build flows under **My flows**, they all appear one below the other, and there is no way of grouping related flows together. Solutions let you logically group the related flows into a single container. So, if your application has multiple flows, you can bundle them all into a solution container, which simplifies navigating and managing these flows.

Getting ready

You must have the following components to create solutions:

- Common Data Service in your Microsoft 365 environment
- An environment with version 9.1.0.267 or later

How to do it...

To create a solution, go through the following steps:

1. Go to your **Power Automate** homepage.
2. Select **Solutions** from the left pane. You'll see all the solutions available in your environment:

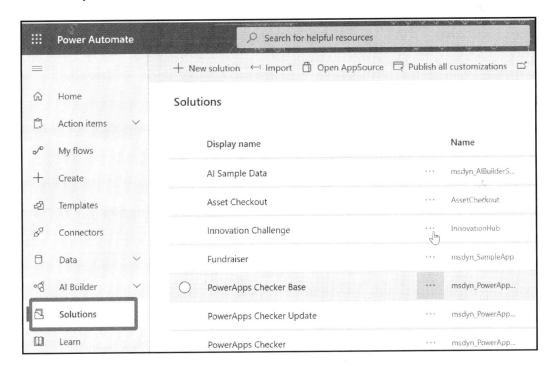

3. Click on **+ New solution** to create a solution.

4. Provide a display name, name (only letters, numbers, and underscores), publisher and version number, as shown in the following screenshot. Click **More options** to enter additional information:

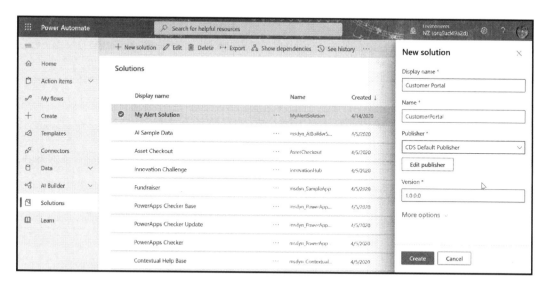

5. Click on **Create**.
6. Now click on the solution you just created. You will be taken to a page that displays the components of the solution.
7. Click **New** to add a new component (which could be a **Flow**, **Power App**, **Entity**, and so on):

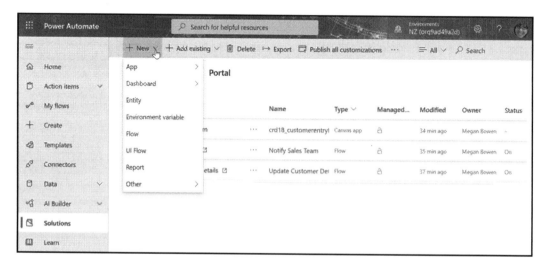

Your solution is ready to be exported, along with its components

How it works...

Solutions provide you with a convenient and efficient way of grouping multiple resources (apps, flows, entities, reports, and so on) together. This method lets the **independent software vendors (ISVs)** deploy their solutions on **Microsoft AppSource**. Creating solutions lets you deploy your components in another environment without having to go through the pain of exporting each individual component and then importing it in.

You can export a solution by navigating to the **Solutions** page and selecting the **Export** option from the context menu, as shown in the following screenshot. Your components need to be published before the solution can be exported:

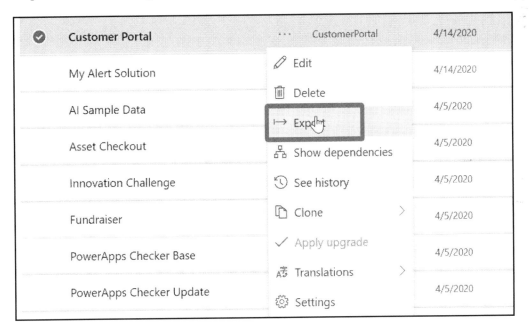

Clicking **Export** launches a wizard that takes you through the exporting process. You need to specify the version number and export type during the process:

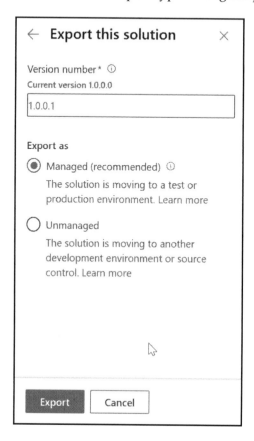

A managed solution only contains customizable solution components that have been customized. We suggest that you first create an unmanaged solution before creating a managed solution.

After exporting the solution, you can move it to a different environment (or even a separate tenant) by importing it. The **Import** option is available on the **Solutions** page:

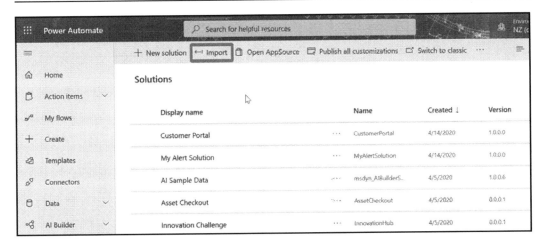

The import process takes you through a series of steps, as shown in the following screenshot. Before running the solution, fix the flow connections:

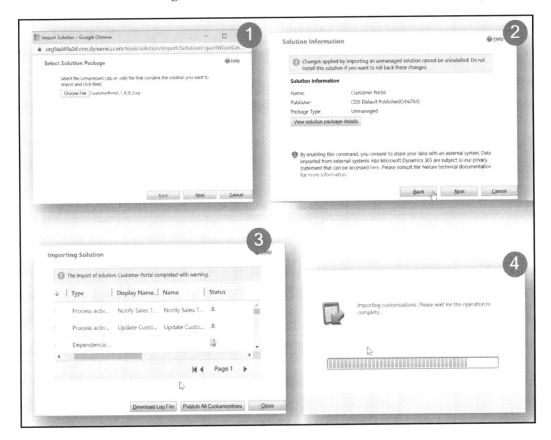

See also

- The *Importing a flow* recipe in this chapter
- The *Exporting a flow* recipe in this chapter

Creating a flow in a SharePoint library

Power Automate is integrated with SharePoint. The Power Automate option appears against every SharePoint list and library. This lets you set up SharePoint-specific triggers right from within the SharePoint list or library. You can use Power Automate to build your custom events, such as the addition of a document, metadata updates, and so on. Within SharePoint, you can run a flow with the following scopes:

- On demand for a selected file
- On demand for a selected list item
- For a specific folder within a library

Getting ready

You need to have a SharePoint license to access SharePoint Online. You also require editing rights for the list in order to add a flow to it.

How to do it...

1. Navigate to the SharePoint list (or library).
2. Select **Create a flow** from the top menu under **Power Automate**:

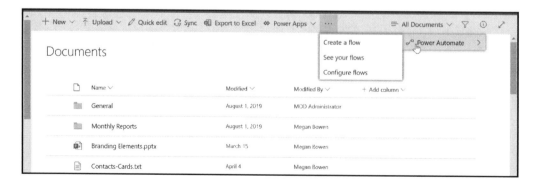

3. A panel will appear on the right with all the SharePoint templates:

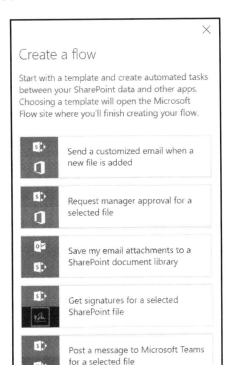

4. Select a template and build a flow as we described before.

How it works...

Selecting a template takes you to the flow designer page. The template provides a basic outline that serves as a good starting point. The flow creation logic is the same as described earlier.

See also

- The *Creating a flow using a template* recipe in this chapter
- The *Editing a flow* recipe in this chapter

14
Power Apps

Power Apps is a form builder that you can use to build rich and powerful online forms for your business. With the help of Power Apps, you can build custom business apps that connect to your business data, whether it's stored on-premises or in cloud storage. Apps built using Power Apps provide a rich user interface that can run seamlessly in the browser or on mobile devices (phone or tablet).

You can build Power Apps using the Power Apps designer for the web. When you build a Power App, you can choose between a web or mobile layout. With Power Apps on mobile, you can even leverage mobile device features such as GPS and the camera in the apps.

Power Apps is a development platform designed primarily for end-users, but developers can take it to the next level not just to create apps for end-users, but also for building "design concepts".

Power Apps is available in two plans:

- Power Apps per app per user per month
- Power Apps Plan unlimited per user per month

 You can check the pricing of these plans at
https://m365book.page.link/pa-pricing.

Power Apps fall into two categories:

- **Canvas apps** are suited to simple processes and forms. They give you the independence to do pretty much anything you want to do. You can tailor the application to meet your business requirements.

- **Model apps** are more suited to use cases where data drives your user interface, such as when you have different components in your Power Apps that are visible to different people based on the data that they have access to. You need it to give you permission to read/write based on your role. You can write a canvas app to achieve this; however, Model Apps provide you a framework to achieve this easily. Model Apps provide you with a layout as a starting point that can then be extended as per your needs.

Build a Canvas app if you want to build an app by connecting to a data source that you already have. Canvas apps let you build pixel-perfect apps as per your requirements.

Build a Model App if you want to build an app quickly using the data models that Microsoft has provided you by default (made available through Common Data Service). You can perform limited customizations on such apps.

In this chapter, we'll learn about the following:

- Creating a template-based app
- Connecting to data sources
- Adding screens
- Creating a canvas app from a blank template
- Creating Power Apps from a SharePoint list/library
- Sharing Power Apps

Creating a template-based app

Power Apps comes with prebuilt templates that let you create functional Power Apps without having to acquire a deep knowledge of Power Apps concepts. This provides you with an opportunity to get a deeper insight into the prebuilt apps and understand the concepts of data binding, data updates, validation, and so on. This way, you could reverse engineer some of the applications that Microsoft and other vendors have developed and shared with the community. Go through the next section to learn about creating apps using a template.

Getting ready

You need Power Apps plan included in your Microsoft 365 subscription in order to build a Power App.

How to do it...

To create an app, go through the following steps:

1. Log in to `Office.com` and click on **All Apps**.
2. Choose **Power Apps** from the list of applications.

3. You will be taken to the Power Apps landing page. Click on **All templates**:

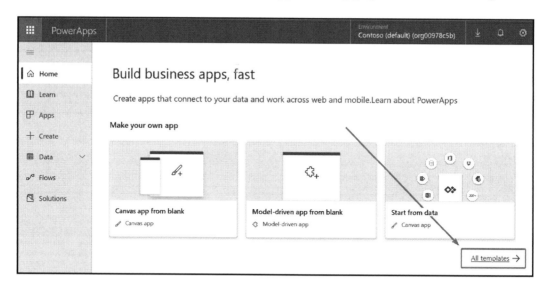

4. There are lots of templates to choose from. Select the one that is closest to your requirement:

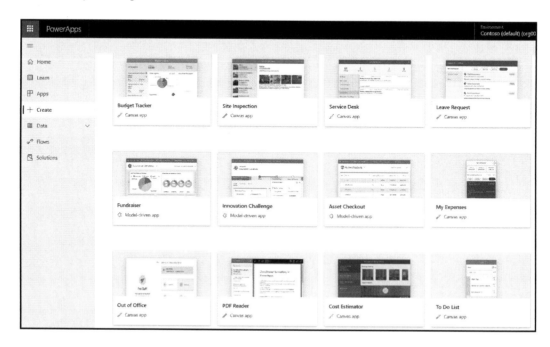

5. Give your app a name and choose the appropriate layout (**Phone** or **Tablet**). Click **Create**:

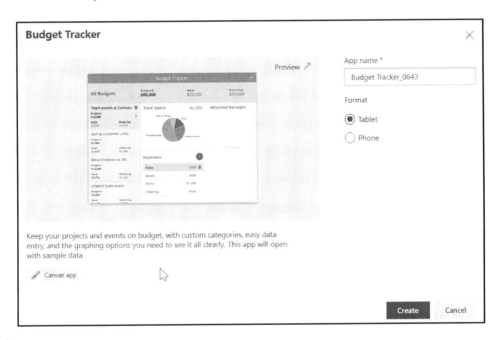

6. The app gets loaded in the Power Apps designer. Press the play icon, as shown in the following screenshot, to see the app in action:

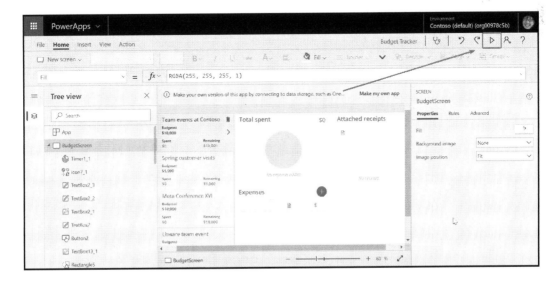

7. Now, if you are happy with the functionality of the app and want to share it with your colleagues or want to extend/change the app, click on **Make my own app**. At this stage, Power Apps will create a copy of the app that you can customize.

How it works...

In order to better understand Power Apps, we need to dive deeper into what the Power Apps designer can do.

Power Apps designer

Let's start with the Power Apps designer's components:

- **Screens**: Screens are the containers for Power Apps different controls. The screen is nothing but the visual frontend of an application designed for user interaction.
- **Controls**: To design Power Apps, different UI elements are required. These UI elements are also known as controls.
- **Properties**: The appearance and behavior of control can be altered by setting its properties—for example, width, height, text, and so on.
- **Connections**: You can access the data in other data sources via a connection—for example, you can read data from SharePoint, SQL Server, or Excel by creating separate connections.
- **Variables**: You can save the state of control or its value using variables. These variables can then be referred to in rules or other conditional logic. Variables can be created using the `Set` function—for example, `Set(x,34)` will store 34 in variable x.

Let's now learn to use the Power Apps designer:

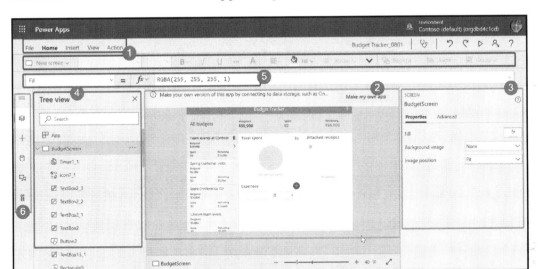

- **(1)** The section marked in blue is the menu bar. We will look at the menu items later in this chapter.
- **(2)** The section marked in yellow in the center panel is used to build the layout of the app. The controls can be placed and arranged in the layout. The center panel also lets you select a control by clicking on it, thereby accessing all the properties of the control in the properties panel.
- **(3)** The section marked light green is the property panel that lets you change the properties of the selected control, such as height, color, and so on.

Please note that the properties of a control might vary based on the control type—for example, the label and text controls have a **Text** property whereas a pie chart control has an **ItemColorSet** property.

- **(4)** The section in red on the left displays all the controls used in the App. You can select a control from here if the controls in the center panel are inaccessible (for example, if a control sits behind another control).

- **(5)** Finally, the section marked in dark green is where a property is set with a given value. You can also specify conditional values, as shown in the following code:

```
If ( Text(Value(ThisItem.Expense)) = "0", "$",
Text(Value(ThisItem.Expense),"$#,##"))
```

- **(6)** The section in light blue lets you perform the following tasks:
  - access controls that you place in the center panel
  - add controls in the center layout
  - add images and media
  - connect to various data sources
  - to test and validate your app

You can learn more about these properties at `https://m365book.page.link/ powerapps-props`.

Saving and publishing

When you build a Power App, remember to save the app before closing the window. This can be done by clicking on **File | Save**. When you save the app, you will be asked to specify a name, as shown in the following screenshot:

You can save your app in the cloud or on your desktop as a `.msapp` file. While saving, you can also specify the **App settings**, such as the orientation, icon, background, and so on:

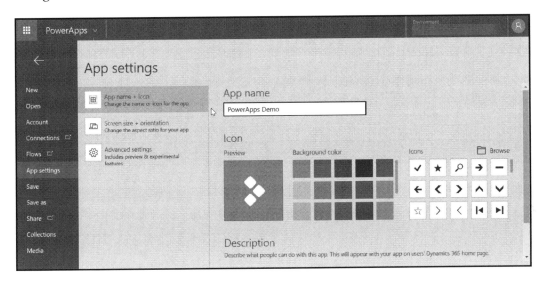

Your app will only be available to you and those who have edit permissions. If you want the app to be available to others within your organization, then you need to **Publish** it, as shown in the following screenshot. You may continue to make changes to the app after publishing; however, the users should use the last published version:

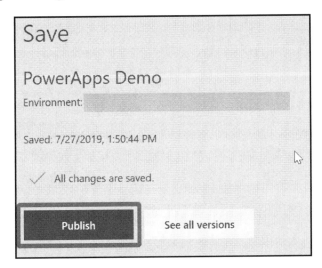

Power Apps also has an autosave feature that enables you to save the app every two minutes. You can enable or disable the **Auto save** setting from the **Account** tab in the **File** menu.

Versioning

Power Apps create a new version every time you save the app. You can only have one published version of the app at a time. If you ever want to revert back to an older version, click **Restore** from the context menu of the app version or from the top bar:

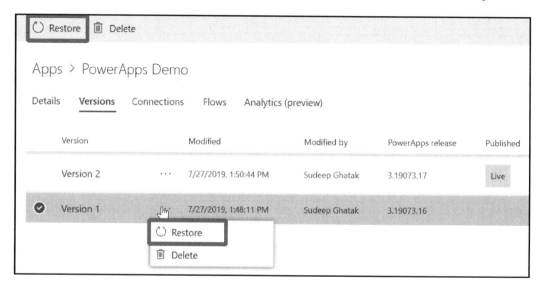

See also

- The *Creating a canvas app from a blank template* recipe in this chapter
- The *Creating Power Apps from a SharePoint list/library* recipe in this chapter

Connecting to data sources

Power Apps lets you build business applications that use data from line-of-business applications. Using Power Apps, you can build apps that work with local as well as connected data sources.

Connected data sources are external to Power Apps such as Excel spreadsheets, SharePoint lists, OneDrive for Business, Dropbox, and SQL Server.

Local data sources save the data in data tables within Power Apps. Collections are one such data source that gets stored within the Power App when the Power App is saved and published.

We will see how you can connect to data sources in this recipe.

Getting ready

You need Power Apps plan included in your Microsoft 365 subscription in order to build a Power App. Download the `Cars.xlsx` file from `Chapter 14` folder in the GitHub repository of this book here `https://m365book.page.link/github` and save the file in your OneDrive for Business.

How to do it ...

To connect to a data source, do the following steps:

1. Open the Power Apps designer and go to **View | Data sources** to open the **Data sources** pane.
2. Expand **Connectors** group and select **OneDrive for Business** and establish a connection by providing your credentials.

3. Select the downloaded file from OneDrive for Business and click on **Connect**:

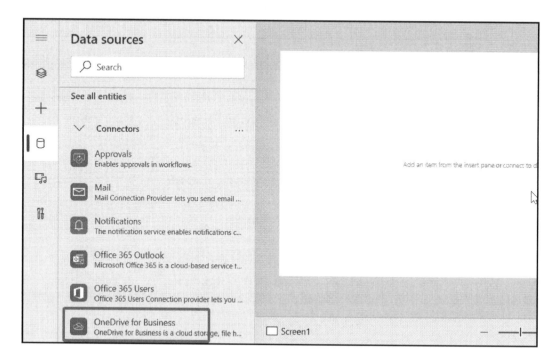

 Some connectors, such as Microsoft 365 Outlook, require no additional steps, and you can show data from them immediately. Other connectors prompt you to provide credentials, specify a particular set of data, or perform other steps—for example, SharePoint and SQL Server require additional information before you can use them. With Common Data Service, you can change the environment before you select an entity.

How it works...

Connectors in Power Apps let you bring data from other systems. Some connectors provide data in the form of tables, some provide only actions, and some provide both. You can store all your connections by going to **Power Apps** | **Data** | **Connections**:

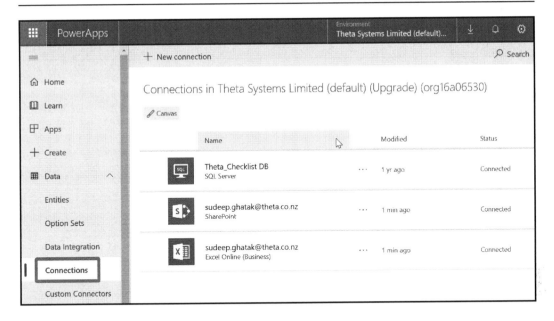

Let's look at the two different types of connections:

- **Data connections**: The data source connections that you make are used by some of the Power Apps controls, such as galleries, dropdowns, and checkboxes. Data connectors have an **Items** property that can be bound to the controls:

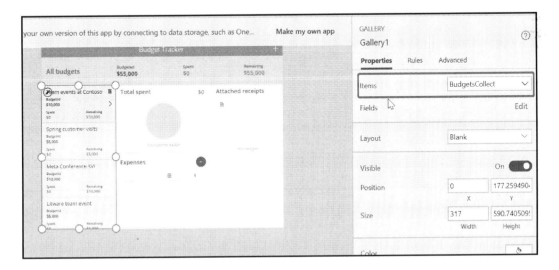

- **Action connectors**: Action connectors perform an action instead of fetching data, like the `Office365.SendEmail()` action, which sends an email.

There's more

It is a good practice to minimize the amount of data stored on the local device. You should always retrieve only the subset of the data required for your application and requery the database only when the user indicates that they want more. This reduces the processing power, memory, and network bandwidth that your app needs, thereby reducing response times for your users, even on phones connected via a cellular network.

Power Apps support features such as filtering, sorting, and so on. These functions enhance the user experience. The way that Power Apps achieves this is by delegating the task of data processing to the data source, instead of retrieving the data into the app and processing it locally. The challenge is that not every data source supports delegation, and not every Power App function supports delegation. If you're working with small datasets (fewer than 2,000 records), you can use any data source and formula because the app can process data locally if the formula can't be delegated. The limit can be changed from the Power Apps settings page by going to **File** | **Settings** | **Advanced Settings**. The default is 500 and the upper limit is 2,000 (at the time of writing this book).

Working with large datasets requires you to use data sources and formulas that can be delegated. The following tabular data sources support delegation:

- Common Data Service
- SharePoint
- SQL Server

Go to `https://m365book.page.link/delegation` to find out more about the functions that support delegation.

You can write a custom connector of your own by following the documentation at `https://docs.microsoft.com/en-us/connectors/`.

See also

- The *Creating a template-based app* recipe in this chapter
- The *Adding screens* recipe in this chapter
- The *Creating a canvas app from a blank template* recipe in this chapter
- The *Creating Power Apps from a SharePoint list/library* recipe in this chapter

Adding screens

A screen in Power Apps is an element that contains a set of controls. Power Apps lets you add as many screens as you like. It also supports navigation between screens based on the user's action. For instance, you could have a screen displaying a list of records, but when the user clicks on an item from within the list, it takes you to the details screen. There could be another screen that lets you modify the list item. The transition between the screens is controlled by the **Navigate** function. In the next section, I will talk about adding screens to your canvas.

Getting ready

You need Power Apps plan included in your Microsoft 365 subscription in order to build a Power App.

How to do it...

To add a screen, go through the following steps:

1. Open the app in the Power Apps designer.

2. From the **File** menu, click **Insert** and add a screen:

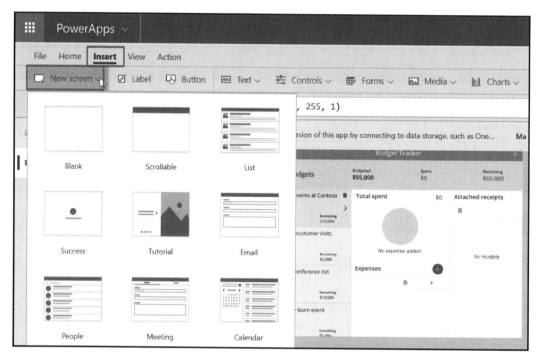

How it works...

Screens act as the interface between the app and the user. There are various types of screens. Some common ones are as follows:

- **Blank**: As the name suggests, the screen does not contain any controls by default.
- **List**: This comes with a **Gallery** control that can be used to display a list of items.
- **Tutorial**: This screen comes with some drawing elements that can be used to provide guided navigation.
- **Success**: This screen can be used to display confirmation messages after an add, update, or delete operation.
- **Email**: This screen provides a template to compose an email.
- **Calendar**: The screen comes with a calendar control.

There's more

Every app that performs get, create, update, add, and delete operations typically requires three screens. You can add more screens if you think this will improve the usability of your app. In order to switch between one screen and another, Power Apps provides two functions: **Navigate** and **Back**:

- **Navigate** lets you transition to another screen of your choice. The syntax of using the **Navigate** function is as follows:

      Navigate(Screen, ScreenTransition, UpdateContext)

  The **first** parameter is the screen that you want to navigate to. The **second** parameter is the visual effect produced when you switch from one screen to another. The **third** parameter is **optional** and is used if you want to pass additional parameters to the next screen—for example, {Shade:Color.Green} will set the Shade context variable to Green.

- The **Back** function just takes you back to the last screen you navigated from. It only accepts one variable: ScreenTransition:

      Back(ScreenTransition)

  The parameter is optional.

See also

- The *Creating a template-based app* recipe in this chapter
- The *Connecting to data sources* recipe in this chapter
- The *Sharing Power Apps* recipe in this chapter
- The *Creating a canvas app from a blank template* recipe in this chapter
- The *Creating Power Apps from a SharePoint list/library* recipe in this chapter

Creating a canvas app from a blank template

Power Apps has several templates that give you a head start in creating an app; however, if you want to start from scratch, you can start with a blank template. The following example demonstrates how you can create an app from scratch. The app queries data from a spreadsheet in your OneDrive for Business. This demonstration only focuses on the basics and doesn't go into detail on building a fully functional solution.

 It is recommended that you start with a template that closely resembles what you are trying to build. This will save you a lot of time and effort.

In the next section, we will build an app that gets a list of cars from an Excel spreadsheet that is stored in OneDrive for Business:

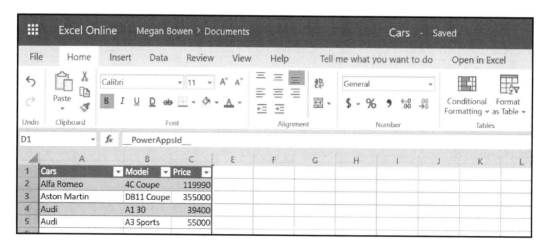

Although we can extend this app to add/update and delete records from the spreadsheet, our intention is to just introduce the users to the concept of a screen, a control, and a data connection.

Getting ready

You need Power Apps plan included in your Microsoft 365 subscription in order to build a Power App.

Download the `Cars.xlsx` file from `Chapter 14` folder in the GitHub repository of this book here `https://m365book.page.link/github` and save the file in your OneDrive for Business. If you are using a file of your choice, note that Power Apps supports excel files that have data stored in tables:

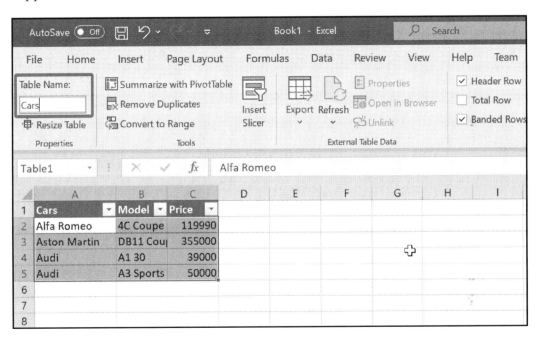

How to do it...

To start building an app from scratch, go through the following steps:

1. Go to Office.com and log in with your organization's credentials.
2. Go to **Power Apps**.
3. Create a blank app and choose the layout that you want—**Phone** or **Tablet**:

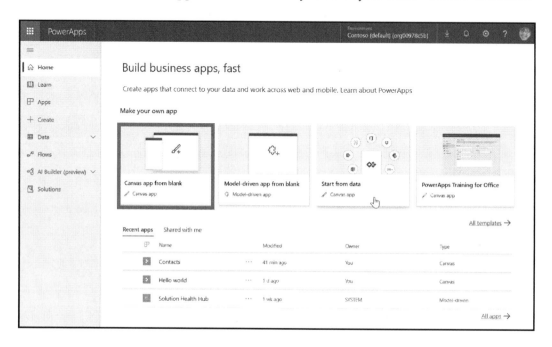

4. You will be taken to the Power App designer. Click on **connect to data**:

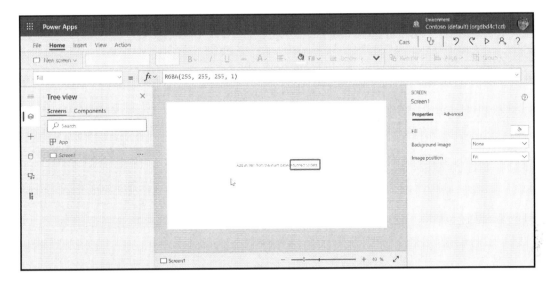

5. A panel will appear on the left of your Power Apps designer window. Type `onedrive` and select **OneDrive for Business**:

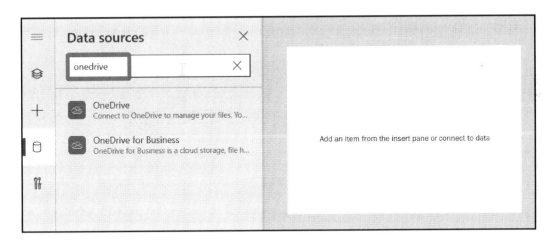

6. A panel will now appear on the right. Click on **Connect**:

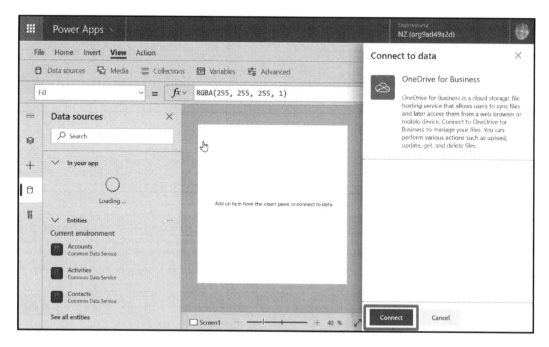

7. Now choose the Excel file that you want to build the Power App with:

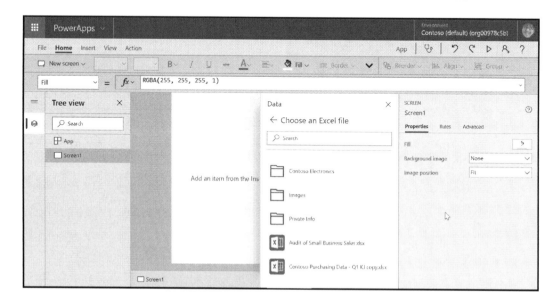

8. Now we need to add a new screen to display the data. Go to **Home** | **New Screen** | **List**. The **List** screen comes with a gallery control:

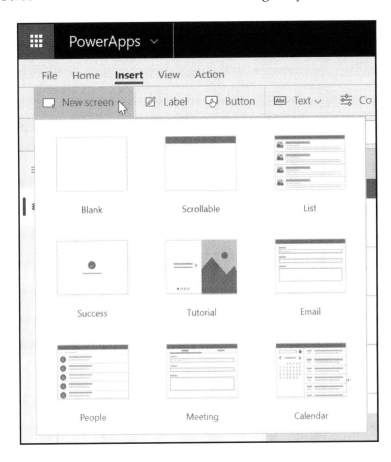

9. Select the **Gallery Control** to bind with the data. From the right-hand pane, select **Items** from the **Properties** dropdown and select **Cars**:

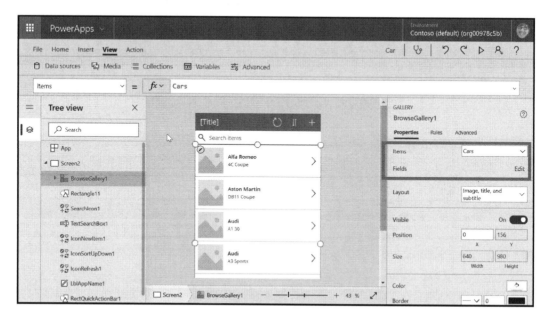

10. Click on the **Edit** link next to **Fields** and add the fields that you want to add to the gallery.
11. Add a label control on the gallery by going to **Insert | Label**. Select the label and set the **Text** property to the formula, as shown in the following screenshot:

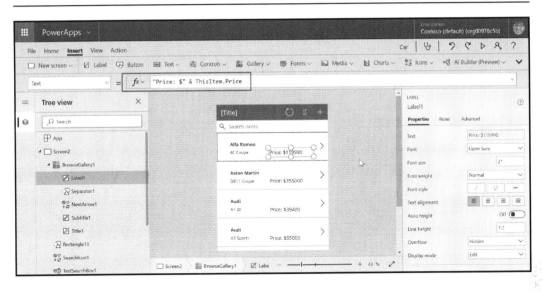

12. A screen to display the data will now be ready. You can add additional screens to add/edit/update operations.

13. Save the app by pressing *Ctrl + S* or through the **File** menu.

14. You will now be prompted to name the app, as shown in the following screenshot:

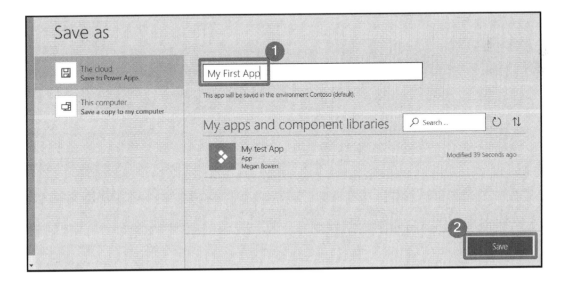

15. **Publish** the app (you will not see this option if this is the first time you are saving the app).

16. Once you have published your app, you can then share it with your colleagues:

How it works...

You can see your app in action by pressing the play button in the top-right corner, as shown in the following screenshot:

Your app will then launch on your device.

 Note that the play button should not be mistaken for a "preview" mode. There is no preview mode in Power Apps, except for the designer layout itself. If the form is submitted, then the data gets added, updated, or deleted in the underlying data source.

Whenever you **Save** changes to a canvas app, only you and anyone else who has permissions can see the changes. In order to make it available to everyone else, you need to **Publish** the app. Every time you save the app, a new version is created. You can access the previous versions on the **Publish** screen:

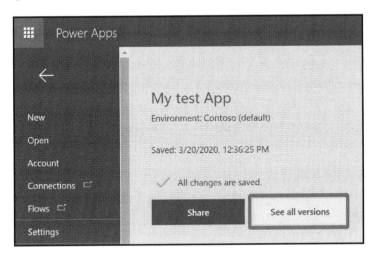

Those who do not have edit rights to the app can only access the last published version. The published version shows **Live** in the **Published** status column. You can restore an older version by clicking **Restore** in the drop-down context menu:

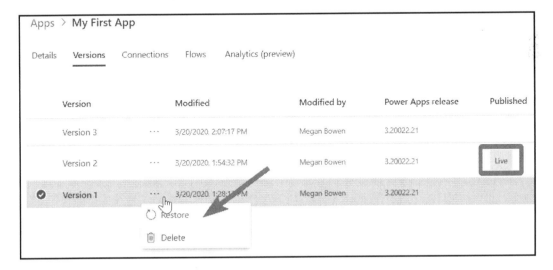

There's more...

The app we built was a simple one. Most apps that you will build will require an understanding of some core concepts, which we will look at in the following sections.

Power Apps events

Events occur when some sort of interaction takes place in the app. This could be a click of a button, the loading of a screen, the submission of a form, and so on. Some notable events in Power Apps are as follows:

- OnStart: The OnStart event is fired when the app loads. This is the first event that fires, and so it is used to prepare the app. The OnStart event is often used to do the following:
  - Set app variables.
  - Navigate to a specific screen within Power Apps.
  - Read values from a query string if Power Apps are accessed from the web.

The OnStart property of Power Apps can be set by selecting the **App** object from the left pane:

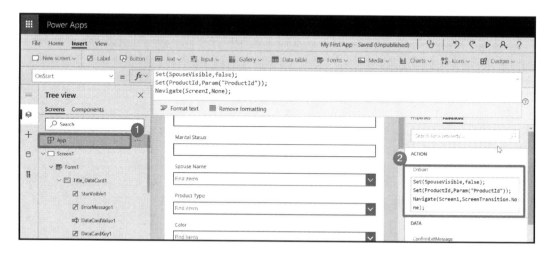

- OnVisible: The OnVisible event is fired when a user navigates to a screen. This function can be used to set screen-specific variables or prefill some field values.

- OnSelect: The OnSelect event fires when a control is clicked by the user. The event is usually used to handle button click events—for example, the OnSelect event of a **Save** button can be used to update the data store and refresh the screen:

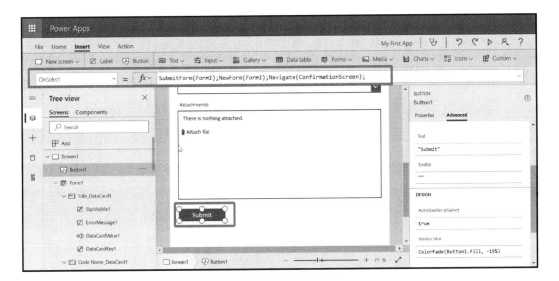

Variables

You can create variables in Power Apps by using the Set function:

```
Syntax:
Set(variable_name,value)
```

Unlike languages where you perform a calculation and then store it in a variable, in Power Apps, the value of a variable can change based on the state of another control or variable—for example, when we want to hide the spouse name if the marital status of the employee is unmarried.

We can achieve this by setting the SpouseVisible variable to True if the user selects Married and False if they select another status:

```
Syntax:
Set(SpouseVisible,if(MaritalStatus.Selected.Value =
"Married",false,true))
```

We then set the `Visible` property of the `SpouseName` field to the `SpouseVariable` variable:

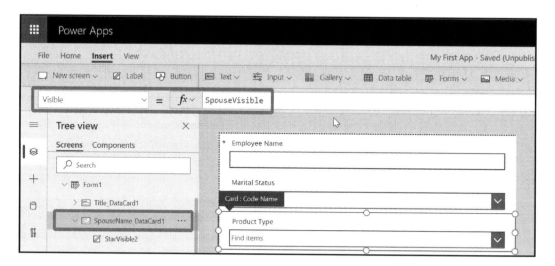

Power Apps continuously evaluates the variable based on the value in the marital status dropdown and changes the visibility of the **Spouse Name** field.

There is a special variable in Power Apps that is known as the `ContextVariable`.

Context variables can hold several data types:

- A single value
- A record
- A table
- An object reference
- Any result from a formula

A context variable holds its value while the app is running. The context variable in one screen is local to that screen and its value is preserved even if the user navigates to a different screen. Once the app is closed, the context variable's value will be lost and must be set when the app is loaded again.

Functions

Power Apps support lots of functions, some that perform string or date manipulation and others that perform mathematical calculations. One of the functions that need a special mention is `UpdateContext`.

The `UpdateContext` function is used to create a context variable. You can set multiple context variables in one `UpdateContext` function using the following code:

```
Syntax:
UpdateContext({ ContextVariable1: Value1 [, ContextVariable2: Value2
[, ... ] ] } )
```

See also

- The *Creating a template-based app* recipe in this chapter
- The *Connecting to data sources* recipe in this chapter
- The *Adding screens* recipe in this chapter
- The *Sharing Power Apps* recipe in this chapter
- The *Creating Power Apps from a SharePoint list/library* recipe in this chapter

Creating Power Apps from a SharePoint list/library

A SharePoint list comes with in-built list forms that let users create or update records in the list. Power Apps gives you the ability to change the form-editing experience. Once the form is customized using Power Apps, it takes over the SharePoint item-editing experience.

The following are some use cases when you should consider using Power Apps:

- Including a logo on the form
- Hiding some list fields from the end-user
- Managing the conditional visibility of list fields
- Adding conditional formatting in the form editing experience

Custom forms for lists are only supported in generic lists at the moment. Custom list and library templates are currently not supported, including, but not limited to, lists such as Announcements, Contacts, and Tasks.

In document libraries, Power Apps only supports editing custom metadata. Editing or managing file(s) is not supported.

In the following example, we use a SharePoint list that maintains a list of customer contacts and change the add/update item experience using Power Apps:

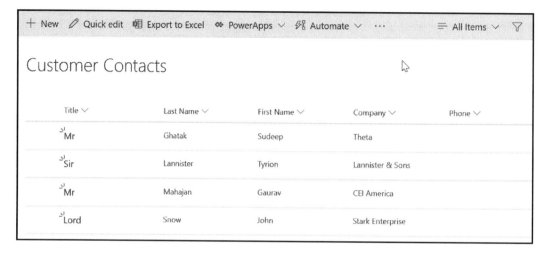

 Please note that not all SharePoint data types are supported in Power Apps. Check out `https://m365book.page.link/pa-issues` for more details.

In this section of this chapter, we'll look at the steps to create an app from a SharePoint list.

Getting ready

People with SharePoint permissions to manage, design, or edit the associated list will be able to create Power Apps list forms.

How to do it...

There are two options available for creating Power Apps from within a SharePoint list, as shown in the following screenshot:

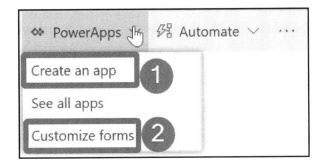

1. **Create an app**: This option lets you create a standalone application that can connect to other data sources. It can be accessed outside SharePoint, made available as a mobile app, and can be embedded inside a SharePoint site.
2. **Customize forms**: This option lets you replace the default SharePoint forms with the Power Apps forms; however, the app is tied to the SharePoint list and cannot be accessed outside the list.

Let's take a look at each option in the following section:

Customize forms

To customize an existing SharePoint list form, go through the following steps:

1. Open the SharePoint site where the list resides.
2. Click on the **Customize forms** option from the context menu in the ribbon:

3. The Power Apps designer will load and a SharePoint edit form will be available for customization

4. From the right pane, click **Edit fields** to include or exclude list fields from the form. Let's get rid of the **Attachments** field because it is not relevant to our use case. We'll also move the **Company** field to the top:

5. To save and publish your changes, click on the **Back to SharePoint** link from the top left-hand corner:

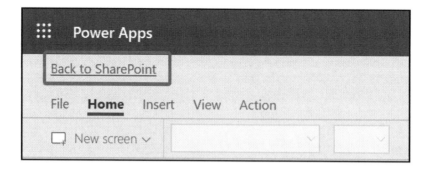

6. Save the App by pressing *Ctrl + S* or go to the **File** menu.

7. Publish the App by clicking **Publish to SharePoint**:

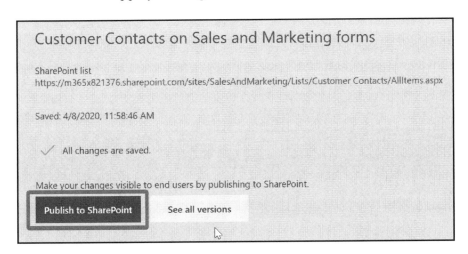

8. You will receive a confirmation message. Click **Publish to SharePoint** again

9. Your changes will now be visible when someone tries to add or update a list item:

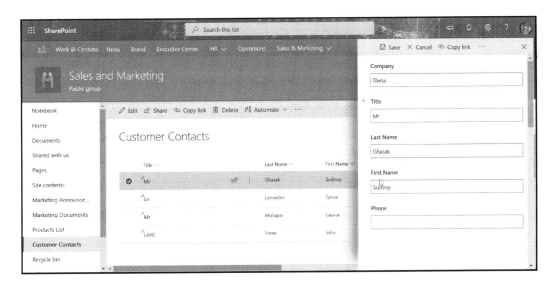

Create an app

To create a standalone Power App connected to a SharePoint list, go through the following steps:

1. Open the SharePoint site where the list resides.
2. Click on the **Create an App** option from the context menu in the ribbon.
3. You will be asked to specify a name for your App. Click **Create** once you have chosen one:

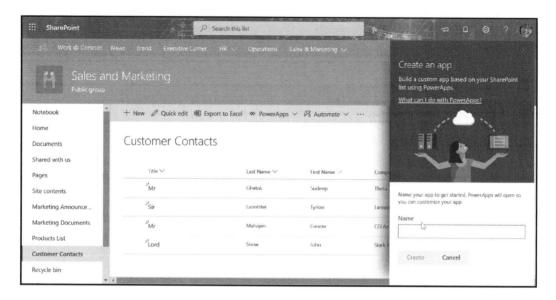

4. SharePoint builds a Power App for you based on the structure of the list. The App has three screens:
   - **Browse**: Displays a list of items
   - **Display**: Displays a single list item in read-only mode
   - **Edit**: Displays a single list item in edit mode

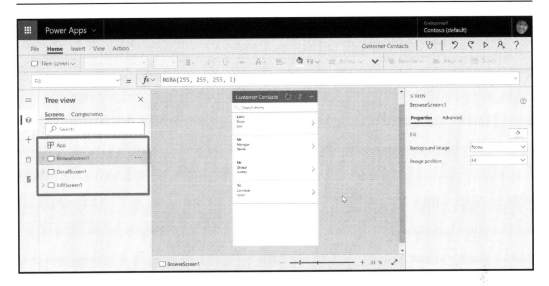

5. Open `BrowseScreen1`, select the gallery, and map the SharePoint fields to the controls in the gallery. SharePoint will have some fields selected by default, but you can change them from here:

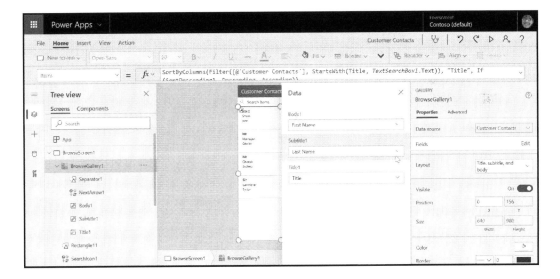

6. Open `DisplayScreen1` and select `DisplayForm1`. Configure the fields that you want to display on the form:

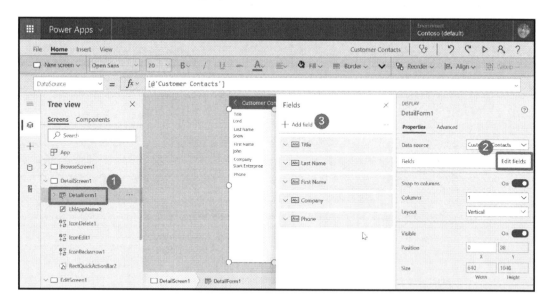

7. Repeat *step 6* for `EditForm1` in `EditScreen1`.
8. Save the app and publish it:

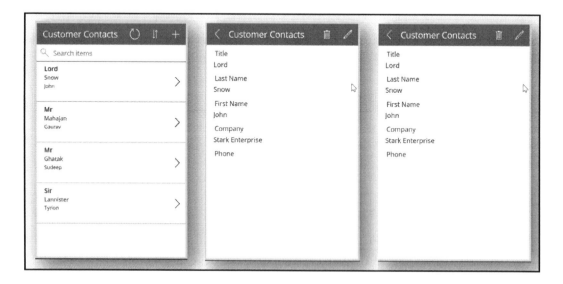

How it works...

When you select the **Customize forms** option, Power Apps creates a SharePoint data source behind the scenes and does all the plumbing for you. If you make changes to the SharePoint list columns and want the changes to appear in the Power Apps designer, then you can do this by clicking the **Refresh** button, as shown in the following screenshot:

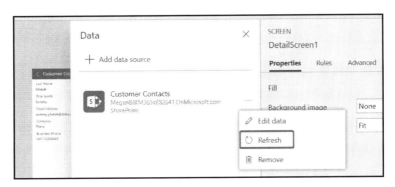

Once you customize a SharePoint list form, Power Apps will take over the editing experience. If you want to revert back to the default SharePoint list experience, then you can do that anytime from the **List Settings**:

1. Select **List Settings** from the gear icon in the top-right corner.
2. Under **General Settings**, select **Form Settings**.
3. On the **Form Settings** page, select **Use the default SharePoint form**, and then select **Delete custom form**:

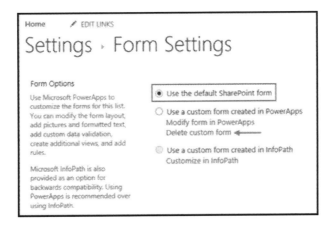

There's more...

Since SharePoint and Power Apps were built as two separate products, there are some limitations, some of which are as follows:

- Power Apps does not support all types of columns from SharePoint lists. The following list shows the kinds of columns that it does and doesn't support:
  - It supports single values for the **Choice** column.
  - It supports single values for the **Lookup** column.
  - It doesn't support **External Data**, **Rating**, and **Task Outcome** columns.
  - It doesn't support columns that have been configured to accept multiple values.
- Currently, Power Apps can only retrieve data from custom lists. It cannot use libraries on any other data stored in SharePoint.

See also

- *The Creating a template-based app* recipe in this chapter
- *The Connecting to data sources* recipe in this chapter
- *The Adding screens* recipe in this chapter
- *The Sharing your app* recipe in this chapter
- *The Creating a canvas app from a blank template* recipe in this chapter

Sharing Power Apps

Once the app is ready and published, you can share it with users so that they can run it. You could share the app with the entire organization if you want to. If you want certain users to make changes to your app, then you can add them as owners. The following section talks about how you can share your app with your colleagues.

Getting ready

You need to be an owner of the app in order to share it with others.

How to do it...

1. Sign in to **Power Apps**, and then select **Apps** from the left-hand side menu.
2. Select the app that you want to share by clicking on it and select **Share** from the banner.
3. Alternatively, you could select the **Share** option from the context menu of the app:

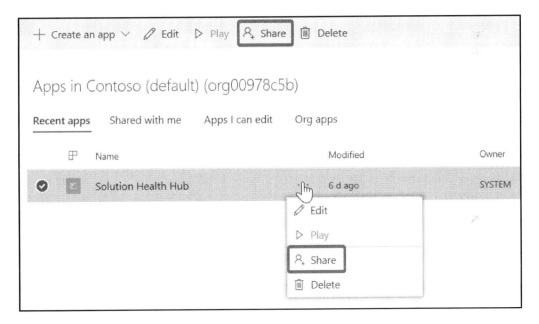

4. Open the **Share** screen.

5. Start typing the name or alias of the users or security groups in **Azure Active Directory** that you want to share the app with. Check the **Send an email invitation to new users** checkbox to notify the users:

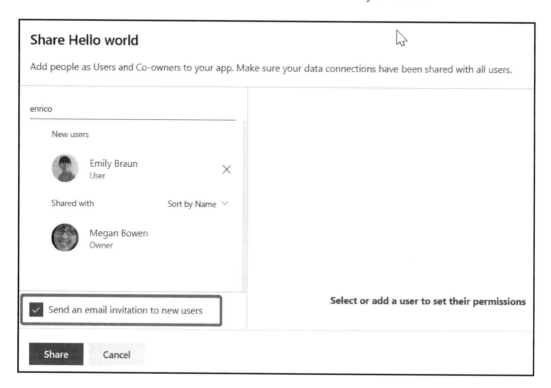

 To allow your entire organization to run the App (but not modify or share it), type `Everyone` in the sharing panel. You can't share the app with people or groups outside your organization.

6. You can assign a co-owner by selecting the user and checking the **Co-owner** checkbox. These users will be able to edit the Power App:

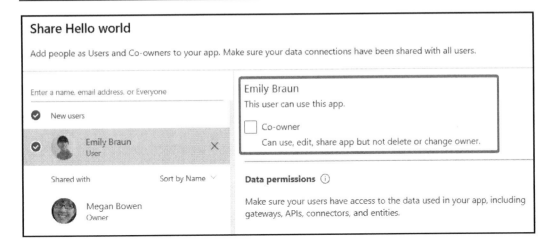

7. If you have built a Model-driven app, then you need to go through some additional steps, as shown in the following screenshot:

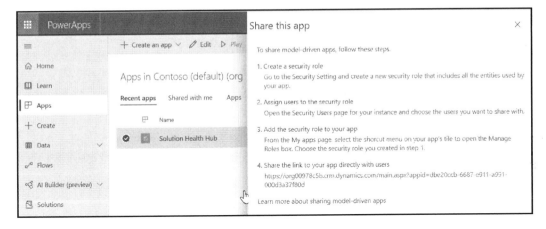

 For more information about managing security for an entity, see https://m365book.page.link/entities

8. To stop sharing the app with a user or group, select the remove (**X**) icon next to the user or group:

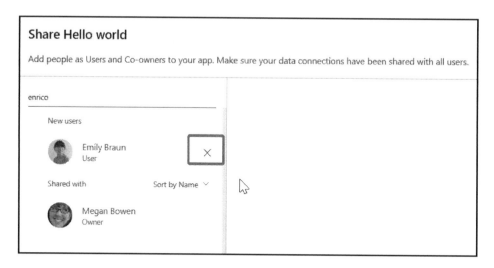

How it works...

If you checked the email invitation checkbox, then everyone with whom you shared the app can run it by selecting the link in the invitation. If a user selects the link on a mobile device, then the app opens in Power Apps Mobile. If a user selects the link on a desktop computer, the app opens in a browser. Co-owners who receive an invitation get another link that opens the app for editing in Power Apps Studio.

 Power Apps doesn't allow co-authoring, and so only one person will be able to open it in edit mode at one time; however, multiple people should be able to run it at any one time.

See also

- The *Creating a template-based app recipe in this chapter*
- The *Connecting to data sources recipe in this chapter*
- The *Adding screens* recipe in this chapter
- The *Creating a canvas app from a blank template* recipe in this chapter
- The *Creating Power Apps from a SharePoint list/library* recipe in this chapter

15
Power BI

Business intelligence (also referred to as **BI**) is all about connecting **business decision making** to **facts about the business** and its **environment**. BI lets you take a deep dive into data in order to make better business decisions.

Microsoft Power BI is Microsoft's BI tool that helps you model, visualize, and share insights. Power BI enables you to analyze information in a more meaningful and intuitive way.

Power BI is a tool for everyone. Decision-makers can use Power BI dashboards for making business decisions, while developers can use Power BI **application programming interfaces (APIs)** to push data into datasets and build data models.

You can build Power BI reports using Power BI Desktop. Power BI Desktop (`https:/ /m365book.page.link/powerbi-desk`) is a free application that you can install right on your own computer.

While Power BI Desktop is a downloadable tool to build reports, the Power BI service is a cloud-based service that lets you share reports over the web with your colleagues. The Power BI service provides limited editing features but lets you collaborate with your colleagues and teams.

If your organization is already using Microsoft 365, then you might already have an Enterprise plan that includes Power BI Pro. Power BI Pro is an individual user license that allows access to all content and capabilities in the Power BI service. Power BI Pro also allows you to collaborate and use workspaces to share with other people, create apps, sign up for subscriptions, and so on.

If your organization has over 500 users using Power BI, you will need to move to a higher plan, which is the Power BI Premium plan. Power BI Premium allows organizations to be able to better administer and manage the resources that are being used with Power BI.

This chapter provides you a basic understanding of Power BI. There are several advanced concepts and topics that were not possible to be covered in a single chapter. This chapter should serve as a good starting point for end users or anyone who is new to Power BI.

In this chapter, we will learn about the following topics:

- Retrieving data
- Transforming data
- Modeling data
- Visualizing data
- Sharing a report/dashboard/dataset

Technical requirements

Power BI Desktop is supported only on the Windows platform at the moment, on Windows 10, Windows 7, Windows 8, Windows 8.1, Windows Server 2008 R2, Windows Server 2012, and Windows. It is available for both 32-bit (x86) and 64-bit (x64) platforms.

You can either download the standalone installer from the website or you can install it from the Windows Store as a Windows app.

Power BI reports can also be viewed on the mobile app (covered later, in `Chapter 19`, *Microsoft 365 on Mobile*), which is available from the Windows, Android, and Apple stores.

 Please refer to the Power BI Desktop guide at `https://m365book.page.link/bi-desktop` for more info.

The examples used in this chapter have been demonstrated using Power BI Desktop.

Retrieving data

Retrieving is the process of fetching data from a location. Power BI has connectors to various data sources, ranging from text and **comma-separated values (CSV)** files to databases, as well as web pages. Some common Power BI connectors are shown in the following screenshot:

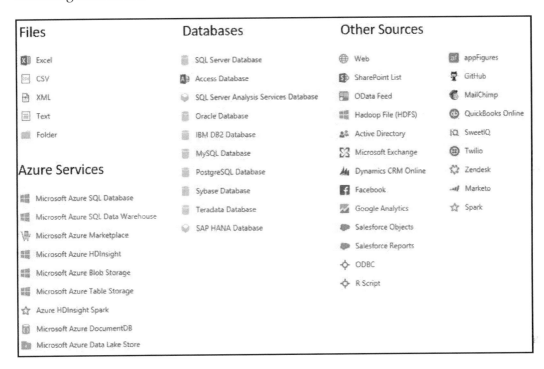

In this section, I will demonstrate how you can retrieve data from a CSV file.

Getting ready

Download the `Products_bikes.csv` file from `Chapter 15` folder in the GitHub repository of this book here `https://m365book.page.link/github`

You don't need any special permission to retrieve data from files such as text, CSV, or Excel files.

> If you are querying a secure data store, you might require additional permissions.

How to do it...

1. Open the Power BI Desktop tool.
2. Click on **Get Data** and select the **Text/CSV** option:

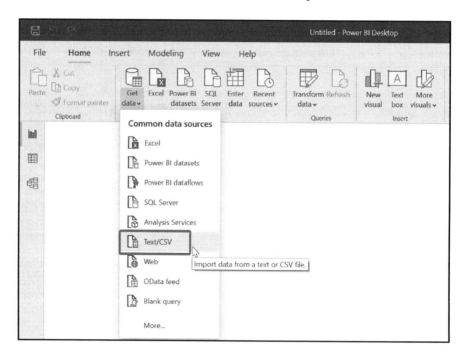

3. Press **Connect**.
4. Browse to the location of the CSV file and open the `Products_bikes.csv` file.
5. Click **Load**.

6. Power BI Desktop will show a preview of the data. Click on **Load**, and the data gets loaded into the tool.

How it works...

After the data is imported, Power BI Desktop lets you analyze the data in three ways:

- By using one of the visualizations on the imported data:

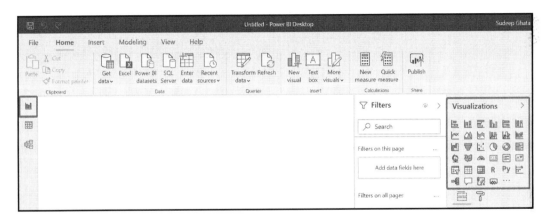

- By looking at the raw data in tabular form:

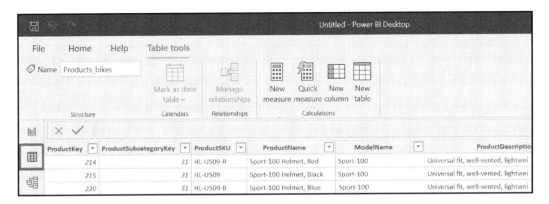

- By looking at the structure of the table and its relationship to other tables:

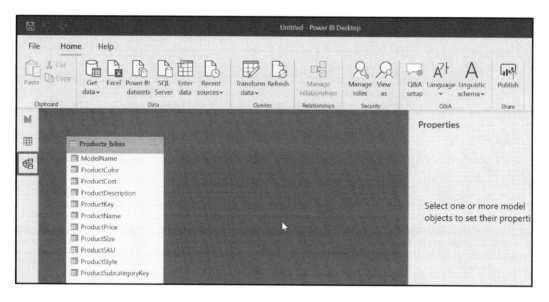

If you import the data once, Power BI Desktop stores the data source details internally. So, if the data in the source file changes, you can just use the **Refresh** option to import the modified data:

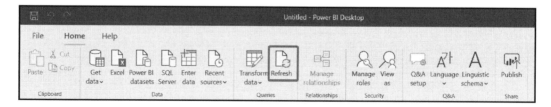

 If you used credentials for a secure data store, they are not saved in the PBIX file itself (but are saved in the Power BI Desktop config). So, if you publish/share the PBIX file, the recipient cannot use your credentials—they need their own.

See also

- The *Transforming data* recipe
- The *Modeling data* recipe
- The *Visualizing data* recipe
- The *Sharing a report/dashboard/dataset* recipe

Transforming data

Data transformation refers to the process of converting data from one format to another. This could require simple or complex data manipulation, based on the nature of the data.

In most cases, the data that you retrieve from a data source is not in a format where it can be used as-is, and you might have to take some additional steps to clean it.

Examples of basic transformations include the following:

- Changing data types
- Filtering (rows and/or fields)
- Creating conditional columns
- Splitting columns
- Renaming/reformatting

Some examples are as follows:

- Getting rid of trailing spaces at the end of a text field
- Reconciling multiple formats saved in a date field (such as Jan-19, Jan 2019, 01-19, and so on)
- Concatenating **Title**, **First Name**, **Last Name**, and so on to get the person's name

Hence, the first step after retrieving data from a data store is to clean the data and convert it into a reusable format. In the following example, we will perform three data transformation activities on an Excel spreadsheet, shown in the following screenshot:

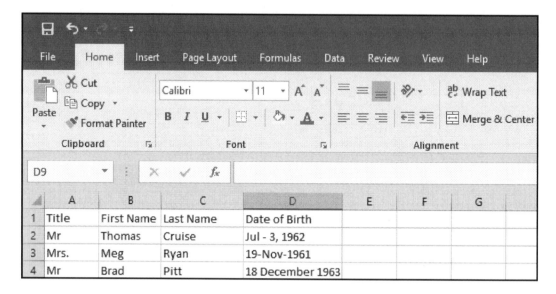

1. Get rid of the . in the **Title** field (where applicable).
2. Combine the name fields (**First Name**, **Last Name**) into one field.
3. Change the dates to conform with a consistent date format.

Getting ready

For this exercise, download the file DOB.csv from Chapter 15 folder in the GitHub repository of this book here https://m365book.page.link/github

You don't need any special permission to perform data transformation on the data that has already been imported.

You should have access to the data if you are querying a secure data store.

How to do it...

1. Connect to a data store and load the data, as demonstrated here:

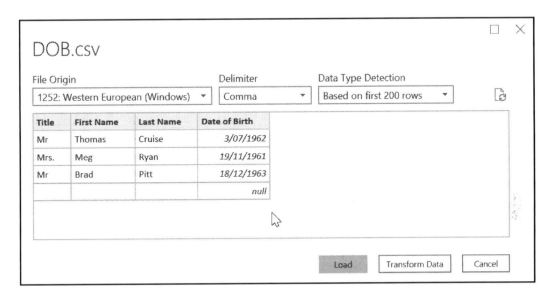

2. Once the dataset is loaded, click on **Transform data**:

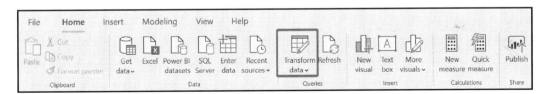

3. You are now able to apply transformations to the imported data:

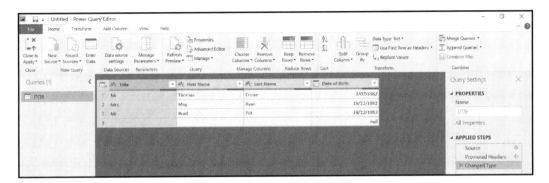

As you must have noted, the Power BI Desktop tool has treated the **first row** in the `DOB.csv` file as a **header row** and the data type of the **Date of Birth** column has automatically been changed to **Date**. Also, you'll note that all date fields now have a consistent date format. We'll explain this in the *How it Works...* section.

4. Next, we need to remove the dot (after **Mrs**) to make the **Title** consistent with other records:

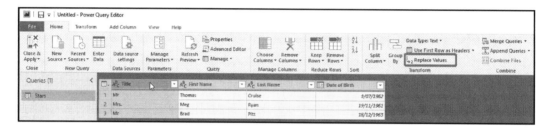

5. The `replace` operation requires you to specify the text that needs to be changed, along with the replacement string. Replace the . with an empty string.

6. Instead of having three name fields, we'll merge them all into one. To do this, select the three columns and click **Merge Columns**:

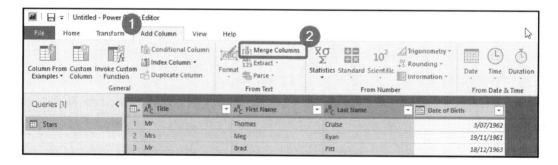

 Note here that the order in which you select the columns will determine the order they are merged. That is, if you first selected **Last Name**, then held *Shift* and selected **First Name** and finally **Title**, it would put the columns in the following order: **Last Name**, **First Name**, **Title**.

7. Use **Space** as the separator between the three columns while merging:

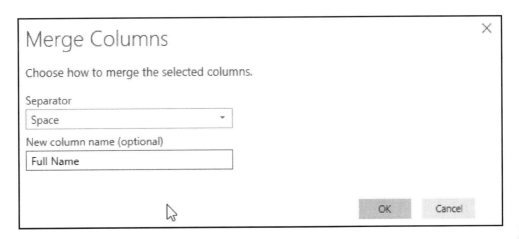

8. A new column should now appear in the table:

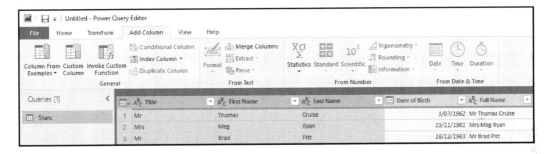

9. Finally, click on **Close Apply** to close the transformation window and apply the transformations to the dataset:

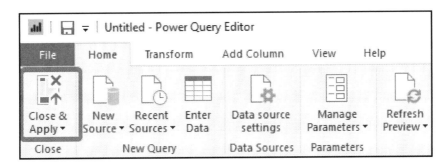

How it works...

Power BI Desktop gets busy as soon as you import data. You saw that in the preceding example. Three operations were applied to your dataset when it was loaded. They were as follows:

1. The first row got promoted to row header.
2. The data type of the **Date Of Birth** column was changed to **Date**.
3. The date format of all dates was set to dd/mm/yyyy.

If you want to use a different date format, change the preferences from **File | Options and Settings | Options | Regional Settings**.

The way Power BI Desktop achieved this by applying a series of steps called **transformations**. The transformation steps can be seen on the lower right section of Power BI Desktop:

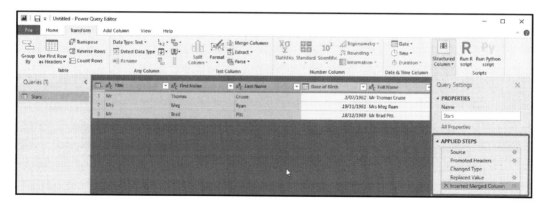

As you witnessed in this example, the first three transformation operations were applied automatically for you. You can change the data type by clicking on the data type selector in the header and assign a particular data type:

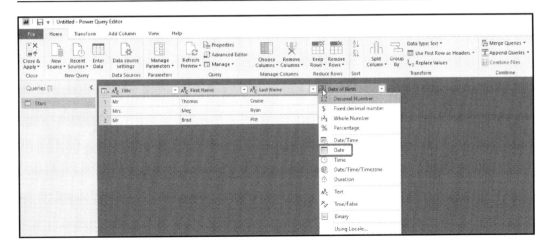

The beauty of transformation is that it eliminates the need to perform repetitive operations on data every time you connect to the data store. Power BI Desktop records all your transformation steps and then applies the steps sequentially every time you query the data store. In other words, you spend time building the transformation steps just once. From there on, Power BI Desktop manages the data cleansing operations for you.

You can see a preview of the data at each step, and you can insert/remove/rearrange steps. When you click **Apply** in Power Query Editor, all the data goes through all the steps and then gets loaded to Power BI:

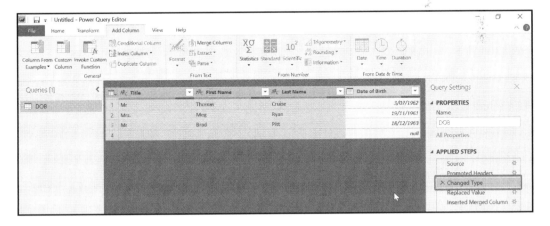

You cannot undo the transformation actions once applied; however, deleting the action takes you back to the state before the transformation was applied.

See also

- The *Retrieving data* recipe
- The *Modeling data* recipe
- The *Visualizing data* recipe
- The *Sharing a report/dashboard/database* recipe

Modeling data

Modeling is a process of combining multiple data sources and setting relationships between the datasets.

To understand modeling, you need to first grasp some key database terms.

Primary key: The primary key of a relational table uniquely identifies each record in the table (refer to `Customers.csv`). A table can have only one primary key. Since a primary key is unique, it cannot be repeated in the same table. Take this, for example:

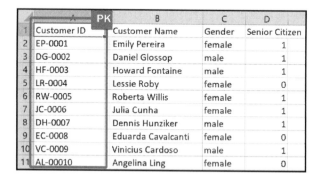

Customer info

In the preceding example, by specifying the customer ID, I can uniquely identify a person. There can be two customers with the same name, but they will each have a unique customer ID.

Foreign key: A database foreign key is a field in a relational table that matches the primary key column of another table (refer to `Product_Sales.csv`). See this, for example:

	A FK	B	C	D	E	F	G
1	Customer I	Customer Name	Order Date	Order ID	Postal Coc	Product IC	Quantity
2	EP-0001	Emily Pereira	4/10/2002	43	35801	102	3
3	DG-0002	Daniel Glossop	18/11/2003	34	99501	127	4
4	HF-0003	Howard Fontaine	28/01/2003	72	85001	18	1
5	LR-0004	Lessie Roby	25/05/2009	75	72201	103	5
6	RW-0005	Roberta Willis	6/10/2011	70	94203	119	2
7	JC-0006	Julia Cunha	14/06/2015	105	90001	90	3
8	DH-0007	Dennis Hunziker	22/10/2007	53	90209	28	4
9	EC-0008	Eduarda Cavalcanti	1/05/2006	59	80201	38	5
10	VC-0009	Vinicius Cardoso	10/07/2012	89	6101	2	2
11	AL-00010	Angelina Ling	15/08/2015	70	19901	91	3

Sales info

The **Customer ID** column (used in the earlier example) becomes a foreign key when used in the sales table. The same person can buy two products, and hence the customer ID can appear multiple times in the sales table. Every foreign key value must always correspond to a primary key in another table.

Fact table: A fact table stores quantitative information and is used for analysis and reporting. In our case, sales info is a fact table.

Dimension table: A dimension table is a collection of reference information about a business. In the preceding example, the customer info table will be a dimension table because it provides additional information about the customer. Similarly, we can have a product info dimension table (refer to `Products.csv`) with more information about the product being sold:

	A	B	C	D
1	Product ID	Product Name	Category	Sub-Category
2	1	Washington Berry Jui	Washington	Fruit Drinks
3	2	Washington Mango D	Washington	Fruit Drinks
4	3	Washington Strawber	Washington	Fruit Drinks
5	4	Washington Cream	Washington	Fruit Drinks
6	5	Washington Diet Sod	Washington	Fruit Drinks
7	6	Washington Cola	Washington	Fruit Drinks
8	7	Washington Diet Cola	Washington	Fruit Drinks
9	8	Washington Orange J	Washington	Fruit Drinks
10	9	Washington Cranberr	Washington	Fruit Drinks
11	10	Washington Apple Jui	Washington	Fruit Drinks

Products info

A fact table usually has information in the form of numeric data. Additionally, this data can be modified quite easily, and that can be done by clubbing together and adding any number of rows. These tables typically have more rows and fewer columns because they store transactions.

Dimension tables, on the other hand, tend to be shorter (because you can only have a given number of customers or products) but have many columns because they store metadata about the entity being stored, such as customer name, age, DOB, phone, address, email, and so on.

Let's say that you want to create a sales report. To build a meaningful sales report, you will need to pull information from other supporting tables. For example, a "Sales Info" table will contain transactional information such as the date of sale, and the number of products sold. A "Products Info" table will store information such as the product category, product price, product color, discount, and so on. A "Customer Info" table will contain information such as customer name, city, and so on.

Power BI lets you combine information from the three tables, thus enabling you to view the report in multiple dimensions such as Sales by Region, Sales by Product Category, Sales by Year, and so on. To do this, you need to define relationships between these tables. This is done using foreign key relationships, as explained previously. Modeling is the process of setting up this relationship.

Power BI modeling lets you do more than build relationships. It also lets you do the following:

- Perform custom calculations on existing tables.
- Define new metrics.
- Perform custom calculations for new metrics.

In the following example, we will create relationships between the product sales data tables

Getting ready

Download the following `.csv` files from `Chapter 15` folder in the GitHub repository of this book here `https://m365book.page.link/github`

- `Customers.csv`.
- `Locations.csv`.

- `Product_Sales.csv.`
- `Products.csv.`

You don't need any special permission to perform data modeling once the data is imported.

How to do it...

1. After the transformations are applied, click on the 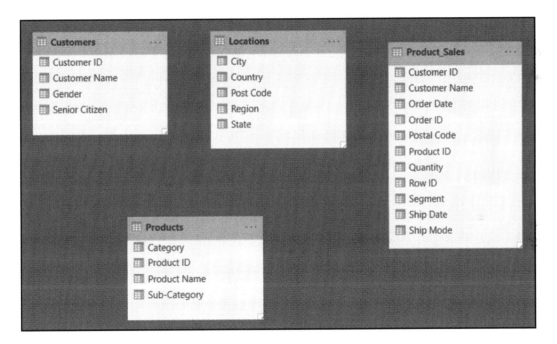 icon on the left-hand side of the screen. You will see all the data sources you have connected to:

2. In some cases, Power BI Desktop will automatically determine the relationships based on the column names. If it doesn't, connect the columns manually by dragging the column from one table to another:

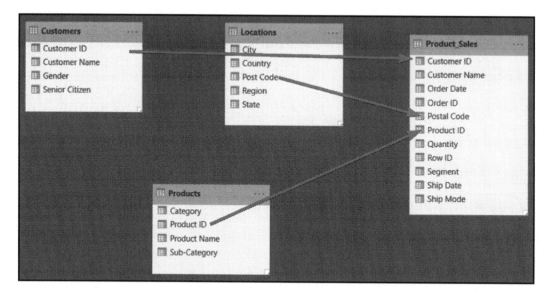

3. Once the columns are connected, your model is ready:

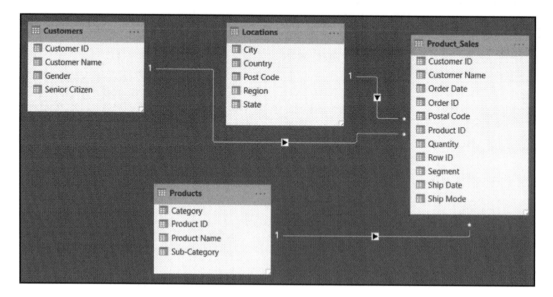

How it works...

The question you might ask is this: *why do we need a model at all?*

A model signifies the relationship between the tables. This enables you to analyze the data by customer, location, or product, or a combination of these. We will see this in action in our next recipe.

For a more detailed view of your data relationships, you could try selecting the **Manage Relationships** option on the **Home** tab.

A pop-up screen, which lists all the relationships in a single view, appears. From here, you can select **Autodetect** to find relationships in new or updated data. Select **Edit** in the **Manage Relationships** dialog to manually edit your relationships.

To better understand the concept of relationships, you need to understand two key terms:

- *Cardinality*
- *Cross-filtering*

Cardinality refers to the relationship between two tables based on the number of unique values in the column. It could be any of the following relationships:

- **One to many**: If the column is a primary key in one table and a foreign key in another table—for example, products and sales relationships
- **One to one**: If the column has a one-to-one mapping of data in both tables—for example, a person and driver license table relationship where there will be a unique record of a person against every driver's license number
- **Many to Many**: When there is a possibility of multiple values in both columns—for example, a student and class relationship, where each student can take multiple classes, and each class can have multiple students enrolled

Cross-filtering is the ability to set a filter context on a table based on values in a related table. The cross-filter relationship can be one of the following:

- **Both**: Where data in one table can be filtered based on the data in another—for example, Sales and Store. A product could be sold in multiple stores; at the same time, a store could have multiple products.
- **Single**: This is a relationship where the filter direction is unidirectional—for example, a Product table versus a Sales table. A sale item will only correspond to a single product, but a product could be sold several times.

Power BI Desktop resolves the cardinality and cross-filtering based on the column values in the two tables. It lets you change the cardinality and cross-filtering if you wish to.

 Assigning incorrect relationship parameters (cardinality and cross-filtering) will result in inaccurate visualizations, so a proper understanding of these concepts is necessary. We recommend watching Alberto Ferrari's presentation on Power BI relationships. The video can be found at `https://m365book.page.link/relationships`.

To create/modify a relationship, go to **Home | Manage relationships**, as shown here:

There's more...

Before we jump into the visualizations, we have got to learn some additional concepts—namely, calculated columns and measures.

Calculated columns

Sometimes, you need to create additional columns or measures within your model to create data for your visualizations. You can create these columns using **Data Analysis Expressions (DAX)** formulas. For instance, if you have been provided the dimensions of a car in feet and inches, you could create a DAX formula to change them to their metric system equivalents (refer to `car_sales.csv`). DAX formulas look similar to the formulas used in Excel, such as the one shown here:

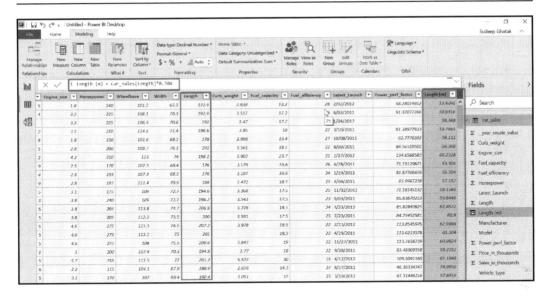

You might also need to create a calculated column to build a relationship between tables when no unique fields exist.

To create uniqueness in data, you can, for example, create a calculated column named "Phone Number" by combining the values from the "Area Code" and "Local Number" columns from your dataset.

> **Calculated column** values are stored in memory. They can cause performance issues if the dataset is too large. Hence, they should be used with caution.

Measures

Measures are usually the numeric fields within a dataset that can be aggregated or used in other ways (such as average, minimum, and maximum) to derive meaning from your data—for example, **total sales** by state; **average sales** by year. Measures are calculated at the time of the query and hence are not stored in the database. However, they use processing power to execute a query at the time of the request. Because measures are not stored in memory, they are generally faster but require more processing power. Hence, calculated columns and measures should be used judiciously.

You can create a measure in Power BI Desktop, as shown in the following screenshot. I am getting a forecast for the next year, based on the average cars sold this year:

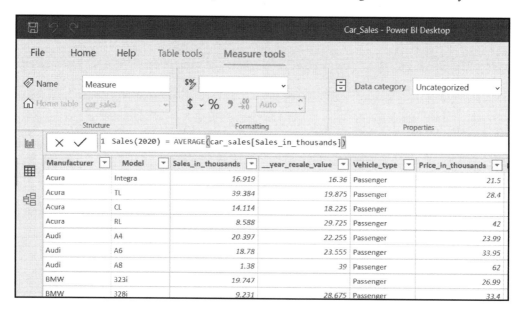

Unlike calculated columns, they don't appear in the model next to other columns, but you can drag them to your visualization window in the **Report** tab, as shown in the following screenshot:

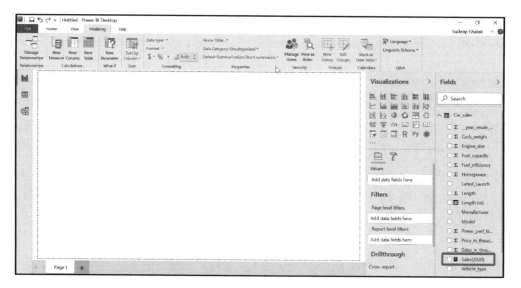

Notice that the measures are context-aware. What that means is that if you drag the **Sales(2020)** field alone, it shows the average sales across all models, but when you place it along with the **Model** field, it represents the breakup by each model:

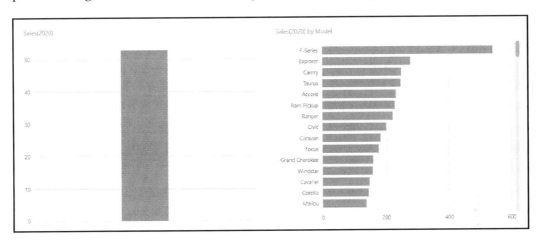

See also

- The *Retrieving data* recipe
- The *Transforming data* recipe
- The *Querying data using natural language* recipe
- The *Visualizing data* recipe
- The *Sharing a report/dashboard/dataset* recipe

Visualizing data

The end goal of any data-crunching exercise is to draw insights from your data. Power BI visualizations provide you with hundreds of visuals (some within Power BI Desktop; others from the marketplace). A Power BI report might consist of a single visual on the entire page, or it might have pages full of visuals.

There are many different visual types available directly from the Power BI **Visualizations** pane:

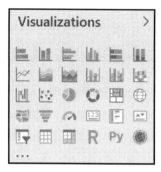

And, for even more choices, visit the **MARKETPLACE**:

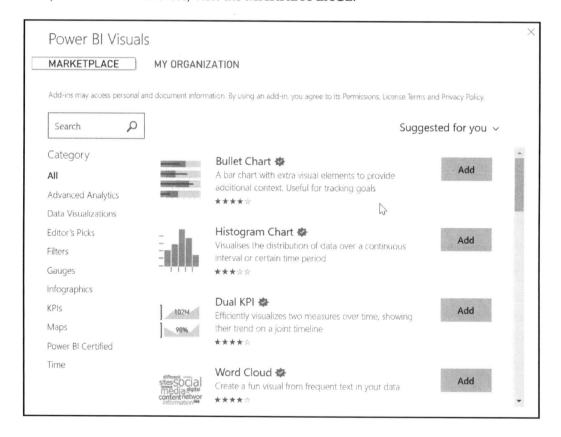

There is an upper limit to the number of fields you can add to any visual. The limit is 100 fields (including measures or columns). If your visual fails to load, try reducing the number of fields in your visualization.

Getting ready

A user can interact with the visual either as a designer or as a consumer.

A designer can add/edit or change visuals using Power BI Desktop. A consumer, on the other hand, can only look at the reports or dashboards shared with them. The consumer can interact with the visuals using filters and via natural language; they cannot make any major changes to the visualization.

Download the file `car_sales.csv` from `Chapter 15` folder in the GitHub repository of this book here `https://github.com/PacktPublishing/Microsoft-365-and-SharePoint-Online-Cookbook/tree/master/Chapter%2015`.

How to do it...

1. After you've completed the modeling of the dataset, click on the icon on your left-hand side of the screen to enter the report view.
2. From the right-hand **Visualizations** pane, pick a visual. We will use a **line chart** for the demo.
3. Pick the fields you want to display on the report.

4. Based on the field type, Power BI Desktop will place them under **Axis** or **Values**. You could also drag the fields as appropriate:

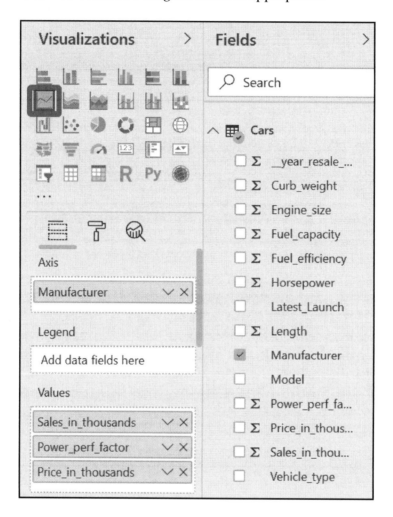

5. As soon as the fields are selected, the report appears on the canvas. You can sort by graph on any of the selected fields to derive insights:

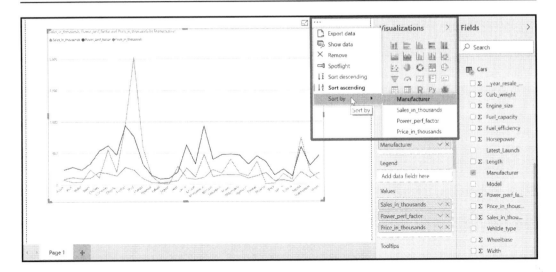

6. You can bring a visual into focus by clicking on the **Focus mode** option. This option displays the report in a full-page view. This is helpful when you have multiple reports on your page:

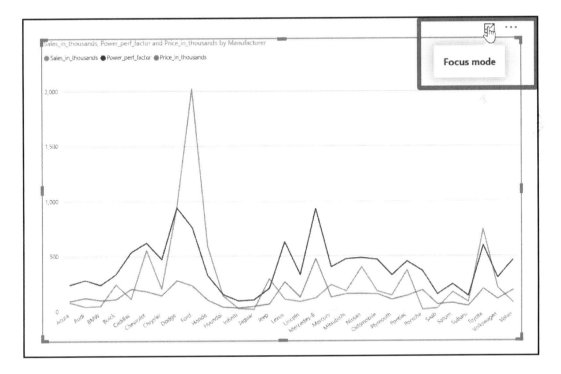

7. To go back to your report, use the **Back to report** option:

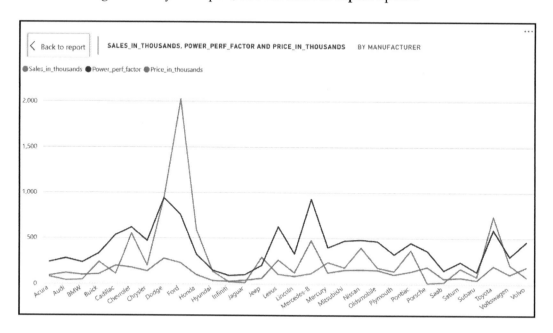

8. Power BI Desktop generates a random report title based on the fields you have selected. You can change the **Title** by updating the **Title text** option:

9. You now have built your first report using Power BI Desktop.

How it works...

Visuals in Power BI Desktop can be changed by simply selecting the report and choosing another visual from the **visualizations** gallery. There are several visuals that are provided within the Power BI Desktop. You can read more about each individual visual on Microsoft's Power BI documentation page, at `https://m365book.page.link/bi-visuals`.

A visualization has three property tabs:

- **Fields**: This tab lets you choose the fields for your visualization.
- **Format**: This tab lets you choose the data colors and labels for your dataset.
- **Analytics**: This tab lets you add additional lines to compare your data points against, such as a constant or an average line across your report.

Filters let you reduce the dataset you want to analyze. Say you want to focus on a specific year or a specific brand of car. Filters remove noise from the visual so that you can focus on the subject of interest. Filters are of three types:

- **Visual-level filters**: These affect only the selected visual but have more options, such as Top N filtering and filtering by measure value.
- **Report-level filter**: This applies the filter on a specific visual without affecting the rest of the page.
- **Page-level filter**: This applies the filter on all the related visuals within the page. The following screenshot shows a page-level filter on the **Manufacturer** field:

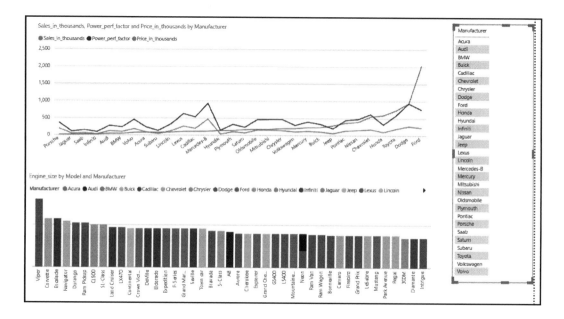

There's more...

Power BI has a powerful Q A feature that can be used to build charts just by using natural language.

You can use this feature by dragging the **Ask A Question** button from the ribbon, as shown in the following screenshot:

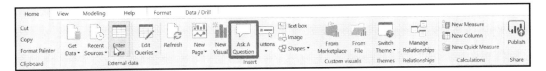

As soon as you drag this menu item on the canvas, Power BI suggests some probable questions based on the data. As you start typing, it even autoselects a visual based on the data:

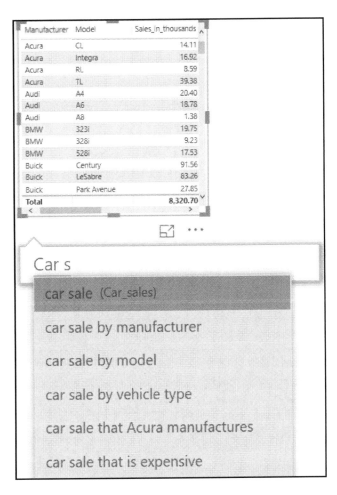

You can change the fields (highlighted with a yellow underline) to view the data in other ways (say, by model), as shown here:

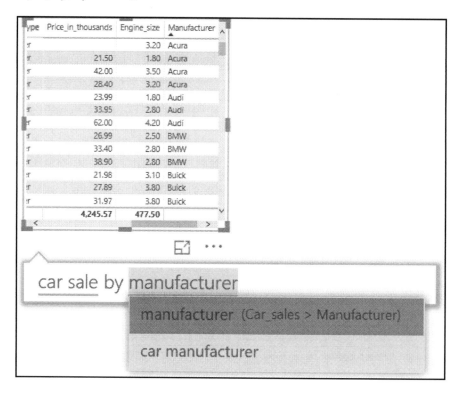

You get the same experience when you use the Q A feature on the Power BI web experience.

See also

- The *Retrieving data* recipe
- The *Transforming data* recipe
- The *Modeling data* recipe
- The *Querying data using natural language* recipe
- The *Sharing a report/dashboard/dataset* recipe

Sharing a report/dashboard/dataset

Microsoft 365 is a collaboration platform. The ability of users to build and share reports is a key factor. The Power BI service lets you share the charts and dashboards with your colleagues in several ways.

The **Dashboard** feature is only available in the Power BI service. It is a non-interactive collection of visuals pinned from one or more existing reports. If you click on a report pinned into the dashboard, the Power BI service takes you to the individual report, which provides a richer and more interactive experience.

Getting ready

In order to share a report, you need to first publish it to your Microsoft 365 tenant. While Power BI Desktop is free, you need a Power BI license to share your report with your colleagues. If you have a Power BI Pro license, you should be able to publish your report to Microsoft 365:

You can publish the report to your Microsoft 365 workspace or to a workspace you have access to. After you publish the report, you can access it at `https://app.` `powerbi.com` and log in with your Microsoft 365 credentials:

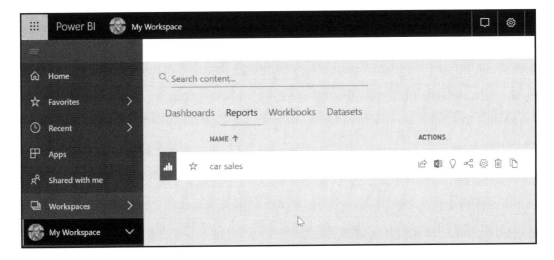

From the workspace, you can share the report with your colleagues. You need a Power BI Pro license to share your content, and those you share it with also require a Pro license, unless your organization has a Premium subscription. Read more about Premium subscriptions at: `https://m365book.page.link/bi-premium`.

How to do it...

You can share a report in two ways:

1. In a list of **Dashboards** or **Reports**, or in an open dashboard or report, select **Share**:

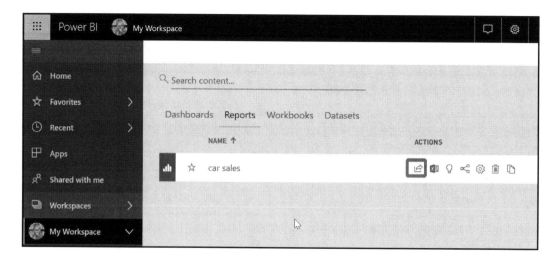

2. You can then specify the colleagues you want to share the report with. You could provide full email addresses for individuals, distribution groups, or security groups. Check the options as applicable:

You can share with people whose addresses are outside your organization, but you'll see a warning. These external users must be added as guest users in your **Azure Active Directory (Azure AD)** if you want to share Power BI reports with them.

How it works...

There are several ways in which you can share a Power BI report. In order to choose the right platform, you first need to understand the following terminology:

- **Share your workspace**: Workspaces provide a common area for your co-workers. You can specify roles to decide who can manage the entire workspace, or edit its content, and distribute its content. Power BI provides a default **My Workspace** area for every user, for them to store their own dashboards and reports. So, while you can, in theory, save the reports in your **My Workspace** area and share it with your co-workers, this workspace is not actually meant for collaboration. It is more like your personal space.

  You should set up separate workspaces to work with your co-workers:

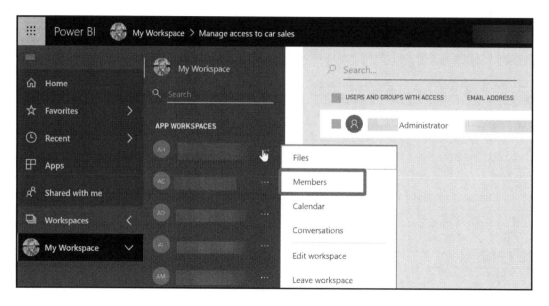

- **Share your dataset**: The dataset refers to the data that drives your visualization. We saw earlier how the data needs to go through transformation and modeling before it can be used within the report. You would obviously not want everyone to go through the same ordeal if they want to base their reports on the same data. So, while this option allows you to save time by sharing the cleansed data, on top of that it also ensures that everyone is building their report based on a single version of the truth.

  You can share a dataset by clicking **Manage permissions**, as shown in the following screenshot:

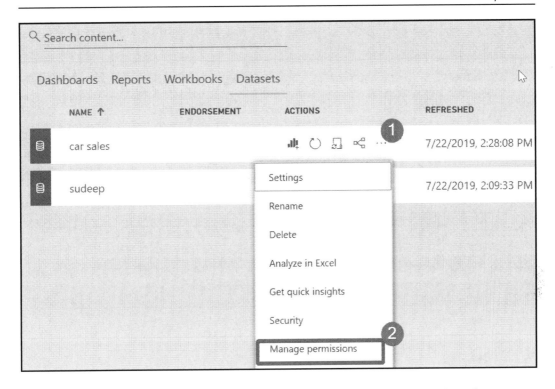

Then, choose the people you would like to share with. You do not need to share reports with people who have access to the workspace already. They will be able to view the reports immediately in the workspace:

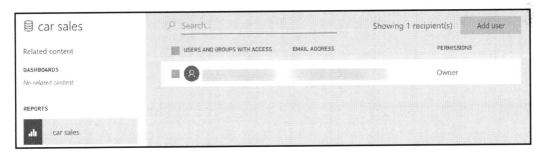

Share your report or dashboard: When you share a dashboard or report, recipients can view it and interact with it, but can't edit it:

See also

- The *Retrieving data* recipe
- The *Transforming data* recipe
- The *Modeling data* recipe
- The *Querying data using natural language* recipe
- The *Visualizing data* recipe

16
Power Virtual Agents

Power Virtual Agents (PVAs) is a **Software-as-a-Service (SaaS)** offering that lets you build smart bots that can answer queries from your customers round the clock. You can design bots by simply using a guided, no-code graphical interface. What this means is that subject matter experts can build bots themselves without having to involve development teams. They can test and debug bots in real-time using the Test Console.

PVAs are a part of the Power Platform, which lets citizen developers build solutions for themselves. As of April 2020, PVA is offered as a separate SaaS offering outside Microsoft 365.

Microsoft already has an Azure Bot Service that lets you build intelligent, enterprise-grade bots. Using the bot framework, you can build bots that range from simple Q&A bots to sophisticated virtual assistants. The bot framework, along with other Azure services such as Cognitive Service, gives you the ability to speak, listen, understand, and learn from your users.

However, building and publishing bots using the bot framework requires developer know-how. You need to write lines of code to build a bot and deploy it. You also have to plan ongoing support to maintain the code in the future.

Using a code-based method poses another challenge. While testing the bot, every time you find an issue, the bot has to go through a development cycle. This slows down the delivery process.

Creating a bot with PVAs is easy and requires no development knowledge. Hence, it lets the subject matter experts build bots without requiring a developer. Citizen developers can build bots and test them using a conversational UI in a matter of minutes, without writing a single line of code. Someone who has experience in building flows using Power Automate can take the bot to an even higher level. PVAs come with a testing console. Since the end-users can build bot themselves, they can test the bots logic in the development cycle itself.

In this chapter, we'll learn about the following recipes:

- Creating a bot
- Creating a topic
- Testing a bot
- Deploying a bot

Let's get started!

Creating a bot

Bots perform tasks that are simple and repetitive. They are much faster than a human and can provide 24/7 support.

Let's see what it takes to build a new bot. We are going to build a bot that will enable our users to register themselves for a course.

Getting ready

You will need a Power Virtual Agent license to complete this recipe. Alternatively, you can sign up for a trial by visiting: `https://m365book.page.link/pva-trial`

How to do it...

Follow these steps to complete this recipe:

1. Go to `https://powerva.microsoft.com/` and sign in with your organization account.
2. If you do not have a license, sign up for a trial.
3. In the **Create a new bot** dialog box, enter a name for your bot. Let's name it `Course Selector`
4. Select **Create** to initiate the bot-building process.

5. If you already have created one bot and want to create another, click on the **Bot** icon at the top and click **New bot**:

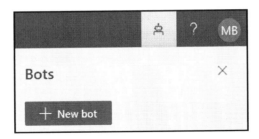

It can take up to 15 minutes to create the first bot; subsequent bots take less time. You will see the following screen when the bot building process is over:

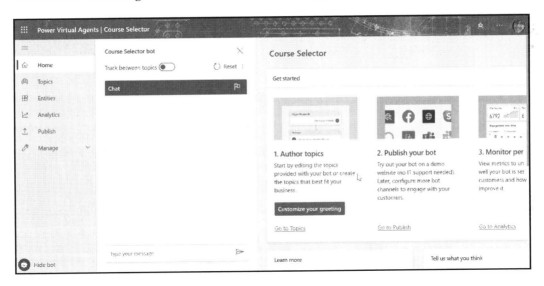

How it works...

By default, the bot gets provisioned in your default environment. You can change the environment during the provisioning process by selecting a particular environment, as shown in the following screenshot:

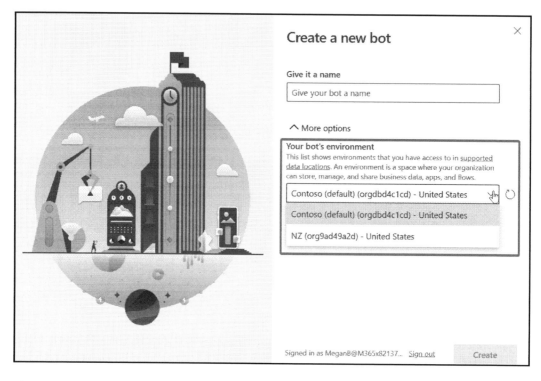

If you don't see all your environments listed in the drop-down menu, this is probably because you do not have access to the environment.

If you encounter an error saying **You do not have permissions to any environments. Please get access from an administrator**, you'll need to create a new environment and use that environment to create your bot.

See also

- The *Creating a solution* recipe in `Chapter 13`, *Power Automate (Microsoft Flow)* (to read more about environments)
- The *Creating a topic* recipe in this chapter
- The *Deploying a bot* recipe in this chapter

Creating a topic

In Power Virtual Agents, a topic defines the bot's business logic and process flow. **Topics** are individual process flows that have a trigger and one or more nodes.

When you create a bot, you will see that some topics are available by default. You get four default user topics and eight default system topics. You can edit both of these topic types in the same manner as the topics you create, but you cannot delete them:

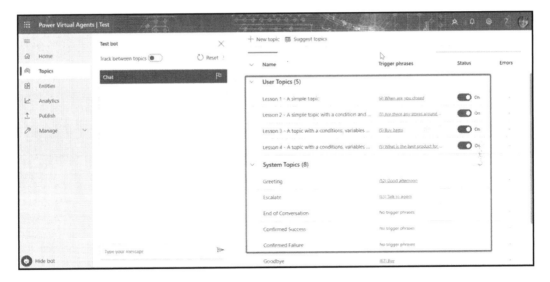

A bot will execute a specific topic based on what the user types. A topic has a number of trigger phrases. **Phrases** are the questions or keywords that the user is likely to type. The bot uses natural language understanding to interpret what a customer wants to know. An example can be seen here.

The topic shown in the following screenshot gets triggered if the user types one of the phrases provided:

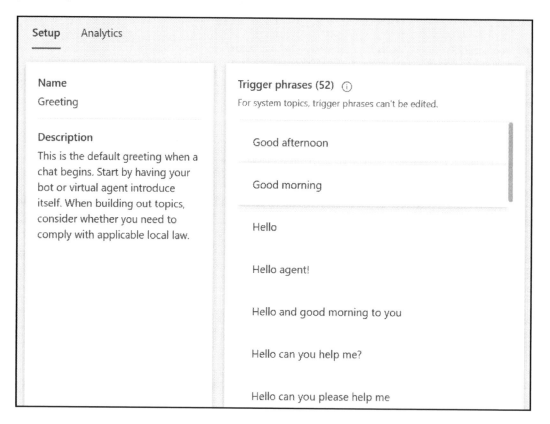

Getting ready

You will need a Power Virtual Agent license to complete this recipe. Alternatively, you can sign up for a trial by visiting: `https://m365book.page.link/pva-trial`

How to do it...

Follow these steps to complete this recipe:

1. Go to `https://powerva.microsoft.com/` and sign in with your organization account.
2. If you do not have a license, sign up for a trial.
3. Click on the link that says **Topics**, as shown in the following screenshot:

4. To create a new topic, click **+ New topic**:

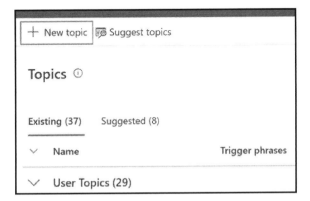

5. Name the new topic Course Topic and add the following phrases to it:

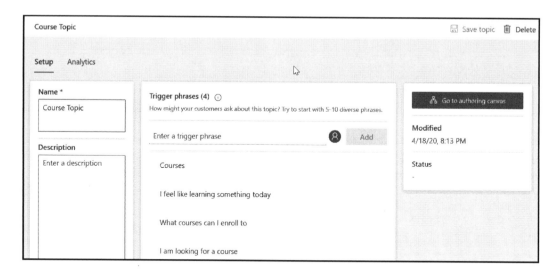

6. Click **Save topic** to add the topic to the **Topics** list.
7. Click on **Go to authoring canvas** to build the logic behind the topic.
8. The authoring canvas displays the topic trigger phrases with a **message** node. Click on the **(+)** icon to add a node:

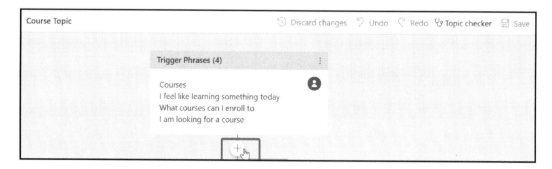

9. When adding a node, you can choose from five options, as shown in the following screenshot:

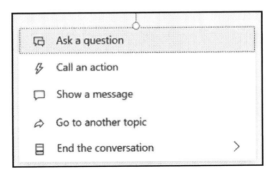

10. Let's pick **Ask a question**. Set the desired question, as shown in the following screenshot. Save the response in a variable. Update the variable name to `CourseName`:

11. Next, add a **Condition** node, as shown in the following screenshot:

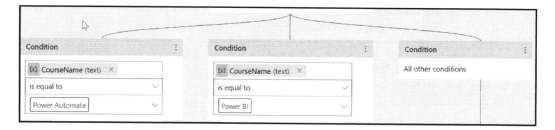

12. Now, we will configure each course branch. For the sake of this example, let's assume that the registration for the Power Apps has closed but that registration is open for other courses:

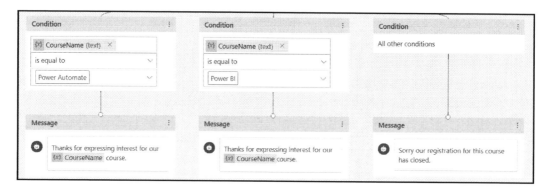

13. Those who expressed an interest in the Power Apps will see a **sorry** message, and then the bot will transfer the user to an agent who'll discuss other options with the user. Here, we need to select **Transfer to Agent** to insert a hand-off node. Enter a private message you want to send to the agent. See how we have used the CourseName variable here to add context:

14. We'll end the other two course branches with a survey:

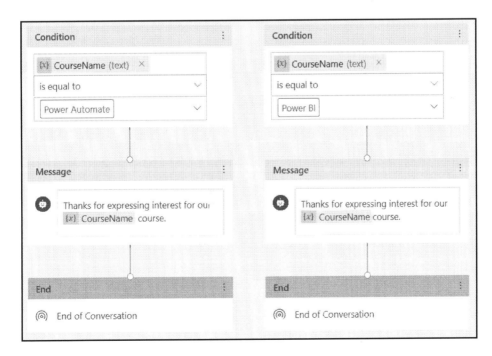

15. Save the authoring canvas logic by clicking on **Save**.

How it works...

Let's take a closer look at some of the nodes that are available for use.

Show a message

This is the simplest of all nodes and simply displays a text message to the user.

Ask a question

In our example, while adding the question, we picked the **Multiple choice options** option. As the name suggests, this option lets us specify multiple options for the user to choose from. We also chose to set the **Identify** type to **entity**, as shown in the following screenshot:

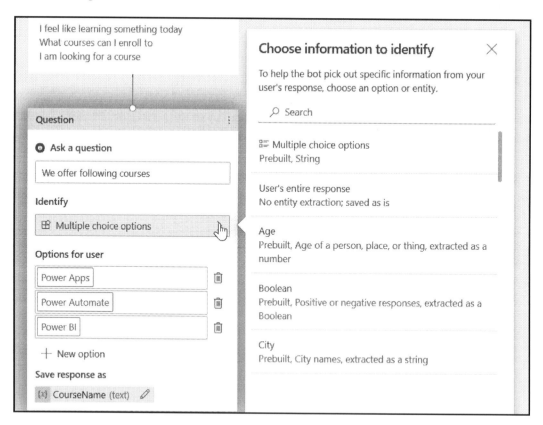

An **entity** enables the bot to extract information units from natural language. For instance, if the bot asks a question that is related to a city, a user can reply in a variety of ways. An entity deciphers the required information from the natural language, as shown in the following screenshot:

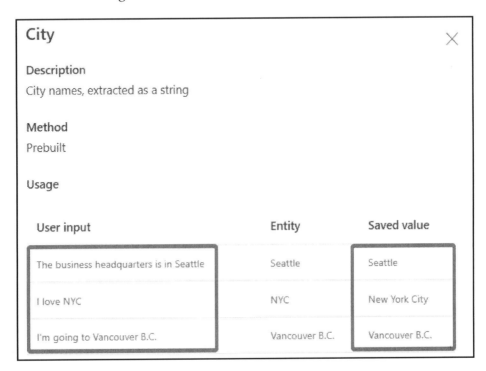

End the conversation

There are two ways to end a conversation. Let's go over them now.

End with a survey

This node will end the conversation flow with a survey to rate the conversation experience, as shown in the following screenshot:

Transfer to agent

As you saw previously, we can hand off conversations to an agent. This can be done seamlessly and contextually within the authoring canvas. Click on the gear icon and choose **Transfer to agent**:

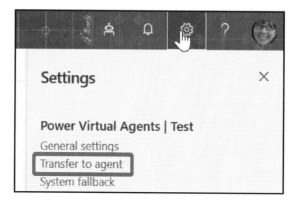

There are multiple options you can choose from to transfer the flow, as shown in the following screenshot:

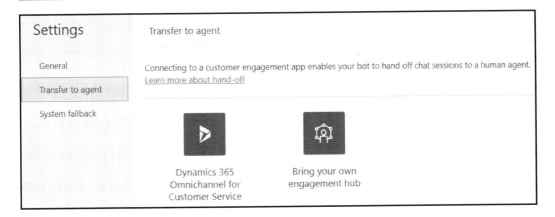

Configuring these engagement apps is beyond the scope of this book. During the transfer process, Power Virtual Agents sends additional information to the agent, along with a transcript of the chat session, as shown in the following screenshot:

Chat session details

User information collected for handoff using the Transfer to agent node.

CourseName	**Power Apps**
va_Scope	**bot**
va_LastTopic	**Course Topic**
va_Topics	**Course Topic**
va_LastPhrase	**courses**
va_Phrases	**courses**
va_ConversationId	**812FCOOEfgP8HvYgycveCj-f**
va_AgentMessage	**The user has requested to be booked for Power Apps course**
va_BotId	**df3653c6-30dc-400b-adc1-1385c089cb2b**
va_BotName	**Test**
va_Language	**en-US**
chatTranscript	Download transcript

Go to another topic

The user is transferred to another topic when they type in a phrase that matches one of the phrases listed in the topic. You can transfer a user intentionally by adding the **Go to another topic** node. With this, the bot transfers the conversation flow from the current topic to the specified topic.

Call an action

This option lets you trigger an existing flow or create a new flow, as shown in the following screenshot:

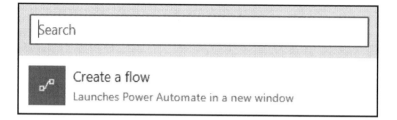

 A flow can only be called from a topic located in the same Common Data Service environment as your bot. Only the flows that are inside a solution in Power Automate can be invoked. You can move flows into solutions so that they are listed in the authoring canvas.

See also

- The *Creating a solution* recipe in this chapter (to read more about environments)
- The *Creating a bot* recipe in this chapter
- The *Deploying a bot* recipe in this chapter

Testing a bot

Power Virtual Agent allows you to build and test bots simultaneously. While testing a bot, you can actually see the required steps being executed. This allows you to find and fix unexpected behavior.

As with any software project, user acceptance testing is crucial. Since it is the subject matter experts who would know exactly how the bot is supposed to behave, they can tweak the bot logic while performing user acceptance testing.

Getting ready

You will need a Power Virtual Agent license to complete this recipe. Alternatively, you can sign up for a trial by visiting: `https://m365book.page.link/pva-trial`

How to do it...

Follow these steps to complete this recipe:

1. Go to `https://powerva.microsoft.com/` and sign in with your organization account.
2. If you do not have a license, sign up for a trial.
3. Usually, the **Test** console is on the landing page itself. If not, open it by selecting **Test your bot**. Once you've done that, the link will change to **Hide bot**, as shown in the following screenshot:

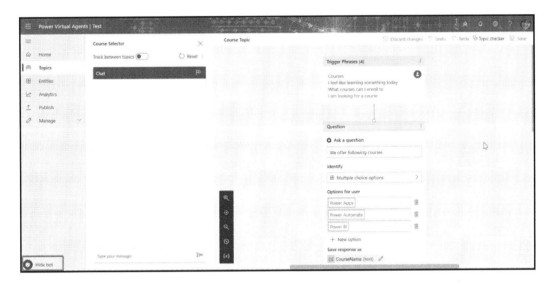

4. Just where the text box appears, enter one of the trigger phrases we defined for **Course Topic**. Let's go with `Courses`.

5. When the courses are all listed, pick **Power BI**.

6. End the conversation by providing feedback, as shown in the following screenshot:

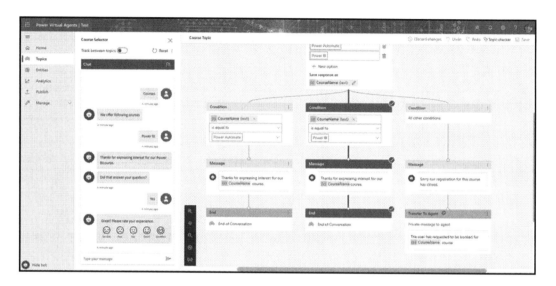

7. Restart testing by clicking on **Reset**.

How it works...

There are three more features of the testing console. These can be seen in the following screenshot:

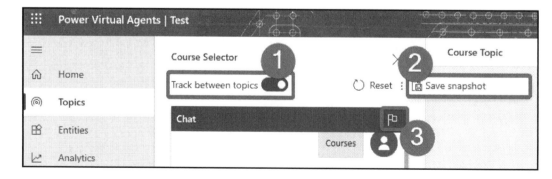

Let's go over these features:

- **Track between topics** lets you follow through the conversation path step by step when your bot moves from one topic to another (**1**).
- If the bot is behaving unexpectedly and you need to have a closer look at the diagnostics, you can click on **Save Snapshot** (**2**).
- If you are having issues with the Power Virtual Agent platform itself, you can **Flag an issue** by clicking on the **Flag** icon. This brings up a dialog box and displays a Conversation ID to help Microsoft debug the issue. The request is submitted anonymously and your test data never leaves your tenant (labeled **3** in the screenshot).

A dialog box will appear to save the snapshot. Click **Save.**

A file named `DSAT.zip` will be downloaded to your device. This contains two files:

- `dialog.json`, which contains conversational diagnostics, including detailed descriptions of errors
- `botContent.json`, which contains the bot's topics and other content, including entities and variables that are being used in the bot:

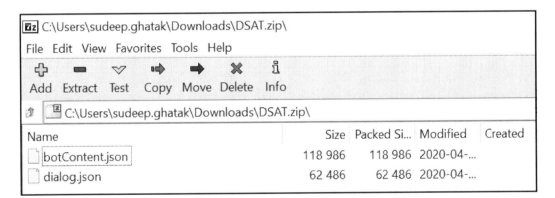

See also

- The *Creating a bot* recipe in this chapter
- The *Creating a topic* recipe in this chapter
- The *Deploying a bot* recipe in this chapter

Deploying a bot

Deploying a bot is done in two stages:

1. Publishing a bot
2. Connecting the bot to a channel

Power Virtual Agent lets you publish bots on multiple platforms or channels, as shown in the following screenshot:

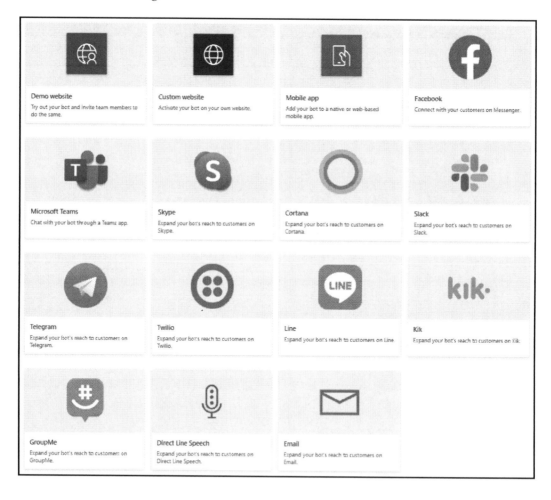

You can connect your bot to as many channels you like, provided that it has been published at least once. Power Virtual Agents lets you publish the bot from within the app. If your bot is already connected to a channel, PVA takes care of publishing the bot to the channels you have connected it to. Once you've published the bot, you can share it with your colleagues and customers.

Let's go through the steps involved in the publishing process. In the following steps, we'll show you how to add the bot to Microsoft Teams.

Getting ready

Install **Microsoft Teams App Studio** and launch it in Microsoft Teams. The app can be download from `https://m365book.page.link/app-studio`

How to do it...

Follow these steps to complete this recipe:

1. Go to `https://powerva.microsoft.com/` and sign in with your organization account.
2. Click **Publish** in the left navigation pane and select **Publish** again from the right-hand pane:

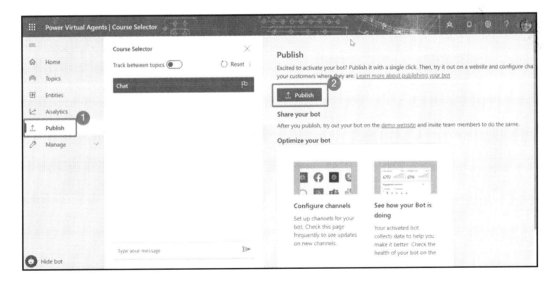

3. A pop up will appear. Select **Publish** again.

4. A confirmation message will appear on your screen, as shown in the following screenshot:

Now, you need to connect your bot to a channel.

5. Select **Manage** on the side navigation pane and go to the **Channels** tab.

6. Select **Microsoft Teams** and then select **Add**. Copy the **App ID** and save it for later:

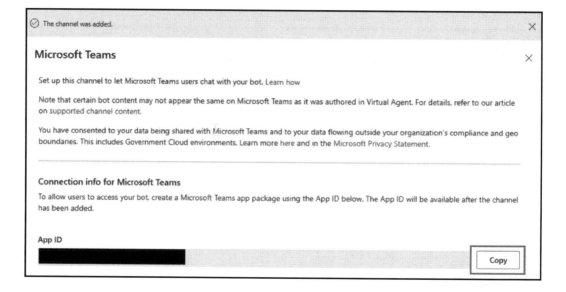

7. Open the Teams app, navigate to **App Studio**, and select **Manifest editor**. Then, click on **Create a new app**:

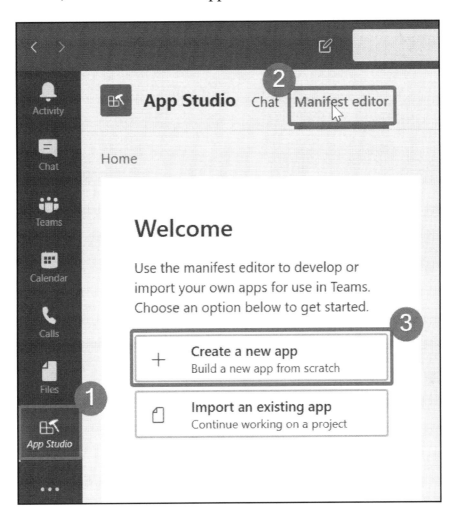

8. Give your bot a name and fill in all the required fields:

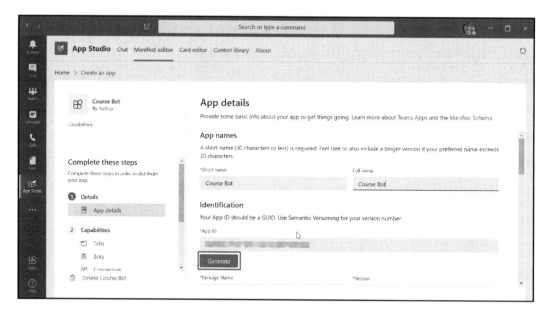

9. Under **Capabilities**, choose **Bots** and click on **Set up**:

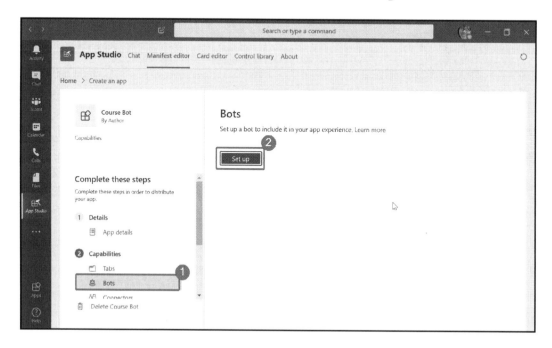

10. Select the **Existing bot** option and specify the App ID you copied in *step 6*. Set **Scope** to **Personal** (if you just want to test the bot experience within Teams). Finally, click **Save**:

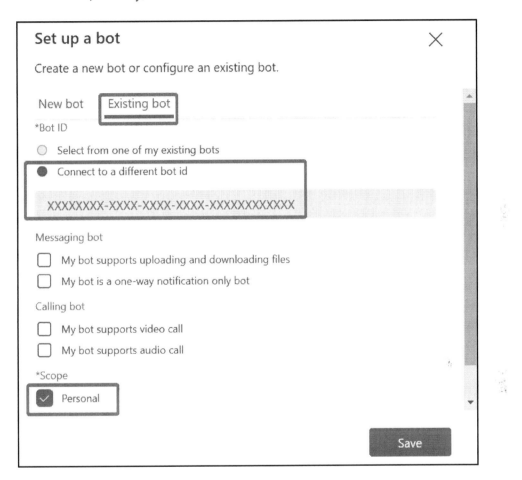

11. Now, your bot is ready to be distributed. The last step is to click on **Test and distribute**:

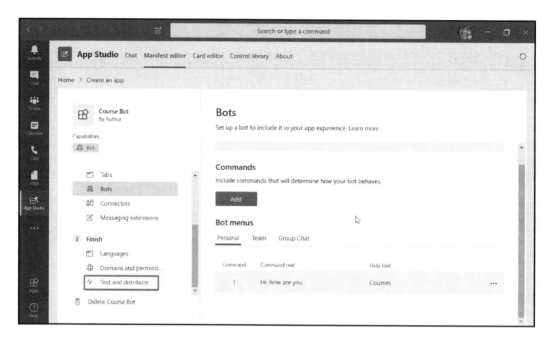

12. Click on **Install** to install the bot on your local Teams client:

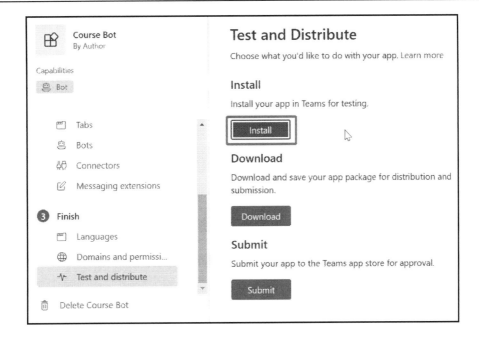

13. Click on **Add** to install the app:

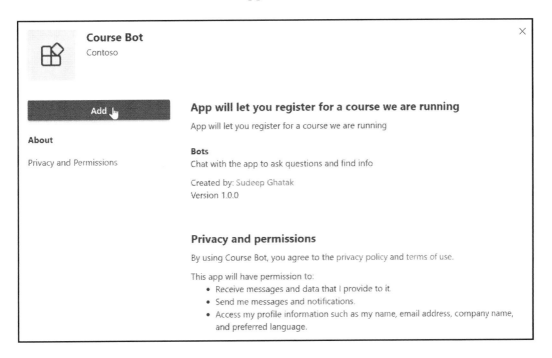

14. The bot can now be accessed by clicking on the **...** link in the left navigation pane:

15. If the app fails to install for some reason, download the package shown in *step 12* and upload it via **Teams** | **Apps** | **Upload a custom app**:

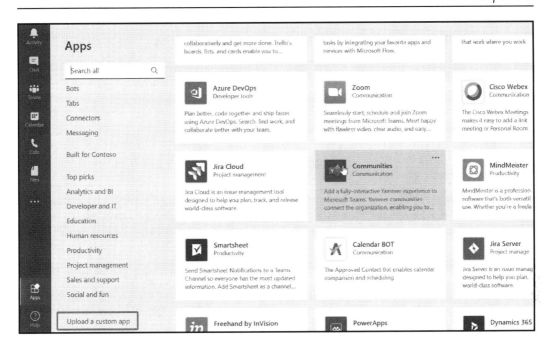

16. You can now use the app in your Teams app:

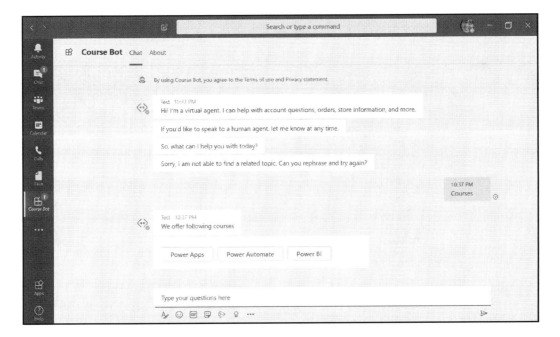

How it works...

The publication process deploys the bot to a demo website by default. The demo website can be used to gather feedback from your peers and customers. The link will open a new tab and display a prebuilt demo website where you and your team can interact with the bot.

This instance is not meant for production deployment. You can, however, share the link with your testers and customers to test how the bot responds to various inputs:

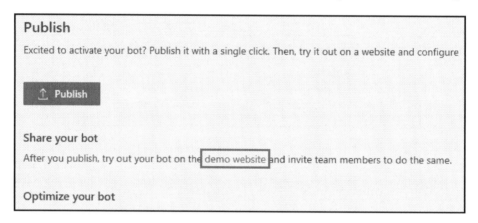

The following screenshot shows what the bot will look like on the demo site:

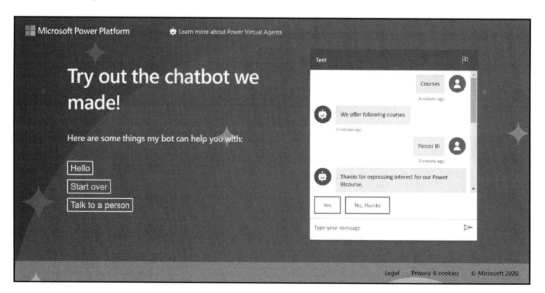

You can change the **Title** of the site, along with the phrases that you want the users to use. You can do that by updating the **Demo Website** channel, as shown in the following screenshot:

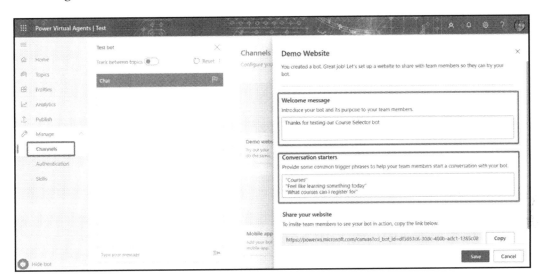

There's more...

Power Virtual Agents lets you keep an eye on how your bots are performing using powerful metrics and AI-driven dashboards. With this, you can easily see which topics are doing well and where the bot can improve, as well as quickly make adjustments to improve performance:

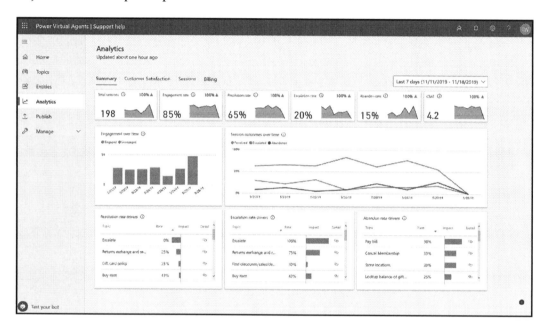

Power Virtual Agents has a comprehensive set of analytics that show you the key performance indicators for your bot.

Multiple charts show you trends and usage for your bot's topics. These charts use AI to highlight the topics that have the greatest impact on your bot's performance.

See also

- The *Creating a bot* recipe in this chapter
- The *Creating a topic* recipe in this chapter
- The *Deploying a bot* recipe in this chapter

17
Planner

Planner is a visual tool that helps you to organize your team tasks. It helps you stay on track, thereby making it easier to manage the ongoing project.

Planner is not a comprehensive project-management solution like Microsoft Project, but it provides lightweight task-management capabilities, such as the following:

- Creating tasks (or cards) and boards
- Assigning tasks to team members
- Specifying due dates
- Sharing files
- Having conversations

Planner also lets you visualize your tasks by allowing you to sort your project tasks by team member, task status, or task bucket, all from the same screen. It does this by laying all your task items on a planner board.

The board is like a dashboard that displays all of the tasks in a given plan. You might want to group tasks together based on an attribute, such as the task status or project phase. You can achieve this by creating buckets within a board.

Buckets let you add cards. Each card represents an individual task. You can move cards from one bucket to another by dragging them or simply by updating the bucket within the card.

You can manage all your plans via the Planner Hub page. The Planner Hub also provides a visual chart of the completed and ongoing tasks. Team members can have task-specific conversations within each card. They receive notifications when a new task gets assigned.

Planner integrates with other Microsoft 365 apps, such as Teams and Microsoft 365 Groups. Together, they offer a rich user experience. Planner is available to customers with Microsoft 365 Enterprise E1–E5, Business Essentials, Business Premium, and Education subscription plans. So, let's dive into it.

We will cover the following topics in this chapter:

- Creating a plan
- Creating tasks
- Assigning tasks
- Adding items in the checklist
- Managing a plan
- Deleting a plan

Creating a plan

Planner can be used to manage an event, research new ideas, track a project, prepare for a customer visit, or just organize your team more effectively.

You begin by creating a plan. There are several ways in which you can create a plan. One obvious way is to create the plan through the Planner homepage. Plans also get created indirectly if you create a team in Microsoft Teams or a group within Microsoft 365 Groups.

Getting ready

In order to create plans, you should have permission to provision a Microsoft 365 group. Administrators can disable this feature in some organizations; however, Microsoft 365 does allow you to selectively grant Microsoft 365 group creation rights to individuals or groups.

How to do it...

To create a plan from the Planner app:

1. Log in to `https://office.com` using your Microsoft 365 account.
2. Click on **Planner**.
3. Click on **New Plan**:

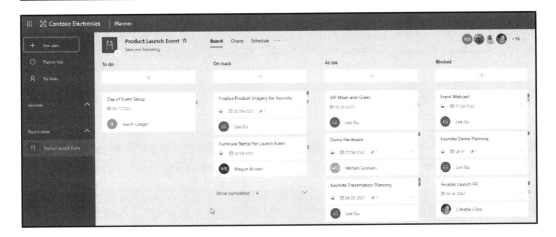

4. Give your plan a name and click **Create plan**:

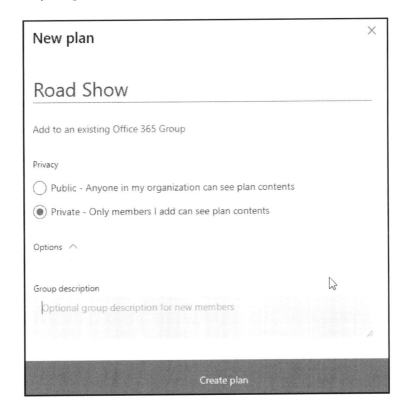

You have now successfully created a plan.

How it works...

While creating a plan, you can specify whether the plan is public or private:

- **Public plans** will be visible to everyone in your organization.
- **Private plans** will only be accessible to members that you add to the plan.

Creating a plan triggers actions in several other apps. You get a Microsoft 365 group to collaborate on your plan, a notebook is created for the group in OneNote, and your group gets a mailbox in Outlook, a calendar, and a SharePoint site.

If you already have a Microsoft 365 group and want to create another plan, then this can be done by associating the new plan with your group using the **Add to an existing Microsoft 365 Group** option.

After the plan is created, you will be taken to the **Board** view (landing page) of the plan.

The board displays all the cards grouped together in columns (known as buckets). Buckets can be project phases, task categories, or any other type that you would like to categorize the tasks by, as shown in the following screenshot:

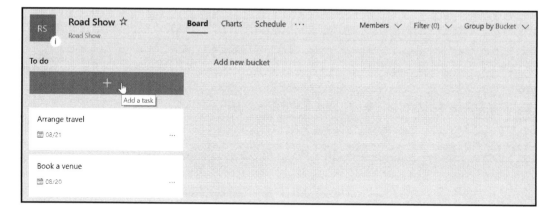

The **Charts** view shows how your plan is progressing. It provides some basic visuals to show what's done, in progress, not started, and late. It also displays the task count by the bucket. You can also create tasks in this view:

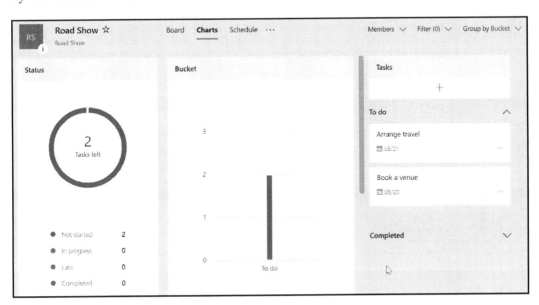

The **Schedule** view displays team tasks and also lets you create tasks within a calendar, as shown in the following screenshot:

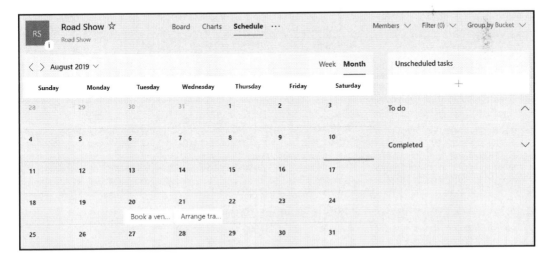

If you click the ... icon, it reveals several options in the context menu, as shown in the following screenshot:

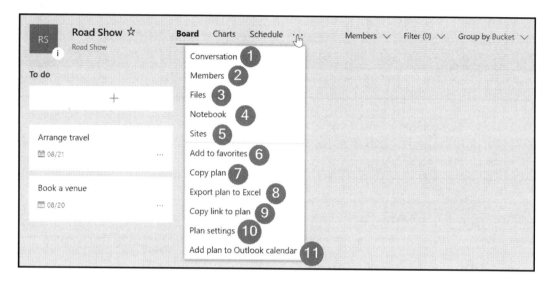

The options under the **Board** view are explained in the following list (the numbers correspond to the labels in the preceding screenshot):

1. **Conversation** takes you to the mailbox for the Microsoft 365 group that sits behind the plan.
2. You can share the plan with your colleagues. This can be done via the **Members** link. It takes you to the Microsoft 365 Groups page where you can add new members using the **Add member** option.
3. **Files** take you to a SharePoint document library where all the group documents are stored.
4. You can access the group's OneNote document by clicking on **Notebook**.
5. **Sites** take you to the SharePoint site sitting behind the plan.
6. **Add to favorites** lets you mark the plan as a favorite so that you can easily find it.
7. The **Copy plan** option lets you clone the plan as a public or private plan. The copy option copies the tasks (along with the task artifacts) associated with the plan. The following table describes what gets copied:

Element	Gets **copied?**
Group	Yes (same as plan)
Group	Yes
Group	No
Group	No
Group	Yes
Plan	Yes (with "Copy of" added to the beginning of the name)
Plan	Yes
Plan	No
Buckets	Yes
Buckets	Yes
Tasks	Yes
Tasks	Yes
Tasks	Yes (all unchecked)
Tasks	No; neither links nor files
Tasks	Yes
Tasks	Yes
Tasks	No
Tasks	No (all changed back to **Not started**)
Tasks	No
Tasks	No
Tasks	Yes

8. **Export plan to Excel** lets you export the planner task into Excel in case you want to share these tasks with an external member or someone outside your organization.

9. **Copy link to plan** copies the link to the plan, which you can bookmark (if you want to). That is not a preferred way of saving links for future reference. Instead, you should mark a plan as a favorite, as explained previously.

10. **Plan settings** let you change the plan name and privacy settings or delete the plan.

11. **Add plan to Outlook** lets you add your planner tasks to your Outlook calendar by adding a subscription.

See also

- *Creating tasks*
- *Adding items in a checklist*
- *Managing a plan*
- *Deleting a plan*

Creating tasks

A plan is no good if it doesn't have any actions. The individual action items in a plan are created as **tasks**. The tasks in a plan appear as **cards**. Every card represents a unique activity with optional due date and an assignee. Tracking the individual cards on the board lets you track the progress of your plan holistically.

Getting ready

Individual tasks can be created by the members of the Microsoft 365 group associated with the plan.

How to do it...

The following are the steps to create a new task in Planner:

1. Log in to `https://office.com` using your Microsoft 365 account.
2. Click on **Planner** and choose the plan you are working on.
3. Click on the **+** symbol on the board below the bucket name:

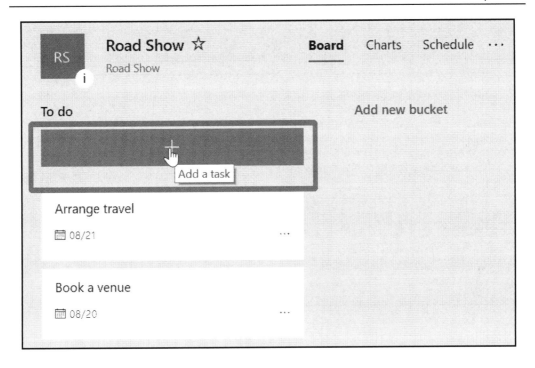

4. Give your task a name and provide a due date (optional) and assignee (optional):

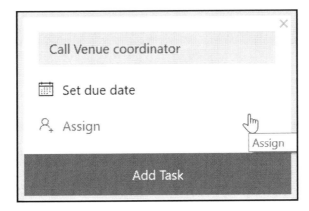

5. Click **Add task**.
6. The task appears on the board. Click to open it.

7. You can now set a start date for the task as well as update the due date, as shown in the following screenshot:

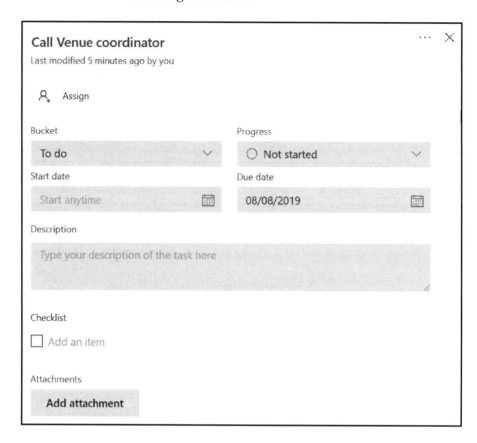

8. Enter the task description. Planner autosaves your task properties.

How it works...

A planner task offers several features that let you manage your task in an efficient manner. You can add a due date to the task, which lets you manage the overall plan. Planner lets you specify a task start date so that the planner can decide which tasks are in progress and which ones are yet to be started. You can mark the task as complete by clicking on the checkbox next to the task name, as shown in the following screenshot:

The card also lets you clone a task. This can be done either from the **Board** view or from within the **Task** view:

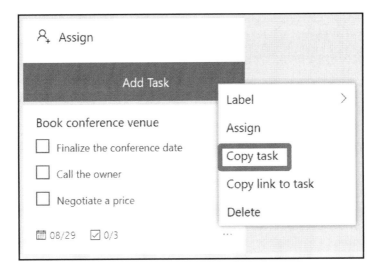

See also

- *Creating a plan*
- *Adding items in a checklist*
- *Managing a plan*
- *Deleting a plan*

Assigning tasks

Planner lets you create tasks without assigning an owner. If you simply specify a task name and press *Enter,* a task gets created without an assignee.

You can see the tasks that don't have an assignee by grouping the tasks by **Assigned to**.

Getting ready

All members of the Microsoft 365 group that is associated with the plan can add task assignees.

How to do it...

You can assign a group member by doing one of the following:

- Update the task.
- Drag the card in **Assigned** to the view.

Both methods are explained in the following sections.

Updating the task

The following are the steps to update a task:

1. Log in to `https://office.com` using your Microsoft 365 account.
2. Click on **Planner** and choose the plan you are working on.
3. Click on the task name.
4. Click **Assign**.
5. A text box appears with the list of group members below it:

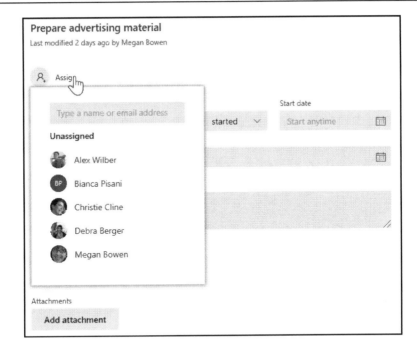

6. Click on one or more group members to assign a task to them.
7. Close the task by clicking the **X** icon.

Dragging the card

You can also update a card by dragging it across to a bucket, as follows:

1. Log in to `https://office.com` using your Microsoft 365 account.
2. Click on **Planner** and choose the plan you are working on.
3. Switch the group the tasks by **Assigned to**, as shown in the following screenshot:

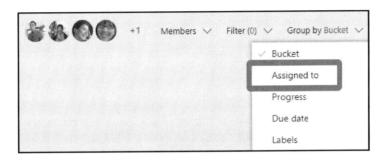

4. Drag a task from Alex's bucket to Christie's bucket. The task assignee gets updated.

How it works...

Planner notifies assignees of the task when they have been added. Planner tasks can be assigned to one or more group members. You can also assign people who are not part of your group by specifying their email addresses.

 You cannot assign tasks to people outside your organization.

See also

- *Creating a plan*
- *Creating tasks*
- *Creating checklist items*
- *Managing a plan*
- *Deleting a plan*

Adding checklist items

Adding tasks on the board meets just one objective. After the tasks get created, they need to be monitored and managed. This is done by organizing the tasks in categories known as boards and tracking the progress of a task by creating checklists within them. For instance, booking a conference room task might involve finalizing the conference date, calling the owner, negotiating a price, so on. These can be treated as subtasks and can be tracked via a checklist.

Getting ready

Checklists can be added by the members of the Microsoft 365 group associated with the plan.

How to do it...

You can add the checklist items by going through the following steps:

1. Log in to `https://office.com` using your Microsoft 365 account.
2. Click on **Planner** and choose the plan you are working on.
3. Click on a task.
4. Go to the section that says **Checklist**.
5. Add a checklist item where it says **Add an item**.
6. Type in a checklist item and simply press *Enter*.
7. Check the **Show on card** option, as shown in the following screenshot:

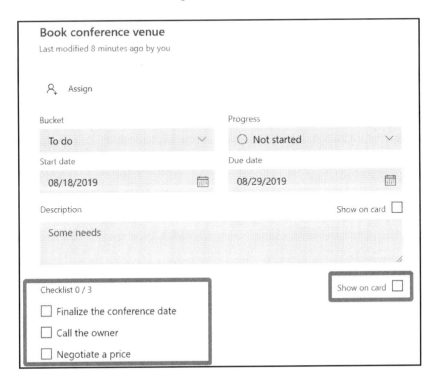

Adding a checklist – checklist items

8. The tasks can be labeled with a color that lets you easily identify a task—for instance, all tasks related to the conference venue, such as arranging food, organizing a projector, and so on can be labeled with a pink color:

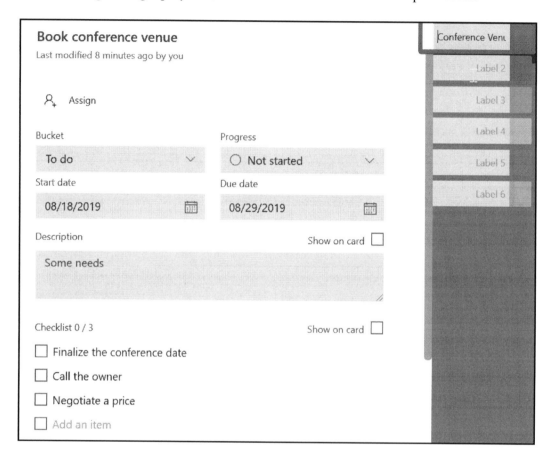

How it works...

While adding the items in the checklist, if you check the box that says **Show on card**, then the incomplete checklist items roll up to the task view. A tiny graphic appears below the rollup section that displays how many of the checklist subtasks have been completed:

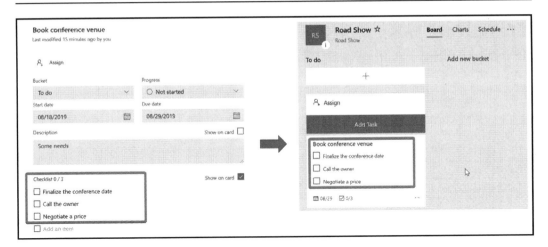

The completed checklist items don't appear in the rollup section; however, they do appear in the task view with a strikethrough:

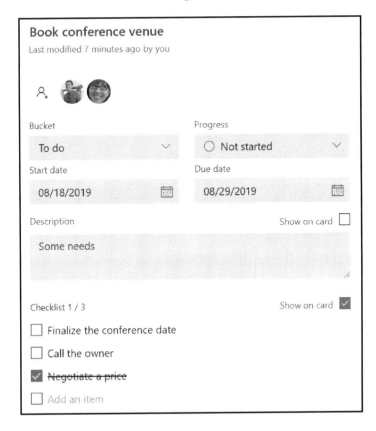

See also

- *Creating a plan*
- *Creating tasks*
- *Managing a plan*
- *Deleting a plan*

Managing the plan

Planner has various features to track and manage your plan. This includes using charts and dashboards. You can view the plans and tasks by bucket, progress, due date, and labels. Planner also lets you visualize the statistics around completed and unfinished tasks.

Getting ready

Plans can be managed by the members of the Microsoft 365 group associated with the plan.

How to do it...

To manage a plan, go through the following steps:

1. Log in to `https://office.com` using your Microsoft 365 account.
2. Click on **Planner** and choose the plan you are working on.
3. Click on the **Board** view to see the tasks by the bucket.
4. Drag the **Collect feedback** card to the **Post Conference Tasks** bucket:

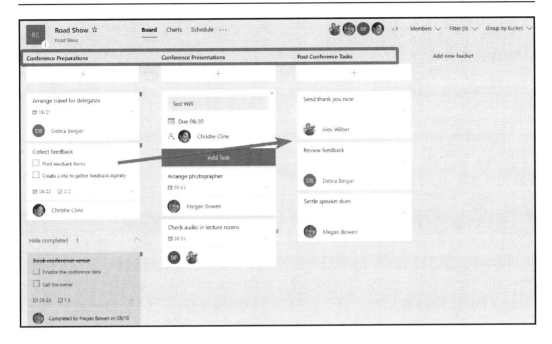

5. Click on the **Chart** view to see the tasks by status. We can see that we have an unassigned task. Let's assign it to someone:

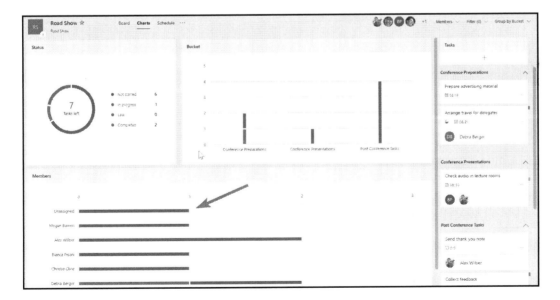

6. Click on the **Unassigned** section. This will filter all the tasks that do not have an assignee:

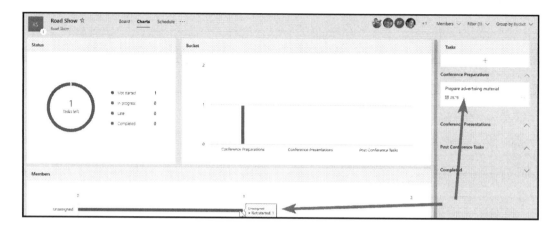

7. Assign a member to the unassigned task by clicking on the context menu:

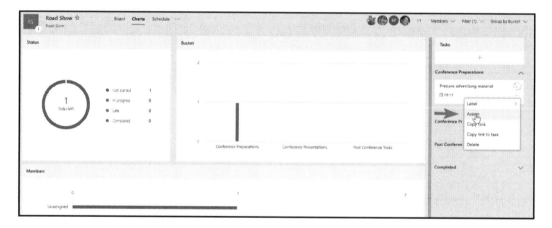

8. Click on the **Schedule** view to see the tasks in the calendar view.
9. To add a task on a certain date, just roll the mouse over the date and click on the + symbol:

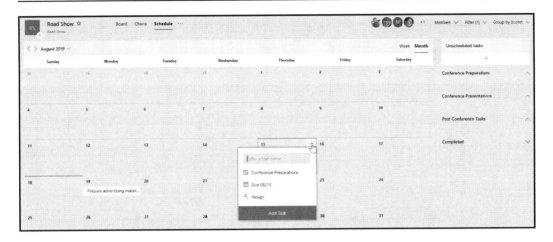

10. Specify the task name and press *Enter*.

There's more...

Besides the three views, you can also visualize the tasks by the following categories:

- **Bucket**: This the default view where tasks appear under buckets. In our case, the buckets are **Conference Preparations**, **Conference Presentations**, and **Post Conference Tasks**.
- **Assigned to**: In this view, the tasks are laid out by the resource assigned to the task. You can change the assignee by simply dragging them under another person:

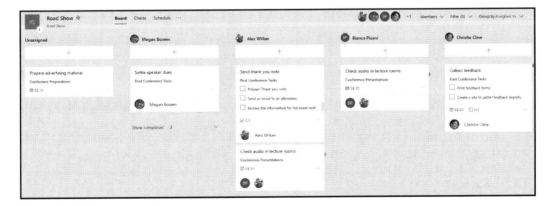

- **Progress**: This view lists the task by its progress metadata. Tasks are listed as **Not Started**, **In progress**, and **Completed**. To complete a task, simply drag the task to the **Completed** section:

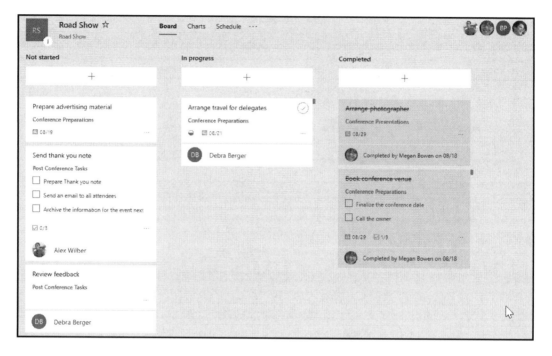

- **Due date**: This view lays out the tasks according to the delivery date. There are five standard categories that a task can fall under:
  - **Tomorrow**
  - **This week**
  - **Next week**
  - **Future**
  - **No date**

The tasks move under the appropriate heading if the due date field is modified. This view is good to use to filter tasks that don't have a due date assigned:

- **Labels**: Labels are useful in identifying the tasks visually. You can use labels to group tasks by an attribute relevant to the plan. You can add more than one label to a task:

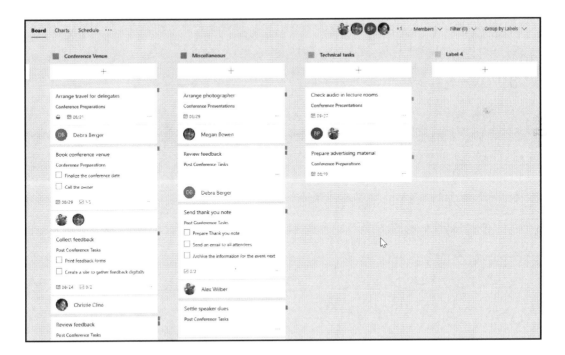

See also

- *Creating a plan*
- *Creating tasks*
- *Adding items in checklist*
- *Deleting a plan*

Deleting a plan

Sometimes the plan falls through and is no longer relevant to the group or the team—for example, if a conference gets canceled because the product that was meant to be launched at the event has been discontinued. In such cases, you might want to delete the plan.

Getting ready

You need to be an administrator or group owner to delete a plan.

How to do it...

1. Log in to `https://office.com` using your Microsoft 365 account.
2. Click on **Planner** and select the plan you are working on.
3. Go to **Plan settings** by clicking on the ... icon:

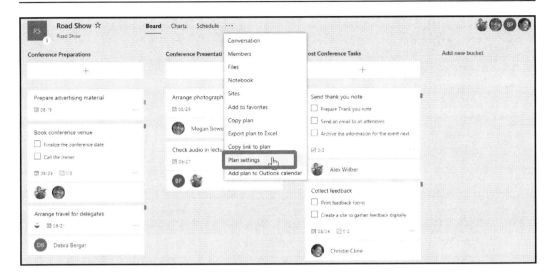

4. On the **Plan settings** page, click on **Delete this plan**:

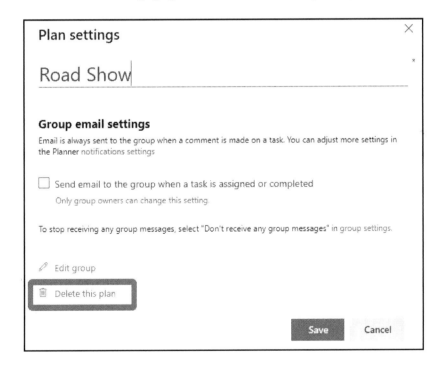

5. You will be presented with a confirmation window. Check the box and click **Delete**:

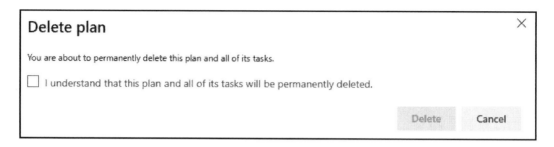

6. If you want to delete the group associated with the plan, click on the **Edit group** after *step 4*.
7. On the **Group settings** page, click on **Delete group**:

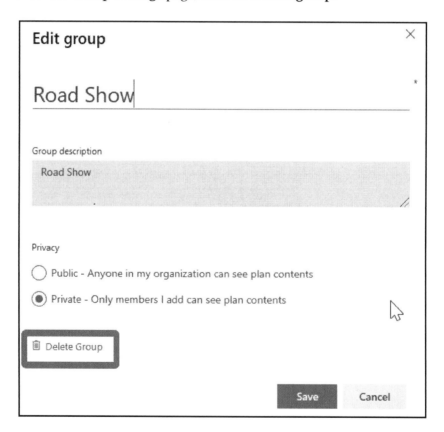

8. You will be presented with the following message. Check the box and click **Delete**:

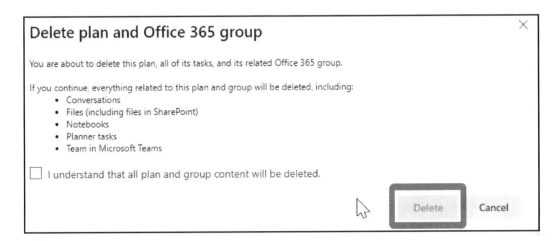

The group and all plans associated with it will be deleted.

How it works...

A deleted plan cannot be recovered, and so you should consult with other members of the group before taking action. If you are deleting the group attached to the plan, then you will also lose all the conversations and group files. If your concern is that too many plans appear on your Planner Hub, then you may leave the plans you don't want to involved in.

This can be done via the **Plan** context menu, as shown in the following screenshot:

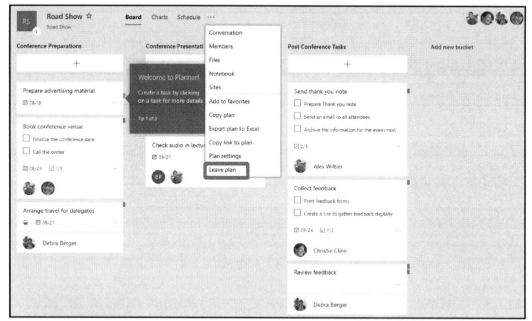

 This option is available to you if you are not an administrator. Administrators will not see the **Leave plan** link.

If you are deleting the plan or group permanently, it is recommended that you back up or move your files and conversations.

See also

- *Creating a plan*
- *Creating tasks*
- *Adding items to the checklist*
- *Managing a plan*

18
Custom Development - SharePoint Framework

SharePoint is a platform that lets you build robust business solutions. Every now and then, however, there comes a time when you want to get just a little extra from the out-of-the-box product. That is when we need to customize it, and for that, we need a development framework. SharePoint has gone through several transformations since it was first launched.

Several SharePoint development frameworks have come and gone. You may ask, why even consider customizing an already proven platform? Why can't we use inbuilt SharePoint features?

Well, the answer is both yes and no. Certainly, SharePoint combined with Microsoft 365 tools should address most of your business needs without having to build a custom solution; however, no product can ever be built that meets every conceivable requirement you can imagine. So, while SharePoint can provide 90% of the requirements natively, you might need to explore the *custom* settings to satisfy the remaining 10%.

However, remember that the decision to build a custom web service should be taken wisely. Note that while customization can tailor a solution as per your needs, it does bring other challenges, such as the ongoing maintenance of the customization, and the impact of future updates and releases on your customizations.

SharePoint has always been a platform that can be extended if needed. Talking of development on SharePoint Online, while other models have not been officially deprecated (such as the app model), the recommended framework is the **SharePoint Framework (SPFx)** and **SPFx extensions** because apart from being completely JavaScript-based, they also embrace open-source non-Microsoft technologies as well, thereby making it easier for developers to pick the language of choice.

Unlike the old days, where you could customize every aspect of SharePoint using full trust code, SPFx runs in the context of the currently logged-in user, which means that it can only do what the logged-in user is allowed to do. Your SPFx code runs on the browser, which means that it does not affect the SharePoint server in any way. On top of that, everything that you build using SPFx is responsive; in other words, it works just the same on your mobile device.

SharePoint Extensions built on SPFX framework can be used to update areas, toolbars, and list data views.

 You can also build a Microsoft Teams tabs using SPFx. Using SharePoint Framework simplifies the development process, as Teams tabs can be automatically hosted within SharePoint without the need for external services.

The SPFx solution consists of a bunch of script files. The script files are bundled into a SharePoint solution. In some cases, the script files are hosted on a separate server and the solution simply contains the URL of the script location.

The following are some other key features of the SPFx framework:

- The code works on both modern and classic SharePoint sites.
- SPFx code runs on both web and SharePoint mobile apps.
- Your tenant administrators must approve an SPFx component before end-users can use them.

By now, you might have realized that this chapter is going to be more technical compared to the rest of the book. In this chapter, we are not just going to talk about SPFx, but we will also touch upon other open source technologies (such as Node.js), toolkits (such as gulp), and libraries (such as React). Since an entire book can be devoted to each of these topics, I can't do justice to them in this one chapter. This chapter assumes that you have a beginner level of understanding of JavaScript.

If you are ready to dive in, let's begin.

In this chapter we will cover the following recipes:

- Setting up the development environment
- Building your first SPFx web part
- Deploying your SPFx web part
- Debugging your SPFx web part

Technical requirements

As I mentioned previously, this is a developer-focused chapter. This means that we will have to get our development environment ready before we proceed.

For our exercise, we will use the following technology stack:

Let's look at the specific requirements for each technology stack.

Node.js

Node.js will be our JavaScript runtime in the environment in which we compile the custom code. You can download Node.js from the official site at `https://nodejs.org`.

There might be a couple of options to choose from, as shown in the following screenshot:

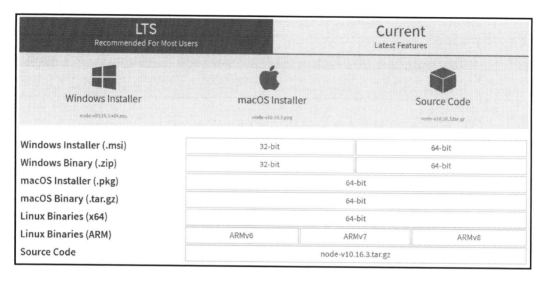

I recommend downloading **LTS** for **Windows** or **Mac** because the **Current** version might contain some features that are not supported by SPFx. Even when choosing LTS, you should check that the version is supported by SPFx by going to `https://m365book.page.link/SPFx-setup`.

Download the 32-bit or 64-bit `.msi` **version** depending on your processor configuration and install it.

Npm

Npm is the default package manager for Node.js. It is installed on your computer when you install Node.js. When you build a project using Node.js, you have to reference several libraries or packages. Npm manages all these packages for you. It has an online registry of all the packages (at `https://www.npmjs.com/`) that you can use. You simply download the package by typing the following:

```
npm install package-name
```

Visual Studio Code

Visual Studio (VS) Code is a lightweight, open-source code editor for Windows, Linux, and Mac. It offers code debugging, reusable snippets, refactoring, and many other features that can be extended via plugins. You can download VS Code from the official site at `https://code.visualstudio.com/`.

Yeoman

Yeoman is a command-line interface that provides common build tools and a starter template and builds you a scaffolding solution that you can begin with and build upon. It can also run your unit tests and provides you with a local development server to test your code.

Yeoman requires you to have Node.js installed. We will learn how to install Yeoman and install the SharePoint Yeoman generator.

Gulp

Gulp is a tool that helps you out with several tasks, reduces your development time significantly, and takes away a lot of the monotonous manual tasks. It can perform activities such as the following:

- Spinning up a development server
- Auto refreshing the browser during code changes
- Merging web assets, such as CSS, JavaScript, and images, into a single file

Gulp also requires Node.js as a prerequisite.

TypeScript

TypeScript is a strongly typed, object-oriented, compiled language that serves as a replacement for JavaScript to write application-scale solutions. It is both a language and a set of tools. It attempts to compensate for the limitations that JavaScript has. TypeScript has now been accepted widely as a language. All TypeScript code is converted into its JavaScript equivalent for execution. In theory, all valid JavaScript files can be saved with the **.ts** extension to convert them into TypeScript files.

PowerShell

PowerShell is a command-line shell and scripting language that is built on top of .NET **Common Language Runtime (CLR)** used to perform a variety of tasks with Microsoft services. We have covered PowerShell in `Chapter 20`, *Appendix,* where we have also talked about various modules it supports. If you are using Windows OS, probably you already have PowerShell installed. You can get to it just by typing `Powershell` in the start menu and looking for **Windows PowerShell**. Here are the instructions to install PowerShell on Mac `https://m365book.page.link/powershell-mac`

Setting up the development environment

If you don't have enough development experience, you could find the SPFx development process a bit overwhelming. I will recommend that you get some development experience with the JavaScript framework before jumping into SPFx development directly. There are several training courses available on Node.js and its ecosystem. If you are familiar with the basics of Node.js, then let's begin.

Getting ready

You need a source code editor, such as VS Code, Atom, or Eclipse, to edit the source code. You also need Node.js installed on your device, which you can do by downloading the installer from the link in the previous section. If you already have Node.js installed, then check the version to see whether it is compatible with your SPFx version by running the following command on PowerShell:

```
node -v
```

The following output is shown after running the `node -v` command:

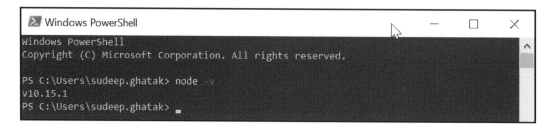

Before starting the next section, I will assume that you have managed to install Node.js.

How to do it...

1. On a Windows operating system, click **Start**, type `PowerShell`, and then click **Windows PowerShell**.
2. Type the following command to install Yeoman and gulp:

   ```
   npm install -g yo gulp
   ```

   You should get the following output:

3. Next, install the Yeoman generator for SharePoint by typing the following:

```
npm install -g @microsoft/generator-sharepoint
```

The output is as shown here:

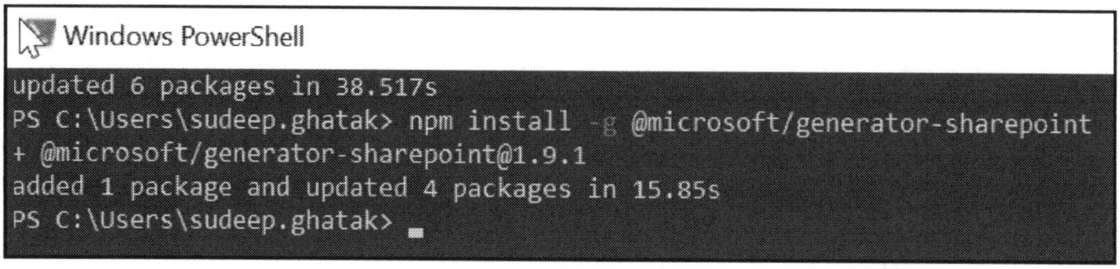

4. Finally, type the following to update npm:

```
npm i -g npm
```

The following is the output:

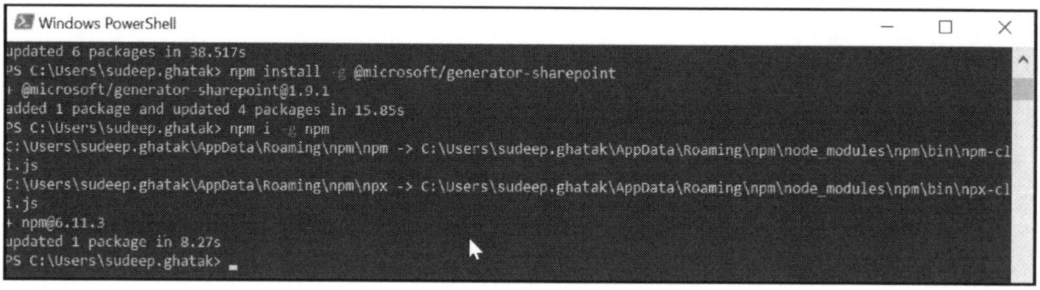

How it works...

Let's now try to understand the commands we just ran.

As you might have already figured out, the `install` command with npm installs the packages mentioned in the command; however, note that I added the `-g` command-line switch, which installs these packages *globally*. If you look in your global directory, you should see the package files there, as shown in the following screenshot:

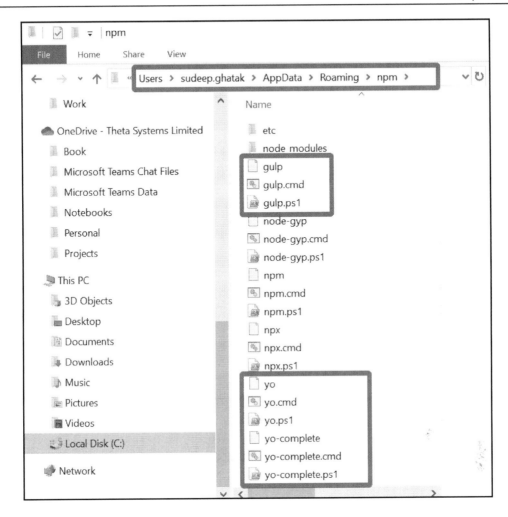

Installing these packages globally would mean that I can invoke the yo and gulp commands from the command line without specifying the install location.

After installing Yeoman, I installed the Yeoman SharePoint generator. Using the Yeoman SharePoint generator, you'll be able to scaffold new custom solution projects to build, package, and deploy SharePoint solutions. The generator comes with code snippets and a local development server to test your code. Note that we have installed this globally as well.

Finally, we just update all of the existing packages that we might have installed in the past by running npm -i -g npm.

See also

- The *Building your first SPFx web part* recipe in this chapter
- The *Deploying your SPFx web part* recipe in this chapter
- The *Debugging your SPFx web part* recipe in this chapter

Building your first SPFx web part

The modern experience in SharePoint provides you with several widgets or web parts that you can add to improve the experience. Shown here is a screenshot of all the components (client web parts) that you can add on a modern SharePoint page:

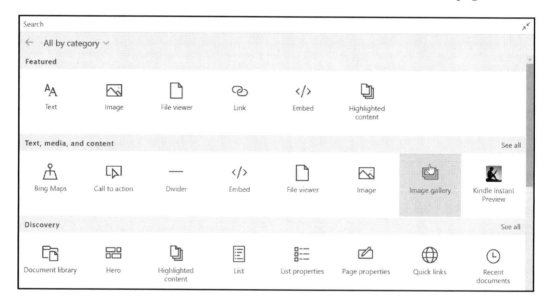

While these web parts offer most of what you need to display on a page, sometimes you need to develop custom functionality. In the past, there were several ways you could do this, but nowadays, the SharePoint framework is your best bet. One good thing about building web parts using SPFx is that you get to use the same framework that Microsoft uses to build the out-of-the-box web parts displayed in the preceding screenshot. This means that you get the same benefits, such as responsive behavior and mobile readiness.

SPFx web parts are compatible with both classic and modern pages.

The project is available for download at `https://m365book.page.link/SPFx`.

Getting started

For this recipe, you first need to set up the SharePoint development environment as described in the previous recipe.

How to do it...

1. On a Windows operating system, click **Start**, type `PowerShell`, and then click **Windows PowerShell**.
2. Navigate to the root folder by typing `cd \`.
3. Create a new folder by typing the following command:

```
Windows PowerShell

PS C:\Users\sudeep.ghatak> c:
PS C:\Users\sudeep.ghatak> cd \
PS C:\> md MyFirstSPFxWebpart


    Directory: C:\


Mode                LastWriteTime         Length Name
----                -------------         ------ ----
d-----        14/09/2019   11:53 AM                MyFirstSPFxWebpart


PS C:\>
```

4. Log in to the folder by typing the following:

```
PS C:\> cd .\MyFirstSPFxWebpart\
PS C:\MyFirstSPFxWebpart>
```

5. Scaffold a web part template by typing `yo @microsoft/sharepoint` and respond to the questions that are asked.

6. Your new web part solution is now ready for deployment. One last thing to do is to install a self-signed certificate by running the following gulp task:

```
gulp trust-dev-cert
```

7. Click **Yes** to install the certificate:

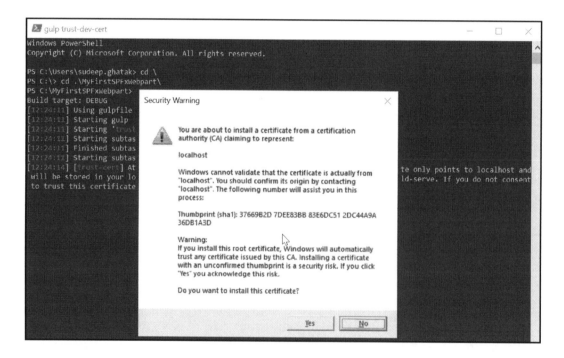

8. You can see your default app in action by typing the following command:

```
gulp serve
```

9. The web part will be launched in the local workbench. Click on the **+** symbol and select the web part:

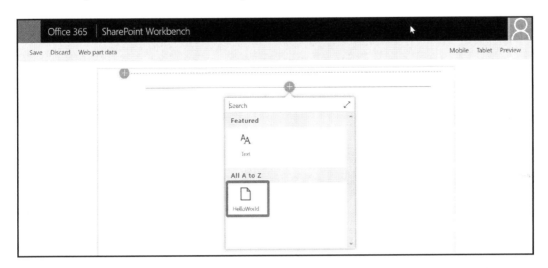

10. The web part will be added to the page, as shown in the following screenshot:

How it works...

So what just happened? Let's investigate what happened behind the scenes. Open the `MyFirstSPFxWebpart` directory in a source editor. You can do this by typing `code` followed by a `dot`, as shown in the following screenshot:

With `code .`, we just issued a command asking your operating system to launch Visual Studio Code from within the folder you are in. As you can see, the project folder has a number of subfolders. Let's look at some of them:

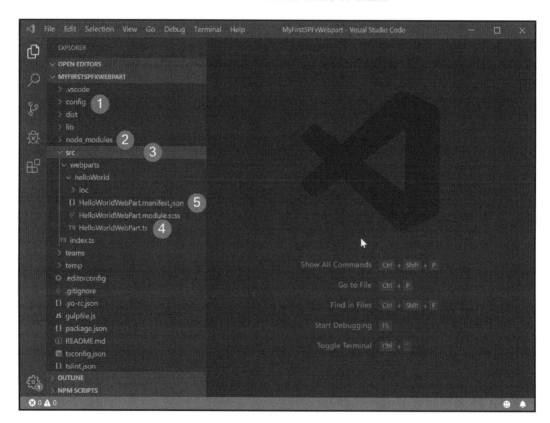

Config folder (config)

The configuration folder comprises files that contain the bundling information along with the components used in the solution. It also specifies the entry point of the solution and the location of the manifest file. If there are external libraries used in the solution, then the references to the external libraries are also stored here, as shown in the following screenshot:

```json
{} config.json ×
config > {} config.json > ...
  1   {
  2       "$schema": "https://developer.microsoft.com/json-schemas/spfx-build/config.2.0.schema.json",
  3       "version": "2.0",
  4       "bundles": {
  5         "hello-world-web-part": {
  6           "components": [
  7               {
  8                 "entrypoint": "./lib/webparts/helloWorld/HelloWorldWebPart.js",
  9                 "manifest": "./src/webparts/helloWorld/HelloWorldWebPart.manifest.json"
 10               }
 11           ]
 12         }
 13       },
 14       "externals": {},
 15       "localizedResources": {
 16         "HelloWorldWebPartStrings": "lib/webparts/helloWorld/loc/{locale}.js"
 17       }
 18   }
```

Node modules (node_modules)

When you install a node package using npm, all the package files and their associated dependencies are stored in the local `node_modules` subfolder of the solution. Read more about node modules at `https://m365book.page.link/node-modules`.

Source code (src)

The `src` folder in the solution stores the custom code that determines how your web part will look and function. In this example, it consists of one web part class, `HelloWorldWebPart.ts`, that is located in the `src\webparts\helloWorld` folder. The web part class extends the `BaseClientSideWebPart` class, which is an abstract class that implements the base functionality for a client-side web part:

```
16   export default class HelloWorldWebPart extends BaseClientSideWebPart<IHelloWorldWebPartProps> {
17
18     public render(): void {
19       this.domElement.innerHTML = `
20         <div class="${ styles.helloWorld }">
21           <div class="${ styles.container }">
22             <div class="${ styles.row }">
23               <div class="${ styles.column }">
24                 <span class="${ styles.title }">Welcome to SharePoint!</span>
25                 <p class="${ styles.subTitle }">Customize SharePoint experiences using Web Parts.</p>
26                 <p class="${ styles.description }">${escape(this.properties.description)}</p>
27                 <a href="https://aka.ms/spfx" class="${ styles.button }">
28                   <span class="${ styles.label }">Learn more</span>
29                 </a>
30               </div>
31             </div>
32           </div>
33         </div>`;
34     }
```

The `render()` method in the `HelloWorldWebPart` builds the HTML that is displayed in the web part when it is added to the page. Note that online number 26, it refers to this object, which contains a `properties` object. The properties are a way of receiving inputs from a user. The properties are defined in the manifest file, which we will see in the following list:

- `HelloWorldWebPart.manifest.json` stores information such as the display name, description, icon, version, and ID.
- `HelloWorldWebPart.module.scss` is the cascading stylesheet that allows variables and rules, thereby enabling the application of styles dynamically.

There's more...

SharePoint provides you with a convenient way of testing your code before deploying it to SharePoint. During the development stage, you can use what is known as a SharePoint workbench.

The SharePoint workbench is a test area that enables you to quickly preview and test web parts without deploying them in SharePoint.

There are basically two forms of workbench:

- Available locally with the SharePoint framework developer toolchain
- Available in a SharePoint site in your tenancy

The first workbench is provisioned on your local machine by the `gulp serve` command. This is your own instance of a SharePoint modern page. You can launch the local workbench by simply typing the following code:

```
gulp serve
```

The second workbench is actually running on your Microsoft 365 tenancy, and can be accessed by navigating to `https://your-site/_layouts/workbench.aspx`, as shown in the following screenshot:

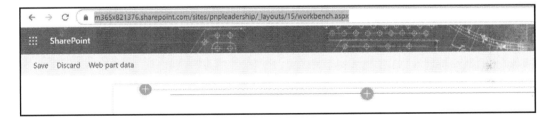

See also

- The *Setting up the development environment* recipe in this chapter
- The *Deploying your SPFx web part* recipe in this chapter
- The *Debugging your SPFx web part* recipe in this chapter

Deploying your SPFx web part to an Microsoft 365 tenant

Once you have tested your web part on your local workbench and are ready to deploy it on the live environment, there are several different approaches that you can take:

- You can deploy the web part to the Microsoft 365 app catalog so that it is available on all SharePoint sites on the tenant or site collection app catalog, restricted to a single site collection.
- You can deploy the web part to the Microsoft 365 CDN.
- You can host the web part on Azure CDN.

In this book, we will only cover the first approach, which is perhaps the simplest. To read about the other two approaches, visit `https://m365book.page.link/SPFx-office-cdn` and `https://m365book.page.link/SPFx-azure-cdn`.

Getting started

To deploy the web part to the tenant app catalog, you need to have the SharePoint Administrator role.

To deploy this on a specific site collection, you need to first create a site collection app catalog by running the following commands to open the SharePoint Online management shell.

 To connect to your SharePoint Online via PowerShell, download and install the SharePoint Online management shell from `https://m365book.page.link/SPFx-powershell`.

To connect to your Microsoft 365 tenant administration site, use the following command:

```
Connect -SPOService -Url https://{your tenant name}-
admin.sharepoint.com
```

You will be asked to provide authentication. Enter your credentials:

Tenant administrators can choose to enable a site collection app catalogs on specific site collections. Solutions deployed to the site collection app catalogs can only be installed in that particular site collection. To provision a SharePoint app catalog, type the following command:

```
Add-SPOSiteCollectionAppCatalog -Site "Url of your site where the app
catalog needs to be enabled"
```

You will see that the app catalog has been created in your site, as shown in the following screenshot:

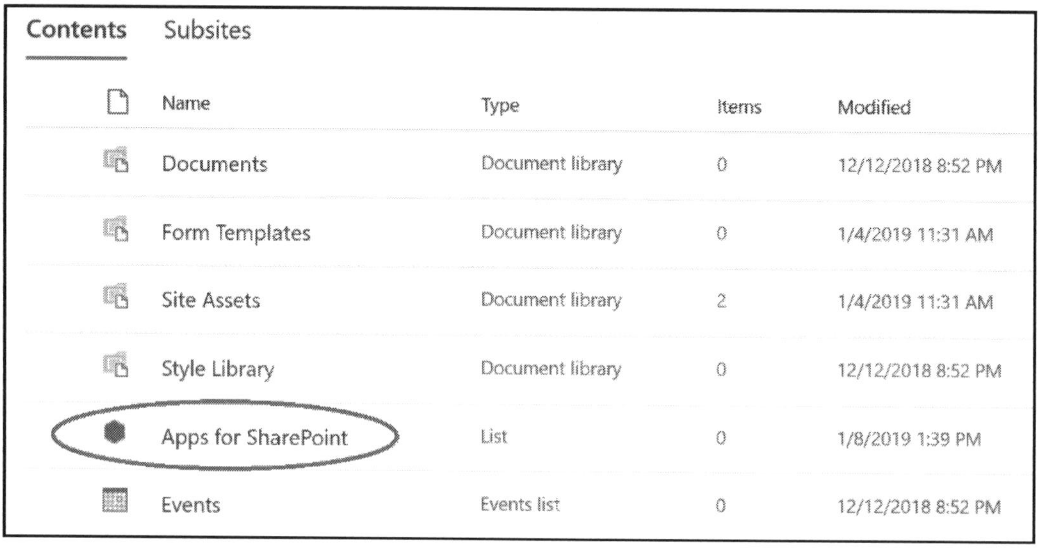

	Name	Type	Items	Modified
	Documents	Document library	0	12/12/2018 8:52 PM
	Form Templates	Document library	0	1/4/2019 11:31 AM
	Site Assets	Document library	2	1/4/2019 11:31 AM
	Style Library	Document library	0	12/12/2018 8:52 PM
	Apps for SharePoint	List	0	1/8/2019 1:39 PM
	Events	Events list	0	12/12/2018 8:52 PM

(Contents / Subsites)

How to do it...

The following sections will cover the instructions to do the following:

- Deploy the web part to the Microsoft 365 app catalog to make it globally available
- Deploy the web part to the app catalog of a specific site

Creating a solution package

Run the following command to create a deployable package:

```
gulp package-solution
```

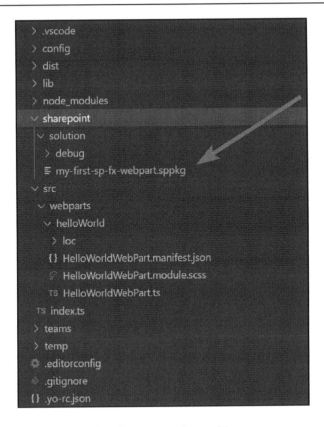

The file with the `.sppkg` extension is your package file.

Deploying to the tenant app catalog

1. Go to `https://office.com` and log in with your Microsoft 365 credentials.
2. Click on **Admin**, as shown in the following screenshot:

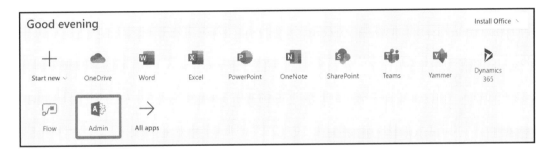

You need to have the Global administrator or SharePoint administrator role in order to see the **Admin** icon.

3. Navigate to the SharePoint admin center by clicking on the **SharePoint** link:

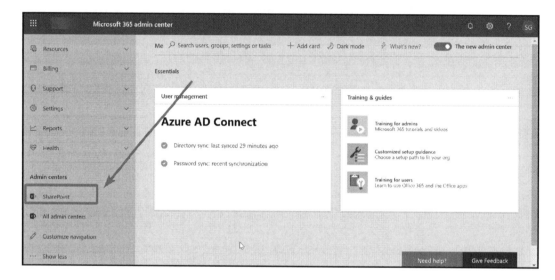

4. Click on **Classic features** on the **SharePoint admin center** page:

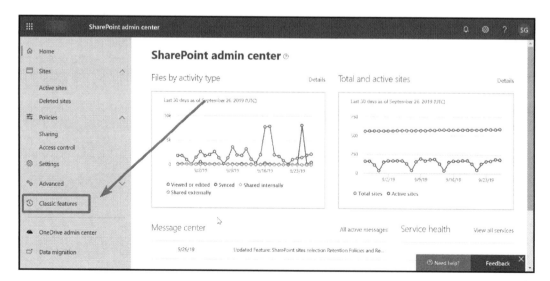

5. Open the **Apps** section:

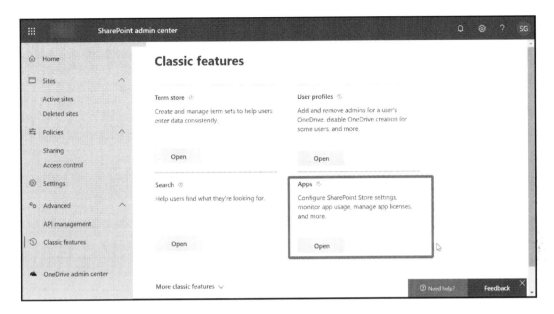

6. Click on **App Catalog**:

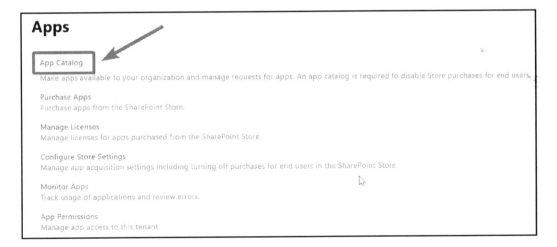

7. You will be taken to the **App Catalog Site**. Click on **Distribute apps for SharePoint**:

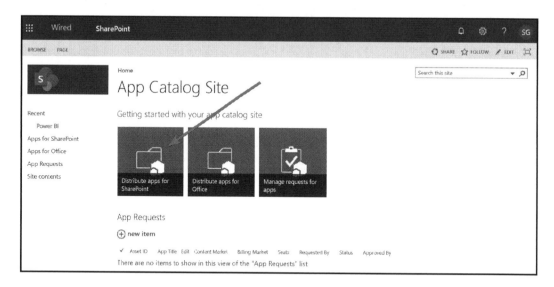

8. You will then be taken to the package library:

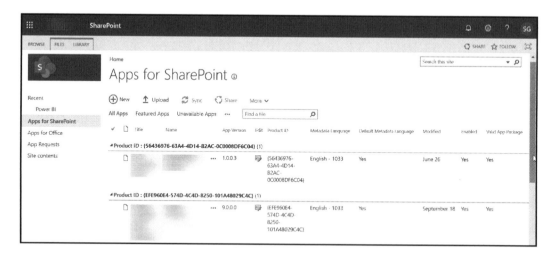

9. Drag your package file from your package solution folder to the library.
10. The web part will now be available to be added on any SharePoint page.

How it works...

The SPFx web part package consists of a **solution package** (a `.sppkg` file) and might optionally include other files, such as scripts, CSS stylesheets, and other assets. The `.sppkg` file is actually just a zipped version of a set of files. If you rename the `.sppkg` file to `.zip` and investigate the contents, you will find that it includes a manifest file named `AppManifest.xml`, which contains a bunch of URLs pointing to the location where script files are deployed.

These files need to be in a location that is accessible to the SharePoint web part running in Microsoft 365. The location could be on Azure Blob storage or the Microsoft 365 public **content delivery network (CDN)**. The other option, perhaps the simplest one, is to host the files in a document library within SharePoint.

Each approach has its pros and cons. CDN delivers pages and other web content to a user based on the geographic locations of the user, so if your users are geographically dispersed, you might want to deploy your assets to an Azure or Microsoft 365 CDN.

Instead of deploying your assets separately, you can choose to package them in the `.sppkg` file itself. You can achieve this by setting the `includeClientSideAssets` property as `true`. After deploying the `.sppkg` solution to the app catalog, SharePoint will unzip the assets to a location in your tenant.

See also

- The *Setting up the development environment* recipe in this chapter
- The *Building your first SPFx web part* recipe in this chapter
- The *Debugging your SPFx web part* recipe in this chapter

Debugging your SPFx web part

No one is perfect, and it often takes several iterations before the desired outcome is achieved. You have to peek into the code in real time to identify certain failure points. Debugging is a skill and can only be mastered with practice.

Debugging is an essential part of the software development life cycle. Not only does it allow the developers to validate their logic, but it also uncovers some areas of improvement. Since all the logic for SPFx web parts exists inside the JavaScript file, we are going to use our JavaScript debugging skills here.

There are two styles of debugging that people use:

- **Logging**: One of the ways to debug the execution flow is by adding `console.log()` statements to your JavaScript file at various places. The debugger prints the messages in the order in which they are encountered.
- **Using developer tools**: This is a more useful way to debug your code by adding breakpoints, watching, and stepping in and out of code blocks.

All modern browsers support debugging nowadays. We will demonstrate some of the common debugging functionalities using Google Chrome.

Getting started

You should download and install a modern browser, such as Microsoft Edge, Google Chrome, Firefox, or Safari, in order to use the browser debugging tools. We will use Google Chrome for our demonstration.

Alternately, you can use the debugging capabilities of your code editor (Visual Studio Code, in this case) by running the following command:

```
gulp serve --nobrowser
```

The process of debugging an SPFx web part within Visual Studio is described at `https://m365book.page.link/vscode`

How to do it...

1. Navigate to the page where you added the web part.
2. Launch the developer tools in your browser by pressing *F12* or *Function + F12*, depending on the browser and the make of your keyboard.
3. Go to the **Sources** tab and locate your web part's JavaScript file. The location of the file will vary based on the deployment method.
4. Since we deployed our web part using the Microsoft 365 CDN, our JavaScript file can be found under `https://publiccdn.sharepointonline.com`.

5. Click on the JavaScript file to reveal the code. Normally, the final packaged solution contains minified files. You can format the output by clicking on the { } symbol, as highlighted in the following screenshot:

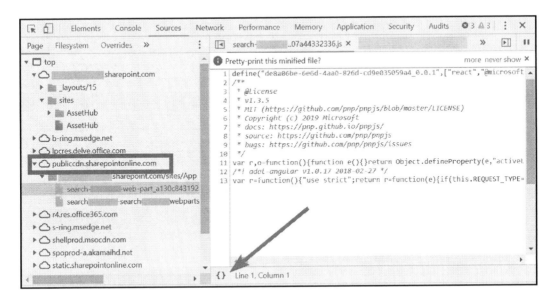

If the code is being debugged from the workbench, then the JavaScript file will point to your local webserver:

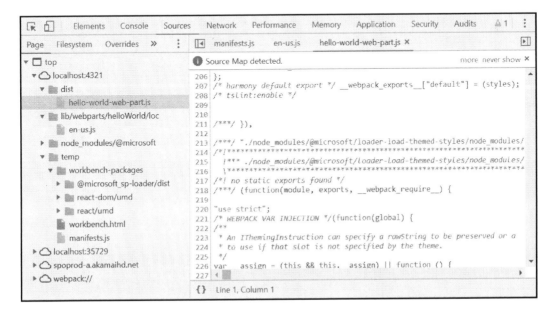

6. In order to debug your code, place a breakpoint by clicking on a line, and then refreshing the page. The execution of the code will pause and the breakpoint will be highlighted:

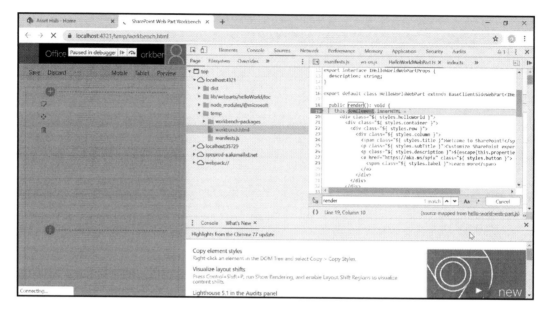

7. Press *F11* to execute the next line.
8. If the next line is a call to another function or method, then the code execution will step into the function or method. If you want to just execute the method without stepping into it, press *F10*.
9. During debugging, you can evaluate the variables by typing them directly in the **Console** tab:

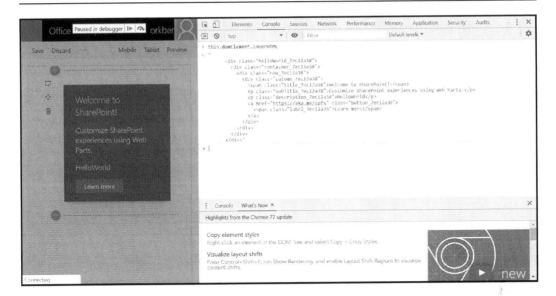

And that's pretty much the majority of what you need to know about debugging.

How it works...

SPFx web parts are built using HTML, JavaScript, and CSS. What this means is that your code executes on the browser, although it appears to be running inside SharePoint. When the page with the web part is loaded, the web part assets get downloaded as temporary files. The web part runs in the context of the logged-in user, which means that you can create personalized experiences for the users using the SPFx framework.

Since the code runs in the browser, you do not need separate tools to debug an SPFx web part. Most modern web browsers have debugging capabilities. JavaScript follows a concurrency model based on an **event loop**, which is responsible for code execution. The code executes in a single thread. During the execution, you can force it to pause through the use of breakpoints. **Breakpoints** allow you to examine variables (in the console window) by typing the variable name and pressing *Enter*. They also allow you to test the conditional logic in the debugging window.

There's more

Besides resolving bugs, developer tools also let you improve page loading and the performance of your application. The **Network** tab can be used to test the following:

- The number of requests that the page is making
- The amount of data transferred during page load
- The resources that the page is loading
- The order in which the resources are loaded
- The time is taken by the resource to load
- The compressed and uncompressed size of the resource
- The performance of the page on desktop versus mobile

The following screenshot shows the performance of our web part in the **Network** tab:

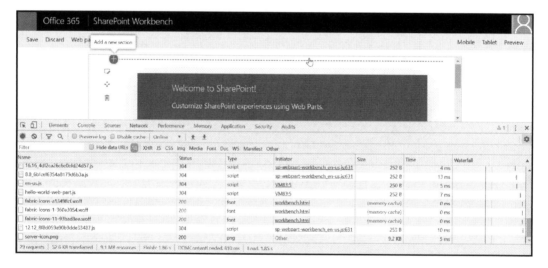

See also

- The *Setting up the development environment* recipe in this chapter
- The *Deploying your SPFx web part* recipe in this chapter
- The *Building your first SPFx web part* recipe in this chapter

19
Microsoft 365 on Mobile

Microsoft 365 is undoubtedly a very rich and diverse productivity solution that covers almost all aspects of an organization's needs. One thing that is embedded in every application of the Microsoft 365 suite is **mobility**. Every Microsoft 365 application has been designed keeping the users of the application in mind. Microsoft 365 caters to users who access Office applications from their workplace, as well as those who are on the go all the time. Some users will connect to the internet using Wi-Fi, while others might choose to do so using their mobile data.

All Microsoft 365 applications are mobile-responsive. What that means is that if you access any Microsoft 365 application on your mobile or tablet browser, you will see that it rearranges the components on the screen so as to provide the best browsing experience on the device of your choice.

In addition to being mobile-responsive, the applications also have native Android and iOS apps that make use of your mobile's native capabilities, such as the camera, the **Global Positioning System** (**GPS**), orientation, and so on.

In this chapter, we will take a look at some of the key mobile apps available with Microsoft 365. These are as follows:

- SharePoint
- Delve
- OneDrive
- Office apps
- Planner
- Power Apps
- Power Automate (Microsoft Flow)
- Power BI
- Microsoft Teams

SharePoint

The SharePoint mobile app helps you remain on top of your work while on the go. You can access the contents of a site, and search for people and documents. The app works with SharePoint Online in Microsoft 365, SharePoint Server (2013 and 2016) On-Premises, and your hybrid environment.

If you have multiple Office accounts, you can switch between them within your SharePoint app, as you can see from the following screenshot:

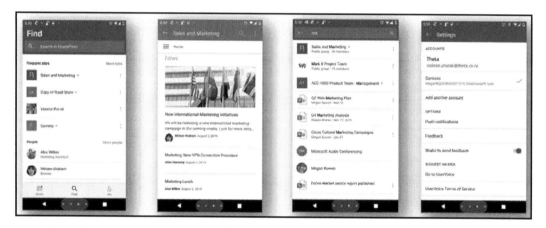

When you sign in to the mobile app, you will see sites you have frequently visited, documents you have been working on, and people you interact with the most. Clicking on the site renders it to appear in the mobile view, where all your page components are lined up vertically. As you search for content, you get the same search experience as on the web.

You can search for content, sites, or people using the **Find** option in the navigation bar at the bottom of the screen. Clicking on **Me** lets you access your recent and saved documents. Clicking on the **gear** icon lets you access the settings page to modify other app settings.

Delve

The Delve mobile app notifies you when your files are updated. You can access recent copies of files in one click. Delve brings the content that is relevant to you on that day, based on your interaction with other colleagues. You can also share documents with your colleagues and team from within the app, as can be seen in the following screenshot:

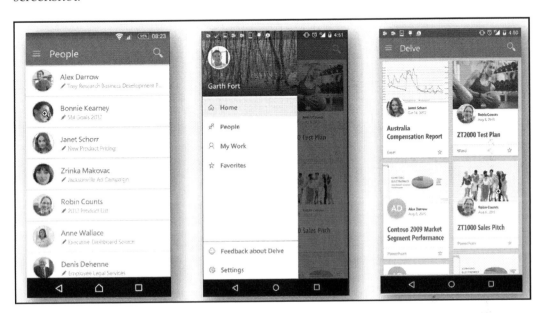

OneDrive

The OneDrive mobile app lets you stay connected to all your files from anywhere and from any device. Microsoft Graph brings all the documents you have been working on, irrespective of where they are located (SharePoint, Teams, or OneDrive) in the OneDrive mobile app.

The app allows you to do the following:

- Upload office documents, **Portable Document Format (PDF)** files, images, and so on.
- Preview documents and images.
- Edit and co-author in native Office apps.
- Mark files and folders for offline access.
- Share documents with your office colleagues as well as external people.
- Delete and recover files directly from your mobile devices.
- Scan whiteboard content, business cards, and receipts, and store them in Microsoft 365, as illustrated in the following screenshot:

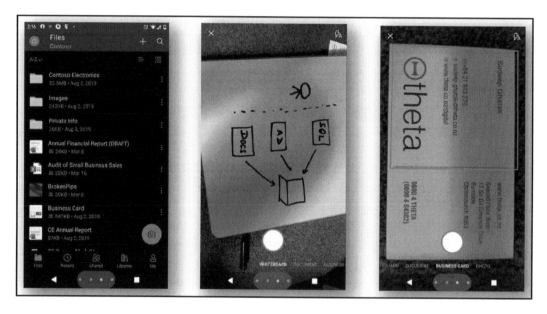

Your OneDrive content is encrypted, not just on the device and in the cloud but also in transit.

Office apps

Microsoft Office has become an integral part of every organization. Word, Excel, PowerPoint, and Outlook have been shown to be the most popular applications. According to Microsoft, there are over 1 billion Microsoft Office users in the world using Office apps on a day-to-day basis, hence it is no surprise that Microsoft devoted its attention to building mobile apps for these applications.

Currently, there are Android and iOS apps for Word, Excel, PowerPoint, and Outlook. However, Microsoft is planning to merge them together into one Microsoft Office app.

The usage of Office apps on mobile devices has gone up significantly. 100 million people (`https://m365book.page.link/office-mobile`) use Outlook on a phone. Having an app on the phone saves you from sitting at your work desk, allowing you to be productive even when you are on the go.

The Microsoft Outlook app lets you connect multiple email accounts in one place and be able to view all your personal and official appointments in one calendar. The Inbox separates out **Focused** emails—the emails that need your attention—from other emails, such as notifications, promotional content, and so on.

Apps for Office applications (Word, Excel, Powerpoint) provide document-editing features on mobiles and tablets with screen sizes of less than 10.1 inches. On your mobile device, you can work on documents stored in SharePoint or OneDrive and leverage the benefits, such as sharing and co-authoring with colleagues. The documents get autosaved, so you can switch between the apps on your mobile device and not worry about losing your changes. With multi-device support, you can pick up your document from where you left off in another device.

The Microsoft Word app renders your entire document, including images and tables. The images and tables open in fullscreen when you click on them.

The Microsoft Excel app lets you add formulas, charts, and tables. You can show or hide columns, use filters, sort, and much more.

The Microsoft PowerPoint app lets you edit your presentations and present them right from your mobile device, as illustrated in the following screenshot:

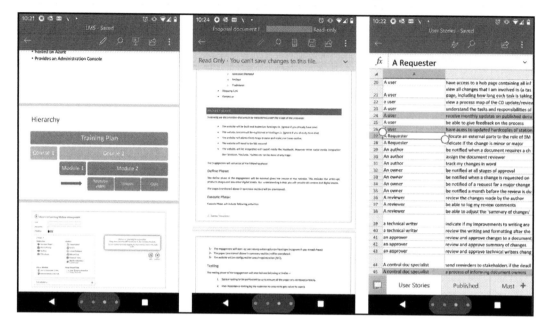

Planner

The Planner app lets users view and updates their plans on the go. It lets you create plans and tasks, assign tasks, share files, chat about what you're working on, and get updates on progress. The app lets you add photos from within your mobile device.

You cannot delete a plan on mobile.

The app offers a task mobile view that displays the checklist items, task status, task priority, and task assignees. You can add attachments, which includes photos from your device. Planner for mobile devices also has some basic charts that show the progress of tasks. The member's chart breaks down tasks by the assignee, as can be seen in the following screenshot:

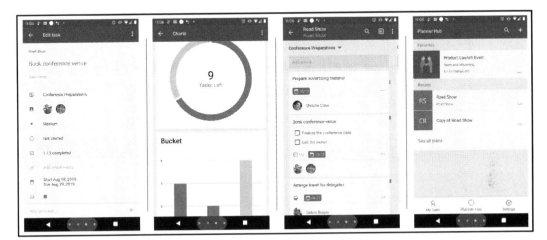

Power Apps

We learned in Chapter 14, *Power Apps*, that Power Apps can be designed for either web or mobile devices. The benefit of the apps running on a mobile device is that you can take advantage of the device's capabilities, such as location services and the camera.

Apps that have been shared with you will appear when you launch the Power Apps app. When you access the app on a mobile device for the first time, you'll be asked to grant permissions to some applications and services, depending on the systems the app is integrating with.

As shown in the following screenshot, you can pin apps to your **Home** screen for quick access:

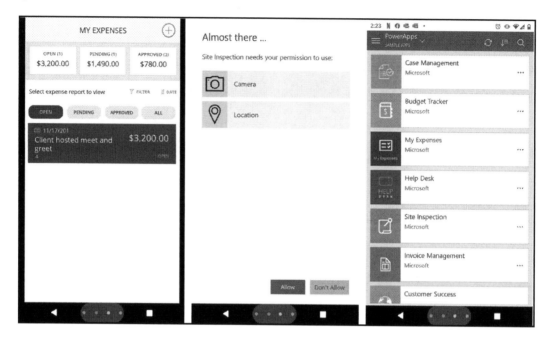

Power Automate (Microsoft Flow)

The Power Automate app on mobile devices lets you do the following:

- **Button flows**: The mobile app lets you build and run button flows to perform tasks such as sending a reminder or getting the weather. There are several templates available to choose from. By integrating with other third-party services, you could even order a coffee or book a movie. An example of this can be seen in the following screenshot:

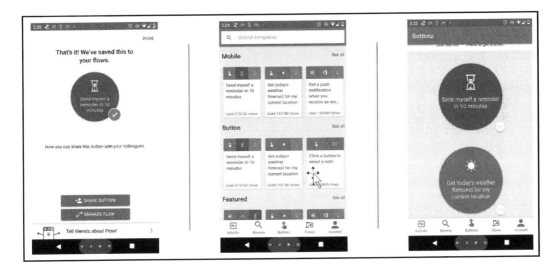

- **Approvals**: You can build approval workflows and receive approval notifications on your mobile device, thus enabling you to approve or reject workflows even while sitting in a cafe or catching a train. The approval notification lets you add a comment (if you want to) and even reassign to someone else within your organization, as shown in the following screenshot:

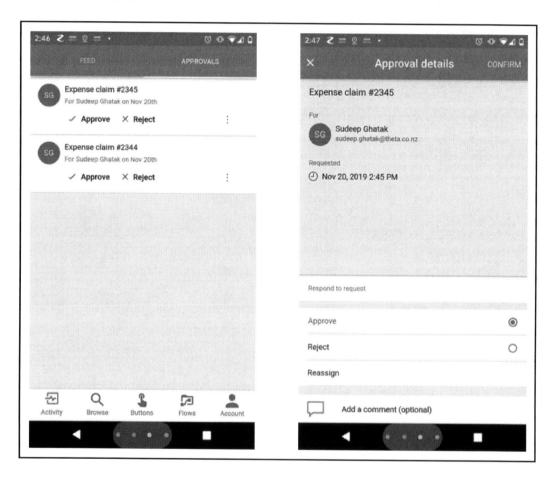

Power BI

Power BI on mobile enables you to look at and analyze your company reports on a mobile device. While designing reports using Power BI Desktop, you can create visualizations for the mobile view. A mobile visualization lets you optimize your screen space.

You can download the Power BI mobile apps from their respective stores, also for free:

- App Store: `https://m365book.page.link/powerbi-ios`
- Google Play: `https://m365book.page.link/powerbi-and`
- Windows Store: `https://m365book.page.link/powerbi-win`

To create a mobile visualization in the Power BI service, launch the report and click **Edit report**, as illustrated in the following screenshot:

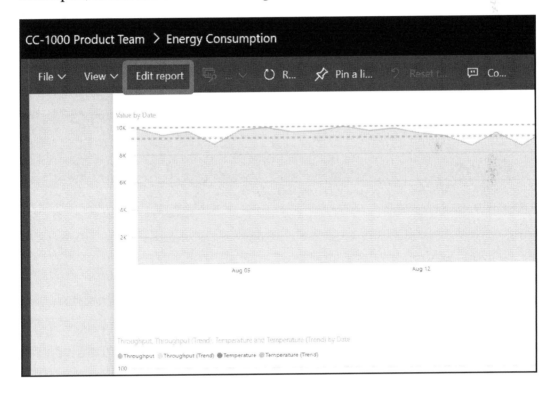

Once the report has been opened in **Edit** mode, click the **Mobile layout** to open the mobile designer window. You can now drag and drop the Power BI visualization components on the mobile layout and resize them to fit the screen, as illustrated in the following screenshot:

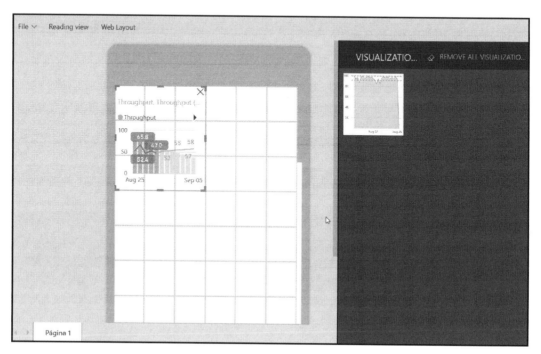

Now, save the report by clicking **File** | **Save**, and you are done. You can now access the mobile-optimized report on your mobile device, as shown in the following screenshot:

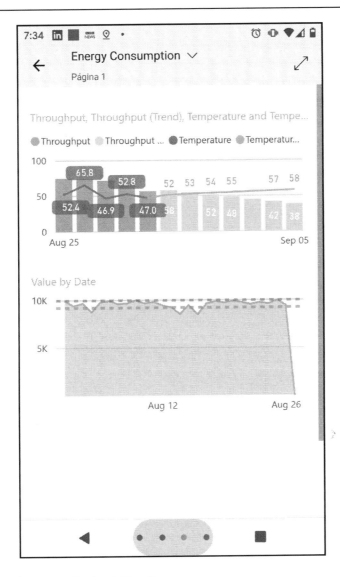

Power BI Mobile lets you do the following:

- Analyze and annotate reports on a mobile device.
- Share reports with your colleague.
- Get instant answers by posing a question.
- Set data alerts and receive notifications.

Microsoft Teams

If you don't want to miss out on team calls, but want to be able to access documents from anywhere and collaborate with your peers without being in the office in person, I recommend you try the Teams app, which is available on iOS and Android mobile devices.

Using the Microsoft Teams mobile app, you can do the following:

- Monitor activities happening across the teams and channels you are part of.
- Attend online meetings, and have audio/video calls and group chats.
- Customize your channel workspace with Microsoft apps and third-party services.
- Collaborate using other Microsoft 365 apps such as Microsoft Word, PowerPoint, Excel, OneDrive, and SharePoint.
- Search your team conversations, files, and chats.
- Set a status message.

The following screenshots show some examples of the Teams mobile app:

Teams' mobile interface is intuitive and easy to use. It is a great way to remain productive even on the go and achieve more as a team.

Appendix

While we have tried to cover all the major Microsoft 365 applications, we acknowledge that new applications are being added to the Microsoft 365 fabric all the time. We have used our collective judgment to promote certain important applications throughout this book while mentioning some other applications that are worthy in the *Appendix* section. Let's go over some of the apps and Microsoft 365 concepts that you might hear of.

OneNote

OneNote is a note-taking application that actually deserves a chapter of its own. The application is rich with features that make it possible to capture ideas, thoughts, and tasks at any time on any device. Since it's part of the Microsoft Office Suite of Applications, it integrates seamlessly with Outlook, Microsoft Teams, and other Microsoft Office apps and services. You can take notes in OneNote during an Outlook or Teams meeting.

OneNote components

OneNote is comprised of notebooks that contain sections and pages. If you are using the OneNote app, the notebooks get synced with OneNote online if and when you are connected to the internet. You can share a notebook with your colleagues to share an idea or meeting notes.

Sections within the notebook are like chapters in a book:

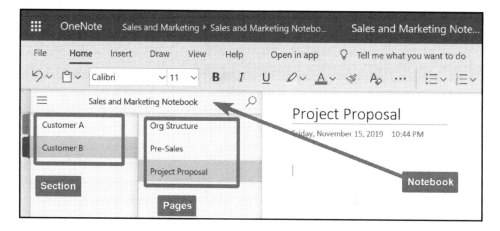

Taking notes

Besides digital notes, OneNote also supports **handwritten** notes (using a stylus) and **audio/video** notes. It can convert your handwritten notes into digital notes so they can be searched for throughout the document. It can also translate notes taken in one language into another language.

You can also insert images, videos, and documents on your pages. You can arrange the content on the page just by dragging and moving it around.

OneNote doesn't have a save button. This is because it autosaves the content, which speeds up the note-taking process.

Sharing notes

You can share a notebook with your colleagues simply by clicking on the **Share** option. This shares the entire notebook, along with all of its sections. You can't share a single section but can copy or move a section from one notebook to another:

SharePoint workflows

So far, we learned how to build processes using Microsoft Flow. Before Flow was included in the Microsoft 365 suite, workflows were designed using SharePoint Designer. SharePoint Designer is a free executable that helps you modify sites and web pages and create workflows with SharePoint. You can download it from `https:/ /m365book.page.link/sp-designer`. Microsoft has not released any new versions of SharePoint Designer after SharePoint Designer 2013, but you can still use it to build legacy SharePoint workflows on SharePoint Online.

SharePoint workflows can be attached to a site, a list, or a specific content type.

To build a workflow, open a SharePoint site using SharePoint Designer:

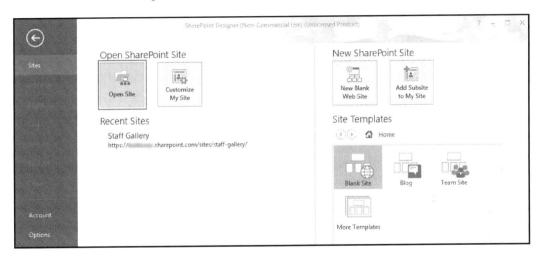

Click on **WORKFLOWS** on the left to see all the SharePoint workflows that have been deployed on the site. From here, you can choose the type of workflow and the workflow designer will load up:

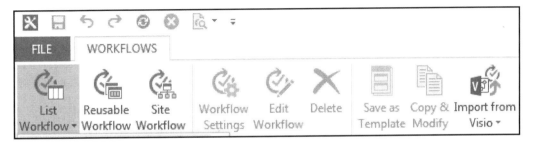

SharePoint workflows use a very old-fashioned editor. It requires you to learn the syntax and the logic isn't easy to debug:

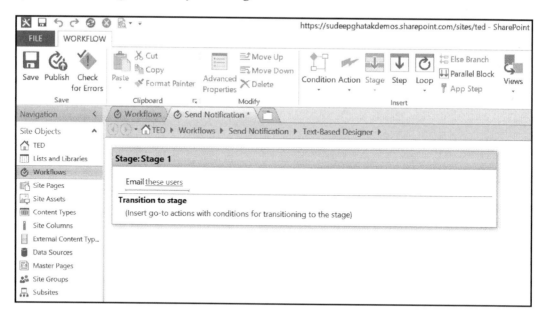

If you are still supporting workflows built on the designer platform, I would recommend rebuilding these workflows using Microsoft Flow.

Microsoft Forms

Microsoft 365 Forms or Microsoft Forms is an application that lets you create survey forms, and quizzes. You can create forms and surveys to get information from your coworkers or even from people outside your organization. To create a form, visit `https://forms.microsoft.com` and log in with your organization account. Once you've logged in, you can create a form or a quiz. The form creation wizard is simple and easy to use, as shown here:

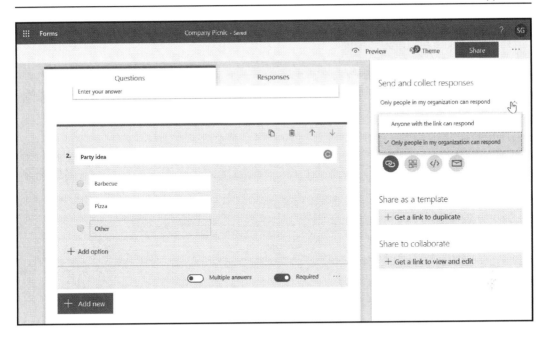

Start by clicking **Add new**, which lets you add questions. These questions could be simple text boxes, radio buttons, date fields, or rating fields. Once you have added all your questions, you can preview the form by clicking on **Preview** on the top banner.

The form can be accessed via a link that is generated when you click **Share**. This link can be public or private to the organization, depending on the sharing settings.

The form creator can look at the responses as they arrive. You can view these by clicking on the **Responses** tab:

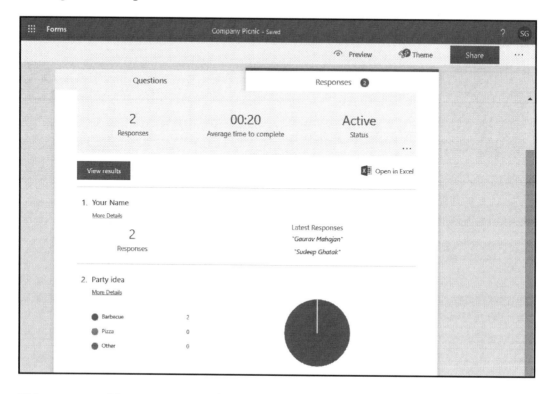

This page provides a summary of the responses. Individual responses can be viewed by clicking on **View Results**. The responses can also be exported to Excel.

Microsoft Stream

Microsoft Stream is an Enterprise streaming video service available with Microsoft 365. Company staff can upload, share, and view video content created within the company. It also supports social features such as tagging and comments, which enable discussions around the video's content.

Microsoft Stream lets you upload recorded presentations and live events for later viewing. Meetings recorded using Microsoft Teams get uploaded to Stream automatically.

The transcript of the audio/video is generated automatically for any Stream video. The best part is that the transcript is searchable, which means you can skip to the point in the video timeline where a given word was mentioned by searching for the word in the transcript area.

Microsoft Teams meeting recordings have another great feature. When a meeting is being recorded, Teams tags the people speaking during the meeting while the video is playing. With this, you can click on an avatar of one of the people from the meeting and be taken straight to the section where the person was speaking, as shown in the following screenshot:

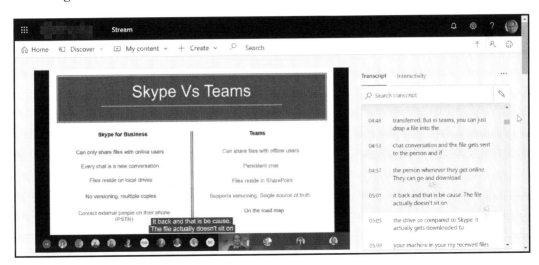

Microsoft Stream video can be securely shared with a group, individual, or the entire company. You can also assign owners to a specific video, which lets them change the metadata information.

You can also embed Microsoft Stream content in your SharePoint pages, as well as Sway and PowerPoint presentations.

Only the video owner has the ability to download the video.

Stream lets you group your videos in channels. You can add videos to a channel to group them logically. You can create channels organization-wide or for specific groups, as shown in the following screenshot:

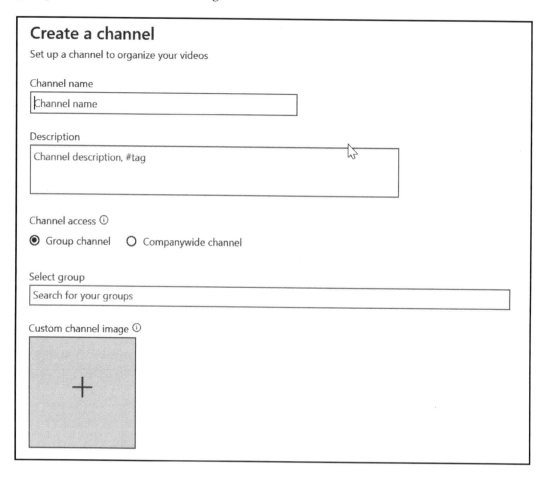

Having the videos added to the channel lets your staff identify them by the category they are in. You can have channels for training, certifications, product launches, and more, as shown in the following screenshot:

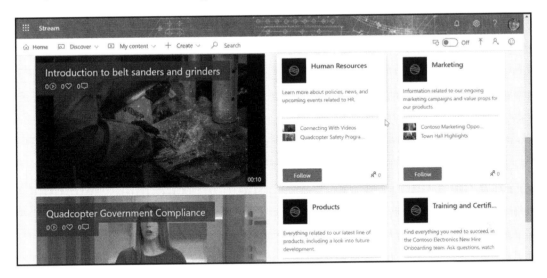

Stream also lets you make screen recordings. So, next time you need to record a training video for your company, try this out:

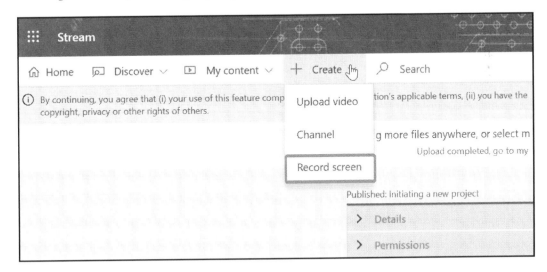

Sway

Sway is a tool that lets you build stunning presentations and interactive reports without you having to worry about the design or the layout. All your presentations will be responsive and render beautifully on any device.

Sway is a free service. However, if you have a Microsoft 365 license, you can do even more with Sway. The following web page compares the free version of Sway to the one that comes with a Microsoft 365 subscription, at `https://m365book.page.link/sway`.

Sway lets you add text, images, and videos to a web page interface that looks pretty similar to a modern SharePoint page. As you add content, Sway will provide you with suggestions, as shown in the following screenshot:

Once your Sway content is ready, you can share it with colleagues or friends. You can build public Sways that people can view without having to sign in. At the same time, you can also create secure Sway content that can only be viewed by people you share it with.

To build your own Sway, go to `www.sway.office.com` and sign in with your personal Microsoft account or the Microsoft 365 login credentials provided by your organization.

To Do

Just like Sway, To Do is a free service available for personal use, as well as a part of your organization's Microsoft 365 subscription.

To Do lets you create and manage your tasks. It lets you capture notes and ideas and tag them with photos, files, and more. You can assign due dates to these tasks so that they appear in your To Do lists.

To Do has a very simple interface, which makes it easy to use.

At its core, you have the tasks screen, which loads when you open To Do. You can assign a due date, add reminders, and provide additional information such as notes and file attachments. A task can be further broken down into steps where needed.

These tasks are added to lists. **To Do** provides some inbuilt lists, as follows:

- **My Day**: You can pick any task and add it to the My Day list so that you can keep track of the tasks you need to focus on.
- **Important**: Any task that you tag as important will appear in this list.
- **Planned**: Tasks that have a due date assigned to them will appear in this list.
- **Tasks**: This is the default list that the tasks get added to when they're created.

In addition to these lists, you can create custom lists and move your tasks to them.

You can create tasks directly from your mobile device via the **To Do** app, which is available on both Android and iOS.

The following screenshot shows what the app looks like on mobile. In the following screenshots, I am demonstrating how, using To do, I can manage the tasks required to author a book:

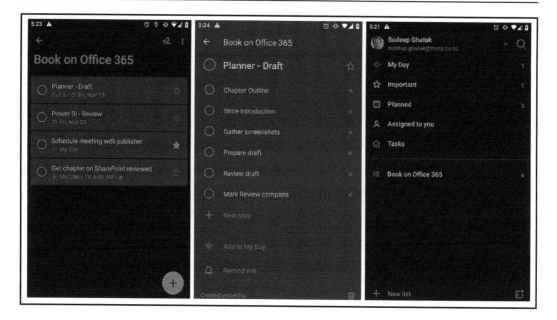

Office development frameworks

Microsoft 365 has a robust development framework that supports customizations being made to various M365 services. The framework is used by Microsoft partners and ISVs who build a rich ecosystem of applications and apps that extend the power of Microsoft 365. For instance, there's an app that lets you receive digital signatures on your documents and an Outlook add-in that lets you save your documents from Outlook to SharePoint.

Companies using Microsoft 365 use the developer framework to customize and build custom solutions that fit their internal requirements. Many such success stories can be read at `https://betterwith.office.com/`.

Let's look at some of the most widely used development features.

Microsoft Graph

Microsoft Graph (formerly known as Microsoft 365 Graph) is a collection of endpoints that lets you build your own applications that interact with data within your Microsoft 365 environment.

Microsoft Graph lets you work with the following:

- Microsoft 365 users
- Social
- OneDrive
- Excel
- Outlook
- Microsoft 365 groups
- Tasks
- SharePoint
- Azure Active Directory

The beauty of Microsoft Graph is that you can interact with all these objects using a single endpoint; that is, `https://graph.microsoft.com`.

The following diagram (borrowed from the Microsoft website) shows how Graph interacts with Microsoft services:

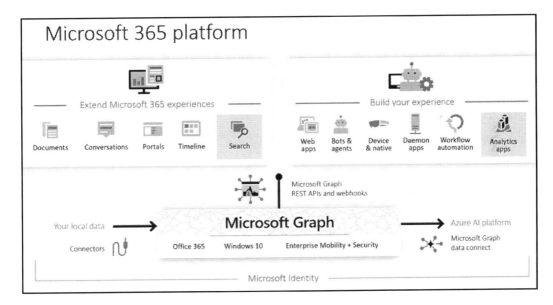

What this means is that you can build applications using the same APIs that Microsoft uses to build its products. By releasing the API to the community, Microsoft has welcomed developers to come up with applications that suit their specific needs.

Microsoft Graph uses REST calls to query information. **Representational State Transfer (REST)** is a widely accepted architectural style that is used to perform Read, Create, Update, and Delete operations using a variety of languages (C#, JavaScript, Perl, Java, Node.js, Angular, and more).

Therefore, irrespective of the language the developer opts for, they can make use of Graph APIs to build custom solutions such as the following:

- A mobile app that creates a summary of what is trending (by looking into Yammer and Teams conversations).
- A resource booking app that helps you identify people who are overbooked, as well as those who are on the bench (based on their calendar bookings).
- A Power BI dashboard showing the usage of Microsoft Teams based on conversations and files exchanged.

If you are planning to build an application using Microsoft Graph, start with Microsoft's Graph Explorer, about which you can find out more at `https://m365book.page.link/graph-ex`.

Graph Explorer lets you test your results by allowing you to log in with your Microsoft 365 credentials and run REST calls, as shown in the following screenshot:

For more information, please refer to the official Microsoft Graph documentation at `https://m365book.page.link/graph-doc`.

PowerShell

PowerShell is a scripting language that lets you execute Microsoft 365 tasks from the command line. Some tasks that you can perform using Powershell are as follows:

- Add users to Microsoft 365 by reading a CSV file.
- Assign licenses to users in Microsoft 365.
- Migrate documents from one SharePoint site into another.
- Provision of a Microsoft Team and create a private channel.
- And the list goes on...

Basically, PowerShell lets you do anything that you would usually do using the user interface in Microsoft 365, provided that the service exposes an API.

You can read more about Microsoft 365 Powershell by visiting `https://m365book.page.link/Powershell`.

Further, in order to work with a specific application, say Teams or SharePoint, you need to install the respective **Powershell module**. Powershell modules are groups of functions that are associated with specific applications. You can install PowerShell modules by using the `Install-Module` command

Some notable modules for Microsoft 365 are:

- **AzureAD**: to work with Azure Active directory
- **MicrosoftTeams**: to work with Teams
- **ExchangeOnlineManagement**: to work with Exchange Online

Specifically, with SharePoint, there are two modules that are often used:

- `Microsoft.Online.SharePoint.PowerShell`: This module is officially supported by Microsoft and contains SPO in the command name (e.g. `Connect-SPOService`). Please refer to the following documentation from Microsoft to read more about the SharePoint Online management shell and to get started: `https://m365book.page.link/PowerShell-SPO`

- `SharePoint PnP`: This module is community-driven with contributions from Microsoft employees and other community leaders. Due to its popularity, we have discussed this module in more detail in the next topic. Due to the open-source nature of this module, you will find that this module is more feature-rich, however, it doesn't guarantee an SLA should you run into issues. You should keep this in mind while running scripts using the commands.

SharePoint PnP

Patterns and Practices (PnP) and is an open-source, community-driven initiative, coordinated by the Microsoft engineering team. This is a wide community of experts and developers from within and outside Microsoft who have built a huge repository of reusable components that can be added to your site, thereby enhancing the user experience of your customers. PnP provides open-source tools, commands, and scripts that you can use for automating various tasks in your SharePoint environment. The following web page provides a good overview of PnP at `https://m365book.page.link/pnp-community`.

These articles give you good overviews of getting started with the two PnP development options:

- PnP PowerShell overview: `https://m365book.page.link/PnP-PowerShell`
- Getting started with PnPjs: `https://m365book.page.link/PnPJs-Getting-Started`

The community runs weekly webcasts, demo videos, tutorials, and other videos and also has a GitHub repository at `https://github.com/pnp/`.

Office Add-ins

Office Add-ins let you build solutions that extend Office applications (Word, Excel, Outlook, and so on) and interact with content inside Office documents. Add-ins can be built using simple web technologies such as HTML, CSS, and JavaScript. As a result of this, they can run seamlessly on all platforms, including iOS and Windows.

If you would like to know more about Office Add-ins, visit `https://m365book.page.link/office-addins`.

Learning pathways

Microsoft 365 learning pathways are a learning solution designed to simplify adoption and increase usage of Microsoft 365 services in your organization. It lets you do the following:

- Install the prebuilt Microsoft 365 training site.
- Customize the services you want to provide training on.

The site is connected to Microsoft Online Catalog, so the training content is always up to date.

The best way to install a learning/training site is to do the following:

1. Get your tenant administrator to create an App catalog. The instructions to set up an App catalog have been provided here at `https://m365book.page.link/catalog`.

2. Wait at least 2 hours and then visit `https://m365book.page.link/learning-m365`.

Click **Add to your tenant**, as shown in the following screenshot:

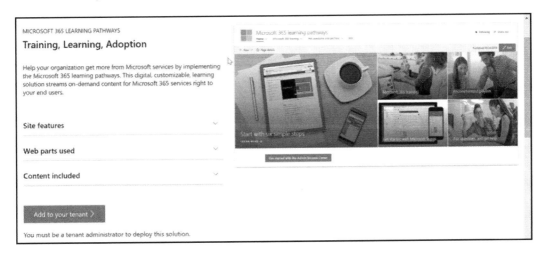

The next screen will ask you to verify the details of your tenant. Click **Provision**, as shown in the following screenshot:

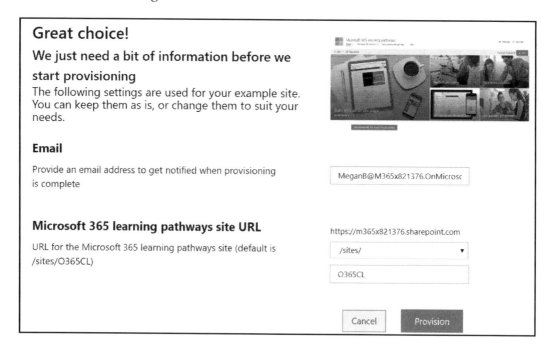

With that, your learning pathways site is ready. Go to the **Microsoft 365 training** link, as shown in the following screenshot:

Click on the **Settings** icon to customize its content:

You can **Show/Hide** content based on your organization's needs:

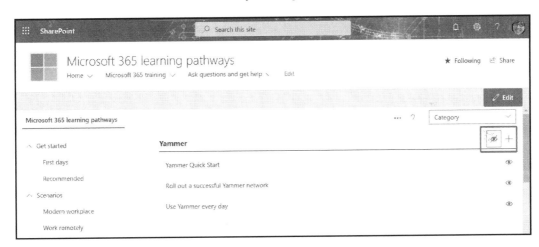

Project Cortex

Project Cortex is a new member that has joined the Microsoft 365 family that uses Microsoft Search and Microsoft Graph to surface contextual information about a specific keyword via topic cards. Imagine that you receive a work email that has a reference to Project ABC (which might be a project running in the company). Project Cortex will convert that word into a hyperlink that displays additional information about what the project is, people involved with the project, and other supporting information.

This reduces the overhead of additional documentation. Project Cortex makes the first attempt at collating information from Microsoft 365 related to the term using artificial intelligence. The SMEs could then go and enrich the content on the pages if they want to. The possibilities it presents are endless. With a tool like Project Cortex, the time you need to onboard a new employee or person joining a new role is reduced. These are still early days for Project Cortex (at the time of writing this book) but watch this space.

The following is a mock-up of how Project Cortex can mine information and provide additional context/information to the end user:

SharePoint spaces

SharePoint spaces is a web-based platform that lets you create mixed reality vision by using 2D and 3D web parts on your SharePoint page. SharePoint lets you add web parts for your 3D objects, 360° images, and videos, 2D images and text, and more.

SharePoint spaces can be used for training staff, organizing virtual tours, engaging classroom teaching, and much more.

To use SharePoint spaces in your site, you need to turn the following **Site feature** on:

Once this feature is turned on, you will get an option to create **Space** pages in the page library of your site. You can now add 2D and 3D elements to your page:

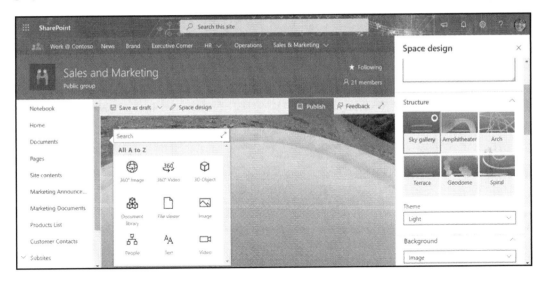

SharePoint spaces look even better when you view them using a VR headset. Developers can enrich the experience even further using the SharePoint Framework.

 SharePoint spaces were in preview at the time of writing this book.

Fluid Framework

Fluid Framework takes collaboration and co-authoring to the next level. With Fluid Framework (which was only recently announced at the time of writing this book), you can add components that interact with each other while you are creating content. It lets you @mention your colleagues and tracks the document changes in real-time.

You can save the Fluid files in your OneDrive or Teams applications and share it with your colleagues. People get access to the document automatically if you @mention them.

There are several components that you can add to your document, some of which are as follows:

- Action Items
- Table
- Person
- Date
- Check List
- Bulleted List
- Numbered List
- Image
- Agenda

Other Books You May Enjoy

If you enjoyed this book, you may be interested in these other books by Packt:

Hands-On Microsoft Teams

João Ferreira

ISBN: 978-1-83921-398-4

- Create teams, channels, and tabs in Microsoft Teams
- Explore the Teams architecture and various Office 365 components included in Teams
- Perform scheduling, and managing meetings and live events in Teams
- Configure and manage apps in Teams
- Design automated scripts for managing a Teams environment using PowerShell
- Build your own Microsoft Teams app without writing code

Learn Microsoft PowerApps

Matthew Weston

ISBN: 978-1-78980-582-6

- Design an app by simply dragging and dropping elements onto your canvas
- Understand how to store images within PowerApps
- Explore the use of GPS and how you can use GPS data in PowerApps
- Get to grips with using barcodes and QR codes in your apps
- Share your applications with the help of Microsoft Teams and SharePoint
- Use connectors to share data between your app and Microsoft's app ecosystem

Leave a review - let other readers know what you think

Please share your thoughts on this book with others by leaving a review on the site that you bought it from. If you purchased the book from Amazon, please leave us an honest review on this book's Amazon page. This is vital so that other potential readers can see and use your unbiased opinion to make purchasing decisions, we can understand what our customers think about our products, and our authors can see your feedback on the title that they have worked with Packt to create. It will only take a few minutes of your time, but is valuable to other potential customers, our authors, and Packt. Thank you!

Index

P

Made in the USA
Coppell, TX
09 December 2021

67615745R00444